NORA HEYSEN

A PORTRAIT

Anne-Louise Willoughby worked as a journalist in a career that spanned thirty years in Western Australia, first training as a newspaper cadet in the 1970s before moving to magazine publishing with Australian Consolidated Press. As a freelance journalist, she was a feature writer for Australian newspapers and contributing WA editor to *Belle Magazine*. Anne-Louise works as a lecturer and tutor in creative writing at the University of Western Australia with a particular interest in memoir and biography. She lives in Fremantle, Western Australia.

Published with support from the Fremantle Press Champions of Literature

NORA HEYSEN

A PORTRAIT

ANNE-LOUISE WILLOUGHBY

For TJW

CONTENTS

LIST OF ABBREVIATIONS

AGB	Art Gallery of Ballarat
AGNSW	Art Gallery of New South Wales
AGSA	Art Gallery of South Australia
AAMWS	Australian Army Medical Women's Service
AANS	Australian Army Nursing Service
AIF	Australian Imperial Force
AWM	Australian War Memorial
AWAS	Australian Women's Army Service
CPA	Communist Party of Australia
HAG	Hamilton Art Gallery
HHFC	Hans Heysen Foundation Collection
MoMA	Museum of Modern Art
NEAC	New English Art Club
NERAM	New England Regional Art Museum
NGA	National Gallery of Australia
NGV	National Gallery of Victoria
NHFC	Nora Heysen Foundation Collection
NLA	National Library of Australia
NPG	National Portrait Gallery
MAETU	Medical Air Evacuation Transport Unit
OWA	Official War Artist
QAGOMA	Queensland Art Gallery | Gallery of Modern Art
RMO	registered medical officer
RA	Royal Academy of Arts (London)
RAAF	Royal Australian Air Force
RAAFNS	Royal Australian Air Force Nursing Service
TMAG	Tasmanian Museum and Art Gallery
VAD	Volunteer Aid Detachment
WAAAF	Women's Auxiliary Australian Air Force
WRANS	Women's Royal Australian Naval Service
WRNS	Women's Royal Naval Service
WPA	Works Progress Administration

PREFACE

This is the story of a life propelled by an all-consuming drive to draw or paint. It is also a story of how that drive prescribed a life. Born in 1911 to artist Hans Heysen and his wife Selma, Nora was raised in the Adelaide Hills, South Australia, in a family home that provided for her natural talent from a young age and enriched her by contact with artistic and erudite visitors. She lived through periods of extraordinary change, and navigated these changes without the loss of creative integrity, and in both collusion with, and separation from, her father and his influential legacy. Nora Heysen was the first woman to win the Archibald Prize for portraiture, Australia's most prestigious and widely acknowledged art prize. The prize was established by Jules François Archibald, owner of the influential *Bulletin* magazine, to support Australian artists while recognising the country's leading citizens and, until Nora entered, winning the Archibald had remained the province of male artists for seventeen years. It would be another twenty-two before a woman won a second time.

Winning the Archibald Prize was not the only first in Heysen's life. She was commissioned as Australia's first woman Official War Artist in 1943, producing over two hundred and fifty hundred works now held in the Australian War Memorial in Canberra that record the efforts of the women's auxiliary services in Australia, New Guinea and the Pacific arena during World War II. She was the sole war artist charged with this extensive brief; it was also here that she met Robert Black, a man who was to change the course of her life.

As an artist with talent, success and domestic support at a relatively young age, one might suppose that Nora Heysen would enjoy repeated successes. But due to a complex conflation of untimely interruptions by the men that held influence in her life, and due to the social constraints of the day, the outbreak of war, and her own responses to all these things, she became sidelined in an art world that was experiencing rapid change.

Her choice of artistic allegiances and her unwillingness to compromise saw her fortunes falter, leaving her widely unrecognised for much of her life, despite her extraordinary talent.

Nora Heysen is a significant figure in the Australian art world. She was brought back into view in the late 1980s by art publisher and curator Lou Klepac. Her 2000 retrospective at the National Library of Australia was a triumph. Both Nora and Hans Heysen's great contribution and significance are now revisited, as posthumous re-evaluation repositions them in their rightful place in the Australian collection. *Nora Heysen: a portrait* is my contribution towards addressing Nora's life and reputation. It is just part of a process of appreciation and restitution which is also visible in current significant institutional initiatives, such as the National Gallery of Victoria joint retrospective exhibition in 2019, *Hans and Nora Heysen: two generations of Australian art,* and those held previously by the National Library and the Australian War Memorial in Canberra.

INTRODUCTION: NORA SPEAKS

> *My memory of childhood was always wanting to draw or paint. This is my earliest memory. It will be my last memory, I think, that I must put something on paper.*-Nora Heysen[1]

The truck driver holds the steering wheel with relaxed confidence. She rests a large, muscular arm on the open window of the truck door, her hands encased in long leather driving gloves. She is wearing air force garb designed for the Women's Auxiliary Australian Air Force—the first group of women, other than nurses, permitted to sign up to the recently formed women's services. Her clothes are loose and masculine in cut. An airman's peaked cap sits squarely on her head; her eyes face forward, her expression is relaxed yet purposeful. She is a professional. She wears red lipstick. She is strong, authoritative and female.

Nora Heysen painted *Transport driver (Aircraftwoman Florence Miles)* 1945 (AWM, *plate 34*) when she returned to Australia from her war artist post in New Guinea towards the end of World War II. Suffering severe dermatitis, a residual effect of the constant humidity and wet muddy environment in New Guinea, Nora was sent home to convalesce. As she recovered, she continued her commission at the Royal Australian Air Force (RAAF) bases in Cairns and Townsville in northern Queensland. While stationed there, she produced paintings that display the power and capability of her women subjects.

In the painting, the viewer sees the mountainous landscape of the tropical north in the distance through the truck window. From a flagpole in the mid-ground, the sky-blue British Air Force Ensign with its red circle roundel floats parallel to the driver's horizontal arm, locating the subject and her allegiance. The artist has used a colour palette that intensifies the light falling on the driver's face from outside the vehicle. Initially the light source on the face could be assumed to be the sun but closer analysis shows sunlight shining on the back of her neck and illuminating the base of the steering wheel. The driver's illuminated face suggests additional light source. Nora is presenting the dawn of a new era for women, casting her subject as an aspirational figure. The woman in the painting is working in the defence of a young nation where every able-bodied contribution counts. She is heading into the light. Despite the sombre subject of servicemen and women at war, the painting is a celebration of women and their capacity. The viewer might feel that he or she—indeed, the nation itself—is in good hands.

In February 1943, age thirty-two, Nora Heysen was appointed to the Australian Women's Army Service (AWAS) as Australia's first woman official war artist (OWA). Her credentials for the job were well established: she had held successful exhibitions since a young age and in 1938 she was the first woman to win the Archibald Prize for portraiture. The appointment was a result of Nora's own negotiations—she felt a strong compulsion to contribute to the war effort.[2] Nine months after being assigned to the Australia-Pacific region, her work started. The Australian Army History Unit regarded Nora as such an anomaly that they initially were unclear about determining her rank or remuneration.[3] While she eventually became a captain, entitled to the same rate of pay as her male counterparts, she noted in a letter to her parents that she received less, although she was promised that would be rectified 'several years hence I should imagine'.[4] In fact, continued correspondence and laborious accounting between departments saw Nora receiving equal pay within months.[5] This did little, however, to alleviate Nora's frustration with the bureaucratic paralysis that slowed her entry to the war:

> … it took them nine months to decide what uniform I was to wear, what I should be paid, what pips would be on my shoulder—and the war was nearly over by the time I got there and then they wouldn't let me get anywhere near the front, as it was called. I could only get with the nursing sisters, casualty clearing stations, and I even had difficulty getting so far up there. They wanted me to stay in the studios in Melbourne remote from the war—what was the *use* of having a war artist![6]

Until World War II, the only women in Australia's services were nurses; their involvement commenced in 1898 with the formation of the New South Wales Army Nursing Service Reserve.[7] In 1900 the first detachment was sent to South Africa during the Boer War following a decision by the British War Office to deploy them to the conflict. This was a direct result of pressure from Queen Victoria's daughter Princess Helena who, in her role as chair of a peacetime committee overseeing nursing reservists, believed they had a role to play in caring for the troops. Initially considered unnecessary, their value would become startlingly evident. The leaders at the War Office were particularly scathing of any plan to deploy nurses. Nurses were not really necessary, one scribe going so far to claim that as civilian nurses had little or no experience of gunshot wounds they would be particularly useless and in the way in warfare. Others wanted to imply that women wanting to assist in this way were essentially going with immoral purposes in mind.

This would eventually be proven incorrect and the nursing units became an indispensable asset. It was considered a victory by those women intent on serving the Empire. Some who missed out on securing a place in the Australian contingent paid their own way to South Africa and joined the British nurses.[8] After World War I, when Australian nursing reservists and civilians were once again recruited, it was clear that the military role of women must expand in order to support any future war effort.[9] When war broke out in 1939, Australian women were keen to contribute to the war effort and several civilian groups were soon formed. They included the Women's Australian National Services, the Women's National Emergency Legion, the Women's Air Training Corps and the Women's Emergency Signalling Corps. Women were not initially considered for the armed forces but, as the war spread and demands for personnel became even greater, Federal Cabinet reluctantly decided to introduce women into the forces. First to form was the Women's Auxiliary Australian Air Force (WAAAF) in March 1941, followed by the Australian Women's Army Service (AWAS) in October 1941 and the Women's Royal Australian Naval Service (WRANS) in July 1942. In 1941 the aircraftwomen of the Women's Auxiliary Australian Air Force constituted the first new women's services.[10] The AWAS would oversee Nora's commission. In 1944 the AWAS became the only non-medical women's service to send servicewomen overseas.[11]

Nora's uniform was straight army khakis, no different in basic styling from her male soldier counterparts. She would come to loathe the colour, proclaiming that 'Khaki is a foul colour to paint and doesn't suit women'.[12] Before making her way north, closer to actual military action, she was instructed to paint the heads of the women's services at her studio in the Victoria Barracks in Melbourne. Professor of Art History at the University of Adelaide Catherine Speck notes in her book *Painting ghosts: Australian women artists in wartime* that despite the disdain Nora held for khaki, 'she wrestled with it and produced quite stunning paintings ... Heysen's portraits quietly but firmly place these women leaders in our military culture as significant historical figures'.[13] Since the women were in uniform there was no capacity to pose or dress them as Nora might for an Archibald portrait. With the constraints that came with the army commission, both in time and setting, Nora highlighted selected details of the uniforms and of her sitters' physical features to impart their individuality. As she worked to find a resolution to the hindrances that curtailed her usual approach to portraiture, Nora wrote to her parents in November 1943, while in the process of painting Lieutenant Colonel Sybil Irving, Controller, AWAS:

> I have been immersed in my khaki scheme and, as if once having mixed the colours, I couldn't get enough of it. I was tackling the whole thing in that tone, with the only relief the red stripes on the lapels and ribbons on the chest. It will either hit or make a very bad miss, and at the moment it is half way between the two, and I feel irritated and on edge. My sitter is overworked and tired, and can spare me a bare hour a day which is not enough, and working in brief snatches like that is very unsatisfactory. One just gets started and time is up, however Colonel Irving has a fine and strong head, domineering and efficient, highly capable with penetrating blue eyes and a sense of humour.

Nora 'battled for the best part of a month',[14] she wrote, and ultimately this attempt was not a success, as she struggled with the unfamiliar colour scheme and the limited and interrupted sittings. She would complete a second portrait of Irving, in keeping with her self-expectations, to enter in the Archibald. Along with the Irving portrait, Nora submitted portraits of the head of the WAAAF, Group Officer Clare Stevenson, and the Women's Royal Australian Naval Service (WRANS), First Officer Sheila McClemans. She worked to complete the second portrait of Irving to deadline, 'as it will not be tactful to show the Heads of both WAAAF and WRANS without the army'.[15] Nora held, from an early age, a sense of propriety in terms of her subjects and a work ethic that informed the perfectionism evident in her paintings.

Alongside the Archibald entries, Nora painted Lieutenant Colonel Kathleen Best, who coordinated the AWAS, the Australian Army Nursing Service (AANS) and the Australian Army Medical Women's Service (AAMWS); Matron Annie Sage, matron in chief AANS; Lieutenant Colonel May Douglas, controller, AAMWS; and Matron Annie Laidlaw, matron in chief WRANS; all are important works on record. Speck observes:

> Their stories are not familiar and their histories are obscured, even though some of the women Heysen painted remained in highly influential positions in the women's services beyond the war years. Therefore as portraits they are paradoxical: they sit uneasily as works that confirm the power and status of their sitters. This is not due to any failing on the part of the artist, nor to a lack of conviction on the part of the subjects, but to a lack of history of Australian women in leadership positions in the armed forces.[16]

In time, such oversights have become the focus of concern and, slowly, rectification in the form of a shift in emphasis towards the contribution of women.

The skill Nora shows in representing the individual qualities of each of these uniformed women is exceptional, in particular in her treatment of Matron Annie Sage. It is a product of her own craft and talent, and her understanding of traditions of painting. The matron's red cape provided great relief to Nora from the khaki that dominated her palette.[17] She wrote to her parents: 'I am working on Matron Sage and am painting her in a white cap and red cape. She has a fine head and the whole thing is like a Flemish Old Master—Van Eyck would have loved her'[18] (AWM, *plate 35*). Speck observes that Heysen captures the matron like a Madonna, 'encapsulating a blend of compassion and experience in the red cape itself'. Speck also describes Nora's portrait *Lieutenant Colonel Kathleen Best* 1944 (AWM) as a 'finely tuned study of the authority and organizational skill of women in senior posts'. She also explores the concept of uniform as a province of the masculine writing:

> ... some critics have questioned the image of women in uniform, suggesting that a uniform is essentially an anathema to the corporeality of a woman's body, that a military uniform is essentially manly and that brass buttons on a woman's uniform can only convey maleness.[19]

Nora has highlighted the precision of Best's uniform, the soft glow of her brass buttons, the press of her starched collar, the precise tie around her neck, and the confident air that surrounds the pips on her subject's shoulders. She uses such details to publicly affirm these powerful women, and to affirm their right to appear in military uniform.

By 1943, 44,000 women had enlisted, but this surge of change in status for many Australian women, and the number of women ranked at the highest level in their services was, as Speck observed, 'short-lived'[20] in the nation's collective memory—where little recognition has, in the past, been given to the works of women depicted in uniform, unlike their male counterparts. Redressing the historical biases that have shadowed women's contributions, in particular to Australian art, has been a crucial project of the past few decades, and this book is a contribution towards that project of restitution.

This exploration of the life of Nora Heysen examines the events that shaped not only the approach she took to her art but also the way she consciously lived her life. While she chose to physically remove herself from her family to pursue life as an independent artist, the immensely influential Heysen name created doubts for Nora for most of her life. Was the name a burden, something to be judged by, or was she its beneficiary? Nora suspected that she would never really know for certain if her work was of innate value or if she acquired success by association with her father.[21] The relationship between Nora and Hans fluctuated in terms of influence. While it was a rich and complementary one, it was often fraught, both personally and professionally. Nora Heysen was a painter who responded to an internal urge that could not be quelled by her doubts, or indeed by her detractors. She committed to the idea that she would do what felt appropriate and allow the outside world its own view.

ONE: IN THE NAME OF THE FATHER

Give me Art that comes from the world that surrounds us, the beauty of which we can see and absorb—a clean beauty that makes us the happier for our experience. –Hans Heysen[1]

She captured a sense of the way these women saw themselves and their place in a unique time. Nora said she wasn't a feminist but she identified with women working in a man's world. –Eugene Schlusser[2]

Nora Heysen was well suited to depicting authoritative women. After all, she was one. Her portraits of the heads of the women's services painted in her capacity as official war artist represent their strength along with her own in the determined brushstrokes she applied to canvas. She was strong in character, sharp in wit and determined to live her life on her own terms. From an early age, she had capable female role models: she, her mother and older sisters all had a part to play in a seemingly idyllic yet hard-working, self-sufficient pastoral life. Her father recognised Nora's talent as a child and encouraged her to draw alongside him in his studio at The Cedars, the 'gentleman's country residence'[3] which became the home of the Heysen family. With thoughtful and disciplined practice, along with practical, if in some ways equivocal, support and encouragement from both her mother and father, Nora became a painter. However, her background was a gift imbued with family contradictions and complexities that were not always constructive.

In November 2000, just over three years before her death on 30 December 2003, a full-scale retrospective of Nora's work was mounted at the National Library of Australia (NLA). In a glossy four-page feature article in *The Australian Financial Review Magazine*, illustrated with large colour photographs including a dramatic portrait shot, the 'art men' around Nora Heysen discussed her position in Australian painting. The journalist David Meagher wrote:

> At 89, Heysen's life has spanned an unparalleled sweep of Australian and international art history. Through her father, she is a living link to the masters of Australian painting; through her friendships—including with Orovida Pissarro, granddaughter of Camille Pissarro—she is separated by considerably less than six degrees from the great post-Impressionists from Cézanne to Van Gogh.

No matter where or in what context Nora Heysen is considered, her father is never far from the discussion. As one of Australia's best-known landscape painters, his work became part of our national imagery from Federation through to the 1960s. In the opening paragraph to his article, Meagher refers to her seventy-year career and her refusal to submit to pressure to change her style or subject matter. He tells us that Nora was 'determined in the face of fashion and even the odd court martial (a reference to her refusing an order during her OWA Commission) to, as she puts it, "Stay on my own bus"'.[4] It might be said that she was not always the driver of the bus, with her father and his friends each trying to take a turn to direct the young woman artist. The men interviewed by Meagher in the lead-up to the 2000 retrospective discuss this marginalisation and its possible causes, including her reluctance to self-promote and the central question of what it means for children to live in the shadow of a famous parent.

In 1989, Lou Klepac, the Australian curator and publisher, revived interest in Nora's work after years of what he calls 'considerable neglect'[5] by the Australian art community. Klepac met with Nora to discuss an exhibition of her father's work in the mid 1980s and later he looked at her paintings. When he expressed surprise that she had never had a solo exhibition in the sixty years that she had lived in Sydney she responded, 'No-one ever asked. And I don't push myself'.[6] The two became close friends. Klepac was a trusted advisor, advocate and manager of her work. In 1989 he published the monograph *Nora Heysen* and curated an exhibition of her work at S.H. Ervin Gallery in Sydney. When Klepac was curating her 2000 retrospective, then director of the National Portrait Gallery (NPG) in Canberra, the late Andrew Sayers, was quoted by Meagher:

> There is something unresolved in her work—that is the relationship of her work to her father's ... I hope that Klepac

> will bring to the exhibition the rigour that is necessary to really understand her.

Meagher also interviewed John McDonald, former head of Australian Art at the National Gallery of Australia (NGA), and he added:

> It could be said that she is more important than we previously thought … From the 1950s and the 1960s onwards the artists that impressed their reputation on people are the ones that made use of their social contacts … she was not a pushy person … Nora suffered the same problem that other children of famous painters have … It's very hard to step out of the shadow of a famous father.[7]

While researching her thesis in the mid 1990s on the subject of Nora's wartime work, Kate Nockels records that Nora revealed a long-held anxiety attached to always comparing herself with her father:

> It wasn't that she was only successful because she was his daughter and that his influence worked in her favour, it was that she was always comparing herself … 'in his shadow' was the phrase she would use and she was always trying to match him … but she went on a different path and you couldn't really compare her still lifes with his landscapes.[8]

Nora's uncertainty was finally addressed after Klepac revealed her work once more at her 1989 Sydney exhibition. In 1993 she received the Australia Council's Award for Achievement in the Arts, a Life Award designed to honour the life and work of eminent but under-recognised visual and craft artists. Klepac had arranged for her to be seen in her own terms and she responded: 'Well, I have produced enough work in my own way … and I would be recognized as a painter separate from my father, I think that's true. I believe it is'.[9]

Nora finally expressed acceptance of her artistic independence. She was eighty-three. Yet eight years later, the 'father–daughter' conversation was still open on the eve of her NLA retrospective. What in her work is 'unresolved'[10] in Andrew Sayers' terms? Sixteen years after Sayers' observation, I put this question to the current director of the NPG, Angus Trumble, and his response was refreshing:

> If it is true that Nora Heysen dwells in the shadow of her father then it's also true that an artist as great as, and under-appreciated as, Orazio Gentileschi lives in the eternal shadow of his daughter Artemisia. So it can actually flow both ways, I think, particularly now when we are inclined to amp up every effort to magnify achievements of women artists for all the right reasons ... My inclination is to take a slightly different position to Andrew [Sayers] and say that Nora Heysen in this evolution of her posthumous reputation is easily able to take care of herself in respect of Hans.

Angus Trumble believes that Nora Heysen now occupies her proper place within the realm of Australian painters, seeing her as 'neither side-lined or over-emphasised'. He refers to the self portraits by Nora Heysen, Stella Bowen and Grace Cossington Smith that hang together in the NPG: 'The point that we make in that part of the display is a general one that it so happens that in various media, not just painting, modernism belatedly finds it way in Australian art, thanks to the efforts of women artists and those three are notables'. Trumble adds that there are other women who have contributed in this way and believes that the NPG has addressed what was a deficit. His final comment to me on Nora is telling:

> It is interesting that she didn't sign her name Nora Black. She had the perfect opportunity to distance herself from the Heysen name when she married Robert Black but she chose not to. It would hardly be surprising if the matter vexed her that she felt both a need to acknowledge her father and his reputation and align herself with that but also be a little bothered about whether that was fair to herself. So it is a tension in her self-projection.[11]

Even so, a change of name would not have been easy. Nora did not marry until she was in her forties. By then her professional name had been established for over twenty years in the eyes of the buying public. She was a woman attempting to produce work in a male-dominated profession, caught between using the name of either of the two men central to her life. Though she used her married name socially, she always signed her work Heysen. The fact that her father was a member of her chosen profession was a complicating factor.

While his daughter managed the role her heritage played in her life, Hans Heysen's own background and his success were a consequence of great tenacity and vision. His past offers us insight into the aspects of his life that had such a profound effect on him and subsequently the daughter that would follow him. Wilhelm Ernst Hans Franz Heysen was born in 1877 in Hamburg, Germany, the sixth of seven children of Louis and Elize Heysen. Two older brothers, Gustav and Louis, died in infancy. His elder sister and two brothers and the youngest Heysen child, Valeska, survived. His parents were relatively secure and comfortable in the early years of their marriage. Louis was the son of a man wealthy enough to provide an education and, as Hans Heysen's biographer Colin Thiele suggests, wealthy enough to live 'a life of some distinction'. Thiele recorded Heysen's memories during a period when the writer was invited to live at The Cedars. Heysen was ninety and his recollections reveal that his father Louis was a man with a propensity for rash decisions and unwillingness to compromise, which would jeopardise what could have been a distinguished way of life. With the support of his own father, Louis became a retailer of sewing machines that could not compete with modern foreign models. The business failed and in the early 1880s he established two drapery stores also in Hamburg, though both of these met the same end. Louis was 'virtually bankrupt'[12] and Elize opened a small drapery on the first floor of their home to keep the creditors at bay. It was then that Louis decided that Australia could provide a fresh start.

Thiele suggests that Louis's health, in particular problems with his lungs, provides the reason for his decision to immigrate to South Australia. Some also suggest his insolvency influenced his decision to leave his family and send for them a year later, once he was established. Emigration had its challenges. He could not make a success of the poor land that had been allotted to him through the land order system in South Australia, and by the time his family was to arrive in Port Adelaide, having left the comfort of their home and its gentle accoutrements, he was penniless. There was no home for them except a wooden hut with almost no furniture. On arriving at these lodgings, Elize's doubts and fears about leaving her home were realised when she entered the virtual slum dwelling that her husband had barely managed for his family's arrival. Before leaving Hamburg she almost wrote to say she was not immigrating to Australia, but her loyalty prevailed. Meanwhile, the former bookkeeper, one-time retailer, failed landholder, dismal accountant and unsuccessful speculative investor in Port Adelaide was now struggling to operate a fledgling pig and poultry run near Rosewater.[13]

German immigration to Australia was initially a result of religious persecution. South Australia and Queensland were the main destinations, and in 1838 Pastor Kavel settled his Lutheran followers in Klemzig, South Australia. In November that same year Captain Dirk Hahn arrived with another 187 Lutheran Germans fleeing a royal edict that would force their church to combine with Calvinists to create a state church.[14] Prussian King Friedrich Wilhelm III and his landowners were concerned about the power and influence of the clergy. Disobeying the edict of the king resulted in systematic persecution.[15] Hahndorf, named for the Danish sea captain that delivered these religious refugees, maintains its German heritage today through the preservation of original buildings and as a busy tourist centre that celebrates its traditions. It would become home to the family of Hans Heysen seventy-three years after the captain's passengers walked alongside their wagons from the port to their future home in the Adelaide Hills.[16]

Louis Heysen's decision to take his chances in the British colony appeared to be yet another error of judgement. But in time, in a desperate bid to provide for his family, he built up a business hawking fish twice a week from the port to Gawler, a settlement fifty kilometres inland. On the trip back to Adelaide, unsold fish were exchanged for eggs and butter that were promptly sold back in town. Finally Louis had a viable enterprise and he was able to purchase a horse and cart. His improved situation meant a series of different homes, each a better version than the last. It also meant school for the youngest children, Hans and Valeska. In 1889, six years after emigration, Louis Heysen finally bought a house. At the rear he set up his trading premises. For the first time since leaving Germany his family would experience a sense of security. He appeared in the Adelaide Directory as 'Produce Merchant, North Norwood'. During the intervening years Hans had attended different schools depending on where the family had taken up residence. In 1890 Hans was enrolled in the East Adelaide Model School where he completed his final days of education, leaving in September 1892 at the age of fourteen.[17]

During these days Hans Heysen's talent for drawing was emerging. There were no formal art classes but in time Hans Heysen's appreciation of the natural world around him and his father's side business of horse-trading produced the drawings that alerted his family to his artistic talent. Louis Heysen bought unbroken horses from station owners, prepared them as best he could and sold them at a profit, keeping those he required to haul his produce carts. As a fourteen year old, stories of the Wild West and 'cowboys and Indians' fed Hans Heysen's imagination while his father's horses provided live models for sketches of an imagined, and sensationalised, American West.[18]

Though his father enjoyed Hans's drawings, even collecting some of his best to keep as samples, no-one, not even Hans, considered art as a means of making a living. At almost fifteen he started work in a sawmill and hardware business, Cowell Bros, on Norwood Parade. Spare time was not plentiful. Hans was using his to engage with his art: 'People called it his hobby. The random sketching of his school days, taking on greater purpose, led him to charcoal and watercolour, and—in a moment of bold experimentation—to oils'. By the time he was sixteen Hans's work was being admired outside of the family and, according to Thiele, it 'had intruded itself sufficiently into the Heysen household to warrant some kind of official recognition'. He began art classes at the Norwood Art School run by James Ashton, the art master at Prince Alfred College in Adelaide. Ashton's tuition validated his gift as an artist and his sense of himself.[19] It also brought him into contact with other artists, something that would not otherwise have happened in his everyday work life. Later in his life Hans would experience a great sense of satisfaction when he asked building contractor Cowell Bros, his first employer, to build his first studio. Hans had left the hardware company aged seventeen, when he and his father were both unhappy as, following two years of reliable work, old Mr Cowell refused to raise his five shilling weekly wage by two and a half shillings. Now Cowell's would do work for him.[20]

Hans Heysen's artistic success was the result of an unusual combination of intelligence, natural skill and application. The encouragement of his family also played a central role. However, his situation was propitious. Adelaide was at that time a small city, and a prodigious talent was likely to be visible. His support came from varied sources: from South Australia's lieutenant governor to Pascoe the pawnbroker, to the philanthropic businessman, Robert Barr Smith, who paid Hans Heysen's tuition fees at the South Australian School of Design. For a time, Heysen juggled his obligations to his father and the produce delivery round with his commitment to his art. Meanwhile his sister Valeska's suitor Oscar Duhst, who was a barber, offered to promote his paintings by hanging them on his city shop walls, facing a regular and captive audience of interested men about town, ready to discuss the merits of the work. The Heysen name became known and sales immediately resulted. During the early period of his career from 1895 to 1899 his work was consistently exhibited and appreciated in Australia; a major surge of recognition came when Ashton submitted a selection of works by his students to the Royal Drawing Society of Great Britain and Ireland. Heysen won first prize with a watercolour landscape, selected as the outstanding work of the year from entries representing 124 art schools across the Empire, as well as winning other prizes in related sections. The works were held over by the organisers to be displayed at national exhibitions and the Paris Exhibition of 1900. He was an extraordinary draughtsman but his ability to represent light in the Australian landscape made his work unusual and exciting. After receiving steady recognition in his home town and abroad, in 1899 four South Australian patrons contributed to a fund that would allow him to study and paint in Europe for four years, facilitating the formal transition to a career as an artist, a somewhat unexpected development for him and his family.[21]

Hans Heysen's personal life fostered his social and artistic standing. When he returned from Europe he opened the Heysen Art School, where he met Selma (Sallie) Bartels: daughter of a former mayor of Adelaide, who became his student, and then his wife. Both were passionate about art and both understood their social context and what the life of an artist dedicated to landscape painting might entail. They had a collaborative connection from the outset. Heysen told his biographer:

> She was wonderful … She knew how to send out invitations, how to address people, what to do and what not to do. I didn't

> know anything; I was a real ignoramus when it came to things like that. Heaven knows what I would have done without her.[22]

Nora recalls her mother's skills:

> Mother was a good organiser and a great reader—very well read indeed and very good at conversation and entertaining. I don't think father could have made a career like that without her. She was the intermediary between the public and the artist.[23]

This marriage was the foundation of a great and socially strategic artistic and cultural progression for the family that facilitated Heysen's own life's work, and the lives of their children, Nora included. Central to this endeavour was the Heysen family home, The Cedars.

I first visited The Cedars when I was thirty-two with my husband, who was a Heysen family friend. At that point, in 1990, it was still a private home. Two years later as a contributing editor for *Belle Magazine*, I would return to write a story and direct a photographic shoot. It was as if the family had just left for a morning walk. The sun streamed in the windows, pale blue and violet hydrangeas were loaded into their vases, abundance and nonchalance paired. Each room was ready to receive visitors: bowls of quinces, roses from the garden—as the eye moved, it registered a tableau from every angle, a still life waiting to be put on canvas. The effect was all prescribed by a sense of a past era: the long-gone artist was guiding my eye as if he were on my shoulder directing me to look. Hans Heysen's favoured Souvenir de la Malmaison, a rose in the softest of pinks, spread lusciously from a glass vase in the master bedroom. My job of directing the angles of the camera had already been done for me. However, the outwardly elegant arrangement of The Cedars, at all times, as with most cultural arrangements, rested on complex and often unspoken compromises: instances of grief and generosity.

1. The Heysen family photographed in the grounds of The Cedars. Seated: David, Deirdre, Freya; standing: Sallie Heysen, Michael, Hans Heysen, Josephine, Nora and Stefan (Lilian deceased). Papers of Nora Heysen, National Library of Australia; image supplied courtesy of Wakefield Press.

TWO: THE CEDARS

The real core of Hans's life as an artist lay in the moment, rather than the day—the first stroke of charcoal on paper, the stub of palette knife on canvas, the utter commitment of the artist as he watched a ray of light moving across a tree trunk. These were the moments of creation and revelation; the living frontier, so to speak, of his own spiritual life. -Colin Thiele[1]

'You're a lucky beggar, Heysen,' was echoed in a hundred letters. They envied him his life, his home, his wife; sensed the simple dignity of his environment; applauded the power of his craftsmanship. Lionel Lindsay had summed it up long before: 'You hold, I take it, most of the cards of happiness'. Hans did. -Colin Thiele[2]

In 1912, after a highly successful watercolour exhibition in Melbourne, Hans and Sallie Heysen had the means to buy the home that Sallie had discovered, and desired, on a country walk.[3] The Heysens were living in rental accommodation in Hahndorf after spending the early part of their marriage living with Sallie's mother in Hurtle Square, Adelaide. The home they would buy was originally named Blackwood, but it was changed to the more bucolic The Cedars, possibly in the 1890s.[4] This was a modest country home at the heart of thirty-six acres of natural bush land and pasture. It would be the heart of the Heysen family for the next century and beyond. The initial asking price for the property was inflated due to the owner's reluctance to sell, but Hans Heysen's Melbourne show of 1912 was such a success that he was able to make the purchase. His form of painting defined a particular, highly popular view of the Australian landscape, and up until the 1940s he shared his successes with contemporaries Gruner, Streeton, McCubbin, Roberts and Lambert as chroniclers of a newly federated Australia.

The Melbourne art world and its patrons had embraced the Heysens, and the implications for the family were immense. The sale of the house to Hans Heysen was completed and the family had its epicentre. He laid out the grounds himself, creating meandering stone paths, beds with borders of quartz and limestone and steps leading to different levels, with the house sheltered by the majestic Himalayan cedar trees that give it its name, planted in the 1870s when the house was built. The effect of Heysen's landscaping close to the home resulted in a European garden rich with the traditions of roses and perennials with which to fill the house. While the flowering shrubs, and bulbs within the boundary fences of the house provided a picturesque surrounding, he remained enamoured with the native bush beyond. In 1938 a highly successful show at the David Jones Gallery in Sydney facilitated the purchase of adjacent land and allowed The Cedars to remain a bush enclave free from urban encroachment. The property surrounding Heysen's studio provided the inspiration for his work that never altered either in subject matter or in approach, a fact that would later prove alienating for the artist as the world around him changed in terms of subject and technique. This same environment deeply influenced Nora, in terms of the physical world but also the philosophical aspects of her father's approach to art. The home as a totality is photographed, but not painted by Hans or Nora. Rather, elements of the home that express the totality by implication are present in each artist's oeuvre.

Hans Heysen is lauded for his immense Australian landscapes, demonstrating the distinctive light of the Antipodes. The paintings concerning his household at The Cedars offer the viewer a different kind of experience. *Sewing (the artist's wife)* 1913, which is today held by the Hans Heysen Foundation Collection (HHFC) at The Cedars, is an oil on canvas that embodies on a domestic scale some of the elements that Hans Heysen worked to represent throughout his life. So much that was central to Hans Heysen's life and his painting informs how we understand his artist daughter. Nora's engagement with the domestic as subject matter is consistently revealed throughout her career, and an examination of her father's treatment of this subject, and of the philosophy that he adopted, leads us to understanding the complexities faced by Nora as an emerging artist in a period of great change as she took her place in the art world in Australia and beyond.

In *Sewing*, Sallie is mother and carer, homemaker and nurturer. Heysen represents the grandeur of the natural world in his vast landscapes. Yet he turned to the domestic for inspiration in *Sewing*. He acknowledges his wife's domestic labour, and reflects on the home the two have created for themselves and their family. Hans Heysen's lifelong quest to represent sunlight, the shadows it creates, and the ambience it produces for the viewer, is delicately rendered with a spill of brilliance through the lace curtains of Sallie's workroom window. The room was in a separate building that overlooked the main house and garden (later it would become Nora's studio) and Sallie takes on an almost beatific role in the painting, where she seems to be a guardian of all that is good and familial. While intimate, and representative of the domestic role many women held at the time, it speaks to bigger ideas of life and family. The woman in the painting is absorbed, working, stitching in her husband's trademark light. Her back is turned to the viewer. This is not a conventional portrait designed to express character through the subject's face; rather it could be compared to the nineteenth-century German Romanticism technique of *Rückenfigur* where the subject's back is presented offering a vicarious experience for the viewer, inviting the viewer into the scene. One of the greatest exponents of this technique of the period is Caspar David Friedrich who claimed that 'The painter should paint not only what he has in front of him, but also what he sees inside himself'.[5] The painting of Sallie Heysen exemplifies an internalised vision of domesticity. Later in 1919 Heysen wrote to his close friend Lionel Lindsay, one of the prolific and successful artistic Lindsay siblings. In Lindsay, Hans Heysen had a sympathetic and admiring contemporary though Klepac points out that Hans Heysen did not share Lindsay's blind prejudice when it came to a mutual suspicion of modernism.[6] The two shared many written exchanges on art and its role throughout their long lives:

> I am only trying to paint as truthfully as I can, and that which my eyes see and perhaps what I unconsciously feel. Truth to Nature after all is the goal but Truth is interpreted through temperament. Of course Light interests me as much as ever, but I am seeking it more under the 'everyday aspect' of nature ... It is surprising what beauty enveloping light gives to the ordinary things in nature and instead of them becoming more commonplace, they become more and more filled with charm—...[7]

Heysen is respectful of the labour that goes into building a life and, by extension, a nation, in his emphasis of the rural: his canvases of farm workers, such as *Ploughing the field* and *The toilers* (both AGSA), painted in 1920, have a similar quality of dignified absorption as his wife at her sewing. Despite Australia's growing urban centres it was the notion of the rural as definitively Australian that resonated with the national psyche at this time, and Heysen was a master of its depiction.

Other paintings offering glimpses inside The Cedars include Nora's *Cedars interior* (NHFC), painted in the 1930s, which depicts a still, luminous portion of a room showing a fireplace, a sofa and other items of furniture and, tellingly, her father's *Zinnias and autumn fruit* 1923 (HHFC), which he would not relinquish to the visiting ballerina Anna Pavlova. It was not for sale, as Heysen had painted it for his wife.[8] In *Cedars interior*, Nora has included her father's painting coveted by Pavlova—and, incidentally, a framed high-quality reproduction ordered by her father from Europe of the famous Vermeer canvas *Girl with a pearl earring* 1665. These elements are central to the domestic space of The Cedars. Both the artists in the family held the Old Masters such as Rembrandt, Velazquez, Titian, Bruegel, van Eyck, and Vermeer in the highest esteem, with Hans Heysen writing: 'It is their understanding of light, life, dignity and character which impresses one'.[9] Heysen held that balance and composition were central to the success of a work and believed in continually honing the skills required of a sound draughtsman:

> ... the art of recording fast what the eye sees. Training the eyes and the hands to do this is one of the most important needs of the artist ... To train the hand to record not only what the eye sees but what the mind behind the eyes sees, is the important thing.[10]

Nora recorded some of her early memories of living surrounded by art in her home and the influence it had on her:

> I was immersed in art as a child. From a very early age I had an intense passion for art—surrounded by paintings and books of my parents. I determined that I wanted to

> paint masterpieces! [I had] an early visual appreciation of fine quality reproductions in my father's studio and in the house—particularly Vermeer, *Girl with a Pearl Earring*, a very early impression. Both my father and I were great admirers of the early Italian Renaissance school, the masterpiece being Piero della Francesa's *Nativity*... and Velazquez's portrait of the Spanish Infanta... Two large Van Gogh landscapes always hung prominently as did *The Gleaners* by Millet—this piece in particular perhaps influenced my desire to portray the people on the land.[11]

Art and family objects are on a common footing. The Heysens appear absorbed in their art in their quotidian spaces. Nora's and her father's flower studies and still-life works reinforce this impression.

As the Heysen family grew, the home was busy with eight children. Josephine, the eldest, was an outstanding horsewoman, her brothers and sisters were active athletes, and outdoor life at The Cedars fostered robust development and an understanding of the natural world. All of them—Jo, Freya, Lilian, Nora, David, Deirdre, Michael and Stefan—had tasks around the property. They were required to help keep the enterprise of The Cedars running smoothly: milking cows, collecting eggs and firewood, working in the garden, and preparing the tennis court for social occasions. Formal education was not a feature for the first five children though there was a series of tutors. Nora recalls:

> We were a wild lot, I fancy. We had a life of our own amongst ourselves and were proper little bush urchins hauled in to say hullo to important persons... We were brought in to be shown off you know, and hated it, and went back bush—building bush houses and whatnot...[12]

From 1915 four tutors were employed to educate and restore some order in the children's world. The first was a British governess who was too iron-fisted for Hans and Sallie. Later tutors fell away. Hans and Sallie

2. Nora, standing, in the lower paddock below the studio at The Cedars with David (left) and Taffy the dog, Freya, Josephine holding baby Deirdre, and Lilian. Papers of Nora Heysen, National Library of Australia.

agreed it was time for a formal school life and the children were enrolled at the Convent of Mercy day school, St Scholastica's, at Mount Barker.[13] One tutor did prove to have some positive influence for Nora in particular. Art historian and curator Jane Hylton notes that Mary Overbury (1860–1932), the 'well respected South Australian artist', conducted Nora's first serious art training.[14]

Social events were frequent at the Heysen home. Visitors, including many socially illustrious folk, were welcomed to an open house on Sundays involving a plentiful supply of homemade German brown cakes and coffee. Hans Heysen's profile and popularity as a collectable Australian landscape painter meant that guests came from a broad spectrum of the international and Australian community. Sunday afternoons at the Heysens' were quite the event. Visitors usually travelled on to destinations in Melbourne and Sydney where their Heysen visits were often discussed. Thiele writes:

> Marie Tempest in the drama, Edward Goll in music, Pavlova in the ballet, Melba or the Italians in opera … It was a ceaselessly recurring pattern of visits filled out by innumerable calls between: Jim McGregor or Howard Hinton, Ifould or McMichael, Moore or Brewster-Jones.[15]

Other notables to call on Hans Heysen and his family were actors Laurence Olivier and Vivien Leigh, the American author and lecturer Helen Keller, and Robert Menzies. A visit from the British actress Sybil Thorndike and her company saw close to forty people arrive on a Tuesday morning, twenty more than they had expected, but according to Hans: 'Still everything moved easily and the inundation was quite successful. The girls managed everything splendidly …'[16] The issue of the domestic contribution of 'the girls' is worth considering. For Nora, the tension between her art and the expectation to be on hand in the kitchen whenever required was never addressed. The home offered a view of the vaguely idyllic, rarefied yet familial, atmosphere surrounding the great artist. In his biographical documentary film about Nora, Eugene Schlusser deemed these visits and events 'theatre'. As much genuine hospitality as a commercial strategy, this 'performance' brought in money through commissions and sales.[17] Nora revealed the reality to McKillup:

> Nora described her mother as a 'skilled and professional hostess, and the entertainment of the guests was left entirely to her … this sells pictures, money for living, with eight children money was involved and very necessary. Mother knew the right people'. When guests arrived the children were all expected to appear to talk a little … then they knew they must disappear and not interrupt or distract the adults again.

Nora also recounted how later in their childhood after they were paraded before visitors they were required to play their roles as support hosts.[18]

But Nora learned far more than the value of hospitality from life at The Cedars. The subtle studious art of observation and the importance of composition were the priority lessons from her father, either in his studio or when she accompanied him on his outdoor painting excursions. These trips were formative for her later work of portraits set in landscape.

The young daughter would experience frustration as her father swiftly set about his work at pencil studies then watercolour paintings.[19] Nora recalls in conversation with Klepac that:

> I used to have my little bicycle with my satchel on my back, and trundle along afterwards for about four or five miles, and I was exhausted by the time I got there … even at that age I wasn't content to paint with watercolours, I wanted to do oils because I found that more sympathetic to what I wanted to do, and by the time I'd got all my oil paints out and my palette fixed up, there was father with a finished picture … I was generally left sitting when father was on another subject, being a very fast worker.[20]

Hans produced remarkable studies of trees, animals and children, drawing on his immediate surrounds. He painted large floral arrangements that were central to the domestic decoration at The Cedars. While flower painting is important in his oeuvre, it would become much more important in his daughter's work. The flowers came from the garden beds that her sister Josephine tended and her floral displays filled the house. In Josephine's regular correspondence to her friend Jacqueline Whyte she refers to her pleasurable outdoor toil:

> Here the weather has been lovely, glorious mornings with heavy dews and mists warm to delightful days with soft breezes and still cool nights. The garden is a riot of colour, the dahlias the best they have ever been. I do wish you could see them massed in every colour, huge flowers too, many eleven inches across. I am kept busy keeping them watered and picked and the dead flowers off.[21]

In a series of hugely financially successful shows in the mid 1920s, Hans realised enormous sums for his work. His popularity was firmly established. By this time Nora had been drawing alongside her father for years and her own precocious talent had surfaced. She would lie on his studio floor as a young child, absorbing by observation and osmosis the nuanced approach of a disciplined draughtsman. Later, as a teenager,

3. Family picnic: Hans Heysen is seated in the centre of his children in 'Heysen Country', Nora is second from the left. Papers of Nora Heysen, National Library of Australia.

she developed her skill while on the receiving end of occasionally less-than-tactful critique. The public, dealers and gallery owners had an insatiable appetite for the Heysen name which was being compared favourably with Henri Fantin-Latour, a nineteenth-century French painter renowned for his classical representations of flowers.[22]

With the resulting financial security, money was 'pouring in spectacularly'. Renovations to accommodate the expanding family could be done. As Thiele points out, The Cedars became a 'beautiful and roomy home. Yet despite its increased size it had an air of compactness, a lived in quality; and like its owners, it was still utterly unpretentious'.[23] In her letters to Jacqueline Whyte, Josephine tells of the many tennis parties and soirées held in the gardens as the Heysen children enacted their position in Adelaide society. The emerging young adult Heysens hosted their own social gatherings. In November 1926, she tells of one large party for sixty-two including friends of her parents, boys from Scotch College and St Peter's College, and girls from Stawell. Her letters read like an excerpt from an Austen novel. On one occasion, after hosting eighteen people for dinner at six o'clock, the girls had to get ready for the arrival of party guests at seven-thirty—'Mr. Roach and Jim Perkins came first and then when the Miss Bennetts arrived we were all in the bath. Not one of us was in a fit state to greet them!' Mr Roach served as temporary host. She goes on:

> We had a gorgeous supper of oyster patties, sandwiches, cream puffs, jellies and strawberries and cream, ice-cream and all kinds of iced cakes and just gallons of fruit cup. I have never seen such a lot of thirsty tigers in all my life. They drank just everything we had in the place. Brewster Gilbert and Jim Perkins acted a Chinese play and Miss Bennett showed mooving [sic] pictures and in between dances we had three competitions.

If there is breathlessness to her storytelling it is because she had so much to tell. Her letter speaks of ardent young men 'forgetting' a scarf in order to have a reason to return, and of visiting boys and girls stealing kisses on the back doorstep out of Mother's line of sight (or so they thought).[24] Nora, nineteen, echoes the excitement as she also writes to her sister's friend in January 1930:

> We are having a most gay and exciting time here the holidays are in full swing, tennis parties, picnics, dances and bridge evenings every day, it seems one rushes to fit as many things into one day as possible. We had a great party here last Saturday and had a jolly time of it, tennis all afternoon then a wild and exciting treasure hunt which covered a distance of over three miles and finished up in a regular scramble in the hay stack. The poor guests who had arrived in evening frocks and high heeled shoes were almost torn to pieces and I am sure would never have come had they any idea of what would happen to them.

In the same letter Nora goes on to describe the 'chief topic of conversation' in the household at the time. 'From dawn till eve'[25] conversation focused on the new acquaintance made with the Balhannah parson's two very good-looking sons. She writes in detail about days at the beach together with the two boys and her siblings. In passing, Nora mentions that she is working on a petunia painting for Pavlova. Growing up with a constant flow of celebrities in and out of her home left Nora completely nonplussed by fame.[26] Her lack of attachment to the idea of notoriety for herself and a rejection of her mother's style of promotional activities likely contributed to her later period of obscurity. Sallie Heysen knew the value of patronage by the rich and famous and was a consummate marketer.

Josephine reported the family's updated circumstances with the news of their first car. The opening line in another letter to Jacqueline Whyte from 1928 reads like a news bulletin:

> Rush! Roar! Thrills! Excitement! We have a motorcar. Really truly ours! A Buick and we have called it Bimbo! Fifi [Freya] is to have the thorough teaching and then she has to set to and explain it to all of us.[27]

So much was left to the young adult children to manage in the home, not the least were the driving lessons. The idea of one sister learning to drive then teaching her siblings points to just how much freedom they enjoyed in the hillside retreat of Hahndorf. David, aged thirteen, drove the family car to the police station in Adelaide to get his licence, there was no driving test, assured the policeman he would not drive until he was fourteen, the legal minimum age, and promptly walked outside to the parked car and drove it home.[28]

Nora describes most winter evenings as spent around a log fire with her family. The rural property provided much of the produce that sustained them: 'cows, eggs, butter, fruit. And we grew all our own vegetables…' Evenings might be spent together to 'pick feathers or put down salted beans. And all the jams were made that way, and the plums were pipped and the marmalade cut. Everybody entered into it. Someone used to read aloud—that's how we got through the classics—mother usually, or the two elder sisters'. The Sunday roast was a tradition from which Nora says

In 1934 Australian photographer Harold Cazneaux photographed the Heysen family and home at The Cedars. TOP: *4.* Freya in the garden sunroom known as the *stoep*. BELOW: *5.* From left: Josephine, Freya and Deirdre Heysen in the garden at The Cedars, Ambleside. Collection of the State Library of South Australia.

that no-one was excused, though she is quick to note that religion did not have a place at The Cedars, and church was not a part of the Sunday ritual: 'We didn't have anything to do with ministers; we were a pack of little pagans. No religion at all ...'—though this detail did not prevent the girls enjoying the friendship of the minister's sons. Hans was clear that his spirituality lay in his connection with nature and the bush that surrounded him. His church was the surrounding countryside and his sanctuary was his home. Sallie and Hans worked in the kitchen together leaving 'yeast cakes ... all round the kitchen stove at night to rise ... and working to make these great big *Stollen*—big round puffy loaves with raisins in them—no one being allowed to make a din in there in case it made them sink ...' Nora and her siblings all carried on the tradition of Sunday roast in their adult lives. Sallie's dream of 'a house in the hills with roses and orchard trees, a place where the children can breathe'[29] was now visible. However, life at The Cedars was less idyllic than this aspiration suggests.

Sallie and Hans Heysen had established a work environment that provided for their large family while it sustained the breadwinner's equilibrium and his desire to be a painter immersed in the beauty of nature without compromise. Sallie Heysen was the designer of the organisational framework that allowed her husband to work unhindered by the tedium associated with running a home and the care of eight children. When his working day was over with the setting of the sun, he left his studio and was embraced at the family table by the children he loved and the wife he adored. The couple had worked hard and strategically to create this situation. However, the Heysens were no more immune to sadness and difficulties than any other family. Hans and Sallie would lose two daughters—one to illness and the other to a set of circumstances influenced by social conventions and ultimately, quite possibly, a lack of required care.

In October 1923, Lilian, aged fifteen, the Heysen's third child, contracted influenza that developed into pneumonia. After months of recovery she was able to participate again in family life.[30] By Christmas of 1924 the family was celebrating a happy and healthy festive season but soon after, it faced shattering events. Heysen described the moment a car took a bend wide, hitting Josephine who was steering the trap pulled by the family's horses, Bob and Mick, onto the main road:

> A car swept up over the small sharp hill to the right and cannoned straight into her. The impact was fearful. It shattered the pole, killed one pony outright and fatally maimed the other, and flung the trap aside as scrap. Jo miraculously was not badly hurt ... Both Bob and Mick gone killed at one blow. I helped bury them on the same night down a mining shaft in dense bush ... it is still a nightmare to us.[31]

Josephine survived, but a few months later Lilian became ill again and underwent surgery for what was described as a 'mastoid'. The mastoid bone is situated behind the ear, and hollow spaces within the bone allow for fluid to drain from the middle ear. Infections on the mastoid are often the result of unresolved ear infections, and sadly for Lilian it would be another three years before Alexander Fleming would make his breakthrough penicillin discovery and another ten after that when Florey and Chain would transform medicine with antibiotics.[32] Sallie Heysen was in Adelaide at the Wakefield Street Hospital writing letters to her husband to keep him informed:

> Then the side of her head was shaved clean—she hated that ... The op lasted until 10 to 8 ... It was a ghastly two hours and I could feel you thinking of us. After a while they sent a message to say they had struck trouble, but the bone had become affected and had to be laboriously tapped and cleared ... Oh I am so glad and thankful it is over.

It was not over. On 8 August 1925, Lilian died, devastating her family. Hans revealed the real cause of her death to Lionel Lindsay in a letter thanking him for his sympathy:

> No thoughts no feeling would come—I was numb. The terrible strain of poor Lilian's death and its tragic aftermath left us both with no hearts to feel with. Even Dame Nature

> could arouse no response, it seemed as if we were living in another world with no sun to give warmth or life … It seems so unnatural that our Lilian should be taken from us that I cannot understand or realise it. It is as if we are living in some terrible nightmare … Meningitis was the real cause of poor Lilian's death and the doctors tell us she had been carrying the dreaded germ ever since she had pneumonic influenza. It seems terribly difficult to realize that in body she will never be with us again—she meant so very much to our home.[33]

Hans would suffer another tragedy with the loss of Josephine in 1938, but the cause of Josephine's death is not so clear. At the time of Lilian's death, Josephine was almost twenty and responsible for the outdoor management of The Cedars. Her energy, great capacity for physical work, and her excitement for life are evident in her extended correspondence with Jacqueline Whyte,[34] a slightly older married woman with no children who lived at Burr Well Station to the north of Adelaide near Copley. Josephine assigned the role of confidante to Jacqueline Whyte, possibly as her relationship with her mother had developed into a tussle between a conservative parent and a more socially liberal daughter. From the late 1920s through to just days before her death, 'Jo Jo', as she ended her letters, shared her life in detail with a woman far removed from her physical world. The letters begin with the youthful voice of Jo Jo ever breathless in her desire to tell her friend everything about life at The Cedars. A number of Josephine's letters refer to her mother's dislike for Max Williams, a horse trainer from Oakbank where she had been a regular competitor as a junior and senior horsewoman. Williams would become central to Josephine's life and remain at the core of the conflict between Sallie Heysen and her daughter. Josephine writes to Jacqueline in early December 1928 after receiving a call from Max Williams suggesting that he and Josephine go for a ride:

> Mother simply flew up a pole, was most frightfully annoyed, wanted to know what kind of friends I was going to make next, [she] thought he had a darned cheek and rowed at me getting familiar with him and Lord knows what not … I can't think of any reason in the world why I shouldn't go riding with Max

> and I can't imagine why Mother should be so wild about it. Really it beats me … I must try and bring Mother to reason. It's all too stupid and unreasonable.[35]

Josephine's prowess as a horsewoman was well known in the community and among the extended Heysen friendship group. She received an invitation in the winter of 1930 to visit the Myers family in Melbourne for seven weeks to work at their stable of racehorses at Flemington and to enjoy the racing and the Hunt Club social scenes. She writes to Jacqueline after returning home to The Cedars:

> I had the time of my little life but managed to get back with no broken bones and actually a whole heart. I met heaps of charming jockeys, trainers, cowboys, bookmakers and owners and have come to the conclusion that you couldn't find a more open-hearted, generous and kind people than the racing crowd … I was up at six every morning and rode two or three horses work [sic] at Flemington. Used to have some glorious gallops and ever so many sprints over four and five furlongs … Twice a week we went out to the hills and galloping over the green slopes at the break of dawning was just glorious … Ps. Haven't seen Max since I got back … must get him to clip 'Jim' for me in a day or two. I didn't have time to write to a soul while in Melbourne hence Max heard not a word from me.[36]

Josephine visited Melbourne again in June 1932. The impression that she was making as a horse trainer was strengthened when her horse, Archeson, took first place in an important hurdle race in the lead-up to the Grand National Steeplechase. Hans wrote to his mother to share Josephine's successes and activities, informing her that in just the first three days of her Melbourne visit she rode almost a hundred miles and jumped a hundred fences:

> … she rides him [Archeson] every morning (on the flat) at Flemington, and besides she is riding in three hunt clubs 'qualifying 8 horses': that means she must ride each horse in 4

> Hunt Club Meetings ... Personally I can't see how she can stand it, and yet it is the very thing she seems to thrive on.

She made the headlines of the Melbourne and Adelaide papers with Archeson as a favourite:

> Photographs of the trainer, Mr. Max Williams, his sister, and Josephine appeared in the turf notes ... The caption 'Woman Rider on Flemington Tracks' was enough to stir everyone's interest ... no doubt Josephine would have ridden her horse herself in the Grand National itself if she'd been allowed to.[37]

Reading between the lines of many of Josephine's letters to Jacqueline, it could be assumed that she had already become attracted to Max Williams though in her early letters she insisted that there was 'not a hint of romance between Max and me we keep strictly to horses while the whole district is imagining Lord knows what ...'[38] Sallie's fears of her daughter being involved with a man of a lower social standing would become a reality. He would become Josephine's track trainer and ultimately more. The association would not have been acceptable in the social hierarchy of the day and it appears from the intimate correspondence between 'Jo Jo' and Jack, as she would come to address Jacqueline, that Josephine was following protocol to a point. Scattered throughout the letters from 1927 onwards are references to 'Max', and horse-related matters. Max appears in her letters more frequently over time, as does the familiarity of tone when she addresses events to do with him. It is clear that Sallie does not approve of the association of her daughter with the horse trainer, though in the day it was acceptable to fraternise with the horses' owners. Evidence of increased friction with her mother over Max Williams is noted in a small exchange with Jacqueline where Josephine acknowledges the support of her friend:

> I have never thanked you for seeing my point of view about Max Williams. It is nice to feel that someone understands and sympathises though it must seem as if Mother has had her way as I have only seen Max once since Christmas.

This was a problem, as horses and racing were Josephine's passion and constituted the world to which she felt she belonged. Hers was an equestrian life. She was more than willing to do the difficult track work, training in all weather, but it is evident that Sallie Heysen was uncomfortable with how Josephine's girlhood hobby had turned into an adult obsession that included Max Williams. Her riding skills were demonstrated during her trip to the Myers as she recounts one of her hunts to 'My dear Jack':

> I got the foxes pad one day and on 'Grey Girl' won the mash which was a thrill especially carrying the bloody morsel around with me for the rest of the day. I am having it mounted so that in the future I'll be able to tell my youngsters what ma did in her young days ... Many of the hunters were old-time steeplechasers. We used to jump 40 to 50 fences. Some of them quite stiff ones too. Stone walls, panels, palings, capped fences and barb-wire [sic]. The horses I had would attempt anything. The country out that way was pretty rough and galloping for your life up hill and down dale through creeks—dodging trees and careless riders and bounding down rocky slopes was enough to make anyone's blood race wildly. Gee it was exciting.[39]

Josephine was fearless. Her father loved the bright and vivacious young woman who capably ran the outside workings of The Cedars, managing the livestock, pastures and the gardens closer to the house, telling his friends in his correspondence what an asset she was to life at The Cedars:

> Jo was the houri, the Ceres of the farm-yard, orchardist, ploughgirl, turkey-keeper, horsewoman—a beautiful lively charmer, full of energy and initiative. Hardly a letter arrived from friends, relatives, or acquaintances ... without making enquiries about her.[40]

There were periods when paid domestic help was not available and Josephine was brought into the kitchen to help deal with the ever-increasing stream of visitors to the Heysen home. Yet in between her domestic and exterior duties Josephine would return to her track work when possible, and to Max Williams, where her heart lay. When she and her sisters travelled to London with their parents in 1934, Josephine was in contact with Williams through a constant stream of postcards. I will return to this later when I trace the family support given to Nora in her early days as an art student abroad.

In an abrupt letter dated 2 May 1938, Jacqueline Whyte receives news without warning from Josephine that she has left The Cedars and is living in Victoria after a hastily arranged secret wedding:

> My dear Jack,
>
> Is it a bombshell or have you heard that I am residing in Victoria as Mrs. Max Williams. Actually I have been married for quite a time but did not want anyone knowing until Max and I could live together and it is hard to credit that a secret like that could be kept in so small a town. Our parents and the minister were the only ones who knew until we left by the express [train] for Melbourne on Thursday night. How far or quickly the news has spread I don't know, but Mother was going to ring the family after we left and let them know. I don't think anyone will faint with surprise.

Josephine writes around the issue of pregnancy saying the reason she remained apart from her husband was that there were no rental rooms or houses 'to be let, bought or stolen near Oakbank'.[41] Two months prior to her leaving, in a letter dated 15 March 1938, Josephine tells her friend that 'I'm getting an awfully fat tummy through lack of riding and would not at all be surprised if I produced twins. All the trotting around the house doesn't seem to exercise the middle'.[42] The letter goes on, suggesting she is oblivious to her situation. She describes recent visitors to The Cedars, her work in the garden and the prolonged labour and post-partum recovery of her sister Deirdre who had married D'Arcy Cowell the year before. Six weeks later the newly wed Josephine had left her home. In October she gave birth to a daughter. In 2015 I travelled to Hawaii to meet this daughter, Josephine Claire. In a conversation recorded in her Maui home, Josephine's assessment was that it was a matter of expediency that her mother marry and then be hastily removed from the judgemental eyes of society. The exercise was orchestrated by Sallie Heysen. Josephine and Max Williams were relocated to a horse training stable in rural Mentone. It is possible that the intention was for the couple to return to Adelaide at a later date with a child of indeterminate age.[43] It was a sad and sudden departure.

Their daughter described the events as a tragedy for her grandfather that she believes he deeply regretted. She felt that he never understood why his daughter had to be banished. This lack of apparent understanding is hard to accept but the strictly weighted social structures of his era underwrote how daily life was lived. To step outside those rules could result in ruin. Hans Heysen likely knew exactly why his daughter was removed and it was the larger societal issue he struggled to accept along with his own acquiescence. Josephine spent her pregnancy in impoverished circumstances, struggling to afford the fresh eggs, milk, vegetables and fruit that she had enjoyed in abundance at The Cedars where they 'couldn't give apples away' but in Mentone were '4 pence a pound'. While gratefully receiving gifts of canned food sent as wedding presents, Josephine wore no wedding ring as there was no money to buy one. Jacqueline sent mince recipes and thrifty kitchen tips for using dried beans and pulses to make Josephine's meagre food allowance stretch. The contrast with her bountiful home in the Adelaide Hills is stark but it is important to note that Josephine was happy. She was in love and expecting her first child. Her change in circumstances surprised her but did not daunt her. She described her house to Jacqueline Whyte as 'small and ugly' but was not perturbed:

> and yet we are as happy as skylarks. I wonder at it because you'd never stop laughing to see me getting in my milk bottle in the morning putting pennies in the gas slot and tripping up the street with my little bag to buy household needs ... It is such a different Jo and yet I'm perfectly content and not hankering after the life of garden and bush that I have left.[44]

Josephine died at Nyora Private Hospital in Mentone on 15 October 1938. Her daughter believes she was suffering from malnutrition, pleurisy and pneumonia when an emergency caesarean section was carried out.[45] Nora later told her goddaughter Meredith Stokes (the daughter of Nora's friend Everton Stokes) that her sister should never have died—and that she had been living in poverty and did not receive adequate antenatal care.[46] At the time, Hans and Sallie were in Sydney to attend the opening of Hans's 1938 exhibition at David Jones Galleries. They received a telegram advising them that their daughter was critically ill. Sallie Heysen arrived in Mentone on the Melbourne Express train and spoke to her daughter just before she died. Hans, driving from Sydney with sons Michael and Stefan, did not arrive in time. Josephine talked about the special relationship that her grandfather had with her mother, suggesting that the two had shared a kind of telepathic connection that surfaced once more when the men were en route to the Mentone hospital. Hans told his son to slow down, that there was no need to hurry as Josephine had gone. He was disconsolate and Sallie was 'wracked beyond relief'[47] at the loss of their first-born. Thiele writes that the baby was taken by her grandparents to be raised at The Cedars as her mother had wished and by agreement with Max Williams. While he agreed for the baby Josephine to be cared for by her grandparents, her father was ultimately persona non grata. She told me: 'Grandmother kept me totally away from that family and would have reared me without even knowing that they existed. My father's mother insisted on walking all those miles [from Oakbank] to the house to introduce herself so that I would know I had another side of the family'.[48] Hans and Sallie Heysen formally adopted Josephine Claire Williams at around the age of four, she believes, and her transition to Josephine Heysen was complete.

In 1990 Josephine requested adoption documents she believed she required for passport renewal in America from the Office of the Principal Registrar in South Australia. She was surprised to receive a Certified Copy of Registration of Birth, not of her adoption. The official practice was to list the adoptive parents on a revised birth certificate and the one sent to her, dated 17 March 1944, not quite six years after her birth, stated that Hans William Heysen was her father, and Selma Heysen her mother, though original documents at the time of her birth list Alfred Maxwell Williams and Josephine Williams as her parents.[49] She was sixteen when she saw her father again. Josephine was dating Derek Jolly, a member of the Penfolds wine dynasty. During the 1950s he was one of Australia's most prominent racing car drivers as a member of Team Lotus, and Josephine said she enjoyed his sports cars and the social life that went with his position in Adelaide. It was Jolly who pointed out Max Williams to her at the Oakbank races and who photographed her with her father. When Josephine returned home and told her grandmother about the meeting, and that she meant to see her father again, there was hostility between them. Sallie Heysen insisted that if she wanted to go to her father, Josephine needn't return. She did visit with her father but also returned home, though in the heat of the moment Josephine told me she intended not to go back to The Cedars. Max Williams expressed regret to his daughter: 'He apologised for not taking responsibility for me. He told me that the war was just starting. He could have been called up. He didn't know what was going to happen and that was his main reason. I said I didn't expect him to. He felt bad'. Josephine and her father saw little of each other throughout their lives, though her cousins on the Williams side, and her aunt, maintained contact with her. Within ten years of meeting her father, Josephine moved to Hawaii, married and had two children. This marriage did not last and Josephine left her husband and two sons, aged eight and six, though she maintained contact. She said that she 'didn't have that adoration of children',[50] that she never learned how to love them as she had not experienced the bonds of parenting.

Hans's grandson, Peter Heysen, eldest son of David and Lyly, remembers his mother speaking of the tragedy surrounding his aunt's death. He reflected that the situation arose out of the social conventions of the day but also as a result of Sallie Heysen's determination to protect her husband at all costs from the consequences once social conventions had been transgressed.[51] The topic was a disturbing one for this compassionate man and one that he said was devastating for the family, not only for the enormity of the loss of Josephine, but also for the effect that her death had on Max Williams, on his surviving daughter, and the extended Williams family.

Peter Heysen told me that in 1900 Sallie inherited £1500 from her father's estate. He revealed that when she died in 1962 his grandmother still held an SA Bank savings account with £1500 and he commented:

> In 1900 that amount would have bought a string of cottages, in 1962 maybe a couple of rooms in a cottage. But she was married to a man who made his money on other people's whims—to buy a picture or not buy a picture—and I think that [money] was her life jacket.

Perhaps here lies the reason for Josephine's removal—that the success of the enterprise of Hans Heysen the artist, and therefore the security of Sallie's family, was at the mercy of public opinion:

> Grandfather, I don't think, was much a part of Josephine going away. She [Grandmother] was a strong lady and her thinking was to protect Grandfather, she would do anything to protect [him]. I think that was the reason for sending Josephine to Melbourne because if that scandal had centred on Grandfather the rich people would have turned away and there was no livelihood. Grandmother was preserving him, his art and his reputation.[52]

This candid appraisal of his grandmother's actions was made with the firm belief that these issues needed to be discussed to ensure they never happened again. As a doctor, along with his obstetrician wife Diana Heysen, Peter Heysen volunteered his services during his years as a general practitioner delivering babies for women at Kate Cocks Memorial Babies Home—a refuge in Adelaide for unmarried girls and their newborns and for infants needing care. He had been deeply affected by the circumstances of his aunt's death and he made it part of his life's work to make a difference for women facing adverse circumstances related to prenatal and postnatal care. His experience of the suffering of many young women compelled to give babies up for adoption stayed with him. He witnessed the disappointment of failed reunions and children demanding to know why they had been taken away:

> I found in medical practice the biggest thing to make things better was the Supporting Mother's Benefit [1973] that made such a huge difference. It stopped them having to put up with [unstable] men—these were people [the women at the refuge] trying to do their best, the babies were whisked away, the heartbreak when children were taken away. The benefit changed that.[53]

Sadly, forty years earlier there was no support in 'good' society for unwed, pregnant women and a 'good' girl was defined as such by the fact that she did not have sex before marriage. Sallie Heysen probably believed she had to move swiftly to safeguard the reputations at stake. Fortunately for Josephine, she and Max loved each other and despite the compromised circumstances they found themselves in, they were ready to make a life together. The tragedy lay in the lack of support—Josephine and Max had been removed and left to fend for themselves and love was not enough to sustain them. Josephine Claire wishes her Uncle David and Aunt Lyly, her cousin Peter Heysen's parents, had adopted her. She missed children her own age and believes growing up at The Cedars with elderly grandparents was not the best environment for a single child. She was isolated and playing alone: she recalls climbing into a tree with a book, *The secret garden*, and imagining a very different life. She was not close to her grandmother, although she loved her grandfather and called him Daddy. Her teen years were spent pushing back against her grandmother's rules, which were out of step with the changing times of the late 1950s and early 1960s. She was unrepentant when she told me she purposefully tried to upset her grandmother with outrageous behaviour. Deeply sad, seventy-seven year old Josephine Wittenburg quietly wept as she stated that she held her grandmother indirectly responsible for her mother's death. Her tears were not for herself, she said, but for Grandfather, 'Daddy', who never came to terms with the tragedy of her mother's death.[54]

Some time passed between my conversations with Josephine in Maui, and with Meredith, Nora's goddaughter, who went to Wilderness School with Josephine in Adelaide. The two women remain friends today. I was struck by a sense of rueful empathy when Meredith described Nora's character to me. Incredibly open-minded, open-hearted and generous, Meredith told how Nora respected people's opinions and ways of living even when markedly at odds with her own.[55] Such a description starkly contrasts with perceived attitudes and behaviours leading to Josephine's situation in 1938. One may easily wonder to what extent these factors that contributed to her death, whether familial, societal or epochal, potentially influenced Nora's decisions about how she would live her own life.

In the year prior to Josephine's death, the Heysen children had begun their adult lives away from The Cedars. An exodus started with Deirdre's marriage to D'Arcy Cowell, the grandson of James Cowell, in April 1937, a match that Hans Heysen found humorous after having been a junior employee with Cowell Bros back in 1892. Michael was studying at Roseworthy Agricultural College and Stefan had aspirations to become an art dealer and was away learning bookkeeping and business administration. David, after leaving home in 1932 to work as a jackeroo at Lyndhurst, north of Adelaide, to prepare for a life on the land, had become engaged to Lyly Refshauge and was ready to start his own family.[56] Hans Heysen helped him to purchase a property in the south-east: Derrymore, near Kalangadoo, which David and Lyly developed into a successful farming enterprise. Deirdre had settled on a grazing property with her husband and she and David would become rural neighbours. It was on Derrymore's walls some fifty-five years later that I would discover the work of Nora Heysen for the first time after it became the home of David's son Tim and his wife Mary.

The events of 1938 represented a seismic shift in what had been an apparently happy, bustling household. Nora had returned from travels to London and left The Cedars to launch her career in Sydney early that year. Josephine had relocated to Mentone with Max Williams. By August the same year Freya's marriage to Edward Booth in Hans Heysen's studio had taken place, and the family had attended David's wedding to Lyly and the newlyweds started life at Derrymore. When Hans Heysen wrote to Lionel Lindsay it was in a wistful tone about his empty home, 'the turn-over has been rather sudden', and Lindsay replied, 'How well I remember my first visit to The Cedars and that wonderful united family—but such unity belongs to childhood and youth, and each must die'. Hans and Sallie were philosophical and remained busy—Sallie with her reading and Hans Heysen in his studio painting.[57]

When Hans prepared for the David Jones show in Sydney in October 1938, The Cedars was empty of Heysen children. Josephine's death changed that. Her baby was brought home, providing some comfort. It was an anxious time for Hans, grieving for his lost daughter, unable to find inspiration to paint, living in a house geared to meet the needs of a newborn, lacking sleep, fretting for his wife who had turned inward on her grief, all while watching the ever-increasing threat of war build amid the rising nationalism in his country of birth. The tranquil environment that had been created for him to work in had for the time being evaporated.[58]

Nora had been working in her Sydney studio preparing for the Archibald after submitting to the Society in September, when her sister died. She writes to her bereaved parents:

> My thoughts are with you all, and I have tried again and again to write but that awful feeling of helplessness to say anything dogs me, and the terrible reality blots everything out. It all seems so wrong, so terribly wrong.
>
> I cannot say anything, but my heart goes out to you and is leaden with thoughts of your suffering. I feel numb and desperate with the reality of it all.
>
> My love and all my thoughts,
>
> Nora[59]

It could be suggested that it was her work ethic and the 'Germanic discipline, from the long tradition of discipline' that she referred to in conversation with documentary maker Eugene Schlusser that helped her to deal with the sudden loss of her sister. Nora told Schlusser that her father distrusted people who let their emotions run away with them.[60] Having always aligned herself with her father, in temperament as well as in deed, it is likely that Nora followed suit, privately dealing with her grief. Her output of work immediately following Josephine's death in order to meet her obligations is testament to this, including completing two portraits to submit for the Archibald Prize two months after the tragedy.

But before these events, Nora's shift from a child with promise, to art student, to award-winning artist was to take a number of turns.

THREE: ART SCHOOL, TWO DEALS AND PAINTING HERSELF

> *They decided that he would stick to the landscapes and she would do the figures, the portraits and still lifes—she didn't do any landscapes and he didn't do any figures after that.* -Kate Nockels[1]

> *Well, I painted myself because I knew her; ... Painting self-portraits is the one time when you can be with yourself absolutely and just paint; you don't even have to get a likeness.* -Nora Heysen[2]

In conversation with Eugene Schlusser, Nora reflected on her childhood and the time of unity that Lionel Lindsay referred to when offering his friend solace, a time when children at The Cedars were surrounded by what Schlusser refers to as 'the elite of Australian cultural life ... all artistic and deeply conservative'. A kind of artistic court was held at The Cedars; Nora described Australian art publisher and NSW Society of Artists President Sydney Ure Smith as a marvellous raconteur, saying 'his stories of artists and people—they were wonderful, wonderful'.[3] Ure Smith championed Australian art at home and internationally, establishing journals *Art in Australia* in 1916 and *The Home* in 1920.[4] Nora recalled, 'The Lindsay family, of course, they never stopped talking and they were very knowledgeable people, the whole family. Norman and Lionel and Darryl—they all used to come over and stay'. Nora also remembered the visits of international musicians like pianist Artur Schnabel, Dame Nellie Melba, and the legendary Daisy Bates: 'I was fascinated, but I was only a kid'. Schlusser asked if this was the reason Nora became a painter of portraits. Nora replied, 'I've always been interested in faces. She [Melba] was interested in me and bought my first picture and gave me a palette'.[5] The painting was a watercolour of white apple blossom against a blue background. 'She wanted to give me something to remember her and her recognition of me ... my first palette and that started me off on oil painting which I really wanted to do'.[6] Today the palette that Nora used throughout her career sits in her studio at The Cedars, a space recreated in the final days of Nora's life and furnished with effects she bequeathed to her Foundation.

Nora's skills as a draughtsman, a term she used to describe the foundation of her work, developed at home with her father; however, she stated that 'He wasn't anxious to teach me, that's why he was anxious to get me to art school ...'[7] Hans enjoyed the artistic rapport he shared with his daughter but her formal tuition was undertaken separately from him, which was essential for her independent development. Despite this, he was not as anxious as Nora was for her to make an early start at art school. It was 1925 and Nora was fourteen in her Intermediate year, traditionally a point in the Australian education system where a student could leave school and take up a trade; for women, it was often secretarial training. Nora was not interested in lessons at St Scholastica's College in Mount Barker, nor in leaving for a course in typing and shorthand. She only wanted to pursue her painting. She shared her father's love of nature and his measured response to formal religion and recalled that the ritual of the school's morning hymn did not sit well with her:

> When we arrived we had to sing a hymn—*Teach, Oh, Teach Us How to Die.* 'When the death clouds around us gather, teach, oh, teach us how to die'. That appalled me even at that tender age, that you should begin the day with this threat.

Nora said that as a child witnessing the rituals at the convent she was impressionable and that she had decided that being a priest would be preferable to being a nun. The disparity in gender roles was not lost on her even at a young age:

> The priests used to come and visit the nuns and had special food cooked for them and you could hear the laughter from the next room where we were all eating. It sounded hilarious, they were having a marvellous time, so I didn't want to be a nun but I wanted to be a priest because they seemed to enjoy life and the nuns didn't.[8]

Eventually she struck a 'deal' with her parents, the first of two, that if she were successful in the Intermediate Certificate exams she could leave school and go to art school. In 1965, oral history pioneer Hazel de Berg interviewed Nora and she told de Berg that she surprised her parents:

> They didn't have much faith in my scholastic ability so they didn't think I had a hope of getting the Intermediate, but they didn't know me really because I studied like mad, sat up all night and studied, and I did get through.[9]

The determination shown by the young Nora foreshadowed a strong personality that continued to develop. She was quite clear about what she wanted to do; perhaps she was not particularly vocal within the large family group, yet she was committed to her art. In a busy household with eight children to feed, clothe, educate and encourage it is possible that her parents did not really *know* her, as Nora suggested, or realise the depth of her determination. She passed her exams and her parents kept their promise. The following year, Nora left St Scholastica's to study at the North Adelaide School of Fine Arts. It appears her father did not want to risk compromising their relationship and the harmonious way they worked together by being her instructor. Nora continued to learn by working near and imitating her father, while he chose a school for his daughter that supported his preferred methodology:

> Father selected this school for me so as to study under the English tutor Frederick Millward Grey [and his] strict academic emphasis on drawing and draughtmanship. I shared my father's studio fairly successfully all things being considered. Two passionate artists. Mother not all that happy with the situation as she was very protective of [Father's] time and privacy. I must have annoyed him but he didn't reprimand me—I used his best paints, paper and canvases! I'm sure he was glad to get me out of his hair when I converted the stables into my own studio.[10]

Nora told de Berg that she used the money from the proceeds from her first sale of a painting at the age of fifteen to convert the stables at The Cedars to her studio.[11] Research suggests that it was not just the sale of a picture that provided the necessary funds and that Nora's studio was also modified with money from the Stow family, Heysen friends prominent in Adelaide who wanted to support the budding artist '... because,' according to Peter Heysen, 'Grandmother [Nora's mother Sallie] wouldn't let any money go into promoting the art of any of the children'.[12] Support from Catherine Stow (whose pen-name was K. Langloh Parker) continued when in 1930 she wrote *Woggheeguy: Australian Aboriginal legends* and commissioned Nora to illustrate the book. Meanwhile, Nora's success in driving her initial bargain with her parents meant that her commitment was tested. No concessions were made for her gruelling daily schedule and her energy was formidable. Every weekday she woke early to milk the family's three cows before walking to the train station a mile through the bush. After attending school for the day and arriving home after an hour on the train around 7.30pm she milked the cows again before her day was finished.[13] Nora said that her father always said physical fitness was essential for an artist. She laughed that it was fortunate she had a strong right arm from all the physical work that was required of her at home, saying an artist needed to be strong not just for painting but to carry canvases and frames.[14]

Shortly before she died, Nora also revealed in an interview with ABC Radio *Arts Today* host Michael Cathcart that her father made it known early to her that he would have preferred that one of her brothers had been the artist in the family. He said painting was difficult, since 'for a woman it would always be a divided interest because biologically they were conditioned to bearing children and running a home and that was what women did'.[15] Female roles at The Cedars were no different to those in most homes of the day. Nora said that when visitors came to The Cedars she would be summoned from her studio mid painting to help in the kitchen: '... if guests arrived I was called away from painting to make scones, I was the scone maker ... if one of the boys had been more interested in painting, they would have been allowed to work on without any interruptions!' She added that she and her siblings would never have dreamed of disobeying their mother[16] whom in her later years Nora described as the manager of everything—of her father, the house, and them.[17] Nora's mother supported her daughter's interests but everyone understood the sanctity of Hans's priority position: 'Mother devoted herself to him and was very protective of his artistic privacy—

a policewoman!'[18] This was ultimately resolved early in Nora's adult career when, as an independent artist, she realised that there was no room at The Cedars for the two artists to coexist. She would leave permanently.

As a teenager, Nora was willing to comply with her assigned duties at home and pay attention to her mother if it meant she could study art. She applied this same stoicism to tackling what she described as the stultifying effects of drawing from plaster casts for three years at the School of Fine Arts, saying they were 'enough to kill an artist stone dead. I survived it because I was very persistent and I knew what I wanted'.[19] She said Millward Grey was a knowledgeable and conscientious academic painter, reliable and safe, 'fresh from England—very tight—he wasn't an inspiration ... you learned the solid way'.[20] In those first few years, before she graduated to life classes, her time working with her father provided the inspiration. Klepac noted that 'Nora was able to compensate for the dull and unimaginative routine of the school' by drawing with her father.[21] Nora supported this observation saying that she benefited returning daily from school to an artistic house:

> We lived art, talked art, drank art and all the visitors were artists so that was my diet when I was young ... On the weekends I could do what I liked—paint in my father's studio, or go out and paint gum trees like Father ... that was my saving—art school could be rather killing, deadly'.[22]

Former Art Gallery of New South Wales (AGNSW) senior curator of Australian Prints, Drawings and Watercolours, Hendrik Kolenberg, who met and worked with Nora in her later life, observed that she had the benefit of her father's guidance along with specific exposure to the artists that he admired:

> At home with Hans she became an accomplished draughtsman inspired by the Dutch Master Vermeer, the Italian Piero della Francesca, and George Lambert—a large figure in Australian art in the 1920s when Nora was first becoming aware of herself as an artist.[23]

Nora told Eugene Schlusser when he asked her how much of her father was in her that her mother had said, 'we weren't intelligent but we were persistent and dogged… and how right she was'.[24] She applied that doggedness and learned artistic discipline with Millward Grey: 'I think one has got to go through that like five finger exercises scales'. She also recalls that after the tedium of the plaster casts—'they weren't even good plaster casts'—the classes only led to working in monochrome: 'you never painted in colour—you didn't learn anything about composition or colour. You had to go to London to find out about that'.[25] Despite the North Adelaide art school's shortcomings, a year after Nora started, Hans Heysen wrote to Lionel Lindsay: '[Nora] is showing remarkable aptitude. She seems to possess the natural talent and endless industry and concentration… She draws quite naturally—has a splendid sense of proportion and a feeling for design… Already she draws better than most of our professional artists'.[26]

Jane Hylton describes how in Nora's second year in 1928, the seventeen-year-old artist was emulating her father in subject choices and in her drafting skills:

> During this early developmental stage, she followed her father's example and naturally looked to her immediate surroundings… she would draw 'the cows about the place, and all my brothers and sisters', still lifes of the produce of the orchard and mixed bunches from the garden. Portraits of family and Hahndorf locals, as well as self-portraits, filled Heysen's sketchbooks and canvases… These rapidly executed, accurate likenesses of family members—her sketch *My three sisters* [1928, AGNSW] for instance—are delineated by confident line work and shading, creating clearly defined facial features.[27]

Years later, when in her eighties, Nora was discussing her mature subject matter (which did not include Hans Heysen gum trees) with art historian and former head of Australian Art at the NGA Mary Eagle, and remarked, 'I can show you a painting so like his style that all I'd have to do is sign Hans Heysen and he'd be the artist'.[28] It is not only Nora who has observed the similarities in the two Heysen artists' command of drafting, composition and 'seeing'. Hylton is unequivocal about Nora's skill:

> Initially she was so extraordinarily talented—it is easy to see—before she leaves 'The Cedars', when she is still very young. You see her drawings next to her father's and they are interchangeable. It is extraordinary.

Hylton describes Nora's drafting skills as equal to those of her father and commented that when Nora painted academically 'she was easily as good as him'.[29] In 1994 in conversation with interviewer Heather Rusden, for Rusden's series of oral histories held at the NLA, Nora revealed that she worked hard to copy her father declaring it 'the sincerest form of flattery ... if you try and copy somebody'. When Rusden asked what he said about this, Nora replied: 'He didn't say anything but

6. *Hahndorf gums* 1930, study in pencil and wash by Nora Heysen, age sixteen. Private collection.

when people mistook my work for his I dare say he felt something!' She describes how visitors to The Cedars studio would marvel at one of Hans's latest works, not realising they were loudly praising the teenage protégé and not the master. Nora confided to Rusden: 'I don't think father felt so much about it—but my mother did. She arranged for me to work outside Father's studio'. Rusden asked if the confusion over who had painted a work was the reason and Nora agreed it might have been one of the factors. Nora's comments suggest that her mother's withdrawal from painting might also have been an underlying issue:

> My mother never painted after she married. She had eight children instead. She was my father's pupil … She wouldn't have had time to paint. I don't think she ever had time to think about it. I think at times she was a bit bitter about it, that she'd given it all away, for married life, domesticity and looking after children.[30]

One of those children had become his unofficial pupil and fellow painter. Sallie was fierce in all matters to do with her husband. It appears she addressed the idea of the great man's work being that of his daughter by moving her out.

An article that appeared in *The Sydney Morning Herald Women's Supplement* in May 1935 featured the headline 'An artist's wife—and the art of being a background'. Sallie Heysen was quoted at length on her role as the woman behind Hans Heysen. It claimed she realised early that she could be more useful as a 'background' to her artist husband than remaining an artist herself. The article continued: '"Besides," she added, with that quiet wisdom which is one of her characteristics, "men don't really like their wives to have careers though some of them may pretend they do."' The article discusses Sallie Heysen's approach to the role parents played in 'moulding' children's choices in life. Sallie claimed that she and her husband had not made 'the slightest effort to guide' their children, stating 'the temptation to interfere must be stifled … or one merely becomes an obstruction' though she does remark on one occasion where she 'put her foot down with a firm hand':

> 'I decided that Nora must have her own studio instead of sharing her father's at our home on Mount Lofty. I found he was taking far too keen an interest in her work and neglecting his own in the process. There are now two studios in our garden'. Again the quiet smile and a firm little folding movement of the white hands and one had the impression that when on those rare occasions Mrs. Heysen did put her foot down it stayed down.[31]

Late in her life, Nora's friend Allan Campbell, The Cedars curator and chairman of the Nora Heysen Foundation, regularly visited her at her Sydney home. She spoke more intimately with Campbell than she had done publicly in the Rusden interview. Campbell kept a journal preserving the conversations they shared. She said that her mother was a remarkable woman and repeated that her father could not have achieved his great success without her: 'I realised this much later in my life than at the time'. She praised her mother's 'wonderful social skills', and that she could converse with anyone on any subject as she was well read and had had an excellent education that included a great appreciation of poetry. Nora highlighted what she called her parents' different backgrounds: 'Mother was reserved and dignified and she didn't mix with the local village folk as did Father'. She admired her mother for 'her exceptional talent', but was clear about the ambitions she held. She also said that her mother never wanted children but that her father wanted them—'she had them for him':

> She was such an asset to him. She should have been a writer or a diplomat. [She] was not a warm mother—her greatest weapon was her tongue—she could lay you on the floor with her tongue! Father was the warmer personality and would play with us children, but not Mother.[32]

Sallie's decision to move Nora into her own studio might have been to protect Hans but it was beneficial for Nora that her aspirations were taken seriously at a young age. In *Eggs* 1927 (NERAM, *plate 8*), the sixteen-year-old Nora demonstrates her understanding of composition and her affiliation with the everyday objects of domestic life at The

Cedars, but her still lifes were often at risk. The purloined objects she was painting could be requisitioned for the making of afternoon tea. She faced similar disruptions later in her own home when well-meaning assistance with 'tidying up' meant a still life she had set up was inadvertently demolished or cooked. Friends quickly learned to leave any arrangement remotely resembling a tableau well alone.

Craig Dubery, Nora's friend and carer in her later years when she lived alone in Hunters Hill, recalls Nora's eye for beauty in the most casual of moments—a bag of apples he had left on a chair in the vestibule by the back door late one night became a beautiful pastel drawing by the time he went to get them the next day; and he recalls a half eaten pawpaw that could not be finished until she had captured it on paper. 'She picked up on things that were natural, random ... like someone had come in and placed them down without intent—she picked up on things like that immediately'.[33] This spontaneity and affinity with the natural order of things is revealed in 1929, when having completed a commissioned egg painting for Jacqueline Whyte, Nora wrote in a letter accompanying the painting of the perils involved:

> Our hens have only just begun to lay again after an unusually long holiday so I had to pounce on the eggs as soon as they were laid, before they were seen and gathered by Michael for kitchen use. I used to hear the fowls cackling from the studio and rush down to get the egg while it was still warm and had that exquisite bloom on it. Sometimes it was days before a special hen would lay the exact shade I wanted for my study.[34]

Nora's plans for her paintings were not only at risk from a cook in a hurry but from a father who had helped train her eye for composition. Having meticulously set up a still life of onions to work on in her spare time, she returned to it to start work after her week at art school had ended. She told Klepac that she was irritated to see that her father had set up his easel and had already painted them. Hans Heysen was also prone to touches of insensitivity in his enthusiasm to guide his daughter; Nora was generous in her memory of him despite finding charcoal corrections covering a freshly finished work:

> ... [he] genuinely tried not to influence me so I could try to develop my own style. Sometimes he couldn't resist, of course. I remember one day I left a painting of a basket of eggs in the studio—which I thought was pretty good—but when I came back I found Father had drawn squares all over it showing where my draughtsmanship was wrong. I was furious. Of course, he was right, but it took me a long time to see it.[35]

Nora told Rusden the eggs she had painted were inspired by a work by George Lambert who had painted a single egg—'and everyone was trying to do eggs'. It is likely she was referring to Lambert's *Egg and cauliflower still life* 1926 (AGSA) depicting a beautifully rendered pale pink shell against the white and green of the highly textured cauliflower. She wanted to do a whole basket of eggs, not just one, and, in her enthusiasm, she 'had modeled them so round they were all over the basket'. Her father said she had lost the strength of her still life and Nora explained the issue:

> I always see things in the round and I'm inclined to draw a curve instead of a square and it goes through my work. Father said you weaken things when you use curves and strengthen them when you square them in and he was always at me for that. I agree with him perfectly now—and this is what I tell other people, not to slide into curves that slide away into curves instead of getting the strength and body of a thing. It was a good lesson to me because I'm conscious of it now. Maybe it's that female element [that] comes into me. I like curves. I still like curves.[36]

Throughout 1928 and 1929 Nora 'filled the house with portraits of every member of the family, sketching and painting with the same indefatigable industry as her father'.[37] Sketching and fastidiously recording her environment were central to Nora's practice but she was also refining her portraiture skills and would often use herself as a model. In her radio interview with Michael Cathcart she told him that she thought that painting a self portrait was like an animal marking out its territory. Each time Nora started work in a new place she started with a self portrait, 'to create my own territory I suppose, to establish myself in my surroundings'. She also told Cathcart that she was trying to set herself apart from her father when she produced the extraordinary self portraits of her twenties:

> I was trying to make my own name then, you see, as against being the talented daughter of the famous Hans Heysen and I think something of that must have crept into it—that I wanted to create myself and by doing a self portrait it was the best way I could think of, that I would make an image there of somebody and that was Nora Heysen, the daughter of Hans Heysen.[38]

Today, these early self portraits painted between 1932 and 1934 sit at the centre of her body of work. Former head of Australian Art at the NGA Anne Gray described these works as being painted by a diffident, strong, serious, semi-shy girl: 'All of them—looking at herself out of the corner of her eye appearing to ask "am I allowed to exist?" ... questioning, analysing, "who am I?", "what can I do?"'[39]

Despite the generosity and encouragement that took place at her father's side, Nora was at a disadvantage because she was a woman. Though times were changing, change came slowly and Nora faced many of the same issues that obstructed women of the previous generation. The pursuit of a life as artist was not widely seen as a serious role for a woman. When writing about artist Vanessa Bell's time as a student at the Royal Academy of Arts in 1902, Bell's biographer Frances Spalding refers to her marginalisation. Spalding quotes Bell as saying she could not share in the New English Art Club male members' apparent grasp of the 'secret of the art universe ... a secret one was not worthy to learn, especially if one was that terrible low creature, a female painter'. Bell, like Nora, was subject to the domestic rules of the day and as a daughter of a widower was required at the household table, leaving her art classes to serve tea and spice buns promptly at four-thirty every afternoon to her father and his visitors. On the death of her father, Bell's situation changed and on her marriage to Clive Bell, who wholly supported her artistic pursuits, she could afford nurses for her children, and cooks and housekeepers. Her situation coupled with her resolve permanently allowed her the freedom to work as an artist without the usual constraints a woman of her day experienced.

But, until then, Spalding notes that the boys in the family, just as in Nora's, did little to redress the imbalance:

> Though the twentieth century had begun, life at 22 Hyde Park Gate was still locked into the mid-Victorian age. The two Duckworth brothers did nothing to challenge [their stepfather Leslie Stephen's] long-established life-style but upheld, without question, all the accepted conventions. As Virginia [Woolf, Vanessa's sister] later observed: 'The cruel thing was that while we could see the future, we were completely in the power of the past'.[40]

Twenty years after Virginia Woolf made this observation Nora's father, as proud and encouraging as he was, spoke clearly about the expected role of women. Marriage, domestic duties, and divided loyalties made it virtually impossible for them to be serious career artists. The domestic role expected of Nora and her sisters in the family home was hard evidence of this. Chris Heysen, Nora's nephew, recalls: 'The shadow of whether she was recognised because she was the daughter or whether she was good in her own right just hung over her. Every time I met with her she talked about it'.[41] Anne Gray argues that Hans Heysen was a product of his generation; that while supportive of her endeavour, he was ultimately patronising to his daughter. Gray suggested that his male ego would only have allowed for him to remain as number one in the group of two artists in the family. While this is at odds with his outward behaviour—encouraging and supporting her study and recognising her natural talent—his actions were designed to influence her choices both in subject matter and technique because he felt he knew best. How would he have mentored a son? The inverse of that question is why did Nora acquiesce in the way that she did? Her social context gave her little alternative. In this era, a girl as career artist was not considered viable, but yes, girls could paint flowers. The fact that the Heysen artists divided their artistic territory, with Nora claiming portraiture and still life, helped Nora to make an independent reputation.[42] That she did not marry until relatively late in her life and did not have children were also factors. Were her successes in spite of her father's support and not as a result of it? The ensuing years would prove complex and fraught as Nora navigated her artistic route.

7. *A portrait study* 1933, oil on canvas, 86.5 × 66.7 cm.
Purchased with funds provided by the Art Foundation of Tasmania, 1986.
Collection of the Tasmanian Museum and Art Gallery.

8. *Eggs* 1927, oil on canvas, 36.6 × 52.5 cm.
The Howard Hinton Collection, New England Regional Art Museum.

9. *Self portrait* 1934, oil on canvas, 43.1 × 36.3 cm.
Collection of the National Portrait Gallery.

TOP: *10. Ruth* 1933, oil on canvas, 81.5 × 64.2 cm. Collection of the Art Gallery of South Australia. BELOW: *11. London breakfast* 1935, oil on canvas, 47.0 × 53.5 cm. Collection of the National Gallery of Australia.

TOP: *12. Self portrait* 1938, oil on canvas laid on board, 39.5 × 29.5 cm. Collection of the Queensland Art Gallery | Gallery of Modern Art. BELOW: *13. Corn cobs* 1938, oil on canvas, 40.5 × 51.3 cm. Collection of the Art Gallery of New South Wales.

14. *Spring flowers* 1938, oil on canvas on hardboard, 75.5 × 65.2 cm.
Collection of the Art Gallery of New South Wales.

15. Nora Heysen's winning Archibald Prize entry
Mme Elink Schuurman 1938, oil on canvas. Private collection.

16. Quinces 1991, pastel, 44.0 × 56.5 cm. Private collection.

When asked why she painted self portraits, just prior to the major retrospective in 2000, Nora replied:

> Well, I painted myself because I knew her; I am only shy with people ... [Painting self portraits] is the one time when you can be with yourself absolutely and just paint; you don't even have to get a likeness. There's this awful thing called a likeness and portrait painters are always up against it with every commission. It has to look like the person and everyone has a different idea of how a person looks ... With self-portraits you can be alone with yourself and not have to worry about another person.[43]

When her father was away on his painting trips in the north, she decamped from her studio back to his purpose-built space with its abundant natural light where she says she painted her early self portraits.[44] Nora's *Self portrait* 1932 (AGNSW) depicts her as an artist at work; she described it being modelled after Vermeer: 'on the walls [of the studio] were several Vermeer prints. I greatly admired Vermeer's works and I wanted to paint like him'.[45] It was gifted to the AGNSW by collector Howard Hinton the year she painted it when only twenty-one.[46] In his review of the travelling retrospective exhibition curated by Jane Hylton, *Nora Heysen: light and life* in 2009, during its Geelong Art Gallery showing, Robert Nelson, art critic for *The Age,* described the work:

> A self-portrait from 1932 shows the artist painting in the studio as if she lived in Delft during the 17th century. Framed tenebrist pictures adorn the wall; the chair draped with blue robe forms a buttress at the bottom right and the statuesque figure is a mighty triangle with light hitting one side of her face. Though pretending to belong to Vermeer's day, the picture is sincere. It confesses her love of an eternally rewarding human attribute: the tranquil gaze of a person concentrating on something marvellous.[47]

The year before she travelled to London to art school, Nora painted *A portrait study* 1933 (TMAG, *plate 7*). British art historian Frances Borzello's exploration of portraiture and subsequently self portraiture led to her writing a history of women working in this genre since the twelfth century, *Seeing ourselves: women's self-portraits*.[48] Nora's 1933 self portrait was selected as the front cover, an extraordinary achievement given the choices that would have been available to Borzello and her publishers. Borzello suggests that self portraits can be viewed as an extension of the idea of 'portraits ... [as] a microcosm of the huge world of painting ... Pose. Colour. Gesture. Composition. Tone ...' The way these elements are treated reflect 'character, conviction or lifestyle':

> ... an artist's studio is a private space, a site of creativity where most mortals have no access. Self-portraits are not innocent transcriptions of what the artist sees in the mirror: they are self dramatisations. Like autobiography, self-portraits attempt to tell a coherent story—not *the* truth, but *a* truth. Like writers, artists construct, create and present and it is this artifice I like about self-portraiture. Because if images are constructed, then it is possible to deconstruct them to see how the artists achieve their effects.[49]

In his *Australian Financial Review* article, Meagher describes Nora's self portraits as showing a 'great sense of determination' and quotes Andrew Sayers as saying 'there is an element in Australian art where artists deliberately set out to work in resistance to something. In her case, it might be her father. But the best things can come from that sense of rigour and pushing up against something'. Each of the self portraits executed over the years by Nora share a common sensibility with other portraits of the strong female subjects she chose to paint. Meagher cites Mary Eagle on the 'enigmatic qualities' of Nora's works:

> She's intriguing, particularly her self-portraits. There's a surprising similarity in all her portraits [of women, including *Motherhood* 1941 (AGB) and the paintings of a woman simply identified as 'Ruth']. All indicate strength, but they are composed, not bullying. They are amazingly positive looking people. They don't necessarily invite you into an exposition of her psychology, but they do invite you in and leave you wanting to know more, and the best art is about all those questions.[50]

In 1999 the NPG purchased *Self portrait* 1934 (*plate 9*) from Nora, a picture that Mary Eagle passed over as a possible acquisition for the NGA. Nora said that this was the first painting she did after she arrived in London and that her 'first response to a new setting was always to start with what she knew best—herself'.[51] During visits to interview Nora at her Hunters Hill home in 1995 and 1996 for her thesis, Kate Nockels reveals that she saw paintings languishing in the hallway of a wooden house she describes as in disrepair, with water running down the inside of the walls and over the pictures. Nockels spoke to Eagle, then senior curator of Australian Art at the NGA, and suggested she pay Miss Heysen a visit with the intention, if possible, to purchase works for the gallery.[52] Mary Eagle subsequently examined Nora's work in October 1996. According to Nockels, another significant painting, *London breakfast* 1935 (*plate 11*), a beautiful study of Nora's close friend Everton 'Evie' (Shaw) Stokes was also at risk in the hallway where vines were growing up through the floorboards. The NGA purchased *London breakfast* in 1996 after Eagle put it forward ahead of *Self portrait* 1934. I discussed the two works with her via correspondence in May 2017 and she shared her notes on the self portrait and was frank about her feelings about her recommendation not to purchase it made twenty-one years prior: 'Looking back, I don't know that I agree with my reasoning of that time. I'm glad that the portrait was later acquired by the National Portrait Gallery'. In her 1996 notes, Eagle reported on the work in detail after her meeting with Nora at The Chalet:

> Self Portrait c1934
>
> not signed
> not dated
> oil on canvas, now un-stretched
> height: the image without the exposed tacking edge … approx. 59 cm
> width: approx. 36.5 cm
>
> In poor condition … numerous small paint losses; faint, feathered cracking of a length of 2 inches beside left forehead. Very dirty. Unvarnished? No, answered Nora, varnished but now very dull. Nora thought she may have put linseed oil on it: at one time it was very shiny.

> Image of a strong face, introspective, mannerist in its simplicity & concentration of sculptural form & psychology. Hair is pulled back leaving the face naked. Plain background. Pale blue, round necked jumper under a brown velvet jacket. I made a brief sketch of the work. (Although I had come to Nora Heysen with an idea of buying the work in mind, I was not convinced that it would be the best acquisition. The work's outstanding quality is that it reveals the artist-subject's wincing vulnerability ... Not only is the painting in bad condition, better paintings of the frontier-type of resolute womanhood exist in public collections. Better to see if we can acquire the self-portrait [painted after her return from London in 1938] held by her [Nora's] Canberra god-daughter, which would present the public with a variation in the theme of the strong-mindedness, showing Nora after the London years, more poised, and with her strength now residing less in the neck than in the windows of her mind.)[53]

The work Eagle was hoping to secure was *Self portrait* 1938 (*plate 12*), which now hangs in the Queensland Art Gallery | Gallery of Modern Art (QAGOMA). It is considered one of Nora's finest works. Eagle was right to have hoped to acquire this work but at the time it was not on offer, as it was held privately by Meredith Stokes, the daughter of Everton Stokes, the sitter in *London breakfast*. It was cleaned and hangs in a central position in the NGA's Australian Collection alongside works by Nora's contemporaries who have also made a significant contribution to Australian art, including Margaret Preston, Grace Cossington Smith, Stella Bowen and Jeffrey Smart.

In *Self portrait* 1934, the work Eagle had decided not to recommend for purchase, Nora is just twenty-three, her face painted square on to the viewer, her head and shoulders visible. There are no accoutrements of an artist, often conventionally enlisted to tell us a painter is painting him or herself. Unlike the 1933 work chosen for this and for Borzello's cover, there is no easel or palette, no brush in the hand. The subject's gaze is engaged directly with the viewer, almost presenting a challenge, yet there is nothing disconcerting about the gaze, which has a disarming modesty. She is constructing her 'truth' in Borzello's terms. Nora's quiet self-assurance is visible. The 'wincing vulnerability' noted by Eagle adds a poignancy to the work when viewed in retrospect, knowing what was ahead for this naive and accomplished woman. Today the work hangs in fine company alongside Stella Bowen's self portrait, also painted in 1934 at the age of forty-one and purchased by the NPG in 2003, and Grace Cossington Smith's intimate and revealing self portrait of 1948 painted when she was fifty-six. Angus Trumble, Director of the NPG, has no reservations about where the young Nora belongs:

> … in Australia, between the two wars, it was women painters who spearheaded the bringing to this country of European modernism, and this group of compelling, small scale, intimate self portraits by Stella Bowen, Nora Heysen, and Grace Cossington Smith bring that theme into vivid focus.[54]

It took sixty-two years for Nora to be hung in the NPG. In her book *Stravinsky's lunch*, Drusilla Modjeska, writing about Stella Bowen, is concerned about the way the establishment had overlooked the artist. It might have taken sixty-nine years for Stella to find her rightful place at the NPG, but now she is rightly recognised. Referring to Borzello's 1998 *Seeing ourselves*, Modjeska felt that Bowen had not been given due recognition, particularly in the light of Nora Heysen being the only Australian artist to be listed 'in a recent book on women's self-portraiture by an art historian from London University'.[55] Nora was surprised at the selection of her portrait for the book's cover and over sixty years after she painted the work she remarked to Meagher:

> I rather like that portrait because it was all sort of handmade; I knitted the sweater and made the skirt … In that period the fashion was that you showed no breast, you had to bind up your bosom so it was flat. When I look at that portrait I think I could have put a bit more in—I had a big one at that time. Why I went along with the fashion I'll never know because I never have since.[56]

Nora appeared in the picture in her handmade clothes. Her works are bold but the domestic realm she inhabited is ever-present. Lou Klepac commented: 'She liked it [the book cover] because it was her work that was being honoured. Nora has always been certain of her own values and remained true to them all her life. Few painters have the same sense of dogged direction'.[57] Klepac noted that Nora was quietly proud of her painting being chosen for the prestigious cover: 'when you consider the women painters they could have used, that pleased her most of all'.[58] He said that Nora was also satisfied that the picture was chosen for an international publication on a topic unrelated to her father and that it had been independently chosen free from any influence he might once have held.[59] Modjeska, writing in 1999, issued a plea for the recognition of Stella Bowen: 'Now that there is a national portrait gallery in Canberra, maybe someone will be inspired to do the thorough search that is needed to place her [Bowen] among her peers as a painter of portraits. Maybe this chronicle of neglect is just another case of the world having to catch up with a woman whose art has long been lost to us'.[60] Thankfully, Nora was also to have her champions.

Over time, as Nora pursued her career as an artist, portraiture and still life, in particular flower painting, became her point of focus as her father pursued landscape—the genre that pleased his buyers. Hylton notes that Nora received her first portrait commission in 1932 for Mrs Janet Simpson and that 'two other portraits in oils that date from this period … show an innate understanding of facial features coupled with underlying structural form as taught by Frederick Millward Grey'.[61] Nora painted *Self portrait* 1932 (AGNSW), establishing the narrative of herself. Early in his career, Heysen's Melbourne-based art dealer and friend William H. Gill was acutely aware of buyer demand—Gill 'insisted on the one hand that he must paint what the public wanted, and on the other hand that he must avoid repetition'.[62] The Heysen artists divided up the genres. Nora offered her siblings a shilling to sit for her[63] and Sallie Heysen played her part, too. According to Schlusser, Sallie 'was helping steer Nora away from her father's landscapes toward portraiture'.[64] Sallie arranged for a local girl from the Hahndorf village, Ronda Paech, whom Nora renamed Ruth for her paintings, who delivered the family groceries, to sit for Nora for a fee. Nora recalled that her mother gave her a book on Renoir 'telling me that one day you will paint like him. Mother was also responsible for the initial idea of me continuing my studies in London'.[65] In conversation with Kate Nockels, Nora tells her of 'the deal', the second that was struck between Nora and her parents after she declared that she intended to make her living as an artist when she was twenty-two in 1933, after a successful first solo show in Adelaide:

> They decided that he would stick to the landscapes and she would do the figures, the portraits and still lifes—she didn't do any landscapes and he didn't do any figures after that. As I understood it from Nora they had a discussion … She loved figures in the landscape—that Renaissance composition, and some of her best [are the] war work, the formal heads of the women's services and Ruth. Hans Heysen did very few still lifes after that so they weren't competing in the same fields.[66]

Artist Margaret Woodward became friends with Nora when Lou Klepac brought the women together at Pens and Pencils, the drawing group he established in Sydney in 1991. Nora's personal situation in 1986 prompted Klepac to start the group including Judy Cassab, the second woman to win the Archibald, John Coburn, James Gleeson and other artists who had become physically and intellectually isolated as their art had become unfashionable, or at least out of the spotlight. At one point, the group had five past Archibald winners as members.[67] Woodward describes Nora's early portraits as having a 'fresh innovative eye in a traditional medium'.[68] The portrait *Ruth* 1933 (AGSA, *plate 10*) and *A portrait study—Ruth* 1933 (NGV) both show a strong-featured girl with a penetrating gaze positioned in a landscape. In conversation in 2000 with Allan Campbell, Nora told him that the period of painting Ruth 'was one of the most satisfying and creative periods of my life'.[69] Nineteen thirty-three was a pivotal year for Nora when her solo show in December raised close to one thousand pounds in sales, enough to fund art school in London for three years, and when she won the accolade of the Melrose Prize for portraiture with *Ruth* 1933.

The much admired works of *Ruth* are the precursor to Nora's goal of painting figures in the landscape. This would be largely denied her as the result of destructive critiques by influential men. The men advising her when she studied in London disparaged her ideas of working with the classical Renaissance composition that she aspired to. Her commitment was somewhat deflated, yet she did not entirely abandon her plan. Her work for the Australian War Memorial is testament to that. Jane Hylton comments that Nora felt the final portrait in the series of *Ruth* was one of her best works. Hylton comments on the recurring theme of female strength that appears in Nora's work:

> Stretching away behind her is a hilly landscape that effectively represents Ruth's territory, a world dominated by a presence symbolising female strength and potential. The female capacity became a theme—particularly that of motherhood—to which Heysen returned over a long period ... it was the first time Heysen expanded the notion of portraiture into something that encompassed not just an image but a concept.[70]

When he reviewed Hylton's travelling *Light and life* exhibition in 2009, Robert Nelson for *The Age* newspaper wrote about *Ruth* 1933:

> Among the many arresting pictures in Geelong is *Ruth* ... How does this woman with plaited hair in three-quarter pose before a dry hilly landscape acquire such astonishing presence?
>
> The composition seems simple with the horizon running halfway through the picture plane. This lets the painter establish some strong juxtapositions. The woman's dark tunic contrasts sharply against the backdrop, and the luminous face is set off against the light sky with the robust frame of hair.
>
> The formidable composition recalls Renaissance painting. The arms are folded gently and the head is tipped somewhat to the side, with a gaze that is both placid and penetrating. Our own position is in the middle of her chest and we therefore look up to her ...
>
> Heysen must have identified with the sitter ... The powerful eyebrows and large eyes, fixed with tranquil certainty, are very like Heysen's own, which you can see in her self-portraits. The gentle but steady gaze reveals exactly the direct and thoughtful attention to which Heysen's paintings testify.[71]

Nora's December 1933 show was held at the South Australian Society of Arts Gallery. Hylton reports: 'An extraordinary range and quantity of her work was shown—sixty-two paintings and drawings in all ... The drawings included several studies of gums and pine trees from around The Cedars, among the last of these landscape subjects that she was to make'.[72] The fact that Nora had a deeply developed understanding of how to render the landscape that surrounded her, and a powerful emotional connection with it, makes the viewer wonder about the direction her painting might have taken if this second deal had not been ratified. What works might have resulted from this young woman's industry and talent? Hylton also observes that Nora's landscapes were influenced by her father as she worked alongside him at The Cedars:

> Her beautiful landscape drawings, more tightly executed and formal than her father's but at times almost indistinguishable from his, indicate a deep understanding of sculptural form and the nature of the bush surrounding her home. In at least one drawing father and daughter worked collaboratively, Nora completing the sheep (or 'accessories' as she later called them) and Hans the trees.[73]

In her later years, Nora pointed out, in conversation with Schlusser, 'Well, I avoided gum trees. Father put a copyright on gum trees'.[74] In an encounter with the Australian governor-general Sir William Deane at the 1997 Australian War Memorial Remembrance Day ceremony, eighty-five year old Nora posed a wry question to Deane. *The Canberra Times* reported that he told Nora, '"We have a painting by your father hanging in our hallway." What was the painting of, Nora Heysen wondered, gum trees perhaps? Yes, gum trees the Governor-General confirmed'.[75] In 1933, family expectations of Nora appear to have cemented her already developing engagement with producing flower pictures and portraiture.

With the proceeds of her early artistic success, Nora was ready to support herself. She left Adelaide on 19 March 1934, with her parents and her three sisters Josephine, Deirdre and Freya, aboard the overnight train to Melbourne. London was their ultimate destination. They sailed from Melbourne for Europe on the *Aller*, a small German 'steamer' as Nora referred to it in her travel diary.[76] The family spent six weeks on a sea voyage that introduced Nora to sights she could never have imagined and others she had imagined would be exactly as they appeared. She struggled when exposed to extreme cultural differences in the scenes she witnessed in unfamiliar ports though she relaxed into European scenery which seemed familiar. She recorded her observations of the picturesque countryside of Holland: '... the flatness, the long even rows of trees ... the windmills, the quaint neat houses, the very green greens and the black and white cows, and dykes along the river bank all exactly as I had imagined'.[77] In contrast, after watching the navigation of the Suez Canal before reaching European waters, on deck as dawn broke in Port Said she writes: 'watched the native coalers coming in on their barges—they came in their thousands huddled together like animals asleep on top of their coal baskets and dressed in filthy black rags. Felt horrified and repulsed by the spectacle'. She describes the market and the main street of the port as 'a lot of sordidness, filth and trash' and she returned to the ship feeling 'disgusted and upset' by what she had seen. The genteel life on board appears to have been a welcome relief when she notes that the ship entered the Mediterranean later that afternoon.[78]

Daily life was repetitive except when land was sighted or there was a scheduled day in a port. Nora's entry early into the sea voyage describes a typical day:

> Thursday 5th April
> A beautiful day spent following the usual routine—breakfast at eight, an early morning swim after breakfast, then tennis then a swim, then German lessons then lunch, then reading writing sewing and studying German lessons, then afternoon tea at four then German lesson then tennis then bath then dinner then games out on the deck then bed at eleven. And so pass the days one like the other—nothing to see but an ever changing blue sea and a pale blue sky.[79]

Reading Nora's entries offers an insight into not just what each day held but also into her mind's eye: the particularity of things she noticed and the way she expressed her observations of nature as if she were composing a scene for a work of art. The painterly descriptions of her views built up a store of images in the young artist's visual imagination while revealing her way of 'seeing'. Her written imagery attests to her keen eye for detail and to the subtleties that she was able to distinguish and relay. While her naivety is on display in her poor capacity to accept different cultural experiences for what they were, her advanced training and level of sophistication of 'seeing' are already evident. They are on show when she writes about the ship's port of call in Malta:

> One of the most wonderful and inspiring days I have ever spent 'Malta' 'The dream city'. At 11 o'clock the Island evolved out of the mist and we entered the harbor in glorious sunshine. Moved and delighted beyond all measure by the great beauty of it all ... Rowed over to the city of 'Valletta' in a delightful painted boat like a goldalier [sic] and landed under a magnificent arch. Drove in carriages to the old capital 'Natabili' and enjoyed a thousand new and delightful sights ... The day was beautiful Springtime and a drowsy warmth in an air filled with the intoxicating scent of orange blossoms and flowers. The buildings were magnificent, beautifully proportioned and a lovely warm colour which gave a wonderfully harmonious feeling to the whole city. Everything was harmony not a jarring note anywhere. The narrow winding streets with their vivid glimpses of shadowed archways and brilliant patches of sunshine on the walls and the blue azure sea beyond, herds of goats moving down the streets—people coming out with their pannikins to milk their own supply ... groups of honey skinned children with dark melting eyes—kindly pleasant faced women sitting in the doorways or spinning ... the botanical gardens in 'Saint Antonio' were a dream—beautiful—a sanctuary of peace filled with flowers and fruits and trees and children, the scent of the orange blossom the drowsy peace laden air. All was surprisingly lovely.

In her dreamy state and with the optimism of youth, Nora ends the entry noting the ships departure at 9.30 in the evening and promises herself that she will return 'to live there for a while and paint there'.[80] The next day was spent watching the coast of Tunisia after sighting Cape Bon and passing the island of Pantelleria off Sicily, and celebrating Hitler's birthday (because it was a German ship). She adds a foreboding note—that three submarines 'like grey snakes'[81] crossed in front of the *Aller.* The ship afforded views of the south-east coast of Spain and the snow-capped Sierra Nevada mountains on one side and the Atlas Mountains of north-west Africa on the other. In the last days of April, following the standard route through the Strait of Gibraltar, the Bay of Biscay and then up the Garonne River with a pilot on board, the ship docked near Bordeaux, and Nora describes her first impressions of France:

> ... the lovely lanes—heard the cuckoos sing and a thousand birds and picked wild flowers ... Saw magnificent old homes, beautiful gateways ... Departed at half-past three and sailed smoothly down the river on a delightful spring afternoon—with a rural idyllic landscape on either side and wonderful old homes along the rivers edge magnificent rows of poplars everywhere and elms and willows and acres of vineyards—[82]

Over the weeks on board Nora had been drawing various passengers. While she doesn't mention her satisfaction with the work, she does refer to finishing drawings including one of the German teacher and a Mr Garland, who celebrated his thirty-first birthday with the Heysens. After an unscheduled stop at Dover and the final stage up the English Channel, the family arrived in Antwerp and Nora observed the 'exquisite beauty of the Antwerp cathedral against a luminous sky',[83] while noting one of the first paintings she viewed on her grand tour when visiting the cathedral was *The descent from the cross* 1612, by Rubens, a good start for her education.

Two and a half months after leaving Australia, the Heysen entourage arrived in London on 3 May 1934. Curiously Nora decided to note her weight on leaving home—8 stone 4 lbs—and again in London, at 9 stone 6lbs. She wasted no time pondering this and no doubt the pace she gathered covering gallery floors saw her rapidly gain fitness after the indulgences of life aboard ship. Day two after settling into accommodation with her family at Berkeley Hall she headed straight to the National Gallery:

> Saw the old Italian Masters (Florentine School) enraptured with the simple beauty of 'The Nativity' by Piero della Francesca and his other masterpieces and still more keenly impressed with Michael Angelo's [sic] 'Entombment'. The beauty and rhythm of the design—the heroic grandeur of the figures and the simple and beautiful colour scheme with the subtle modeling of Christ's body—a masterpiece that thrilled me ... an altogether thrilling and inspiring morning.[84]

With her visual education immediately underway Nora writes of enthusiastic responses to the National Gallery, the Royal Academy of Arts, the Royal Institute of Oil Painters, the Wallace Collection, of visiting exhibitions by Duncan Grant (the partner of artist Vanessa Bell, both founding members of the Bloomsbury Group) and Maurice Lambert (a sculptor and son of painter George Lambert whose work Nora admired), and a visit to Kew Gardens all in the first four days after arriving. By the end of the week she had included the Tate Gallery, two visits to the picture theatre, a night at Queen's Hall to hear works by Schubert, Strauss and Wagner, and visits to both Westminster Cathedral and Abbey. She commented that at the Tate at Millbank she experienced 'a rare artistic treat'—and claims to being 'very interested in Spencer's "Resurrection"'[85] —apparently referring to English painter Stanley Spencer's neo-romantic hallucinatory representation *The resurrection of the soldiers* 1928–29, a homage to the fallen of World War I.

The month of May passed at exhibitions, at the theatre, films and concerts, visits to the National Portrait Gallery, and repeated return visits to favourite works at the National Gallery. These included: 'the Veroneses & the Titian *Bacchus and Ariadne* 1523 ... I specially looked at the Alfred Stevens portrait of a woman and was more than ever in love with it. So beautifully and sensitively modeled and full of fine reserve and dignity'.[86] Nora made her way to the Victoria and Albert, and British museums and then on the first day of June to the Chelsea Flower Show.

Her diary provides us with a clear sense of her constant engagement with the art she is viewing. For a young person she is not afraid to have an opinion on works by established names. After a visit to the Dulwich Picture Gallery she writes that she was 'charmed with the intimate atmosphere' that the pictures were 'good' and that she was 'particularly impressed with the Velasquez [sic] portrait—dignified and subtle in colour scheme'. She was also taken with a Gainsborough describing it as 'naive and full of charm'. After viewing these works she attended the ballet at Regents Park noting that fellow South Australian 'Bobby [Robert] Helpmann danced beautifully'.[87] But the modern works that she approached challenged Nora. In 1926 Glaswegian art dealer Alex Reid and London dealer Ernest Lefevre established their gallery Reid and Lefevre in King Street, St James's. Reid had studied in Paris with Theo van Gogh and lodged with his brother Vincent. Reid and Lefevre would become the pre-eminent dealers of the day in French impressionist and European modernist work. When she visited the Lefevre Gallery, as it became known, Nora was comfortable assessing Corot's and Renoir's work—the Corot 'beautiful quality, big in feeling and well designed'. She was uncertain when challenged with new styles and wrote in her diary 'the Cezannes, Van Goghs and Picassos left me bewildered. Chaos. Ridiculously high prices'.[88] Her visit to Germany with her family before commencing her studies provided her with the opportunity to engage with the art that reassured her—Rembrandt, Vermeer, van Eyck and Dürer.

Her days were not entirely filled with visits to galleries. The Heysen family had many social invitations and these included lunches and dinners with aristocratic peers, and the establishment of the Academy art world. A close friend of Hans Heysen, Dr Shirley Jones, escorted them to lunch where Shirley's relative Lady Fox 'served in style with two butlers to wait at table and superb china and silver'; then they proceeded to meet Lord and Lady Dugan who were preparing to leave for South Australia to take over from the Hon. Alexander Hore-Ruthven, who was retiring as governor. Nora writes of her vice-regal meeting in her journal:

> Felt awkward and hated the afternoon … In the evening went with Daddy and Mother to Mr. Anderson's home and spent a most delightful time in Mr. Anderson's studio listening to [him] & Daddy & Mr. Bateman discussing art. Heated argument about Epstein. Felt very happy to be in a studio atmosphere again.[89]

James Bateman was a painter and member of the Royal Academy, a contemporary and friend of Hans Heysen. Hans Heysen relished discussing art. On this occasion the subject was the sculptor Jacob Epstein. Epstein had become entranced with the Epping Forest near where he lived and had produced a large collection of watercolours that was exhibited at the end of 1933 at Arthur Tooth & Sons in London.[90] His work was known to challenge audiences and these paintings had received wide acclaim. Heysen was an advocate of painting *en plein air* that Epstein had adopted for these watercolours—it is possible that the more conservative Bateman was at odds with his friend. Epstein's style confronted conservatives. It is ironic and sad that the comfort Nora felt in the studio with James Bateman and her father would later be replaced with disquiet and upset when her father's friend had little encouragement for her student work.

17. Nora with Hans and Sallie Heysen, 1934, in Wales during their travels before her parents return to Australia after establishing Nora in her London studio. Papers of Nora Heysen, National Library of Australia.

FOUR: TRUTH, ART AND HITLER

So many painters today express what they feel they 'should' see rather than what they 'feel' they see. If an artist is not honest with himself, God help him. -Hans Heysen[1]

To look. To see. To really see—it is the ultimate result if you do it well enough, and contribute something of the imagination and the real knowledge to anything you do—it must have an effect on the viewer... you don't just look—you see, you feel. -Nora Heysen[2]

The London Nora arrived to in 1934 had been able to ride out the worst of the Depression years. In the 1920s, England had experienced a period of relief from the ravages of conflict. The surviving generation that had been too young to fight in World War I, along with those that had returned, was eager to live for the moment after the supposed 'War to End All Wars'. The era of the Bright Young Things, the British equivalent of the flappers and Gatsby era of the United States, was a time when the children of the wealthy and middle class pursued pleasure:

> The party set were obsessed with jazz which they saw as modern, raw and anti-establishment. They drank to excess, took drugs such as hashish, cocaine and heroin and indulged in licentious behaviour. They frequented the cocktail bars, jazz clubs and night clubs of London where they danced and drank till dawn.[3]

By 1931 the Bright Young Things were no longer receiving attention from the press they had once been accorded. Their behaviour was not indulged amid the deprivations that so many had suffered after 1929. Nora and her family arrived to a country in distress. The British government was working haplessly to avoid another devastating war through its failing policy of appeasement as it responded to the rise of the National Socialists in Germany.[4] At the same time that Jewish émigrés were arriving to escape danger and discrimination, Oswald Mosley was gathering support for his British Union of Fascists, and the Communist Party, while putting its political support behind Labour, had celebrated the fiftieth anniversary of Karl Marx's death with the opening of the Marx Memorial Library in Clerkenwell Green.[5] Intense pressure was also coming from unions desperate to improve working-class conditions. The National Unemployed Workers Movement held marches drawing attention to their plight from 1929 through to 1936.[6] By 1934, relieving workers' housing stress was a priority for the London County Council, though conservative politics and interest groups hindered a speedy solution.[7] Seemingly impervious to the political and social turmoil around her, Nora was focused on her studies and the excitement that the extraordinary city of London held for her. Her travel diary and later her letters home address little of the social issues facing Britain, although they do form the context of her life in London.

The strength of Nora's commitment to her art underpinned all her actions. For Nora, art was about what she designated as 'truth'. This notion of 'truth in art', which may seem so imprecise to a contemporary reader, was learned from her father and would later be a central tenet discussed between the two as artists, engaged in a lifetime of dialogue. In her conversations with Eugene Schlusser, Nora reveals that her father 'wanted me to be free of influences, but he couldn't help himself … he did influence me, and I was influenced by his work quite apart from anything he told me about it'.[8] At critical times, as she developed her own style, she would question his firm beliefs, though they were of central importance to her. In 1922 Hans Heysen had written to his friend Lionel Lindsay, 'I cannot help feeling that my heart lies with these men who see intense and almost religious beauty in simple Nature that surrounds us—in the beauty of the skies and the mystery of the earth'.[9] This was a view of the time held by Heysen and those of his contemporaries who admired the work of John Constable and the Barbizon School of the 1820s. The Barbizon School, including Théodore Rousseau and Jean-François Millet, broke away from a narrowly prescribed code of landscape painting in the Neoclassical tradition that purported to 'emulate artists of the Renaissance and classical antiquity' attempting an 'idealized nature inspired by ancient poetry'. The French village of Barbizon, where these breakaway artists stayed, is on the edge of the Forest of Fontainbleu, a landscape favoured by those who were committed to working *en plein air* 'to fully experience nature, to look rather than copy, to feel rather than analyze'. [10] Heysen regularly discussed his goals for his work with friends and fellow artists. He shared his philosophy about what art should hold for the viewer, and how the artist should approach the process. All the while, Nora was observing and absorbing her father's fundamental tenets, honouring them, but the time would come when the young woman would question them.

Heysen's iterations can be read as a man constantly putting his case at a time when new trends in the art world were challenging and confronting him and his fellow artists. Modernism represents a string of artistic movements that had their origins in Europe beginning in the late nineteenth and early twentieth centuries. These movements included cubism, surrealism, abstractionism, expressionism, fauvism, dadaism, *de stijl* to mention some—but all were based on an underlying principle:

> A rejection of history and conservative values (such as realistic depiction of subjects); innovation and experimentation with form (the shapes, colours and lines that make up the work) with a tendency to abstraction; and an emphasis on materials, techniques and processes.[11]

European modernists were all striving to find new ways to represent a changing world. They included dadaist Marcel Duchamp, Pablo Picasso, and Georges Braque who were exploring new territory, breaking established rules in the early 1900s with provocative cubist works; German expressionists such as Kirchner, Heckel and Kandinsky; and Italian Futurists Marinetti, Carrà, Severini and Boccioni. Modernist agendas 'were often utopian, and modernism was in general associated with ideal visions of human life and society and a belief in progress'.[12] In the aftermath of the devastation of World War I, modernism continued to evolve across Europe. Jane Hylton observes that Heysen's ideas 'derived from European art and humanist philosophies, as well as his personal sense of place in a rapidly changing world'. She adds that:

> ... a fixation on European masters as artistic source, a retreat from modern life and modernist ideas, the trauma of wartime

> anti-German prejudice and family loss and a determination to be ever-true to nature—ultimately tipped the balance of power and influence of his work towards the anchoring classical elements of balance, form and composition.[13]

And so Heysen was maintaining his philosophical ground in Australia.

These were the inherited influences and understandings Nora took with her when she travelled abroad. As late as her trip to study in England in 1934, the academic tradition was still firmly entrenched in the establishment art schools Nora would attend, and it would come to be a challenge as she developed between the influences of the new and the old. For his part, Hans Heysen was clearly not enamoured with the new. He expresses his feelings to Sydney Ure Smith, at the end of 1934 after returning from Europe and viewing collections in England, Germany and Holland:

> Men like Derain, Picasso, Utrillo frankly left me disappointed and unfortunately I did not see any of Severini's work, which has long interested me ... Braque and Co left me entirely cold and I saw an exhibition in Liverpool of 'Unit One' Society ... which evidently was an outcome of Braque and Co's influence. A collection of flat patterns—in black, grey and white—with no hint of representational form, no plastic form and no recession. It was all a conundrum to me ... I wonder what the general public thought of it.[14]

In her diary, Nora recorded the visit to Liverpool with her parents as the guests of Dr Shirley Jones. It was an interesting exercise for a young woman intent on absorbing and observing as much as she could at every opportunity with the privileges that came with travelling with her famous father. Her observations tell us just as much about Nora as they do about those under her observation. Another of Shirley Jones's guests, a Mr Cohen, the chairman of Liverpool's Walker Art Gallery, was responsible for Hans Heysen having the opportunity to view the *Unit One* show. After a stimulating dinner and champagne Nora wrote that Cohen had a 'brainwave' and suggested he open up the gallery that night for his friends which she said was greeted with 'loud applause of enthusiasm':

> Arrived at the 'Adelphi'—excessively luxurious—Dined with Dr. Jones and Mr Cohen ... Sava Botzaris [sculptor] also of the party a thick set strong and energetic little man with a big forehead and protruding dark brown eyes and a row of very white teeth. First thing I saw were the teeth. Spoke ten languages but on this occasion spoke mostly about himself. Also Dr. Littler Jones brother of Shirley was of the party. A clever surgeon. A question was put by Mr. Cohen 'What was the greatest thing in life?' Some of the answers 'Love' 'Health' 'Happiness' 'Birth' 'Death' 'Sense of Humour' 'Art'. Interesting.[15]

She describes how they all responded immediately to the suggestion to visit the gallery that was lit with electric light for the viewing—for the first time in its history. It had been closed for extensions for two years, reopening in 1933. The gallery's collection dates from 1819 and holds Italian and Netherlands works from between the 1300s and 1500s, European art from the 1500s including Rembrandt, Poussin and Degas, and a large pre-Raphaelite collection.[16] Nora was in her element with this private access:

> We all tore through in evening dress admired the bigness and beauty of the well lit rooms and the well chosen pictures. Everything looked surprisingly good. As a top off we saw the work of a group of Modernists who called themselves Unit One—which was funny and childish—Quite a thrill—very excited. Left with my head whirling with a first unusual impression of a fine spacious gallery and a feeling of satisfaction at the thought that there were still people interested enough in art to give their time and energy and money in presenting such a fine collection for the pleasure and education of the public.[17]

While Nora was more lenient than her father, with her touch of youthful condescension for the Unit One modernists, she did hold strong views after visiting an exhibition of German expressionists at the Hamburg Art Gallery. Her views corresponded with his extreme response to the same show. Hans Heysen had arranged a few weeks in Germany after the family spent three months taking in the sights and events of a London summer. Along with Josephine and Deirdre (Freya had joined a different private tour up the Rhine),[18] and her mother and father, Nora visited people and places significant to the family in Hamburg, Berlin and Nuremberg. Nora was vehement in her dislike for the expressionists: 'repulsive, the worst rubbish ever seen and an insult to one's intelligence'.[19] Her father, writing to his mother in Adelaide about the Hamburg Gallery, was also decisive and commented that 'there are some quite interesting pictures, much rubbish, and many terrible modern works which would want to make any honest painter commit suicide'.[20] Engagement with Vermeer at the Kaiser Frederick Museum in Berlin enthralled father and daughter.[21] Nora went with her father to the Pergamon Museum to view the collection describing it as 'beautiful and thrilling', though she savaged the gallery itself:

> Saw the Kaiser Frederick collection—some beautiful masterpieces amongst them—Vermeer's Pearl Necklace deeply impressed me and a lovely Terboch [Gerard ter Borch] with a lady in a magnificently painted silver skirt—also some fine Rembrandts and Botticellis & a wonderful Van Dyck portrait of a man—Pictures badly displayed—rotten gallery badly lit & arranged—shocking taste.[22]

Hans Heysen concurred, suggesting that the London galleries displayed their collections with a better understanding of how to show a picture to its best advantage, and describing the Berlin gallery 'with walls the wrong colour, the rooms too small, and the lighting *too crude*'.[23] The family left Berlin for Nuremberg and once again Nora described the scenes she viewed en route in her painterly style:

> ... the country was very charming and delightfully picturesque more hilly & wooded and a beautiful patchwork quilt effect of yellows of corn & greens of grass & rich purples of ploughed earth & each colour in infinite varieties laid in narrow strips on the slopes of the hills white oxen ploughing women working in full blue skirts with white hankerchiefs [sic] tied round their heads reminded me of Millet's gleaners—delightful and peaceful rural scenes ... carts piled high & children running after the carts.[24]

The influence of her father is evident in Nora's reference to Millet. Lou Klepac lists French painter Jean-François Millet as one of Hans Heysen's major influences 'from whom he inherited a grand vision of form'.[25] Nora recalls that Nuremberg was marred by flags covering the buildings and houses, and that the streets were crowded with 'sightseers and soldiers marching'.[26] The city was in a flurry of final preparations for the September 1934 Nazi Party rally where 700,000 supporters would converge in the following weeks. After visiting the home of Albrecht Dürer, she went to the museum where her exploration of the great traditional painters continued in what she described as a 'beautifully arranged' space: '... full of treasures—exquisite wrought iron work—early German wood carvings of Madonnas full of a primitive charm. A wonderful Van Eyck Madonna and child. Too much to see—Albrecht Dürer head of his master very fine'.[27]

The family had arrived in Germany mid 1934, an unsettled period with reports of shootings and imprisonments, though they did not see any unrest. The Heysens had begun their tour of family reunions and art discoveries just four days after Hitler had ended a week-long purge of SA officers and others he deemed disloyal to his dictatorship. This was known as the Night of the Long Knives.[28] Hundreds were murdered, but the Heysen family had arrived to a seemingly peaceful nation.[29] Nora's diary entry after a fifty-mile drive from Nuremberg to Rothenburg belies the underlying tension in the country:

> A lovely fresh morning with a few white clouds—passed through beautiful countryside—saw it under ideal conditions —everywhere the peasant people hay-making in their picturesque costume ...—bullocks and cows all a biscuit colour or white ... Saw delightful family groups all working together at their plots of land. Everything done in a primitive way. The crop mowed by hand—the women cutting with the men or helping to tie up the bundles of hay with ropes of twisted stalks, while the children minded the herd of geese ... The villages were charming and fitted in so perfectly in the landscape. The houses squatting close to the ground their roofs almost touching it. The old tiles a lovely warm red ... looked down on the valley ... and the old walled city of Rothenburg—looked

> like a city in Grimm's Fairy tales full of romance drawing in the old world atmosphere of the Medieval age—entered the gate and were in a world of the imagination—walked round dumb with wonder fascinated with the quaint houses ... lovely doorways & gay window boxes & the winding streets ... & the towers & churches & the lovely wrought iron work and beautiful fountains in the streets & the signs wrought most beautifully & all the lovely designs so original & unique everything to the smallest detail considered & a work of art—Lovely little peaceful garden overlooking the valley of the Tauber.[30]

Reading her diary gives an impression that sometimes Nora did not have the words to adequately express what she was seeing but she is attempting to record the scenes, and her impressions, as accurately as possible. Her comment about the designs of the village's wrought iron signage 'everything to the smallest detail considered' offers us, through her observation, an indication of what mattered to her at that time. In later life, she abhorred all repressive social structures, including the strictures of class delineation.

Nora writes on her arrival in Hamburg that they were met by her mother's relatives Aunt Annie and Uncle Paul: 'first time we had all met for over 15 years ... all stared at each other and noted resemblances—Margot quite good-looking—very slight and small and delicately made—felt a huge country bumpkin in comparison'.[31] Like many of the women in her portraits, Nora was handsome and majestic, close to five feet ten inches (178 cm) tall. She continued to maintain her diary and wrote of more than a few picturesque villages they encountered during their German tour: of the beer gardens by the river, the coffee and *kuchen* they regularly enjoyed; and the 'disgusting exhibition of German modern art' at the Hamburg Art Gallery while adding that in the evening they listened to broadcasts by Hitler.[32]

Josephine wrote numerous postcards to Max Williams back in Oakbank expressing her dismay at the ugliness of London, confessing to being unable to 'get a thrill out of London despite its history', suggesting her 'lack of English blood' could be the reason for her antipathy. From Nuremberg she asks Williams his view of Hitler:

> I wonder are you in favour of Hitler—you and I never talk politics so I don't know. To Germany he is the angel that is delivering them from destruction. They worship him blindly. I'd love to see him, they say he is marvellous and has the most fascinating eyes.[33]

On another card Josephine writes that the family is scheduled to leave Nuremberg the next morning, the day Hitler was due to arrive prior to the rally at the Luitpold Arena, the setting for the Leni Riefenstahl propaganda film *Triumph of the will*. What would Josephine have made of *Lichtdom*, architect Albert Speer's *Cathedral of light* epic installation of anti-aircraft searchlights casting vertical lights into the sky around the Zeppelin Field?[34] She writes to Williams: 'I am terribly disappointed as I did want to catch a glimpse of him and feel the intense excitement of the crowd'. Running in tandem with Josephine's naive commentary on Hitler are her observations of her German surroundings: 'On the lakes and parks, bordered with shrubbery and blossoms gracefully glide white swans. Roses are in full bloom and filling the air with fragrance. These trees on the card are the trees I love so much they are in flower now and the scent is enough to touch the hardest heart. No wonder Germans get homesick for their Fatherland'.[35] Josephine's romantic observations, removed from the political reality, underline the protected world she and her sisters inhabited.

While Nora and her father are busy rejecting artworks and Josephine is describing the many beauties she observes in the German landscape, their innocence eerily provides a backdrop for the position Hitler held that 'National-Socialist Germany … wants a German Art of eternal value …' In 1937, Hitler took his position to the people:

> Adolf Hitler defined 'modern' art by opposition to ethnic art … 'as nothing but an international communal experience, thus … killing altogether any understanding of its integral relationship with an ethnic group … we desire for ourselves an art which takes into account within itself the continually growing unification of this race pattern and, thus emerges with a unified, well-rounded total character'.

Co-authors Mary Eagle and John Jones in *A story of Australian painting* observe that the Americans and the Russians, though diametrically opposed on so many fronts, also both held to a narrative of 'earthy identities':

> ... these countries promoted an image of homely folk ... in contrast to the sophisticated foreign import, abstraction. Italy and Germany proposed an ideal humanism as their national styles, Germany looking to the Aryan ideal and Italy to the classical. Here [Australia], as elsewhere, national identity was a preoccupation of official culture. Australia alone virtually ignored the human motif ... finding her national identity in the landscape and specifically in the light that gave colour and atmosphere.[36]

Margaret Plant, Emeritus Professor of Visual Arts at Monash University, has explored Australia's relationship with modernism. She explores the appeal of Heysen during the Federation years, his skill at embracing the 'homely and heroic' that reflected what she describes as '*gemütlichkeit*'[37] (an atmosphere of comfort, peace and acceptance) in the rural and picturesque. Eagle and Jones comment on the way that modernist ideas precipitated feelings of disquiet:

> The post-war nostalgia for an earlier way of life ran counter to the forces for change through modern technology. Fear of change, fear of disruption, the need for reassurance were strong emotional factors in deciding attitudes to modern art. Modernism nonetheless represented a contemporary reality ... like every other western country, Australia was committed to modernity through its acceptance of electricity, radio, the aeroplane and functional design. Modernity was the way the world was going.[38]

In Australia, modernism faced a slow rate of acceptance evidenced well into the 1940s. Sydney artists were more conservative, while in Melbourne, there was a willingness to engage with change. Art patrons Sunday and John Reed challenged a public and an art establishment largely unwilling to consider work verging on the experimental when they established an avant-garde enclave at Heide in Victoria. The artists central to the Melbourne modernist movement were all members of the Angry Penguins, part of a broader collaboration between John Reed, then head of Victoria's Contemporary Art Society, and the surrealist poet Max Harris. Harris was the original publisher of the movement's avant-garde magazine that sponsored the group's name; all were influenced by the works that had disturbed Heysen and his contemporaries. They made it their mission, through their political and aesthetically challenging approach, to contest the establishment ideals of what constituted art:

> The aim of the group was to modernise Australian creative arts and poetry, and challenge traditions they saw as restrictive in Australia in the 1940s … The symbolic surrealism in the works by Nolan, Boyd, Hester and Tucker added a new and exciting dimension to a somewhat stagnant Australian art.[39]

In contrast to the European artists' response to war, Margaret Plant suggests that World War I, along with the Federation years, frustrated the rise of modernism in Australia, with painters such as Rupert Bunny perhaps the closest to expressing some kind of modern view in his work that reflected the Australian attitude of the day, that of one which embraced an idea of 'belonging' in the newly federated country:

> Necessarily Australian art was closed off from modernism, seeking traditional and reassuring beauties. Paris modernism in the first decade of the twentieth-century—in Braque, Picasso, Matisse, Derain—was necessarily aggressive, destructive, for only through attack could it eschew tradition.[40]

During this period in Australia, Hans Heysen provided these 'traditional and reassuring beauties', offering a safe alternative to the fear of the unknown and the modern, and he would continue his life's work based on the principles that he established early in his career with the goal of representing nature and the 'glory' it held for him. All the 'isms' that would encroach into his art world, he rejected as 'unhealthy':[41]

> How terribly tired one gets of all this lifeless and soulless conglomeration of lines and cubes which really mean nothing at all. How full of humanity—life and romance and fresh air—when I think of our mutual friend Constable. The more I see his work the more I love it and respect the man ...[42]

For Heysen, 'truth' in art lay in the capacity to observe nature—not to represent it as in photorealism but to understand it and represent it with what he regarded as a balance of emotion and with his sense of fidelity—'I doubt the value of a painting unless it has that "inner feeling" that is the result of a love for the thing seen and painted ...'[43] The symbolic surrealism subscribed to by the modernists did not inspire the 'inner feeling' he held at the core of his aesthetic, rather it appears that it added a sense of disquiet and imbalance. His aesthetic was established early in his career after his formal training in Europe. In an address to members of the South Australian Society of Arts in Adelaide in 1906 he delivered his paper 'Observations on art' and noted: 'A glance at Nature would indicate that it would be foolish and impossible to paint in every detail. To know how much to conventionalise and yet retain truth could be acquired only by close study and comparisons between Nature and the works of the best masters ...' Thiele points out that the 'truth' that Hans Heysen referred to was the apparent truth of realism, and that it was this steadfast adherence to this belief system for the role of the painter that might have eventually marginalised Hans Heysen from the progressive art world of later years. According to Thiele, Heysen 'rejected out of hand' the idea of the imagination impacting on the physical world 'if it meant distorting its natural forms', a conviction which some of his later critics were to seize on as the basic and stultifying weakness of the whole Heysen philosophy. Heysen maintained that:

> ... the 'truth' lay in shape, form and colour which could be observed and recorded, which was palpably and demonstrably 'real', he had little patience with what he called 'concoctions of the mind'. He was a landscape painter in a realistic tradition—an academic tradition—with the strengths and weaknesses of the premise on which this was based.[44]

It is notable that both Hans and Nora Heysen were engaged by the work of Cézanne,[45] and Plant's writings offer a possible explication for why this might have been the case when the two were grappling with the changes around them and the conflicting philosophies that they were forced to consider. Plant suggests that Cézanne's approach to the modern allowed for the comfort of the familiar:

> Federation necessarily frustrated modernism. Cézanne—the major figure for Australian modernism, such as it is—is preferred because his safety net is capable of repetitive, diagrammatic application to the safe genres of landscape, portrait and still-life. Cézanne remains acceptable as the key model even to post-Second World War Australian artists such as Godfrey Miller and John Passmore. Ours is a *gemütlichkeit* modernism.[46]

In a letter to Sydney Ure Smith, Heysen wrote that 'Cézanne and van Gogh were intense and great individualists, and I liked the bulk of their work immensely', although he added that he had reservations about some of Cézanne's paintings and was sometimes disappointed in them, finding them 'too static'. Heysen did, however, discover 'recompense in [Cézanne's] colour',[47] asserting 'I believe in the modern movement so far as its insistence on design and essential form, instilled with life and vitality are concerned, but not where it tolerates crude craftsmanship'.[48] He wrote in his letter to Ure Smith that 'No doubt we owe a deal to Cézanne for his determined fight against the impressionists who had run their objective to its extreme limit, and it was time a definite reaction set in to stop the "dry rot" of disintegration'.[49] The idea that Cézanne acted in some way as a brake on what Heysen perceived as the dangers of the modernist approach put Cézanne on the right side of progress in Heysen's view, despite his reservations about the work of the Frenchman.

According to Eagle and Jones, post–World War I Australian painters assisted in Australia finding a national identity. Hans Heysen, along with Arthur Streeton and Elioth Gruner, dominated the genre:

> In human terms the war was a disaster from which society recovered only very slowly. For some years afterwards Australian painters expressed themselves most feelingly when portraying the landscape. And so the war contributed to an already existing tradition whereby the landscape rather than the people was used to express human emotions as well as national aspirations.[50]

These factors contribute to understanding why Hans Heysen's work remained popular with the art-buying public for as long as it did in the face of swiftly changing views in Europe, but Nora was engaging with this new sensibility and finding her own way as an art student in prewar London of the mid 1930s.

During her time in London, Nora was introduced to Australian-born artist Roy de Maistre, who had immigrated to England in 1930 as he was unable to make a living from his art that was based in a form of 'academic cubism'.[51] De Maistre changed his name from Roi de Mestre because he thought it was a modern version and more in keeping with his modernist aesthetic; it also allowed him to link himself to the philosopher Joseph de Maistre.[52] Nora met him in 1937 in London, where he enjoyed a reputation as 'a modernist of some note'.[53] Throughout her life's correspondence with her father, the topic of discussion was predominantly art, both the shifting trends and the personal aspects of each other's work. She wrote to her parents about finding de Maistre interesting to speak to at their meeting:

> He is a rank modern, thinks that Picasso and Henry Moore are the two great men of the age. Picasso is holding an exhibition at present. I went to see it and came away feeling that he was a charlatan. I simply couldn't take the work seriously… but there you are, another man can come along with intelligence and knowledge, and find expression and meaning there which he finds satisfying and interesting. What strangely conflicting views there are about.[54]

The irony lies in the fact that all three artists claimed to be searching for the 'truth' in art. Truth is clearly a subjective matter, and each formulated their own versions. While de Maistre was in France, just as with the two Heysens, Hans before him and Nora after, 'he learnt to admire the French for finding "the Good, the Beautiful and the True"'. While it seems that Nora did not know this about de Maistre, her observations of him suggest that she held a more open approach to the notion of another 'truth' than the one her father claimed. While de Maistre might have left Nora puzzled, at the same time he was a pivotal influence on Australian writer Patrick White, introducing him to his ideas on modernism. White's biographer David Marr tells us, 'De Maistre's paintings were the great lesson for the young man [White]. They were abstract, fractured and difficult, but de Maistre's aim was not to paint patterns on canvas but to show the real world in a fresh light'. It was 1936, the year White met de Maistre, the same year White read James Joyce, 'making more sound than sense at times' in *Ulysses*.[55] Both events were turning points, with White describing Joyce 'as practically God' and de Maistre the painter as his 'intellectual and aesthetic mentor … he persuaded me to walk in the present instead of lying curled and stationary in that over-upholstered cocoon the past, refuge of so many Australians then and now'.[56] Perhaps it was de Maistre's guidance of the young Patrick White that allowed him to embrace the *enfant terrible* of the 1960s, Brett Whiteley, forty years later. White found his work in 1970 '"staggering"': '"He's the only Australian painting on the same scale as Nolan, with equal diversity in his imagination"'.[57] The cross-tensioning between artists that hold different aesthetic views is interesting to observe. Nora's archived papers include carefully cut-out stories on Brett Whiteley.[58] According to Meredith Stokes Nora 'loved' Brett Whiteley's work.[59] Nora might have been surprised to know that she shared more than just the same prize with Whiteley. Both are on record as looking to Piero della Francesca for guidance. Ashleigh Wilson, in his Whiteley biography, refers to this:

> [Whiteley] did not like abstraction 'for the sake of abstraction', nor did he like aesthetics or paintings created 'wholly from other art + not from life' … He liked pictures that 'evoke human activity' and expressed many things at once … He wanted a 'solidity in the picture structure' through a network of

> integrated planes that stopped the viewer halfway in, as in the works of Duccio, Sassetta and Piero della Francesca, and did not 'disappear' into illusionist perspective.

Wilson goes on to quote Whiteley directly:

> I like above all a sense of poetry and quietude. This is achieved through a complicated reference to scenic space, so that forms are selected and invented, then arranged in an order that is essentially modern in concept but which remains attached to the principles and disciplines of traditional art.[60]

Hans Heysen could have written these words, minus 'modern in concept', thirty years before: they evoke the squares he drew on Nora's eggs. Composition was central to the success of a work for all four artists, as well as the writer Patrick White. Marr observes that 'However complex the surface of de Maistre's paintings and White's prose, behind them lay the same quest for freshness, simplicity and truth'.[61] For the two Heysens, the comfort as described by Plant, indeed White's 'over-upholstered cocoon', was not an easy refuge to vacate, though Nora would find her own space to inhabit between the two worlds, her 'truth', while Hans held fast to his.

Nora's travel journal comes to an abrupt halt soon after her parents' departure for Australia in September 1934. Before leaving Europe, Hans made sure Nora took in a few last artistic treats. A brief visit to Bruges allowed her to view an important van Eyck: 'Madonna & child … one of the most satisfying pictures I have seen—perfect in every detail—perfect craftsmanship drawing & colour & composition. Truly magnificent piece of work greatly impressed as fresh as if it had been painted yesterday—a miracle …'[62]

Satisfied that her final visit to a continental gallery had revealed Europe's best to her, Nora writes in contrast that she was 'struck by the sick appearance of London, crowded streets and traffic'. The family had arrived back in the city a day before they attended the opening of the second

Empire Games on 4 August 1934 and Nora notes that 'Edwards—the British New Guinea representative ran beautifully—lovely to watch'.[63] The games had been originally awarded to Johannesburg but were moved to London to prevent a political crisis over black and Asian competitors attending the games. The Heysen travels had been undertaken in a period of challenging political and social upheaval.

The family searched for a suitable studio for Nora. It was a difficult and often disappointing exercise and they took refuge in more visits to museums and galleries. Lodgings were eventually secured, which Nora notes in her diary. Her capacity for incisive character portrayal is on display when she follows the description of her flat with an entry about a visit to a family acquaintance: 'Found a studio at last & arranged to take it for a year—a nice studio & homely little place—few trees and quiet. [In the] afternoon had tea with Miss Gladys Potts—came home frozen with her inhospitality—cold as ice'.[64] This stab is reminiscent of another comment in her diary: she was happy to be leaving Weisbaden 'after an uninspiring day—glad to say goodbye—awful waiter terribly ugly spoilt my appetite'.[65] This bluntness was characteristic of Nora and as she matured it was not only expressed in the privacy of a diary.

On 6 September, after a few weeks of shopping for necessities and dealing with utility services and unreliable workmen, Nora moved in, recording simply 'slept there for the first night—liked it'.[66] Her mother, writing to Hans Heysen, who was away in Oxfordshire for a week, tells him that Nora has 'fallen heavily for a pair of Cromwellian leather chairs—just like the Vermeer ones', suggesting that they were a good investment should she need to sell them later. These chairs feature in much of Nora's London work and were shipped back to Australia when she finally returned. Colin Thiele writes that Hans Heysen was satisfied with the events of the six months that he had toured with his family. He had successfully purchased works for the South Australian Art Gallery and settled his daughter in London ready to start her next phase of tuition. He had also revisited the collections that meant the most to him and reaffirmed his connection with the works that 'became an even more dominant influence in his judgment of landscape art'[67]—mainly those of Constable. But while he consolidated his position, Nora was open to change.

FIVE: PISSARRO, EVIE AND THOSE OTHER MEN

Women coped with the prejudice against them by denying it existed—as was officially the case—or by getting on with their work regardless. -Frances Borzello[1]

Yesterday afternoon I went in after work to see a few shows ... I cannot arouse any enthusiasm about Holmes' work and have no sympathy with his outlook. Now I understand why he disliked my work, his pictures are low in tone and gloomy. There seems to be no joy in nature for him, but perhaps that is bias, for I still smart when I think of his remarks about my work. -Nora Heysen[2]

I wanted to paint figures in Australian landscapes but art teaching in London knocked it all out of me. I sometimes wonder if it would have been better for me (my art) not to have gone to London. -Nora Heysen[3]

Many young Australian artists went to London to broaden and complete their art studies. Tom Roberts was the first Australian painter to be selected to study at the Royal Academy of Arts in 1881 and his contemporaries Arthur Streeton and Charles Conder were among the pioneers of the regular artistic exodus to Europe. In 1899, Nora's father set sail for Marseilles en route to his Paris education. Art historian Janine Burke refers to the period just prior to World War I and the years between the two world wars as the time in Australia when 'a generation of women artists emerged ...' Burke writes that many of them were born during the 1880s and 1890s and that they 'were to have an extraordinary impact on the course of Australian art'. These were the women that directly preceded Nora and laid the groundwork for her ambitious desire to live and work as artist, which until their day was rarely an option, with marriage, Burke says, being 'the single, most consuming career for women':

> This group of women, who formed part of the first two waves of modernism to reach Sydney between 1913 and 1930, includes Norah Simpson, Grace Cossington Smith, Thea Proctor, Margaret Preston, Dorrit Black, Grace Crowley and the sculptor Eleonore Lange. They were instrumental in introducing post-impressionism and its antecedent avant-garde styles into Australia … These women were, both in their art and their lives, the radicals of the day. Of seven only two married … They numbered among them the best informed, most articulate, influential, widely-travelled and most 'advanced' artists of that time.

These women travelled, studied and worked overseas for many years and, according to Burke, 'they devoted their lives to their art, virtually to the exclusion of all else'. It was a practice that Nora would emulate during her years in London, diligently working at improving as an artist. Both Burke and historian Bernard Smith write that the reason for the prominence of women artists between the wars was the stark fact of 'the thinning out of a whole generation of male artists' due to World War I. Burke maintains that it was also due to the advances made by the feminist movement 'informing and consolidating the role of women' at the end of the nineteenth century up until the 1920s: 'The women artists of this period are not some isolated out-crop of female talent but the culmination of forty years of growing feminist awareness and increasing liberty for women'.[4] In 1894, writer Sarah Grand coined the term 'the New Woman' referring to independent, educated women moving away from the expected role of the domesticated female in a male-dominated society. Grand addressed the double standards of Victorian marriages where the woman was expected to be a pillar of virtue while the same did not apply to her husband: 'The New Woman was a real, as well as a cultural phenomenon. In society she was a feminist and a social reformer; a poet or a playwright who addressed female suffrage'.[5] Nora vehemently maintained throughout her life that she was not a feminist, but it is evident that she benefited from these women who went before. Just thirty years before her arrival in London, the idea of her attending art school unchaperoned would have been an impossibility. The progressive women of the Victorian *fin de siècle* undoubtedly assisted her ambitions.

Before her departure for London, Nora had added to her funds raised from her solo exhibition with sales of her paintings to the state galleries in South Australia, New South Wales and Queensland at exhibitions held by the Society of Artists in both Adelaide and Sydney.[6] Nora was well positioned to make a success of the endeavour, being financially secure (with the added security of help from home if an emergency arose) as well as socially connected thanks to her father. Unlike many others, Nora did not take on menial work or suffer any real degradation as a struggling artist, though funds were low towards the end of her time away and unrequested help from her father came as a welcome reprieve. She had been in London for just over two years when she announced to her parents that she would extend her stay by a year. Her father referred to her decision as a 'rude shock' though it was clear from his response that he recognised this was a crucial period in a young artist's life, since his own travels and studies in Europe were instrumental in his formative years.[7] Though initially daunting, it was an exciting time for Nora; her first time away from the close-knit Heysen clan and a time of freedom where she was able to make her own decisions, moving away from the subject matter she had shared with her father, particularly his gum trees—'so I went the other direction … I wanted to stay in London four years, like my dad, who studied in Paris four years. But I wanted to be recognised in my own right, too!'[8] Already there appears to have been a gentle tension surfacing for the young Nora. She wanted to be independent but at the same time was drawn to emulating the actions of her father when he was starting out. Her funds did not quite see her through and her time abroad was six months shy of her father's four years.

When Hans and Sallie Heysen delivered Nora to London, she was twenty-three. Until then their daughter had lived an extraordinarily sheltered life. Sixty-two years after Nora's arrival in London, art historian Mary Eagle, then a curator at the NGA, met with her to discuss acquiring her work. Nora confided in Eagle that when her father left her in London in 1934 he told her, 'Your innocence will be your protection', to which Nora 'commented bitterly' to Eagle:

> 'Like fun! I'd spent only one night away from home [from the protection of her family] before being pitched into London

> on my own'. Continuing the subject of how ill-prepared she had been for city life, Nora told a story about how a man had approached her after the theatre asking whether he could carry her handbag for her, he escorted her home, and when they arrived he kept hold of her bag with the key to her flat. She kicked him in the groin, grabbed the bag—last thing he said, 'I'll be here when you come out next'. She stayed in her room for days too scared to venture out.

Nora was open about her naivety. It is remarkable that she survived her time away relatively unscathed. The large windows of the flat chosen by her parents not only provided light for her studio but also views of unwelcome exposure. Eagle recounts:

> Nora said she knew nothing about sex, not even the physical details, before going to London. [She] did not recognise the sexual significance of 'a man standing legs apart wagging his penis, looking up at my window, standing there every time I looked out'. But she was 'soon taught the facts of life in London, from artists, from students who had deviant sexual tastes'. She was 'shocked and disgusted' by lesbian approaches—[she] found the man masturbating 'less upsetting'.[9]

At this point, referring to notes she took during the conversation with Nora in 1996 at her Sydney home in Hunters Hill, Eagle asked herself in 2017:

> Did Nora feel a need to clarify the question of her sexual proclivity for the record? As I recall, the feminist movement of the 1970s was hung with questions of women artists' supposed lesbianism ... Did she feel she owed the return of success to the feminist movement? Did she associate feminism with lesbianism? Did she feel she was regarded as lesbian?[10]

This conflation of the two states—one conceptual, one physical—is fraught, but Eagle's question is linked to the idea of one being seen as bound to the other through stereotyping. In his 2004 obituary for Nora, emeritus curator of Australian Art at the AGNSW Barry Pearce writes that the last time he saw Nora a few weeks before she died '… she said, in that resonant, plain-speaking voice that could raise one's neck hairs "Come and see me more often. I AM NOT A FEMINIST!"' I would suggest that she was *not* declaring 'I AM NOT A LESBIAN!' as for her there was no confusion. Pearce adds that he 'felt suitably chastised'; he suggested that it was a response to the renewed interest in her from academic quarters with researchers seeing her as 'a hero of sorts, a tough self-determined one, perfect for a new generation anxious to correct the historical neglect of women'.[11] Nora always maintained that this was not her—she was an artist, and she was not polemical, though she did say that she supported greater recognition of the status of women artists in Australia.[12] Perhaps her chastisement of Pearce was the result of irritation with questions about which she had long been on the record. David Meagher referenced a similar moment during his interview in 2000 for *The Australian Financial Review Magazine* when Nora bristled: 'As the interview concludes, Klepac asks Heysen if it has tired her. "It's not a matter of being tired," she says. "It's a matter of being interviewed."'[13]

Eagle's suggestion that Nora might have told her the story 'for the record' is perhaps the accurate one, an echo back to the assertions that her parents made about her friend, a young widow Evie Shaw (later Stokes), during her London years, who was at the centre of so much concern due to Nora's mother's belief that she was a lesbian. Sallie feared that Nora may be seen as lesbian, too. For the record, Nora's goddaughter Meredith Stokes said that Nora told her that people thought she and Meredith's mother had been lovers: 'Nora said to me many times "we were so close, really close, but it was never a sexual relationship between us"—she said it many times, she must have been aware of the accusations'.[14] These accusations started in the Heysen home. In the 1930s lesbianism was largely viewed by society as aberrant and unacceptable. This attitude in Australia was the result of nineteenth-century religious views that had dominated the social structure of the new colony where same-sex relationships were declared a sin:

> Sexual activity between women became an increased focus of social anxiety in the years after European settlement. Throughout the nineteenth century, religious notions of sexual activity

> between women as sinful and immoral dominated social attitudes towards the subject.[15]

It is not difficult to understand why Nora's parents would be concerned for her reputation given the attitudes of the day, arising from long-held religious views that framed the societal attitude that the family was subject to. The Heysens were not religious but lived in a conservative culture in a small town where public opinion mattered. This was evident in their attitude to Josephine. Gossip and judgement were not welcome.

Not long after Nora was settled in London she made decisions counter to her parents' wishes. Evie arrived from Adelaide in December 1934. It was not a relationship that met with senior Heysen approval. Nora writes to her parents:

> I have never talked about this friendship, perhaps if I had it would have been better, feeling your intense dislike for Evie. I never wanted to, it was something I had apart and I suppose I resented not being able to have her at home, or to see her when I liked, or be able to talk to her or anything.[16]

Evie Shaw was viewed by her parents as a threat to Nora's character and reputation. In December 1934, after Nora had felt the loneliness of living without her large family and its rituals of coming together around the kitchen table along with the continual array of visitors to The Cedars, the two women decided to share Nora's flat-cum-studio in Dukes Lane, Kensington. They both attended classes in London at the Central School of Arts and Crafts, Nora for her painting and Evie as a sculpture student.[17] Hans Heysen wrote to Nora in February 1935, directly pointing out his perceived risks of his daughter's association and his disapproval, along with the guilt-laden assertion that Sallie's ill health could be attributed to Nora's actions:

> Mother lately she has not been as well as she should be … I am afraid that Mother is worrying and feeling apprehensive about Effie's [Evie's] entrance into your studio … Unfortunately this apprehensive feeling has been aggravated by information that has come to her through others. You know exactly what we feel

> about the whole matter and there is enough evidence to show that our suspicions are justified. There is a very true saying 'that love is blind' and this may not only apply to when that state exists between man and woman but it is equally true and can happen between two persons of the same sex. Your letters sound perfectly happy—almost as if you were under such a spell.
>
> I am writing quite openly dear Nora about my impressions, for I want you to be candid and open with us—it is the only way that our mutual love and an honest respect for your parents can be kept alive. Your Mother feels the position keenly and has taken it all very much to heart, and I am hoping a change in circumstances may soon clear the air and free her from her anxiety, which I feel is partly responsible for her health, which should be better than it is ...[18]

In her letters of response Nora expresses her sadness and disappointment in the silence from her mother: 'This week at last brought no home letters and I feel rather sad. I suppose I know the reason well enough, no one will write while Evie is here'.[19] However, Nora never acquiesced to parental urging to end the association, rather holding firm in her position while underlining her loyalty to her parents who appear to have suggested that they had been duped by their daughter and her arrangements:

> She [Evie] was ill before she left, and, I did not know till actually she had arrived at Port Said that she was coming. You say you could see the cupidity of the move and how you had been hoodwinked, I cannot see that there was anything of that in it. I simply thought that if we were both here together studying we could be very happy living together. So I asked her to share with me. I knew you would not like it, but I did not think you could object to it so strongly and that it would cause so much upset. My love and loyalty I have for you will always be there.[20]

Kate Nockels suggests that Nora was selective about the information her parents received. She was twelve thousand miles away and regular letters took up to a month to arrive, and another month was required for a response by return mail. This meant a lot could happen in the intervening period:

> Nora was circumspect when writing to both parents. I'm certain that Nora self-edited, writing what they wanted to hear. She [Nora] told me the backstory about Everton Shaw. She was older than Nora by four or five years and was in fact Josephine's friend … and was introduced to the family. She also befriended Nora. I gather Everton was a very strong personality … The official story was that because [she] had transferred her affections from Josephine to Nora she was disloyal and not to be trusted. But the understory was that she had a reputation as a lesbian and was someone to be wary of within Adelaide circles. This is what Nora said quite clearly her mother said, but she [Nora] didn't believe it.[21]

Meredith Stokes believes there was another factor that rendered her mother Evie an unattractive proposition as a companion for Nora Heysen. Evie's parents were successful caterers in Adelaide, sharing the big end of town business with Balfours. Her father was the Wallace of Cook and Wallace Caterers and a large part of his business was providing food services to the racing industry. Meredith Stokes described her mother's family as nouveau riche—owning their own horse and carriage was an open sign of their wealth. Stokes expanded: 'But that was not in the art circle—Pavlova was *not* going to visit *them*. They were not the crème de la crème of the art set. They were low status. It was very much the time, and establishment Adelaide was incredibly class conscious …' Stokes added that both the families were staunch conservatives, but shared politics did not equate to a shared space.[22]

It is apparent from the letters between the two women that Nora was not completely transparent with her parents, despite her protestations. Nora knew well ahead of Evie's arrival in Port Said that she was destined for London, though just quite when might have been in doubt. Whether the plan to live together was discussed before the sculptor left Adelaide is not clear. The friendship was a priority for Nora; the letters between the two women in their twenties show a deep connection based on a mutual understanding of the role of art in life and its practice as central to each of theirs, and to beauty as observed in the natural world. In October 1934, a short time after Nora's parents and sisters had left by ship for Australia, Evie writes a response to Nora who has expressed her loneliness in London:

> You talk of being depressed and impossible to be near—you shall laugh—I'll make you—laughter cures everything—but in the meanwhile Norrie you will often be very lonely—and it disturbs me to think of that—you must go out—see a musical comedy—talk with people. There are times when we are all alone—but that is the way of things and in those brief intervals we probably see things in a different perspective, find the few essentials … write to me—and you can get it all off your chest—I'll understand. About Xmas dinner—what shall we eat and can I have a bon bon?—a little bon bon—that wouldn't be too extravagant if I bring little ones.[23]

The opportunity to have a female contemporary with whom to share her artistic aspirations was clearly a strong aspect of the friendship. Until meeting Evie, Nora's key influences were her father, the artists she admired from history, and her teachers at art school including Frederick Millward Grey—all well meaning, but perhaps lacking in empathy. They were patriarchal figures. To be full of youthful vigour and expectation for the prospects that lay ahead during her 'grand tour' and to be able to share them with a like-minded friend would have held great attraction for both women. Evie Shaw had also suffered a great loss, and the friendship with Nora must have been important. She had been married to a young World War I fighter pilot who, according to Meredith Stokes, after many successful missions had been retired to train other pilots towards the end of the war. He was killed during a training exercise in Queensland six weeks after their wedding. Stokes said her mother asked her to give the Australian War Memorial his flight log book: 'So I did, but I read it first in masses of tears because he was a poet and it was beautifully written'.[24] It is difficult to comprehend the young woman's loss and at the same time the rejection of her by another family. This rejection was grounded in anxieties about women's sexuality and class that are perhaps better understood in the social historical context of their time.

The friendship between Nora and Evie was underpinned by unconditional support and understanding of the other's needs. It was a deeply valued connection. Nora had grown up with her siblings as her major point of social contact within a shared friendship group that presented itself for visits and special occasions. The opportunity to find a person that shared her interests so intimately outside of her family would have been limited and Nora was not willing to relinquish this. An example of the connection can be read when at one point while writing from London to Evie, Nora appears to have discussed undertaking modelling [sculpture] but Evie urges her to concentrate on her painting. Eagle noted in her meeting with Nora that 'Nora said she wanted to draw figures from the inside out—physiology not psychology' and that in London 'she had been determined to study sculpture, to get a proper knowledge of form'.[25] At a later stage while the two women study Nora does take a class in sculpture but in the meantime Evie writes from Adelaide:

> You haven't the spare time if you really do want to paint that mother and child—using your own experience of that subject—imitating no-one—the test is for an artist of our period to set his own style and see if it will stand the criticism of a future generation—of a few generations.[26]

We must imagine the letters Nora wrote that elicited Evie's responses. Evie's letters are in the collection of Nora Heysen Papers as a matter of public record, at the behest of Nora, in the NLA. They reveal that Evie is the one person that a 'shy and introverted'[27] Nora could openly convey her feelings about art and life. Evie has the voice of a confident woman and at times writes philosophically. She was a few years older than Nora and also more progressive in her views about art in terms of how much exploring she has done in developing her own aesthetic. She shared her intimate thoughts with Nora:

> There is a bowl of roses on my desk—the faintest creamy pink with deeper centres—they resemble camellias and you would like them under the warm glow of the lamp—too delicate in colour, too fragile in composition to be real—some time ago

> I slipped into a dressing gown and bed can be resisted no longer—wanted to talk with you first. I went to the library and buried the head in Japanese prints … they had the secret of portraying rhythm and grace in a few lines—deleting any unnecessary discordant details that tends to imitate; and returning home I found myself looking at the pear tree in flower seeing only the pear tree and a few attributes, the remainder of the scene fading out of existence—it was a strange sensation, perhaps I'd better not repeat the visit.[28]

These words are written close to the time the women knew they would soon be reunited. Nora had left Adelaide months earlier, and Evie's letters indicate the deep affection each held for the other. The letters tell the story of a friendship founded on mutual interests, the opportunity to safely share private thoughts, and loyalty, despite opposition. At Easter in March 1934, Evie writes to her absent friend who at this time has only recently left the country:

> It was a grey day with a sharp little breeze that made me quicken my pace towards sunset, when the sun broke through the heavy bank of cloud, outshining the Mount Lofty ridge with brilliant light whilst the lower half remained in deep lilac shadow. Suddenly I felt that you were not just over the other side of it, and a loneliness pervaded the whole scene. Tonight is a full moon in a clear warm sky—almost daylight, and the firs are soft and feathery like down. The landscape is a veritable fairy land. I walked out to gaze down at my valley—which the moon had covered in soft veils of mist, touching the faces of the slumberous little hills with a profound peace. It is all too beautiful so I came inside. I miss you so much that it is difficult to write without wailing about it.[29]

The women are aware of the other's sensitivities. Nora had given a record of German songs to Evie, leaving the record under her pillow at a hospital where it appears from the correspondence that Evie was training as a nurse for a time. Evie writes again to Nora on 23 April:

> There is a mixed bowl of dahlias under my lamp which I badly want you to see—so my glance lingers on the brilliant reds and yellows, pinks and mauves—for you—a little longer on the white ones.
>
> Norrie, 'Morgen' ['Tomorrow'] is so lovely I play it more than anything else listening is a dream. I realized how much you have become a part of my existence—couldn't live very far out of touch with you—for long—no-one to be rude to me in galleries or to fight under poplars with ...[30]

The song that Evie is referring to appears to be the widely recorded tender love song based on the poem by John Henry Mackay with music composed by Richard Strauss that speaks of a longed-for reunion. On Evie's birthday in May, Nora writes in her travel diary: 'Bought a bunch of forget-me-nots for E. Birthday celebration'.[31] Nora also spent hours creating a camisole for her friend decorated with delicate needlework and Evie responds earnestly: 'Surely there is nothing more warming as a great friend. Norrie, it is almost definite that I leave [for London] in November—that is all being well'.[32] It is date marked 11 May 1934. Despite a delay, Evie arrived three days before Christmas, presumably with bonbons in hand.[33]

Nora tells her parents of the pleasure of Evie's company, about how sharing the experiences of school and life in London was the richer for it. Anxious to take some heat from the situation, she wrote to her parents in late March 1935 that Evie would be going to stay with her mother. As readers of Evie's letters we are now privy to each woman's dependence on the other for much of their happiness and the sting in Nora's words is potent:

> Evie leaves me in a day or two ... that will be good news for you. All this worry seems so useless, we have been very happy together. Is it not better to be happy, and have companionship, than to be lonely and miserable? We all have to branch out for ourselves at one time or another. I have chosen Evie for a friend; whether it is just a spell, as you think it is, I don't know. It has lasted too long and stood too much to be just that.[34]

Late in her life when Nora delivered her demonstrable and unprovoked clarification about not being a feminist to Mary Eagle, the outburst might have erupted from a deep and long-held desire to defend the right to make the choices she did, and the rights of others close to her. It is likely that Nora's distress was about the very direct sexual approaches made to her in her student days when, by her own admission, she was blatantly ill-equipped to deal with any sexual advance—heterosexual or homosexual—and perhaps also about a perceived injustice initiated by her parents against a dear friend, sixty years earlier. It appears to be less about homosexuality or her position on the subject and more about her ignorance of sexual matters—how her 'innocence' offered no protection from any quarter, and how her father's proclamation rang hollow. Her lifelong adult relationships with gay friends and her love for her 'adopted' gay 'son' are evidence of her acceptance of the sexuality of others. Another factor in Nora's outburst on feminism to Pearce and Eagle is that she maintains the concept did not feature in her upbringing, though in her later years she could see where sexual discrimination had taken place.[35] Feminism was also something that would ultimately create friction between Evie and Nora. Evie's daughter Meredith Stokes says that when she became a political activist and feminist in the 1970s, her godmother Nora—described by Meredith as 'extremely broad-minded'—while not judging her, and while listening to her views, did not take on her position. Evie Stokes vehemently opposed her daughter's views and activism to the point of disowning her. This caused significant strain between Nora and Evie, which might provide another reason for Nora to distance herself from avowed feminism. Meredith suggested that Nora did not want to provoke further antagonism with her old friend while never outright rejecting her 'Marmalade Princess', her nickname for Meredith.[36]

When he returned to Australia, Hans arranged for Nora to meet with Orovida Pissarro in order to purchase a work by her father Lucien Pissarro, son of the renowned Camille, for the Adelaide Gallery. Lucien Pissarro had lived in London as a child with his family during the Franco-Prussian War before returning to Paris in his formative artistic years.[37] He settled permanently in London in 1890, married and had one child,

Orovida, who also became a painter. Coincidentally, before her father had made any arrangement for them to meet, in 1935 Nora wrote to her parents about a painting she had viewed at the Royal Academy by a woman called simply Orovida. The woman concerned had decided on this *nom de peintre* in an attempt to distance herself from the famous Pissarro name and to claim some independence as a painter.[38] It is not surprising given that she was surrounded by successful family—her famous grandfather, her father, and four uncles also painted. She was the first Pissarro woman to take up a brush.

Orovida and Nora shared some commonalities when it came to famous men in their artistic lives. The work by Orovida caught Nora's eye in an exhibition that she felt was inadequate. Nora wrote that the work appealed to her more than the Spencers, Sickerts and Johns on display, describing it as 'a native mother and child with magnolia flowers ... a most lovely and decorative thing. I could just see it in my studio ... it was only £42'.[39] Heysen made a point of acquiring the painting for his daughter and it forms part of Nora's archive in Hahndorf. When Nora met Orovida for the first time, her characteristic bluntness delivered a bohemian caricature but also confirmed Nora's priority:

> I had tea with Miss Pissarro and thereby hangs a long tale. I got a shock when she met me at the door, a great hulk of a woman in a brilliant red jumper and a mottled skirt and old slippers on her feet, a fat rosy face with short curled black hair, glasses, altogether the most unattractive presence imaginable ... However, once in her studio and talking art I forgot her appearance and saw only her alert intelligent eyes.[40]

The Pissarro father–daughter team influence would prove a turning point for Nora and lead to a new approach to her use of a higher-keyed palette, away from the base of browns and blacks traditionally prescribed and preferred by her father and his contemporaries.[41] Margaret Woodward notes that Camille Pissarro influenced Cézanne and said that Nora would have received some of Camille's teachings through the meetings with Lucien and Orovida: 'I think these things have got to permeate through families that are very conscious of painting ... so there's her [Nora's] father and also the legacy of Camille

Pissarro working in her consciousness and her work'.[42] Camille Pissarro held that 'It is only by drawing often, drawing everything, drawing incessantly, that one fine day you discover to your surprise that you have rendered something in its true character'.[43] Hans and Nora Heysen would have concurred with this, though Pissarro's son's and granddaughter's modern ideas appear to her father as a distraction for Nora.

Nora's enthusiasm for the Pissarros' guidance is clear but she maintained her personal views without being completely bewitched by the new influence:

> I don't intend swallowing all she said, but it does no harm to have a change of palette and experiment with new harmonies ... It is amazing the depth and richness of colour that can be got without using brown or black. It is a valuable hint to me—though I don't think I will ever desert the earth colour, to me just as beautiful harmonies can be achieved with them if used rightly.[44]

Hans Heysen, while diplomatic in his response, gently encouraged her experimentation: '... it is wise from time to time to make a change ... not that you need to definitely discard your black and brown, these also have their proper place'.[45] Still, he went to considerable lengths to re-establish the academic approach, even sending three of his small paintings to her in London 'to remind her of her origins both in life and art'. However, Nora was invigorated by the suggestions of Lucien Pissarro according to Hendrik Kolenberg:

> Lucien advised her to lighten her palette, to become more aware of light, the shimmering qualities ... it brought an ecstatic, joyous quality to her work which was watchful and serious earlier. Orovida bluntly said her academic realism was fifty years behind the times. She believed in Nora's talent and gave her a list of colours to use: cadmium, red, ultramarine, *vert composé*, cobalt and crimson. Nora was delighted in the new depths in her paintings.[46]

In her later years, Nora acknowledged the lessons learned from her father along with the unwavering commitment to the work ethic he taught her. While she responded to insights from other artists in relation to technique, it was in the fundamentals of good practice that she deferred to her father. She spoke dismissively of those who did not understand a draughtsman's work:

> I got there by sheer persistence and hard work. So did Father. Very disciplined and very hard workers we are, my father, and likewise myself. Didn't come out of the sky—fall on you. People think that you're talented and it just drops out of the heavens or something. But it's just continual working at it. Having an aim and working at it.[47]

Nora applied herself to learning as much as she could from her teachers as well as from the great collections in London. She was determined to make a life as an artist, just as Preston, Proctor and Cossington Smith had done before her, and she faced numerous obstacles from those who should have been guiding her, due to their discriminatory views of the shifting trends in art and of her gender. It is curious that in later life Nora commented that she was not conscious of any discrimination against her. She perceived herself simply as a student artist being directed by her teachers: 'I was not at all feminist because it wasn't in my home and I didn't meet up with it in London—amongst artists it really wasn't apparent that women were being thought of so poorly in the art world. We were all students together and I wasn't conscious of it'. This conversation between Heather Rusden and Nora took place when Nora was in her eighties; Rusden asked her what Adelaide was like for women artists in the 1920s and Nora's answer possibly explains her lack of awareness of the issues facing women students during her time in London. She grew up in a home where her male role model and mentor accepted her as an artist along with his male friends who encouraged her:

> I think it was pretty tough—but I was away up in the hills—and quite remote from Adelaide so I wouldn't have known the struggles of the women artists but I've learnt now they weren't even admitted into some exhibitions. Women's work wasn't

> even shown—can you imagine that? I was separate from all that. I wasn't even aware of the feminist bit at all.[48]

There is a great quantity of documented evidence recording the barriers women artists faced as they undertook art studies throughout the centuries and Nora was not spared, despite apparently being oblivious to discrimination.[49] She put her difficulties down to possible poor skills and a need to work harder in order to improve. But the arrival in London of Evie Shaw from South Australia made her far-from-unique struggle easier. It was not just from her teachers that Nora faced resistance.

Though Evie left Dukes Lane, it was not a permanent departure and she was soon back sharing the flat with Nora. For most of 1935 she acted as Nora's main model for her portraiture. Both women sat for each other—a mutually beneficial and productive generosity is evident in the work both produced.[50] They were hiking companions in the country, and fellow students attending art classes. Meredith Stokes describes their time together:

> They used to go to the Shakespearean plays—they stood up in the gods to see John Gielgud and everybody because they didn't have any money. Always right up the top and they stood through all the performances. They did have a lovely time, you can when you are students even without money, as long as you're not on your own and not lonely. They had no [spare] money so they went for long walks in the Cotswolds in winter with sandwiches in their pockets that froze. When they travelled my mother did all the organising, she had the temperament and Nora was a bit shy. She [mother] always said they complemented each other, yin yang. She said Nora wouldn't have travelled without her, and she made all the arrangements, motivated her and got her there. They went to Paris and Italy as students. It was a very productive time for both of them. My mother ... did quite a few sculptures of Nora, and Nora did paint my mother.[51]

For the month of June in 1935, Nora and Evie went to Paris where Nora was introduced to the collections at the Louvre, and the Musée du

Luxembourg, which at the time was devoted to works by living artists. When the women arrived, the Italian exhibition, as Nora called it, was open and she writes excitedly about spending seven straight hours there: 'The whole thing just took my breath away. All the pictures I had admired in reproduction … The Raphaels were wonderful and the Leonardos and the Michelangelos and the Botticellis'.[52] Nora would have viewed the impressionist collection that included works by Camille Pissarro, Sisley, Cézanne, Monet and Renoir in the Louvre, as it was moved from the Luxemburg in 1929. Today the impressionist collection is synonymous with the Musée d'Orsay, its home since 1986. Cézanne would become a major influence for Nora. The pair revisited Paris a year later, again in June, and Nora comments on the tension in Paris 'probably owing to the political situation', the half-empty cafes and the higher cost of living. She reviewed the works that she maintained were her favourites, including the sculptures *The winged victory* 190 BC by Pythokritos and Alexander of Antioch's *Venus de Milo* 101 BC, Vermeer's *Woman with a pearl necklace* and Fra Angelico's paintings; she also celebrated a small van Gogh street scene, 'a joyous lively thing that fascinated me …' Nora also took in a retrospective of Corot, a favourite of her father. She wrote: 'There is a tenderness and beauty in his work that no other painter possesses'. The Musée du Luxembourg's role as the contemporary art gallery of Paris was coming to a close but in its final year before the completion of the purpose-built gallery in the Palais de Tokyo in 1937, Nora had the benefit of viewing the working artists of the day:

> I found the paintings in the Luxembourg very stimulating. There were hundreds of ideas in the work but badly painted, but the French painters get something in their work that the English never get. They have ideas and imagination.[53]

Nora was twenty-five and developing her own view as she seized every opportunity to observe and learn. When the women returned to England, they spent the summer months of 1936 living and working at their respective disciplines at Rempstone Farm in Dorset, enjoying the country life so familiar to Nora. She was making the most of life in London, too. A few days before boarding the train for Wimborne in Dorset she went to see Chekhov's play *The seagull* and described the cast as 'all-star'—Gielgud,

Edith Evans and Peggy Ashcroft were the leads.[54] The domestic space in the Dukes Lane flat created a number of opportunities for Nora to paint Evie while she experimented with colour schemes and compositions—in particular *London breakfast* 1935 (NGA) and its partner painting, *Interior* 1935 (NLA). Jane Hylton describes *London breakfast* as:

> a fine example of Heysen's growing mastery of compositional complexity. Evie, engrossed in reading, enjoys a pot of tea and starts her day with a simple meal of bread, butter and jam … The pinks in the mat and Evie's slippers create overall warmth that can be read as a reflection of the gentle domestic pleasure Heysen and her friend enjoyed together.[55]

Sixty-four years later, Mary Eagle would make an offer in order to acquire it for the National Gallery. It is appropriate that Evie, the woman at the centre of so much discord for Hans and Sallie Heysen, would be the model in the work that so well represented Nora's talent. It hangs prominently in the Australian Collection in Canberra. Eagle's official documentation goes a long way to explaining why this work was exceptional, examining the personal drivers that helped Nora produce such a subtle piece. In her submission for acquisition to the NGA, Eagle writes:

> The painting shows a young woman seated at breakfast in a room furnished with oak table and Cromwell chairs. All told the composition has a formality that imposes itself on the image as a whole, a sign of a detached and reflective mood.
>
> In London, in a series of paintings of her small flat … Nora emulated Vermeer's approach to subject matter, painting her room, its furniture, *objets d'art* and textiles, according to strict compositions in which every cubic inch of space seems carefully weighed. Like Vermeer, she painted the room under various conditions of light. She used a modern version of Vermeer's palette—expressly his cerulean blue. In these ways she imbued her images with an air of passionate but detached observation.
>
> Examining Vermeer's two late paintings in the National

> Gallery, London, *A lady standing at the virginal* and *A lady seated at the virginal*, Nora Heysen was able to form an idea of his technique at that stage of his career when the merest dabs and brisk strokes had become a shorthand manner of describing the play of light on textured surfaces.[56]

The notes that Eagle had taken in conversation with Nora when she prepared her report were central to informing the administrators who would make the final approval to purchase. The detail that Nora paid to every aspect of her work including her fastidious choice of a frame stands out:

> *London breakfast* … prompted me to ask [Nora] about Vermeer: 'I was so smitten with Vermeer when I first went to London that I had my frame-maker make exact copies of Vermeer's frames in the National Gallery [London] … She [Evie] is sitting in the Cromwell period [leather and wood upright] chair I [always] sat in to have coffee. The painting has never been exhibited. I had it framed in a Vermeer frame'. [It is] signed 1.1.1935. 'Evie is in my blue dressing gown'.[57]

Nora's parents had gone to some lengths to arrange for Nora to receive the Jaeger dressing-gown she mentions to Eagle. They had entrusted their close friend, Australia's largest wool broker and art patron James McGregor, with the task of choosing it and delivering it to Nora.[58] Jaeger's flagship store was established in Regent Street, specialising in high-quality wool garments. It had received a Royal Warrant in 1910; by the 1930s it was considered a luxury brand.[59] Nora writes to her parents:

> This is a simply lovely present you have given me. I was so excited when it came, it is a beauty, the most gorgeous dressing gown I have seen, so soft and warm. It is the colour I love best. A lightish soft blue grey … with a buff coloured lining. Did you tell Mr McGregor exactly what I wanted?[60]

I wonder if it irked them when Nora wrote to her parents saying she was painting Evie wearing the gown. She might have been a little provocative in her choice of costume for her sitter in at least two works that are known, *London breakfast* and its partner picture *Interior* 1935, a work barely a foot square, imbued with the same intimacy of the larger piece.[61] There is a touch of willfulness in her choice, whether conscious or not. *London breakfast* was never exhibited and this fact appears in the provenance report for the NGA. It had been in the artist's possession since it was painted. Nora had kept it for herself but in 1996 she was happy to have it go public. Eagle describes the painting further in her submission:

> The serenity, amounting to exaltation, of this and other London images, was new in Nora's art and probably owed more to personal circumstances than to the criticism of Central School art instructor Bernard Meninsky who told Nora her drawings lacked any emotional quality. After her parents left London in 1934, Nora, who had spent one night apart from her family, was thrown headlong into loneliness and fear. The trauma this naïve and reserved young woman experienced through exposure to the sexual advances of a man in the street and the sexual behaviour of one of her neighbours, was only relieved when an Australian friend Evie ... arrived in London. The *London breakfast* shows how Evie's presence settled Nora, allowing her to achieve the serenity and absorption in her art that had been disrupted by loneliness and fear. She became, says Nora, 'my alter ego', and was the model for some incandescent images, portraits and interiors, including *London breakfast*. She is always shown wearing blue. The blue of her eyes, her Jaeger dressing gown, her woollen jacket [seen in *Portrait of Everton (Evie)* 1936], is airy and uplifting.[62]

This domestic pleasure was not something Nora was willing to relinquish under pressure from her parents. She was financially independent and making her own way. One particularly beautiful work Nora produced is *Portrait of Evie* 1935 (Meredith Stokes gifted this drawing of her mother to the AGNSW in 2008), a wistful and delicate drawing in brown conté crayon on ivory wove paper, a preferred medium of Nora's, capturing the soft beauty of her friend. Evie has her long hair loose, out of its usual chignon, draped over her shoulders, evoking intimacy and informality.

18. Portrait of Evie 1935, conté crayon on ivory wove paper, 34.0 × 26.0 cm. Collection of the Art Gallery of New South Wales.

Though Eagle personally considers the work 'too saccharine',[63] it offers an insight into the tenderness and sensitivity between the artist and her subject, of a calmness and technical control. Nora wrote to her mother and father in September 1935 when she was happy and productive, working on a flower piece that she described as 'ethereal' as a result of how she treated light and atmosphere in the work. She wondered if it would appeal to her parents. Her parting paragraph is a pointed final report on Evie:

> Evie is staying with me until December when she is marrying. It is wonderful to have her, and we do not get tired of each other. I think it a very good test if two people can share a flat, and be happy and work together. She helps my work. You will not believe *that.*[64]

Nora wrote to her parents about her loneliness but it is not clear whether they were aware of the fearful aspect of that loneliness or its cause. Her unpreparedness for the sexual advances of men and women, the blind trust that resulted from her lack of worldly experience combined with an inability to recognise a threat had rendered her vulnerable. She had left behind the sanctuary of her home in the hills and its full and lively family life for a solo existence in one of the world's most sophisticated and potentially isolating cities. Perhaps Nora did not want to add worry to her parents' concerns should they have known that their daughter had faced some personal risk. Having a close friend to share the experience and to feel safe with must have been a transformative element in her overall experience of being away from Australia. Eagle suggests that this friendship and the security it provided Nora was central to the equilibrium she was able to find and that it showed in her work. Such a feeling could not be surrendered when the alternative had left her bitterly unhappy. In her final comments regarding *London breakfast* and its 'Place in Artist's Corpus' for her submission for acquisition, Eagle finishes with:

> Nora Heysen was at her best in the 1930s (before, during and after the trip to London), when she produced a group of remarkable portraits. The intimate, reflective *London breakfast*, though less immediately gripping than the single portraits, is a fine painting in its own right, and will achieve a ready recognition from the public.[65]

As head of Australian Art at the NGA from 2001 to 2016, Anne Gray curated the touring exhibition *Face: Australian portraits 1880–1960* in 2010 and included *London breakfast*.[66] *Face* was the partner exhibition to the successful 2007–2009 *Ocean to outback: Australian landscape painting 1850–1950*. Gray endorsed her predecessor Eagle's decision to choose this work for purchase by the NGA in 1996 when she selected *London breakfast* for this important exhibition. Both Heysens were showcased in their respective genres: Nora in *Face* keeping pace with her father after Hans Heysen's *In the Flinders—Far North* 1951 (NGA) was selected for the landscape show. The accompanying publication for the portraits carries Gray's commentary on this seminal work in Nora's oeuvre:

> There are white flowers in a blue vase on the breakfast table, and there is a blue and white plate on the bookshelf behind. Heysen was concerned with arranging forms and colours—opposing blues and yellows, keeping the colours as pure as possible.
>
> ... In composition Heysen adopted some of the features of Whistler's famous portrait of his mother; but instead of Whistler's subdued palette, Heysen used bold contrasting colours, and in place of the master's spare composition, Heysen filled the space with practical objects. The portrait is also a homage to Vermeer, whose reproduced works hung in Heysen's family home. As in so many of Vermeer's paintings, Heysen's subject is dressed in blue and engaged in a tranquil occupation, a pearly light comes into a domestic scene from a hidden window on the left, and there is a careful placement of objects in a clearly defined architectural space.[67]

Nora and Evie's time of living together in London ended with Evie's marriage to Reuters journalist Henry Stokes[68] but the two women would continue to travel together in the countryside in England, taking walking tours in Canterbury and Tunbridge Wells, following Evie's marriage.[69] Nora wrote to her parents about these trips openly, in a confident tone; it was as if she kept writing of regular events between two friends with the goal that acceptance may be the result:

> I'm safely home again and feeling ever so much brighter after three days of tramping under the sky ... Heavens it was too wonderful to smell the country again, all the old familiar smells of apples, of cows, of sweet hay and clover. [We] arrived here at eleven last night. You have never seen two more weary individuals than we were then.[70]

After Evie left, Nora did not look for a new housemate to limit the loneliness: 'There were few people whose company she was as comfortable with as Evie's'.[71] The two enjoyed an enduring friendship throughout Nora's life and would be reunited in 1938 as war was looming, and a pregnant Evie was evacuated to Sydney, after her husband was assigned as a war correspondent to Singapore. The two women shared a flat once more in Sydney where Nora would become godmother to Evie's daughter who affectionately became known as Merrie.

In January 1936 in London Nora received late wishes for her November birthday from her parents. The friend who had caused her parents so much consternation was now respectably removed from their daughter's studio but a tone of defiance remains discernible in Nora's correspondence. While thanking her parents for their wishes she makes a declaration on two levels—one as an adult woman, and the other less directly, but no less pointedly, as an independent artist with her own defined approach to her work. On 7 January she writes that '... I want to work out my life here. I want to work and justify myself and find myself, until I have done that I will not feel free to return. I want to absorb as much as possible to experiment to learn ... I feel as if I am only just beginning to paint'.[72] Five days later she writes again and follows with a bold opening:

> Dearest Mother and Daddy,
>
> Well I'm now 25, a great age. I'm a young woman now and feel that I have left girlhood far behind. This last year of living here by myself in London and making my own decisions and having my own responsibilities has made me grow up three years in one. You probably celebrated the day more than I did. I spent it painting a self portrait.

She goes on to describe the painting in unequivocal terms that stand counter to Hans Heysen's advice to her about not abandoning her artistic roots. In response once more to her father's earlier effort to bring her back to the conservative fold, Nora is clear about her intent, directly referring to his preferences but in non-negotiable terms:

> I'm painting it all in a higher key using no black or brown on my palette and only a very little ochre ... I am doing myself in a blue smock against the wall and a part of my pink roses,

> the colour scheme is beautiful and I hope to make something good out of it.[73]

Nora's enthusiasm and commitment to the piece leave little room for her father to respond critically, nor does it appear that she is asking for his input. Rather she is telling him as a woman and as an independent artist what she is working on; and a week later she follows with, 'This morning I painted on my self portrait, it is almost complete and I think it is the best self portrait I have painted. It is all very high in key'. Hans Heysen appears now to cease urging Nora to readdress her palette, perhaps thinking it wiser to keep the flow of communication open. At the end of January, a week after her report on the self portrait, Nora writes that she visited 'the Chinese exhibition' and is full of the impact it had on her referring to 'a new base of life' and stating 'there is no end to what I am going to do'.[74] She refers again to the 'high keyed palette' that she adopted for a new work of Evie when she was inspired by what she had seen 'trying for life and vibration of colour'. Nora is clearly enamoured with the techniques she has just seen and writes as if to punctuate her commitment to developing her style as distinct from her father's:

> That Chinese work has taught me a very great deal already. Their work is so refined, their outlook so aesthetic and beautiful, and they are masters of design and have such perfect taste. It is an object lesson to see how they conventionalize nature and make a picture of the simplest things, a twig on a blade of grass, and the thing is perfect.

Nora goes further, telling her father that she has compared the new work of Evie, which she described as 'delicate and subtle' and 'more alive than anything I have ever painted', to the last 'head' she had painted describing it as 'dirty brown' and looking 'rotten'.[75] The 'rotten' head went straight to the rubbish bin. It appears that Hans, as caring father as well as artistic mentor, took the line of least resistance: 'It's wonderful to read of your enthusiasm for your work, its ambitions, high hopes and disappointments'.[76] It could be suggested that Hans was willing to retreat in order to take the longer view, perhaps understanding and remembering the flush of excitement that came with his own studies and discoveries as a young student in Europe, while hoping his daughter would work through her infatuations, both artistic and personal. The disappointments that Hans Heysen referred to were recent rejections by the Royal Academy. Nora had submitted paintings for exhibition consideration; a portrait was accepted but due to lack of hanging space would not be shown and another flower piece received no mention at all.[77] He reassured his daughter by way of recalling that he, too, was 'Rejected for lack of space' by the Academy when he was a student.[78] Further challenges to Nora's confidence manifested themselves in the form of her father's colleagues. It could be suggested that these men were also ultimately responsible for the subjects that would dominate her oeuvre, more due to what they discouraged her to paint than the opposite.

Frances Borzello writes that by the twentieth century, women could expect to take their place as artists, indeed that 'a woman could regard a career in art as her right'. But that right was not a given outcome of a male-dominated world despite the fact that 'on the surface there was no longer any difference between male and female artists'. Men and women could enrol to study art at the same institutions, draw from a naked model, take commissions, enter and win competitions, and take on travel scholarships, says Borzello:

> … the theory was that talent would out. The trouble was below the surface. Equality of opportunity turned out in practice to be rather an illusion. Firstly because the artistic power structures remained male: despite the odd exception, it was the men who ran the art schools, had most power of patronage, were the most respected critics, chaired the trustees of the local museum. And secondly because the women who entered the art world did so against a background of unhelpful ideas about women and art—the same old ideas but modernized, with Freud brought in to support the 'difference' of women, and social realities used to argue for women to breed after two World Wars.[79]

Borzello discusses a number of factors that cumulatively represent blatant prejudice against women painters, stating that even as late as the 1960s there were 'teachers who believed that their women students lacked originality, did not take art seriously or were only at art school to catch a husband'. Borzello also shares how the theory of talent being genderless was subverted by the male view. The mainstream powers observed that there were enough successful female artists to support the false perception that talent was genderless. This notion was also used against women when the male establishment contended that prejudice was not the reason there were fewer women teaching in art, fewer female art academicians and fewer females exhibiting and represented in art journals and books, but that 'their poor showing was due to their lack of interest in putting themselves forward, the diversion of their creativity into motherhood, their inability to wield the knife in institutional politics, the fact that they were just not good enough'.[80] Nora was a young and naive woman in her twenties in London, facing the barrier of male judgement that had been centuries in the making. It is not surprising the experience was gruelling. The question could be asked at this point: was it helpful to have a father widely successful in the art world? Might Nora have had a less battered experience without the direct entrée to the powerful men Hans Heysen introduced her to? Would she have been better off incognito, without the special audiences and appraisals, and left to her own devices and development?

Borzello comments on a number of women artists and their experiences in the early third of the twentieth century at art schools in the United States and the United Kingdom:

> Officially there was equality. Unofficially they had to find their way through a tangle of assorted attitudes. There were supportive teachers ... but for every one of them there were probably ten whose attitudes were less than helpful. Nearly all of their teachers were male ...[81]

Nora would experience these 'tangled attitudes' right from the start of her time at the Central School. Her first teacher, Bernard Meninsky, gave her a 'scathing [response] ... the worst damning criticism'. It is heartening to hear the young Nora questioning and being unwilling to accept his verdict while discussing the issues only in terms of art and work, ignorant of any gender issues:

> I don't know how far he is right, but it appears that he does not see my point of view at all ... It is very difficult to know how far to trust one's own judgement ... It isn't much good going to a school unless one is ready to knuckle under and learn from them, but on the other hand I don't want to give up my point of view for his, and we are both striving for something so completely different. He draws very well and I admire the solidity and movement he gets, but I don't want to draw like him.[82]

Nora's skills as a draughtsman were acknowledged well before she left for London. Perhaps Meninsky could not bring himself to give the young woman before him the credit due to her. In contrast Nora's even-handedness is evident in the generosity she affords him when corresponding with her parents. In these moments a 'blind' viewing, like a tasting of wine where the names are concealed, could have made for interesting assessment.

The painter Ethel Walker foreshadows what was to come for Nora. According to Borzello in *A world of our own*, Walker's oeuvre consisted of 'portraits, women, flowers, landscapes and seascapes and large decorations ...' At her peak of recognition in the 1920s and 1930s, she was Britain's best known woman artist, but she would disappear from view. 'Well known in her day and forgotten now', she did not fit within what Borzello refers to as the twentieth-century art styles written to 'follow each other like a Biblical genealogy'. This orthodoxy left little room for the woman artist and the realms of the domestic where she so often practised. Nora persisted in attempting to survive the crippling criticism that would come her way, as she tried to define her own way of seeing 'truth in art' apart from her hugely influential father and her peers. She would develop a style that, like Walker, as Borzello describes it, was 'not attached to any of the major stylistic movements of the twentieth century'.[83] Neither Walker nor Heysen could be categorised, and as a result both would fall into obscurity until close to the new millennium, a time about which art historian Janine Burke commented: 'We are facing a renaissance in women's art in this country at the beginning of the 1980s: we must not lose sight of it'.[84] Nora Heysen's story is a case study in the demise of the woman artist and the social structures and world events that prescribed that demise. Borzello reflects further on Walker:

> The fact that the stylistic advances of the avant-garde are the organizing principle of twentieth-century art history does not detract from her talent; it merely makes her invisible ... all through the period, women artists managed to make their way in an art world that neither actively hindered them nor put itself out to welcome them.[85]

Henry Tonks, Borzello reports, taught many women between 1892 and 1930 at the Slade School of Fine Art in London. She quotes his views on women students from a letter to his friend:

> Speaking generally they do what they are told, if they don't you will generally find they are a bit cracked. If they become offensive it may be a sign of love. They improve rapidly from 16 to 21, then the genius that you have discovered goes off, they begin to take marriage seriously!

Borzello asks, 'One wonders what theories explained the serious women who did well and went on to make a career. The fact that a male tutor might pick out a talented male student to encourage and a talented female student to seduce was seen as life, not sexism'.[86] It is possible that Nora's male teachers might have shared similar views as Tonks.

Not all Nora's teachers had a negative effect. She undertook sculpture study in order to represent the human figure three-dimensionally to help her draw it with a deeper understanding in two dimensions:

> ... at the Central [School] I wanted to learn sculpturing [sic] under Alfred Turner. I was very interested still in form, and wanted to get a full knowledge of form. In fact, I got so interested in sculpture at one period I wanted to give up painting all together ... I actually hacked out a whole life size figure in stone which eventually got so cumbersome I put it into the Thames because it was too expensive to cart around. However, to get modelled figures cast into bronze was a very

19. Everton Stokes wrote on the back of this photograph: 'Bust on left Miss Heysen's on right mine ... Nov–Dec 1934'. Papers of Nora Heysen, National Library of Australia.

> expensive proposition and always putting the figures back into the bin when I'd finished them didn't encourage me ... and I went back to my painting with, I hope, a fuller knowledge of form.[87]

Alfred Turner and John Skeaping were her tutors and Turner encouraged her with positive comments about her work.[88] Traditionally students were left to their own devices, occasionally receiving input from tutors, often harsh. Meninsky was a member of the New English Art Club (NEAC) that Vanessa Bell had referred to and that was linked to the Bloomsbury Group. Her portrait had been painted by one of the NEAC jury members, Charles Furse, whom Bell thought was one of the men—along with Henry Tonks and John Singer Sargent—actively protecting the secrets of the 'art universe' from women painters. Meninsky's style reflected his bohemian associations, having moved away from the academic and towards the impressionistic—he counted Rodin, Picasso and Modigliani as the greatest draughtsmen of his time, 'all of who had the power to evoke a solid form by means of a single binding line'.[89] Nora's feelings about Picasso could only have led to a fraught relationship with Meninsky. The NEAC was set up in reaction to the conservative Royal Academy and its unwillingness to embrace any forms of modernism. Many of its founding members had studied in France and the club reflected that sensibility.[90] Meninsky's work, with a widely acknowledged basis in sound draughtsmanship, was unappealing to Nora with its impressionistic and unbroken strong lines. Meninsky suggested that she would improve if she were to draw in his mode, fundamentally forcing a modernist technique on Nora. It is not surprising, given the climate within the male-dominated schools, that the non-compliant Nora would not be 'welcomed', as Borzello notes was so often the case. Nora writes to her parents:

> He said that I had a good idea of drawing and proportion but unfortunately I had been taught the wrong way but it was likely with a few years of training I might be able to see the way he does and do Meninsky drawings.[91]

In today's terms of how we understand the role of the artist, this is quite a conceit. It is ironic that the NEAC by the beginning of the twentieth century 'had become as hidebound as that of the RA'[92] and while it is still a highly regarded organisation today offering the figurative and realistic, it is the Royal Academy that has embraced abstract and conceptual art. What neither Meninsky nor Heysen could know was that, like Meninsky in World War I who served in Palestine with the Royal Fusiliers and then in 1918 with the Ministry of Information as War Artist, Heysen would be commissioned as an official war artist in the Australian Army six years after leaving his classroom. Bernard Meninsky was just the start of the series of unfortunate and unhelpful masculine artistic interventions in Nora's career.

It was not only her teachers who challenged Nora. Like her father, Nora was passionate about nature and the transient beauty of flowers and it would be a subject that would sustain her throughout her fluctuating career. She claimed her religion was 'growing things and sunshine. Light and life'.[93] Her love of nature was the essence of her flower pieces and still-life works that she turned to in her darkest hours. But her path to these more intimate works, dominant in her oeuvre, was influenced by two men, recommended to Nora by her father while she studied in London, who would have a devastating effect on her sense of worth and artistic ability. The first stinging criticism came from the Royal Academician James Bateman whom Nora had enjoyed listening to in conversation some eleven months earlier with her father in a fellow artist's London studio. Nora wrote home to her parents on 19 May 1935 that Bateman and his wife had joined Nora for dinner at her studio and he took the opportunity to review her work. The trio was headed to the theatre afterwards but how much Nora enjoyed that is in doubt:

> I got a gruelling criticism from Bateman. He doesn't like my work evidently, and hasn't a good word to say for it. He thinks that it lacks tone, that my technique is mechanical and that I am trying to get light and vibration in the wrong way. All of which is very disheartening. But then he is very biased against women painters ... we nearly came to blows discussing women artists and their merits. In wishing to condemn someone's work he said 'Oh just like a woman's work' and that made me furious, and I stood up for them and defended them with all I had ... Probably his criticism will do me a lot of good. At the moment I feel sore about it and a little resentful ... his words didn't tally at all with what Miss Pissaro [sic] thought, so where is one?[94]

Despite her bravado, Bateman's thoughts and words on her work would strike another devastating blow during a second visit by him to her studio. She succumbed to Bateman's follow-up attack that alleged her work was 'mannered' and 'superficial'.[95]

Sir Charles Holmes, director of London's National Gallery, dealt a 'devastating' blow in late 1936 when he reviewed Nora's work and delivered 'a very adverse criticism'.[96] Nora had studied at Central School since 1934 and, while suffering from Bateman's criticisms, she had still managed to push on, realising that although she was not convinced about new approaches, the constraints of the conservative Academy discipline also had drawbacks. Jane Hylton notes that Nora addressed the criticism with a clear reply when she viewed Bateman's 'vast Academy picture' which she had seen at his studio, when she found it 'too worked out and precise. I would have liked to have seen the subject treated more vigorously with freer handling'.[97] But it was her meeting with Holmes that most affected her.

> I took my work to Charles Holmes. My father had made contact and made an arrangement ... that he would advise me as to how I was going ... He asked me what I wanted to do ... and I said figures and landscape—he just laughed at me, and it crushed me. Absolutely. It was a very untimely criticism. And, well, I lost my confidence entirely. I [went] on painting, but my big ideas, you know, Australian landscape and figures ... it was very sad, and devastating. Devastating.[98]

Nora makes this frank comment to documentary maker Eugene Schlusser, when she is in her eighties, seated on the verandah of The Chalet, her home in Sydney. As she delivers these lines her head shakes slowly from side to side as she relives the blows delivered by the man who would be dead not long after their meeting. How was Nora, an impressionable young woman, to react to the contempt of the man who was known as a great watercolourist, oil painter, author and critic, a man she had been sent to for advice by the father she loved and respected and looked to for guidance? For her twenty-first birthday in 1932 her father had given her an inscribed copy of C.J. Holmes' *Old masters and modern art*, and here she was, at his mercy. She was aware that there were many ways to paint, to express one's creativity and vision of life and nature, but the males around her were a formidable force. She wrote in a bewildered tone to her parents:

> There were several items in Holmes's criticism that I still cannot fathom. He said that my paintings of flowers looked dead and had no life as if I'd taken no pleasure in painting them. I can't understand it, if there is anything I love doing and find the greatest joy in doing, it's in painting flowers. Especially the one

> I took him of *Spring Flowers*, which I painted at the highest pitch of excitement, and enjoyed every moment of. I can't help but feel that some of what I felt is in the work, and I can't agree with his criticism on that point.[99]

Ironically, Charles Furse, a member of the NEAC jury responsible for choosing works, was closer to Nora's position than she would ever know. He challenged the 'antiquarian taste' of a fellow jurist Roger Fry as he supported 'the merits of a sober brown painting of a barn by Charles Holmes'.[100] Holmes had his detractors well before Nora was exposed to his criticism. It appears he was out of touch as well as very ill. Hans Heysen had unwittingly sabotaged his daughter.

Margaret Woodward observes how deeply affected Nora was by the criticism of the men whom her father believed could guide her, describing their actions as 'extremely cruel ... absolutely inexcusably cruel ... she was particularly sensitive at this time and it was a very unfortunate and sad thing to occur'.[101] Nora knew there was more to painting than the Academy style of all of these men, including her father, but Schlusser tells us after making a second trip to Paris 'she surrendered to Holmes and enrolled in the respectable Byam Shaw School and retreated to old-fashioned objectivity and a certain distance from passion, studying the chemistry of paint, and life drawing'.[102] It is at this moment one might ask, what might have been? If it had not been for Orovida Pissarro and her father Lucien, Nora's self-belief might well have been completely lost.

Art patron and close family friend James McGregor learned that Nora intended to return home, having exhausted her financial reserves. He believed that Nora should see the great Italian works before her European adventure ended and he funded a six-week tour during June and July of 1938. Evie and Nora started in Rome and then travelled by car to Orvieto, Assisi, Perugia, Siena, Florence, San Gimignano, Padua and Venice.[103] From Venice, her last stop was Milan, and then she returned to London. Her father's tour of Italy had lasted twelve months and the postcards written to his mother document his entrancement with Venice and Florence.[104] On hearing about her proposed trip to Italy, Hans Heysen wrote:

> The memories of these places are still the clearest and strongest of my life and so they will be with you. What you will see will but whet the appetite.
>
> In the end every artist must solve his own problems in his or her own way. But I see from your letters that you have come to this conclusion yourself. Your letters have been most interesting to me throughout, to feel the gradual change and development in your outlook and your reactions to the different schools of painting. They are not dissimilar to my own reflections and thoughts at that period of my studying years, and have revived many old memories.[105]

It appears Nora's itinerary was a close match for his, albeit covered at a faster rate. She wrote home to her parents about her 'thrilling' encounter in Arezzo with works by Piero della Francesca and Tintoretto as just a couple of the highlights. After leaving Milan with a deep impression left by Bellini's *Pietà* (c.1465–1470), the two women visited Paris together for the last time. In the same letter she writes about an exhibition of van Gogh paintings discovered after walking miles while covering what she referred to as the Great Paris Exhibition. In fact it was the important Exposition Internationale des Arts et Techniques dans la Vie Moderne, a showcase of the achievements of many nations, a hotbed of nationalistic pride and competitiveness with the various pavilions constructed to project national strength. Nora's focus had not shifted and despite the intentions of the exhibiting nations she continued to immerse herself in art, not politics or national prowess, and affirmed her admiration for van Gogh:

> There was one glorious golden landscape with a blue cart that was so alive I could smell the grass. His work has a strong vitality and always leaves me excited and stimulated. I walked into that room feeling utterly weary after miles of walking in trying to find the place, but the moment I saw those canvases all so alive, so vital and intense, I forgot it all. Also saw an exhibition of very modern work—Braque, Picasso, Vlaminck, Modigliani, Maillol and others.[106]

20. *Down and out in London* 1937 resurfaced among Nora's collections of long-forgotten paintings when she told the story of the important work to Jane Hylton in 1994. It is pictured above on an easel in The Chalet's garden in its unstretched state as it was 'rolled and squashed' for the journey home nearly sixty years before. Papers of Nora Heysen, National Library of Australia.

On returning from Paris, her final days at Dukes Lane must have been difficult. Within a few weeks of arriving back in London she would leave her friend Evie; her time in London had not been all she had hoped for, she had no money and was in debt to her father for her passage home:[107] 'The money I have is not going to see me through ... I will be called upon to beg yet again another loan from Daddy. My debts are mounting fast. The first thing I will do when I get home is mount a show and pray that the people will buy'.[108] The last work she painted before leaving was *Down and out in London* 1937 (AGSA). A self portrait, it shows a despondent, tired woman in the domestic realm.

Like her self portrait of 1934, there is no easel, no painter's smock, palette or brushes to identify the individual at the centre of the work as an artist, but the confident and focused young woman of the earlier portrait is also absent. Instead the viewer is presented with a dismal scene of a cramped kitchen with washing strung up above a gas stove behind the figure as she sits perched on the small kitchen table staring off to the side, disengaged with the viewer, an empty glass by her hand. The sombre tones of the painting underpin its mood, perhaps a direct reflection of Nora's state of mind just prior to her return to Australia. There is an ambiguity in the evidence for this downheartedness as she writes home about the painting in a positive voice having just completed it before traveling to Italy,[109] but much lies beneath the surface unsaid to her parents and expressed instead on canvas. She was leaving London in a state that was not what she had imagined—as a trained artist with a defined approach and clear view forward, and the title she gave the work speaks for itself. Schlusser comments: 'Is that where they want her? In the kitchen? She looks uncertainly across the frame, her face blurred but questioning and full of emotion. It is a modernist work but it seems to reflect the confusion of her tangled artistic identity'.[110] During her time in London Nora had been hurt by the repeated rejection of her work by men who were indignantly watching the world they understood start to tilt as a result of the forces of change. Could it be that a talented woman with fresh ideas was one challenge too many for them? The painting fared little better than Nora's crushed confidence. She revealed in 1994 to Jane Hylton that the painting had been 'rolled and squashed' on the journey home to Australia 'lost amongst my debris ever since' and that she was pleased that the picture could be restored after such a period of neglect.[111] A grant from the South Australian government was made available and the painting is now held in the AGSA collection. It is a pity that the restoration of Nora's confidence could not have been as satisfactorily reinstated forty years earlier. She would also suffer a protracted period of neglect, out of sight though not quite under the bed.

SIX: NORA TAKES HER LEAVE

Nora told me she loved her mother but felt at times her mother resented the close relationship she (Nora) had with her father. –Phyllis McKillup[1]

Nora made her way back to Adelaide by ship, the *Thermopylae*, departing in August 1937 with a scheduled arrival in Adelaide in early October. Nora noted to her parents in a brief letter before she left that she would be home in time for her father's birthday on the eighth of the month. She told them that James McGregor had been 'invaluable' in helping to get her home including providing her with letters of introduction to the captain. Nora writes wistfully that her studio is empty but it is clear that she is ready to return, saying that she will sail that night before spending the following day in Antwerp: '… so it is the Channel for me tonight and then all aboard for home. The studio looks bare and desolate with a huddle of suitcases in one corner … I'll soon be with you all'.[2] During her years in London she had witnessed changes in the art world and also in the fabric of British society. When she arrived in 1934, the British parliament was dealing with a plethora of social and political issues following the Depression years, including mounting tensions between Ireland and Scotland and the establishment of the Scottish National Party with a view to secession.[3] By 1936, under Stanley Baldwin's government, public sympathy for the poverty-stricken families of the north-east was mounting; Edward VIII declared his abdication to marry Wallis Simpson; and the unthinkable prospect of another war with Germany was looming. Nora experienced the death of her host country's king, the abdication of another and the coronation of George VI in a tumultuous year for the British people. She wrote to her parents on 30 January 1936:

> London is looking particularly bleak and drab, everything is draped in black and purple. The effect is too depressing for

> words and everyone is dressed in black to lend a still more dismal air. The funeral must have been a deeply moving spectacle. I was too busy painting to make an attempt to see it, but I turned on the wireless and heard a description of the whole thing. London is black in mourning her King.[4]

Nora had spent three and a half years abroad wholly dedicated to her studies. She remained committed to her chosen career despite the men who might have derailed her. It is unclear whether a comment in a letter home about it being hard to believe that she was '… twenty-six, old enough to be married and have a few children …' was wistful or an expression of achievement in remaining unattached.[5] In London, she had stared the poverty of the artist's lot in the eye, often talking for hours to other artists about the predicament for artists when a public was not buying— 'all together we were a little group all with ideals and no money'.[6] She described how Australian artist John Passmore was representative of many trying to make a living:

> A Mr Passmore, also a Sydney scholarship winner, was there. He has been over for four or five years and is now working at a business job in the daytime and studying art at an art school in the evening. J. Cook they say is doing the same—the same old story, no one seems to make a living out of art. It is a wrong state of affairs.[7]

Nora had been comparatively fortunate in that the small works she sent home (mainly flower pieces) were popular and sold, though she was never able to sell a piece in London. Her father's contacts in Australia no doubt helped in keeping her solvent to the point that she did not have to work in a secondary job. She also had the benefit of her father's financial backing when she asked for it. This was a level of security most of her fellow artists did not enjoy. The loan she required for her fare back to Australia was something she could have been certain of, but what she would find when she returned was not so clear.

Her last days in Paris, after the Italian tour courtesy of James McGregor, might have been filled with viewing art but a troubled world was being established in microcosm in the grounds of the Trocadéro, in the

16th arrondisement, the *palais* that had been dismantled and rebuilt as the Palais de Chaillot for the *Exposition Internationale des Arts et Techniques dans la Vie Moderne*. The political crisis that culminated in World War II just two years on was visible at the exposition, in the massive grounds where Nora had sought out the paintings of van Gogh. History shows that one chapter of the Italo–Abyssinian War had ended in 1936 with Italy taking Addis Ababa. This highlighted the weakness of the League of Nations with paltry sanctions against Italy; accordingly, Italy used these sanctions to limit alliances with Britain and France and to move closer to Hitler's Germany. It had violated the Treaty of Versailles and entered the Rhineland and by October 1936 the alliance between Germany and Italy was agreed. The same year the Spanish Civil War began and the German–Italian alliance backed the Nationalists while the Republicans were supported by the Soviet Union. Japan was at war with China.[8] Another kind of face-off between Russia and Germany occurred as a result of the two nations' pavilions being situated directly opposite each other in the Jardins du Trocadéro in the middle months of 1937 in a Paris that wanted to be seen as still prevailing 'when it came to matters of taste' and as a 'cultural authority'.

> The 1937 *Exposition Internationale* faced some of the most important dualisms that divided humanity against itself: the split between Paris and the provinces, between France and her colonies, between art and science, between socialism and capitalism, between fascism and democracy. The official philosophy of the exposition still paid homage to the twin gods Peace and Progress, as all parties at the great ceremony in Paris intoned the faith: no matter how bleak the world seems to be, the twin gods will see humanity through to a glorious future ... By June of 1940, Paris would belong to conquering Nazis.[9]

The fact that the planners of the exposition situated Germany and Russia directly opposite each other was a curious decision. Perhaps they had opted for equality of location without considering the potential for symbolic confrontation in each pavilion's design. While there appears to have been some unsanctioned German viewing of the secret Russian designs, the French planners were busy utilising the ready home talent throughout the pavilions. Nora might not have known it, but the city that had prided itself as 'the home and center of fine art' had undertaken a program of employing artists to decorate the pavilions of the exposition to 'alleviate the widespread and growing poverty' among them, hiring two thousand artists as mural painters. The last exposition had been purely a celebration of the modern decorative arts in 1925, but the arts would not feature in the same way in 1937. According to historian Arthur Chandler, 'The Great Depression—and the trend among painters and sculptors towards "unpopular" abstract art—the number of buyers to support the arts had declined sharply'. The 'widespread' poverty among artists was the result. Likening it to the United States' WPA (Works Progress Administration) that employed artists, musicians, writers and directors in large works initiatives—including a young Mark Rothko and Jackson Pollock before they were known—Chandler writes about the French government program:

> Artists gratefully accepted this public support; and some of the most renowned French artists of the period—painters Robert and Sonia Delauny, Albert Gleizes, sculptors Henri Bouchard and Alfred Janniot—staved off starvation with government commissions. But there was a subtle price attached to this patronage: modern painting and sculpture at the *Exposition Internationale* were reduced to the status of architectural embellishment. First the superiors, then the equals of industrialists, artists had now fallen to the level of plaster molding manufacturers and furniture decorators.[10]

If Nora had visited the Spanish Pavilion she would have viewed Picasso's *Guernica*. He had been commissioned by the Republican government to create a mural for its pavilion as was Joan Miró, and sculptor Alexander Calder created his *Mercury fountain* for its ground floor. Having read accounts of the bombing of Guernica by Italian and German air forces in May, Picasso completed the work in early June and it was on display in July[11] when Nora was there. It is possible that she did not seek out Picasso's latest work, having referred to him as a charlatan to her father in a letter in April the same year.[12] The tension at the exposition was further evidenced by the facing Russian and German pavilions and the significance of each design could not have been lost on Nora. The German pavilion was designed by Albert Speer, Hitler's favoured architect, responsible for the Nuremeburg rally grounds. Records regarding the exposition reference his subterfuge in creating a pavilion that dominated its Russian neighbour:

> On a visit to Paris several months prior to the exposition's opening… Speer 'stumbled into a room containing the secret sketches of the Soviet pavilion'. Upon this good fortune he designed a pavilion that was intended to firmly counteract the assail of the *Worker and Kolkhoz Woman* [a massive bronze sculpture by socialist realist sculptor Vera Mukhina on the top of the Russian Pavilion depicting a male and female worker, ten metres tall on a high platform, boldly striding forward, jointly raising a hammer and sickle] … Speer created an indomitable vertical mass, capped by an eagle perched atop the swastika.[13]

The level of unrest that Nora had lived through in her time in Europe was reaching a crescendo. Her departure was timely. While Australia was not yet embroiled in any conflict in its own region, as part of the British Commonwealth the threat was real from afar. What the European conflicts around her might mean for her country was not the focus of Nora's attention at this time. Returning home to an uncertain artistic future would have been uppermost in her mind. While she was away, the politics of the art world in Australia had not been static. The rise of modernist movements and reactions to them had resulted in philosophical and practical artistic conflict, with many feeling the need to choose sides.

During 1936, Hans Heysen, along with Robert Menzies, at that time attorney-general, and Heysen's friends including Sydney Ure Smith, Lionel Lindsay, and Robert Henderson Croll, had been establishing the poorly conceived Australian Academy of Art. Modelled on the British Royal Academy, it failed to receive a royal charter despite its goal to be the 'expert body' on the country's artistic matters. Officially founded on 20 June 1937, by 1946 it had held its last exhibition and was disbanded.[14] Hans Heysen had arranged membership for his daughter. Whether Nora wanted to join or not was immaterial. Once again, she was following her father's precepts, although he was from another painterly age. She had expressed her reservations about the establishment of such an organisation in a letter home in mid 1936 and her observations proved prophetic: 'It seems as if the Australian Royal [sic] Academy will only be a weak replica of the English. It will cause more wrangling and jealousy than it is worth. I can't see the sense of it, or really what good it is going to do'.[15] It appeared that her father would have settled for no royal charter though he conceded it would lend the Academy weight saying, '... it is the only "*sign*" that will give it the authority that it must have to do any good at all'.[16] In 1938, the Contemporary Art Society of Victoria was established, according to its own declaration, 'in protest at the perceived conservatism of the dominant Australian Academy of Art, with primary and paramount objectives being the fostering and promotion of contemporary art, to further the understanding of it, and to encourage and stimulate artists'.[17] Menzies' political and sometimes legal rival, Labor politician and former High Court judge H.V. Evatt, supported the Contemporary Art Society and officially opened its inaugural exhibition in Melbourne in 1939. Kate Nockels notes:

> He attacked the Academy and its supporters for their 'unwarranted assumption of pontifical authority'. In bringing such high level politics into the art world, the divisions between academic traditionalists and those artists exploring the new ideas emanating from Europe ... became even wider and more hostile.[18]

After two years as the Society's president, artist George Bell made way in 1940 for art patron John Reed and the 'radical' artists of the day including Arthur Boyd, John Perceval, Sidney Nolan and Albert Tucker, all Melbourne based. The Academy membership was made up of recognised artists, ten from each state except Western Australia, patrons, and collectors with strong representation from Sydney-based men active in the art world including Ure Smith, Lionel Lindsay, Douglas Dundas, and Lloyd Rees. Robert Menzies had been appointed the provisional chairman. Opposition from the Contemporary Art Society blocked the Academy's application for a royal charter.[19] The Contemporary Art

Society's 1941 exhibition was held at Hotel Australia in Melbourne and its catalogue reads like a manifesto for modern art:

> Great art has never been produced by merely copying Nature. Man not only sees, but feels. What he feels is as fundamental to the art he creates as what he sees. Man to-day sees and feels differently to man of yesterday. His art is different. Imitation of the art of yesterday is worthless. This exhibition is of the work of artists of to-day, 1941. The Contemporary Art Society offers absolute freedom to the Australian artist, imposes no limitations and refuses no work, except that which has no aim other than representation. It is essential that opportunities should be provided for showing the work of artists trying to break new ground.[20]

The intent is clear and the gauntlet is thrown down in the Academy's path. Initially many artists, including moderns de Maistre, Wakelin, Proctor and Cossington Smith, were willing to take advantage of the audiences attracted by the high-profile Australian Academy of Art and the potential for sales. The demise of the organisation was a result of the lack of support by artists that 'saw the Academy as stifling the artistic expression and strengthening the power of the establishment'. The Academy's promotion of 'academic naturalism' seen by many in contemporary groups as 'sterile mimetic art' saw it 'falter and wither … under the onslaught of critics and *avant garde* artists …' according to Kate Nockels.[21] Nora was returning to a more disputatious and fragmented artistic community than the one she had left behind.

Nora's return from London would precipitate a physical parting from her father. Back in Hahndorf after almost four years of independent living she realised there was only room for one artist at the family home. Clashes with her mother did not help matters.[22] During conversations recorded with Nora for her PhD thesis, Phyllis McKillup discussed Sallie Heysen's protective attitude to her husband. From the beginning of their relationship, Sallie had made it her business to sustain interest in and promote Hans Heysen's work. Of course, her own aspirations were submerged in the family enterprise. Nora told McKillup, 'Father believed painting made too great a demand on a woman, to allow her to give enough time and commitment to the family. In my case this did not apply … She [mother] was leg-roped to the kitchen, and never able to use her self-expression'.[23] McKillup suggests that Sallie might have resented Nora 'not only for her close relationship with her father, but also the closeness of their professional relationship which Sallie understood as an artist herself'.[24] Alongside the mother–daughter tension, Nora's work was taking a different direction to her father's. This all combined to precipitate a move. Kate Nockels suggests that Nora did not want to contradict her father.[25] Her proximity to him made that a challenge. Meredith Stokes said that over the many years of conversations she shared with Nora, her affection for her father was clear though she rarely spoke about her mother: 'Nora adored her father, they were very, very close'.[26] McKillup noted that 'Nora and her father were very similar in their personal reserve, and Nora says herself she could never talk intimately to him about personal feelings or emotions'.[27] This admiration and the accompanying inability to communicate openly must also have exacerbated Nora's position. It would not have been possible to tell her father that she was questioning his approach to art, given their shared reticence. Her understanding of a modern view of painting and her exposure to influences from abroad all contributed to her need for her own work environment, removed from The Cedars. Despite this, Klepac reports that in the few months that she spent living in the family home, working in her old studio, 'She painted some of the loveliest of her works there, characterised by an intense emotional determination'.[28] In this period she produced *Self portrait* 1938 (*plate 12*), purchased by QAGOMA, and *Corn cobs*, purchased in 1987 by AGNSW (*plate 13*); and the painting Klepac describes as 'the very post-impressionist' *From the kitchen window, The Cedars* c.1940 (Private collection):

> These works signal the emergence of an original painter, but fine as they are, her father found them to be too light a key. She loved and admired him, but she knew that she belonged to another world. If she was to make a life for herself in Australia, she must move.[29]

However, throughout her life's correspondence with her father, Nora accepted his guidance on many issues and held to his belief that the 'truth' in art sat within the artist's capacity as 'draughtsman', who must be able to see and draw what is observed. As a result of this belief an extraordinary work ethic was embedded in both of their modes of practice, a continual striving for the very best of representations of 'truth'. Kate Nockels puts that Nora was never completely free of her father's influence:

> In the last decade of her life, when I knew her, I think he was always on her shoulder. He was there. She was loyal, she didn't want to confront him when she came back [from London]. Nora was caught between the two schools.[30]

The two schools are represented by her father's academic realism on the one hand and the modern art movement in Australia. Schlusser refers to 'an artistic break' with her father as 'inevitable' and Nora responds:

> I didn't realize that until I came back from Europe—that I wanted to stand on my own two feet, and be recognized as I thought—apart from my father. I was always called the talented daughter of the famous Hans Heysen—and then I got an urge to be recognized. I didn't know how I stood in my own work—I wanted to be recognised.[31]

Hylton agrees with others' observations about Nora's move for independence, maintaining that during Nora's years in London 'her work had shifted away from the influence of her South Australian teachers, including her father, and taken on a gentle brilliance of light and colour that she could truly call her own'. Hylton, along with Klepac, observes that when Nora returned to her studio at The Cedars in October that year, leaving the gloom of London weather and arriving to the garden bursting with flowers, she responded by producing 'a number of high-keyed works including a floral still life, a self-portrait, and *Corn cobs* one of her most dynamic compositions ...'[32] Nockels comments:

> Nora Heysen had changed her approach and technique significantly as a result of her time in London. Her palette was lighter and she had absorbed the Post-Impressionist ideas on divided colour. Her composition now acknowledged the

> Modern emphasis on form and mass and her picture plane was flattened. She could, in fact, have joined the 'Modern camp' along with Preston, Crowley and Cossington Smith and felt at ease. However unless she publicly distanced herself from her father, she was inevitably placed in the pro-Academy camp … As it was Heysen opted to remain in what she saw as the dominant art discourse, Academic realism, where she was affirmed as a 'sane modern'.[33]

Living back at The Cedars and as a new member, largely by default, of the new Academy, Nora elected to exhibit *Corn cobs* and one other 'sane modern' work, *Still life, apples* 1938 (Private collection), at the inaugural exhibition. Klepac points directly to this choice as a key moment in determining her future: 'The fact that Nora Heysen exhibited with the Academy of Art in 1938 and not with the Contemporary Art Society has in a way left her out on an historical limb for a long time'.[34] After this exhibition, the separation between father and daughter became clear. Klepac tells us: 'She owed him much, but from now on she knew she was the better judge of her work and its future'.[35] Hylton also acknowledges the shift in the relationship between Nora and her parents and to the discomfort Hans held for 'her looser painting style and the very high-keyed palette she had adopted. She was also no longer the young woman that needed cosseting against the world …'[36] In her correspondence to her parents from London she had signed her letters 'Norrie', once home that changed and she became 'the mature, independent Nora'.[37] Nockels confirms that there was also friction between mother and daughter, with frequent arguments, not necessarily about art but more to do with two adult women both with strong views: 'She wasn't going to fit into the obedient daughter mould … Sallie was a strong personality and Nora was no longer going to buckle under and do as she was told. She'd been away from home … and she had survived'.[38] After living independently for three years on the other side of the world, the necessity for Nora's departure was clear. Her choice of new home was calculated:

> I thought of Melbourne, I didn't really like Melbourne. I thought it was too dull at that period and most of Father's friends, the artists who had visited my home were from Sydney.

> I knew much more about the artists of Sydney and what was happening [there]. I didn't like the Meldrum School [in Melbourne] particularly for the tonal work. I thought Sydney would suit me much better. There was much more *lift* in Sydney. There were my father's friends who wanted me to come over so that they could keep an eye on me sort of thing ... Ure Smith was a great help and Jim McGregor ... a great friend of my father, and Lionel and Norman Lindsay.[39]

Artist and teacher Max Meldrum was the main exponent of Australian tonalism in the 1920s, a theory in direct opposition to those of colour and narrative behind the Heidelberg School: 'he argued that painting was a pure science, the science of optical analysis or photometry by means of which the artist, in carefully perceiving and analysing tone and tonal relationships, could produce an exact appearance of the thing seen.[40] Lionel Lindsay could not tolerate Meldrum or his theory and called him 'the mad mullah' while Norman Lindsay used him as the basis for his character McQuibble in his 1913 comedic novel, *A curate in Bohemia*.[41] Nora did not warm to Meldrum for stylistic reasons, and within a few short months of her move to Sydney he would prove to be an unattractive antagonist in her life.

Nora's works of the late 1930s are central to her oeuvre and her sustained appeal. Seen by many experts as her best work, they represent a pivotal moment in her artistic life, one where she is claiming her independence. Nora repeatedly said that the most important aspect of any artist's life was that they found their own way of saying something.[42] Her vibrant *Self portrait* 1938 was painted just months before departing for Sydney. It was held by Meredith Stokes until 2011. Nora had given it to Evie. It is an extraordinary work that was never in the public realm until a determined effort to secure it was made by the QAGOMA. Nora's centenary year produced a surge of interest and activity in her work by major galleries in Australia. There is a second work *Self portrait* 1939[43] now held in the important Cruthers Collection of Women's Art at the Lawrence Wilson Gallery in Perth that appears to have been painted in close succession to *Self portrait* 1938. This second head-and-shoulders portrait, with its subtler vibration due to a different background treatment and being less closely cropped, presents a similar gaze and resonates with Nora's new-found assertiveness. With the assistance of Lou Klepac, Angela Goddard, director at Griffith Artworks, then curator of Australian Art at QAGOMA, approached Meredith Stokes who, in consultation with her family, agreed to it finding a new home in the public realm at QAGOMA: 'I talked the family into doing it, as they were the only major gallery in Australia without one of her self portraits. We thought thousands of people would see it instead of just a few'.[44] Klepac describes it as a work 'that represents a determined stand by the young artist who has reached an important point in her life ... the paint ... has a charged energy about it, while the artist presents a restrained and controlled expression. The bright eye and sensuous mouth suggest a deep inner life'.[45] The approach she took did not sit well with her father. It is fitting that this particular work was held by the daughter of Evie Stokes, the woman who was central to so much of what was successful about Nora's time in London. It is also fitting that it is now available to the public as a work central to Nora's oeuvre.

Goddard recalls she had been in contact with Klepac in relation to the exhibition she was curating on the work of husband and wife artists Ethel Carrick Fox and E. Phillips Fox. She recalls that this was when the conversation with Klepac around Nora began:

> Earlier that year [2010] a major [Nora] Heysen had come up for auction—a self-portrait with a palette and a dramatic tonalist chiaroscuro. Because I had been working on the Ethel Carrick exhibition I was very interested in women artists and I think Lou responded to that. We [QAGOMA] didn't go for that picture [*Self portrait* 1932]; it went for a huge sum in comparison to anything that had been at auction from her before, so that set an indication. After that auction I couldn't get it out of my head. I started poring over all of the texts and looking at what might have been still in private hands. My approach to Lou was that we didn't have a major work by Nora Heysen while the other major collections in Australia did ... and that it was a gap for us.

Goddard added that while permanent hangs can 'change a lot' she expressed a strong view to Klepac that if QAGOMA, which in 2011 held nothing of Nora's, were successful in acquiring a major work over a larger gallery there would be greater likelihood of that work being more accessible to the viewing public and less likely to be hidden on a rotation in storage. She recalls that Klepac listened to that argument and told her that there was a significant picture still in private hands but that he didn't know if the family would be willing to let it go 'because they are very close to it and very close to her [Nora]'. Goddard wrote a letter on behalf of the gallery, and Klepac made the approach to Meredith Stokes. It was a successful strategy. The self portrait, one of two works considered by many experts as Nora's most outstanding, the same one that Mary Eagle had identified as a major work of interest for the NGA fifteen years earlier, was granted to QAGOMA. Goddard remembers the impetus for attempting the purchase:

> Ethel Carrick Fox … was in a strange position of being an expatriot where she's not really claimed as an English artist, she's not claimed as a French artist or even as an Australian artist and I've always found that quite sad, and in a way I saw that kind of intrepid ambition in Nora Heysen as well [and the subsequent neglect?—'yes'], and then those women who gave up all sorts of things they could have had in their lives in order to make work—I felt that kind of identification with the work [by Nora] … It is an impressionistic picture, the broken brush strokes, it's very frank, there's a strange kind of patterning of light across the face, and this really strange dab of green right under her nose … why would you do that to a portrait of yourself? It's a really brave painting. It's not huge, it's humble in size but it sparkles … Yet it doesn't have all the kind of mise en scène of all the other works—the palette, the smock, the serious expression.[46]

The successful acquisition was a coup for QAGOMA.

The major Nora Heysen work auctioned in 2010 that highlighted the need for Goddard to examine acquiring a Heysen for QAGOMA was *Self portrait* 1932. It was purchased by the NGA whose team described the work as 'bold and brilliant',[47] referring to her self portraits as 'arresting images of a modern, independent woman that are exquisitely executed with a distinctive and refined realism'. It is the first self portrait by Nora the NGA purchased with funds from the Masterpieces for the Nation Fund,[48] stating at the time, 'The National Gallery of Australia aims to represent art from each state and territory in Australia and has, for some time, sought to better represent this significant South Australian-born artist'. Nora was twenty-one when she painted the work. It depicts her as artist, modestly dressed in a cream pullover and box-pleated woollen skirt in a taupe and brown tartan weave. To focus attention on 'her and her art as the subject'[49] Nora painted a deep blue curtain backdrop:

> In this work she combines her interest in Italian Renaissance art and classicism with her sense of herself as a modern woman committed to her art. Heysen depicts herself with a focused determination that became a characteristic of her self-portraiture; her blue eyes are fixed in a piercing gaze. The look expertly captures her confidence as well as her self-containment and down-to-earth humility (the latter also suggested in her attire). In her hands, she holds two brushes and her treasured palette, given to her as a child by her father's patron, Dame Nellie Melba.[50]

Sotheby's in Sydney had listed it with an estimated price of between $60,000 and $80,000—it realised $168,000, an unprecedented price for a Nora Heysen. In 2010, seven years after her death in 2003, there was a groundswell of interest in Heysen's work and it continued to grow, reflected in auction prices realised during the following seven years, culminating in two sales occurring during the writing of this book. On 3 May 2017, the other painting of Evie at the breakfast table titled *Interior* 1935, the partner to *London breakfast* purchased by Mary Eagle in 1996 for $35,000, realised an extraordinary $146,400. The NLA was the purchaser at auction and Nat Williams, director of exhibitions at the Library, writes that 'there is a poignancy in the fact that the painting that depicted and stayed with [Evie] during her life has now joined our archive of letters which traverse their [Nora and Evie's] life together in London 80 years ago'.[51] Almost half the size of *London breakfast* at just over thirty centimetres square, and considered a study for the larger work,[52] *Interior* is evidence that Nora's position as a major contributor to Australian art can never again be in doubt. The provenance listed by Sotheby's Sydney notes Meredith Stokes as the seller having also inherited this painting from her mother who had received it directly from Nora.[53] Further cementing Nora's pedigree a week after the sale of *Interior*, the 1934 portrait Nora painted of her sister Josephine in London *Interior with Josephine* (Private collection) realised $92,045 on 11 May 2017, sold by auctioneers Menzies in Sydney.[54] Nora's work is now sought after.

Another significant sale in 2011, just eleven days after *Self portrait* 1932 (NGA) realised $168,000, occurred in South Australia when a painting that was thought to have 'gone missing', was auctioned by its owner. The Adelaide *Advertiser* ran the following article on 15 May 2011:

> NORA Heysen's *Still Life with Cauliflower and Vegetables from the Artist's Garden* [1930, Private collection] has sold for a record amount and will stay in South Australia.
>
> The still life, which was missing for 50 years, yesterday sold for $50,500 at the Elder Fine Art auction on Melbourne St.
>
> Elder Fine Art proprietor Jim Elder said the bidding price was initially placed from $18,000.
>
> 'The price we achieved is actually a record for that artist [for a still life] so that's a great achievement for us and for the artist,' he said.
>
> 'It puts her where she should be put, high up on the list of artists in Australia. Not just Adelaide but Australia'.
>
> Mary Henderson was the successful bidder for the oil painting which attracted a crowd of devoted art lovers that filled the auction room.
>
> 'I've always liked her work because she was so young I think when she started and so successful,' she said.
>
> Seller Margaret Leppnus bought it in 1948 for about pound stg. 4. It was much later during a visit to The Cedars in Hahndorf that she realised she had the 'missing' painting.
>
> 'I've had it for so many years and I'm now in a nursing home so I don't need the painting,' she said.[55]

According to the auctioneer, the discovery was significant as it represented Heysen's early career. It was with this work that she won her first prize, at age nineteen.

Nora had visited Sydney in 1931 with her mother and father, and this experience possibly helped to inform her later decision as to where she would live. It appears that Hans was fostering his daughter's interests as a career artist and he included her in the trip to view that year's show of the Society of Artists and visit the galleries. It was perhaps an early twenty-first birthday treat—a valuable experience by her father's side in the inner sanctum: 'Nora was introduced to the art world of Sydney in a way that would not have been possible otherwise, and her father was able to renew his association with all his friends there …'[56] Her move to Sydney, where she remained until her death, marked the start of her adult professional life: 'I owed my father because he paid my fare back from London. He bought a flower piece of mine—35 pounds I had in my pocket to start my way in a big city'.[57] Nora left Hahndorf not quite financially independent, since she was effectively underwritten by Hans Heysen and his friends were waiting for her, ready to help her launch. She would be able to repay her debts sooner than she imagined.

SEVEN: MAD MAX, MARY AND THE ARCHIBALD

If I were a woman I would certainly prefer raising a healthy family to a career in art. Men and women are differently constituted. Women are more closely attached to the physical things of life. They are not to blame. They cannot help it, and to expect them to do some things equally as well as men is sheer lunacy.-disgruntled Archibald entrant Max Meldrum protesting against Nora Heysen's success in the Archibald Prize[1]

Art's art to me, no matter who does it—men, women or what!-Nora Heysen in response to Max Meldrum[2]

Nora arrived in Sydney shortly after the city had hosted sesquicentennial celebrations marking one hundred and fifty years of European settlement in Australia on January 26 1938 with a grand parade under the banner of 'Australia's March to Nationhood'. Celebrations were planned to continue through to April. Records show that floats depicted various aspects of white settlement and progress including the wool industry, the explorers Burke and Wills, convicts, steam trains, and trams and bicycles.[3] On the same day, Sydney witnessed the first national Aboriginal civil rights gathering. The pamphlet promoting the event at the Australia Hall in Elizabeth Street (organisers had been refused permission to meet at the Town Hall) was titled 'Australian Aborigines conference sesqui-centenary day of mourning and protest'.[4] The rally was attended by Aboriginal men, women and children from around the nation and had three aims: full citizenship rights, Aboriginal representation in parliament, and the abolition of the NSW Aborigines Protection Boards. The Protection Boards were government agencies that were charged with overseeing the welfare of Indigenous Australians and which in reality were closer to agencies of persecution than protection, instrumental in the processes that resulted in the 'Stolen Generation', children forcibly removed from their families and communities.[5] The result was that then prime minister Joseph Lyons agreed to meet a delegation of leaders, and major reforms were made to the Protection Boards but it was not until 1967, almost thirty years later, that the referendum held to decide the question of Aboriginal people's right to full citizenship and the altering of the Federal Constitution to acknowledge their existence in their own country returned a resounding 'Yes'.[6]

These two events in Sydney in January 1938 were followed by the opening of the Empire Games on Saturday the fifth of February, while the following day became known as Black Sunday when huge numbers of visitors arrived at Bondi Beach, and it was reported that approximately two hundred people were washed out to sea by three freak waves. Five people drowned, and the Bondi Surf Bathers' Life Saving Club records show 180 were rescued by its club members in an extraordinary operation.[7] Nora had arrived in noisy and chaotic London of 1934 to the opening festivities of the Empire Games; she might have timed her arrival to avoid a repeat experience in Sydney four years later. She did not see 'Dashing Dess', Decima Norman, the Western Australian female track-and-field athlete, take five gold medals,[8] but she might have read reports of the Royal Commission set up to investigate the treatment of poliomyelitis in Australia. In 1938, art critic Robert Hughes was born, as was the poet Les Murray. Each would play a significant role in the arts for a developing nation; Hughes would not become an ally of Nora or her father. Aside from sporting competitions, protests and celebrations, the year of Nora's arrival in Sydney coincided with Australia's participation in talks in Evian, France, as a member of thirty-one allied nations. Australia agreed to take fifteen thousand refugees from Europe.[9] It was also the year that attorney-general and minister for industry Robert Menzies received his nickname 'Pig-Iron Bob' for attempting to force waterside workers to load pig iron for export to Japan; they refused, believing the cargo would end up in munitions.[10] The Empire Games would not be held for another twelve years after the 1938 Sydney closing ceremony. In September 1939, as prime minister, Robert Menzies announced Australia's involvement in World War II.[11]

Evie Stokes left London in 1938 on the last available ship. Her husband was stationed in Singapore and, as I noted earlier, Evie returned to Sydney expecting her first child. She and Nora became flatmates once more.[12] In a letter to her parents, Nora described the difficulties in finding accommodation but sounded buoyant discovering the Elizabeth Bay flat that met her requirements and budget. She wrote in a positive tone that despite the place being boxy and very small, it had a view over Rushcutters Bay and good morning light. Its high position afforded an airy interior with breezes circulating off the harbour water and Nora was relieved that it had running hot water. She had landed herself a place in close proximity to friends in the art world, including fellow South Australian Arthur d'Auvergne Boxall who by then, after his time away in Europe, was teaching life drawing at the East Sydney Technical College:[13]

> Flat hunting here is just as depressing as in London, rents are high ... there are no studios and well-lighted rooms are rare as masterpieces, or rather I should say for the price I want to pay. Then this turned up. Boxall has his quarters only two doors away, and Beaumont is within cooee. McLeay Street runs parallel, so Mr Ure Smith is almost a neighbour. Also [flamboyant designer] Hera Roberts lives down the same street.

Speck notes that at the time Nora was flat hunting there was a paucity of letters from home that appears to underpin 'some form of disapproval'.[14] In the same letter telling of her happiness at finding a flat, Nora describes several repeat visits to the bank, as well as her previous address at a Cremorne Point hotel, in the hope that mail from home might have turned up. It appears a marriage and pregnancy for Evie had not ameliorated the Heysens' view of Nora's friend as she and Evie once more shared living arrangements. Nora continued corresponding with her parents as if all were well. Again she was forging ahead with her life in the way she saw fit while at the same time keeping the lines of communication open. Later she writes of her gratitude for her father's consummate packing as her belongings arrived safely from Hahndorf and at last she is able to thank him for a letter with news of home;[15] but there would be uncharacteristic silences from Hahndorf with Nora writing apprehensively about her letterbox being empty for two weeks.[16]

Nora had arrived in Sydney ready to start life as a professional artist, and once her easel, paints and table had arrived from home, the flat looked more like an artist's home-cum-studio. The business side of painting and selling art was a subject regularly discussed between Nora and her father and now the work would begin.[17] *The Ming bowl* 1938 (Private collection) Nora painted in this first flat, and she described the picture as one she was doing to 'get my eye in so I can start on some flowers'.[18] Faced with the downside of leaving behind the abundant flower beds of The Cedars and with no garden around her flat in Sydney, Nora's resourcefulness surfaced. The director of the Botanic Gardens gave Nora permission to paint in the gardens and also 'to pick one flower from every bed to make a mixed bunch for her flower paintings'. The retirement of the director meant this arrangement came to an end and Nora reported that the new director responded to her request with an emphatic *no*: '... if I want flowers for my wife I buy them'. She claimed that 'bureaucracy makes thieves of us all' and defiantly took a paper bag to hide pilfered blooms during visits to the gardens.[19]

Despite the initial positive report on her first home, within a few months the two women moved. The apartment was too constricting as Nora used one of the two rooms as a studio. Sleeping and eating with the smell of turpentine and linseed was a problem. Hans Heysen wrote that he was pleased that Nora had resettled: '... good health is absolutely essential to a painter's job and you cannot retain it if you have to sleep and live with your canvasses, in fact live on the smell of paint. Lead is extremely injurious to both the stomach and lungs ... it pays to be careful in this subject'.[20] Nora and Evie were the first occupants of a newly built flat in Onslow Road just a short distance away and Nora enjoyed the fresh interior, modern kitchen and plenty of storage, going so far as to describe it as 'a luxurious place after this little box of a doll's house'.[21] The location meant Nora retained the view over the harbour that held so much appeal for her. She missed the country—'I sigh for the trees and the bush and the garden'[22]—and the water views compensated for the negative aspects of life in the city. It was here that Nora painted the two Archibald entries.

In the first week of December 1938, with the deadline for submission to the Archibald just weeks away, Nora hosted a drinks party as a house-warming. Her father's friend Shirley Jones, whom Nora had spent time with in London, was there and Nora introduced him to benefactor Howard Hinton who went on to buy a number of her works. John Lane Mullins, the subject of one of her Archibald entries, was also at the gathering and Jones and Mullins hit it off.[23] Mullins was a politician in New South Wales and a patron of the arts involved in the administration of the AGNSW and the Society of Artists. Two months after the painting of Mullins was completed, Nora was shocked to hear that he had died, but in her pragmatic manner writes to her father in the following sentence that her next sitter had arrived and she must get back to work.[24]

Another artist who would join her expanding group of friends was William Dobell. In early 1939, a year after Nora had arrived in Sydney, Dobell returned from London and settled in a two-room apartment in the ANZ bank building in the heart of Kings Cross—'the one place that at least felt like Europe, with its cluster of apartment blocks and a scent of the cosmopolitan', a place where artists could find like-minded contemporaries. Dobell's top-floor balcony provided views the length of Darlinghurst Road, views that Dobell made good use of as material for his work. Dobell biographer Scott Bevan describes the Cross of Nora's and Dobell's day as 'hanging around the fringes of Australian society ... Kings Cross offered that rare taste of somewhere else for those who had never been anywhere else, and it provided potent reminders for those who had been elsewhere'.[25] Nora and Bill Dobell met in May 1939, four months after she had been announced winner of the 1938 Archibald Prize, through the art publisher John Brackenreg who brought Dobell to Nora's nearby flat. It is possible Dobell looked across to Nora's building in Onslow Road from his eyrie in the Cross. The more respectable address of Elizabeth Bay was perhaps a deliberate move on Nora's part while it kept her closely located to those in her artistic circle including Elaine Haxton, Donald Friend and Russell Drysdale. She wrote home of artist friends visiting and keeping her up to date with talk of what others are working on, and upcoming shows. She also enjoyed the invitations she received to dine with her friends and broaden her circle.[26] For a brief time she painted in a studio on the floor below Dobell in the same bank building. She wrote to her parents about their initial meeting, saying Dobell had little good to say about Australian painters, and that he was keen to return to Europe as soon as he had the funds. She added that 'I nearly came to blows with the young man' (though he was in fact twelve years her senior) when they did not see eye to eye on the standard of Australian art, particularly concerning his opinion of portraitist George Lambert whom Nora held in high esteem. In the same letter's postscript she adds that she was feeling almost wealthy having just received her Archibald cheque of £422.[27] Little could Dobell possibly know that in just a few years he would be at the centre of controversy surrounding the great prize. For now, it was Nora who had caused a stir.

In July 1938, before submitting to the Archibald, she was preparing a still life to enter for the Society of Artists show. She had sold a large flower piece and was receiving requests for more.[28] In her letters home it is clear she is settling into the life of a professional artist, referring to 'more commissions in the wind'. Despite her recent entry into the profession she understands an artist's worth. Refusing a lower offer for a work was a matter of principle. At the Society of Artists show she was offered £8 less than the asking price for *The chestnut tree* c.1938 (Private collection) 'but that I cannot accept, as it is not fair to those that pay the full price, and I don't approve of bargaining with pictures'.[29] Nora's principles and sense of fairness were evident throughout her life. Meredith Stokes said that many of the artists at the time were struggling and that her mother and Nora had gone to visit Dobell: 'Between them they scraped together £18 and bought a little painting of his of a woman scrubbing steps—they had no money and he had no money, they weren't famous and they weren't getting the prices they did until they died'.[30] The Dobell is an engaging work and today hangs at The Cedars in Nora's studio.

Two years earlier in London Nora declared winning the Archibald as one of her goals: 'Why can't someone paint a better portrait than Longstaff… I'd like to win that prize away from him one day'.[31] John Longstaff was a Melbourne-based portrait artist in the academic style and had won the Archibald five times between 1925 and 1935.[32] By August of 1938 Nora was working on two portraits with the Archibald clearly in her sights. The prize for portraiture was established in 1921 using the proceeds of a trust fund of over eighty thousand pounds bequeathed in 1919 by the journalist and founder of the *Bulletin* magazine, Jules François Archibald. His publication was seen as radical at the time and came to serve as an opinion shaper on matters affecting the nation, its culture and its identity. Archibald had a lifelong interest in art and the role it played in a society's development—the aim of the prize was to support artists, foster portraiture and celebrate great Australians.[33] No woman had been able to wrest the prize from the establishment males, but that was about to change. Nora had completed her training abroad as so many of them had, and she was ready to compete on home ground.

Lou Klepac judged that Sydney was the right choice for the young artist when she made her move for independence. Her earlier experience in the city with her parents would have been a good foundation and helped in the forming of relationships that she would cement later on her own terms:

> It was the home of *Art in Australia* [established in 1916 by Sydney Ure Smith and Bertram Stevens then sold to Fairfax and Sons in 1934],[34] which had always been favourable to Hans Heysen, and it was the home of the influential Society of Artists of which Sydney Ure Smith was the driving force. It was at the Society's annual exhibitions that she had launched her career, for it was from the 1930 exhibition that her works were acquired by the state galleries.[35]

As Ure Smith was a close friend of her father's, Nora benefited from the people he could introduce her to. His broad interests in the art community and his position within it provided her entrée. Klepac pointed out that Ure Smith promoted her membership of the Society of Artists in September 1938 when the Society was 'in its heyday … and represented the whole art world of Sydney'. Klepac also reveals that a relative of Nora's mother, Anita Smith,[36] married to the famous aviator Sir Keith Smith, introduced her to influential friends in Sydney including the consul-general to the Netherlands, whose wife would become the sitter for Nora's winning Archibald portrait, and to Ursula Barr Smith—later to be Lady Hayward—a renowned collector and patron of the arts along with her husband Sir Edward Hayward, known as Bill.

The Haywards would become close friends of Nora's and in her return travels to England after the war in 1948 she would connect with them and fellow artists Jeffrey Smart and Jacqueline Hick.[37] The Haywards, along with Heysen friend James McGregor, the powerful wool broker, were regular travellers to London to buy for their art collections.[38] It was fortunate for Nora that Ure Smith was receptive to the changing tide of the modern art scene. While the Lindsays and Hans Heysen adhered to their traditional artistic persuasions, Ure Smith had been actively encouraging new membership in the Society of Artists advocating 'measured progress in Australian art',[39] publicly declaring his position when he opened the 1919 Wakelin–de Maistre show. In 1923 he supported the society's travel scholarship being awarded to the modernist de Maistre. In the same year he arranged an exhibition in London of works by members of the society. His profile in the changing art world was heightened when he defended works by Norman Lindsay that were selected for London. They were subject to a challenge for exclusion on moral grounds that was put before the New South Wales minister of public instruction.[40] It was a hostile court injunction lodged by a group of disgruntled Victorian artists that wanted their work to be considered for the show to be held at Burlington House in London. Lindsay's work focused on the representation of the nude female and his particular style was also not enjoyed by the women of Sydney's Feminist Club. Miss Sara Hynes addressed the conference, maintaining it was not representative of Australian art: 'It may be a man's idea of Paradise, but it isn't woman's. Are those kinds of pictures fit to send to London?' Her rhetoric received a resounding 'no', reported *The Register* newspaper in Adelaide.[41] Ure Smith pressed ahead despite the protests. His support also extended to other contemporary groups in Sydney and also to the 1939 exhibition in Melbourne of contemporary French and British art. While this might have put him at odds with his friends Heysen and Lindsay, the three were in accord rejecting abstract art.[42]

In Sydney, Ure Smith was also publisher of *Home*, a periodical that 'fostered "good taste" in contemporary architecture, interior design, photography and graphic design, with covers usually by Thea Proctor or Hera Roberts'. Distanced from the conservative realms of Adelaide and Melbourne, he maintained his lifelong friendships with Lionel Lindsay and Hans Heysen while remaining a relevant commentator and possibly 'Australia's most diversified art patron'.[43] It could be assumed that Nora was able to learn from Ure Smith about the changing art scene with less pressure than she would have been able to under the continued influence of her father. Ure Smith opened her world to new ideas as well as doors:

> On Monday evening I met Syd Ure Smith and had a chat with him. Cousin Anita invited him and Evie and myself to a sherry and we had a pleasant time. Syd Ure Smith is entertaining with his wonderful stories … I'm waiting until I get straight before inviting people here, but next week I hope to do a little entertaining.[44]

Under Ure Smith's mentorship, Sydney art circles quickly embraced Nora. James McGregor, who generously financed Nora's final leg of her foray in Europe with her trip to Italy, continued his support of his friend's daughter and Nora was happy to be included in gatherings that included fine wines and food along with the chance to privately view exceptional works in McGregor's private collection at home. Nora stepped out boldly when she invited all the guests at one McGregor luncheon to her flat for sherry. It may be that she remembered her mother's art of hospitality and networking when it came to marketing but it was her good manners that dictated reciprocity:

> Lunch at McGregor's was a handsome affair and ah, the wine—some rare old vintage in whose presence one could but talk in whispers and sip in ecstasy. Mr Ure Smith was a guest and Hera Roberts, Mrs Rutherford and a Peter Whitehead. Mostly I enjoyed his collection of pictures and fell in love with a little Lambert flower piece …
>
> I have asked the whole party in to a sherry on Friday evening, I don't know where they'll sit, or stand for that matter, but it is the only way in which I can return any hospitality.

Sherry parties appear to have been the order of the day, with Nora regularly reporting to Hahndorf which new acquaintances had been made—often Ure Smith hosted them. He was making sure Nora connected with artists at similar stages of their careers to hers including Adrian Feint, John Brackenreg and Dobell. By September she was not only a member of the Society of Artists but also a successful exhibitor at the 1938 show where the National Art Gallery of New South Wales (as it was then) purchased her *Spring flowers* completed that year (AGNSW, *plate 14*). With another private sale that week, Nora was feeling a sense of security—'I'm off the rocks and feel almost rich'.[45] Her father had submitted two large watercolours to the same show. He was never far away. In a letter home, Nora comments that his paintings are well hung and that they stood out from other works. Her view on Picasso and Marie Laurencin has not altered, saying the two works on show 'leave me cold'. By the end of the first week of the show, McGregor had offered Nora a large room to paint her portraits in and access to his vases, presumably for her flower pieces.[46] There is no doubt that her father's friends were of great assistance as she started to gain momentum in her professional life. It was just over a month later that the loss of Josephine would devastate the family. Nora's professionalism would be tested with Archibald sitters to be accommodated and commissions to be completed.

In the years that followed her move to Sydney, Nora demonstrated her independence both in her approach to her art and in how she would live her life. The central events that illustrate that independence were firstly her choice of subject that would win her the most prestigious art prize in the country in 1938; a decision she made that would see her commissioned as Australia's first woman official war artist in 1943; and finding love with a married man. The third event remained pivotal to the choices she made for her life, and the ramifications of this love would prove to be profound.

When Nora won the Archibald, she was twenty-eight and the youngest entrant at that time to have secured the prize. She also ended seventeen years of male winners. That year the competition received 145 works from eighty-four artists, a record for the time. Hylton observes that the field was 'particularly competitive … Heysen herself considered the other of her two entries, a portrait of John Lane Mullins, the better painting, but was nonetheless overwhelmed and delighted to have won'.[47] Nora experienced difficulties with her winning portrait when after only two sittings her subject, Madame Adine Michele Elink Schuurman, refused to sit: '… after that she was always tired, had a headache or an excuse, and I had to bully her into returning … She was a very spoilt social butterfly and sat there weeping while I finished her portrait'[48] (Private collection, *plate 15*). Hylton observes: 'Perhaps this is why Heysen was able to capture the seeming vulnerability of her subject, the result being a sensitive image full of life and colour, qualities that many other entries lacked'.[49]

Madame Schuurman was twenty-five with small children and invariably unavailable to sit for Nora due to domestic and social arrangements which interrupted the portrait process.[50] After her win Nora said: 'Of course, Madame is elated. She came in radiant and all the trial of model and artist were forgotten'.[51] These two young women had executed a major coup in the establishment art world. Nora's patience, and at times resignation, in accommodating her sitter had eventually paid a handsome dividend. John Lane Mullins was recovering in bed after surviving a heart attack at the time of the announcement and Nora visited him:

> The biggest surprise of all was the portrait of Madame Schuurman winning it, and not John Lane. I hadn't in my wildest dreams entertained the thought of her doing it. Poor old John was terribly disappointed. He is in bed with the after-effects of a heart attack. I went to see him yesterday, and it was quite sad to see him trying to cover up his disappointment. I feel that I have let him down.[52]

The win was announced on 21 January 1939. The Adelaide *Advertiser* described other entries in lacklustre terms stating: 'In the midst of these sober surroundings Miss Heysen's portrait stands out in joyous style'.[53] Nora was swimming in Watsons Bay, oblivious to the controversy her win was causing. In conversation with Kate Nockels in the 1990s, Nora recalled that she had no expectation of winning and told how James McGregor

> ... came to the rescue and shepherded her through the bevy of reporters and camera people, through this very public moment in her life—she was not exactly out of her depth but somewhat overwhelmed by it all. McGregor provided a car and a chauffeur and gave her time to get out of her bathers ... then whisked her off to the gallery to receive the prize.[54]

An artist with an expedient eye to self-promotion would have seized this moment but for Nora it was just all too much fuss. While she was very pleased with her win, acrimony arose from fellow entrants who felt her subject and her execution of the work were not worthy of the prize. Nora recalls:

> In those days it was the be all and end all if you won the Archibald Prize. My [painting] wasn't really eligible, it had no pretensions of being [of] an outstanding Australian. She was just a social butterfly and I used her to hang that beautiful Chinese coat on her. And they were all men judges, it was a very fresh portrait amongst all the others.[55]

An article published in *The Australian Women's Weekly* on 4 February 1939 highlights what women artists of the time faced as they worked to be taken seriously. The headline read: 'Girl Painter Who Won Art Prize is also Good Cook'. An accompanying photograph of Nora peeling vegetables at her sink captioned: 'MISS NORA HEYSEN, a talented cook, who collects recipes from many countries, at work in her kitchen'. Perhaps underestimating the broader interests of their readership, the editorial staff gave the historic win a culinary twist. Nora, with her usual grace, responded to their request for her favourite recipes and she submitted three, which comprised the bulk of the story surrounding her extraordinary achievement. Whether the significance of her response was lost on the journalist or not, it appeared in print under the sub-headline 'Nora Heysen Gives Recipes for Her Favorite Foreign Dishes—There is scope for artistry in the kitchen just as there is in the studio'. The foundation subject of the article is inserted as a sideline, as Nora's statement is reported: '"Most artists can cook even if all cooks do not paint," says Miss Nora Heysen, who, with her portrait of Mrs. Elink Schuurman, is the first woman to win the Archibald Prize'. Despite the *Weekly*'s attempts to guide the tone of the piece, Nora deftly steered the report back to art:

> 'Artists learn to be good or fairly good cooks out of sheer necessity during their student days, when they are nearly always poor,' she explained … 'There are probably people much cleverer than I am who can do two jobs at once, but I can't.
>
> 'If I have some exotic creation cooking on the kitchen stove

I can't possibly paint, and if I am painting I cannot turn my mind to how the dinner is cooking.

'Thousands of years of domestic routine have trained women to do their housework in the morning and I generally do my housework and meal preparations early and leave the afternoon free for painting.

'I discipline myself, whenever possible, to working hours for painting just as one has to in any sort of job.

'When working on a portrait, I paint for several hours in the afternoon, but if I am painting flowers, for instance, I paint for perhaps eight hours until the flower, or myself, have wilted'.[56]

21. Nora with her winning 1938 Archibald Prize entry. Papers of Nora Heysen, National Library of Australia. Photograph: Tim Clayton / Fairfax Media.

The article also carried a photograph of Nora at work in her studio alongside her recipe for Hungarian goulash and instructions for 'Duck with Olive Sauce'.

Nora's friend, Craig Dubery, recalls a passing comment Nora made about the criticism of the winning work and the fact that her other portrait of Mullins better suited the competition—'You're right!' she responded. 'The one they threw out should have won!' Dubery reflects that Nora simply did what she felt was right for her art:

> At the time there was a newer quality coming into Australian society that hadn't been [there] before, and that's our Nora pushing the boundaries without thinking—not on purpose as in 'I'm going to do this for the Archibald specifically'—it's just what she did. She broke down barriers for women and people's equality… extraordinary, without big noting herself or wanting to be known for that.[57]

Fellow entrant Max Meldrum did not hold to the idea that women artists could aspire to paint as men could. The city newspapers carried reports of his comments immediately after the announcement of Nora's win:

> A great artist has to tread a lonely road. He needs all the manly qualities, courage, strength, and endurance. He becomes great only by exerting himself to the limit of his strength the whole time. I believe that such a life is unnatural and impossible for a woman.[58]

Despite this, Nora seems to have retained a degree of equanimity. In a letter to her parents immediately after receiving the news of her Archibald win she reflects on the commotion attached to the moment:

> After two days of rather bewildering notoriety and excitement, today the reaction has settled in and I'm glad to spend a quiet day in my studio. I have been beset with reporters and photographers, and their battery of cross-questioning. Now I have a vague idea of the life of a movie star. Thank goodness

> that it lasts for a brief day … and I can settle back and paint in comfortable obscurity …
>
> You'll laugh at the attack of Meldrum's. The reporters all want to urge me into battle defending women's rights, but I have no wish to be drawn into it especially as it becomes personal.[59]

It is clear that Nora did not believe in capitalising on the adage that any publicity is good publicity and was keen for the attention to end. In conversation with Eugene Schlusser, Nora recalls artist Max Meldrum's reaction to her win: 'Was he angry! Max Meldrum said a woman's place was in the kitchen! … I thought *my goodness gracious*—fancy taking that view! Art's art to me, no matter who does it—men, women or what!'[60]

Despite Meldrum's position on Nora's win, she was generous praising his entry. Though she reserved some criticism, she thought his was the best entry. She remained self-deprecating, suggesting it was a fortunate year for her, as Longstaff, whom she had decided to challenge for the prize, had not entered. Into March she was still on the receiving end of public backlash about her selection as winner but remained sanguine:

> This Archibald Prize has brought not only blessings on my shoulders, but by some trick it seems to have made me a few enemies. There are still irate and seething letters in the papers against my portrait and the judges' decision, the papers rang to know what I think of it. I have nothing to say, so probably they will grow tired of it.[61]

The portrait must also have been too much of a departure for Nora's parents. Although they were proud of her, Nora wrote to them after they had viewed it, 'I'm sorry you don't like my portrait of Madame Schuurman'.[62] She moves quickly on to another topic and there is no further discussion. Her friend Dobell would suffer a controversial court challenge to his win in 1943 that sparked a wide and lively debate, a challenge brought about by two Royal Art Society members, one being Joseph Wolinski and the other, the same woman named as Nora's major critic. Both times the complainants were unsuccessful in overturning the result. Margaret Woodward commented:

> A number of artists who were strongly against her, and who hadn't won the Archibald Prize, thought they should've done by that time … it was Mary Edwards who was particularly vitriolic about Nora's winning painting … and suggested to her that she hand the money back because her painting was 'so inept', which was a load of nonsense.[63]

Hylton reports that Nora exclaimed to her parents, 'The woman's mad,' and that 'Edwards had written an apologetic letter to her [Heysen] … that the attack was not personal but that … all the artists in Sydney had been wronged by [Heysen] gaining the prize'. There were 'disgruntled' male artists who did not believe the Archibald should be open to women artists, according to Hylton, who also notes that it was 1960 before Judy Cassab was the next woman artist to win the prize.[64]

There was no argument for Nora as to how she would live her life. While her upbringing was conservative, it also offered a certain freedom that came with a rural home and the capacity to safely roam and learn from the natural world. Released from any religious teachings, it could be deduced that she looked to her surroundings and the example set by her parents and their peers as to how she would determine her values. Exploring her art at her father's side, experiencing the broad spectrum of visitors and the news and views they introduced to her realm, observing nature without the constraints of suburbia—all are factors that might have contributed to Nora's even-handedness when dealing with the contradictions that her adult life held. With a healthy and expected respect for her elders, Nora was still able to evaluate and decide for herself her position on many cultural and social issues in a period of great change. The most apparent aspect of Nora's quest for 'truth' was that she did not broadcast her position on matters important to her but simply put her head down and carried on—and perhaps it was to her detriment according to Nat Williams, formerly the National Library's director of exhibitions, and responsible for the Nora Heysen retrospective exhibition in 2000:

> … you know it's one thing to be a good artist, there are many people who can paint and make art but they can't sell themselves, and they have to be a commodity and she found

> that difficult. You read about when she won the Archibald she... lacked the capacity to push herself forward into the limelight—she was dogged, stubborn [in her approach] and probably able to but would not push forward.[65]

Within weeks of her Archibald win, Nora was immediately immersed in new work. Rather than promote herself or let the win change her perspective, her humility was on show as she confided in her parents that she was grappling with a new sitter:

> All is once more normal and the feeling of momentary success has been thoroughly swamped by the difficulties and problems of another portrait. I don't know how a portrait painter can ever hope to buoy himself up with conceit. The very fact of being confronted with a person of whom one has to portray on canvas, their character their atmosphere, with all the subtleties of flesh painting of God knows what else, is to humble one to dust.[66]

Later Dubery reflected on the egalitarian quality that Nora exuded and her willingness to accept others without judgement or prejudice. Schlusser says of Nora:

> History is littered with the spiritual corpses of children trying to emulate successful and famous fathers. Only Nora made an attempt in the Heysen family. Naturally shy, a woman, and surrounded by forceful men used to getting their way—her father, her husband, and Australia's male establishment—to achieve a sense of self she fought a long battle with herself and the Australian art world.[67]

This is a complimentary view of Nora's tenacity. However, her motivation was oblique in terms of gender disruption. She was singularly engaged with her work and this was deeply sustaining.

During the months following her Archibald win, Nora continued to work on portraits and her still-life flower studies. She had learned that good coffee and cake in her studio while a potential buyer considered her work was conducive to making a sale. Her mother's skill hosting afternoon coffee at The Cedars had provided the template but this was as far as Nora's marketing skills would progress: 'Mrs Malcolm Reid rang the other day and asked if she could see my work, as she wanted to buy a flower piece. She bought [sic] along a sister and friend and I fed them cream cakes and coffee and I believe I sold a mixed bunch. She is to come and have another look tomorrow morning and finally decide'.[68] By May 1939 she was planning a solo exhibition but as the months progressed and tensions relating to war rose, Nora was anxious. She was nervous about producing enough work for her self-imposed deadline and as world news worsened, the idea of an exhibition became less feasible. In August she wrote to her parents:

> ... now it seems that only a miracle can save the world from another 1914. I find it all too disturbing—somehow even over here, with all this glorious sunshine, one can't even remain impervious to the shifting of world powers and the terrific anxiety and strain that has gripped England and Europe. One thinks war an impossibility—and yet?
>
> Everyone over here is depressed. Brackenreg came down on Monday looking very gloomy and despondent. It has just dawned on him that artists are in for some lean years and that prospects are desperate.[69]

Just weeks later, on 11 September, Nora writes that she has postponed her show until November assuming events allowed. War had been declared a week before and her thoughts immediately went to her young unmarried brother Michael. The relief she expressed when she heard that men would not be sent from Australia would be short-lived: 'One can only hope and pray that this terrible madness will stop before we are too far in to withdraw. Every morning I awake to realise it afresh'.[70] James McGregor was also concerned for the welfare of the country's artists, telling Nora 'it is indeed a poor outlook'.[71] She stopped reading newspapers and tried to settle down to some work despite her anxieties but later in November she would confirm to her parents that her show would most likely be held the following year. For now, it was a case of finishing a portrait commission that was causing her concern: 'One wants a great deal of patience besides the hundred and one gifts to succeed at this game. At the moment I vow I'll never take another commission, or if I do I'll see that I make a few clauses before I begin'. She added that she was looking forward to Christmas at The Cedars, that 'it would be good to get home and quietly paint some flowers … I'm longing to try the pink roses again …'[72] While she worked she continued to study the art that was available to her in travelling exhibitions such as the French impressionists at the Sydney David Jones Gallery. She wrote to her father to discuss what she had seen—'better examples of Van Gogh, Gauguin and Utrillo and Matisse than I had expected. It will take another visit to sort things out …'[73] These shared discussions on her work, his, and that of others, were the mainstay of their communication.

After her Christmas visit home, Nora returned to Sydney and life with Evie. During 1940 she continued with her flower pieces and portraits. In March she was pushing to meet the deadline for the Academy show. She also expressed her scepticism to her parents about the inclusion of more than one woman on the selection committee: 'Margaret Preston, Thea Proctor, Douglas Dundas and Lloyd Rees. It seems ridiculous to have two women on the same committee'.[74] The work she had been struggling with was a portrait of James McGregor's friend, a Mrs Nesbitt, and when it came time to submit, McGregor, who had been tracking the work's progress and had not been happy with the background, eyes and mouth, advised her against entering the work. She was left frustrated with two flower pieces entered instead. The Academy exhibition was opened by Robert Menzies, one of the key members of the group behind its establishment. Nora wrote home of a varied response and of criticism 'scathing in the paper'. The show closed after poor sales and after what Nora ultimately described as receiving a 'lukewarm reception' amid dropping prices.[75] Her year was filled with commissions for portraits, often through introductions from James McGregor; she finalised her successful portrait of artist and friend Adrian Feint; and she took on a young student—though she never thought she would teach, the income was welcome.[76] The year ends with a warning observed by Nora that came in the form of over eleven thousand visitors to a contemporary art exhibition—she suggested that 'the Society of Arts will have to wake up and take *notice*'.[77] She was referring to the Contemporary Arts Society show reported by the *Sydney Morning Herald* as 'Art of Youth' in its headline, and that went on to state that 'This is the art of youth, of idealistic daring, of prodigal vitality ... Where there are no prosy pictures to act as wet blankets, the fancy of the spectator as well as of the artists can soar fast and free'.[78] In August 1940 the Victorian Contemporary Art Society under John Reed's direction had held an exhibition at the National Gallery of Victoria of two hundred works and in September the same year, for the first time, brought its exhibition to Sydney's David Jones Gallery.[79] Nora continued to write home about the controversy surrounding the show: 'a fine stir and everyone is having a ding-dong go at each other'. The impact of the exhibition could not be ignored—'Sydney is going modern with a vengeance', claimed Nora.[80]

As Nora approached thirty, entering a new decade, news from home included letters with photographs of new babies and she refers to being an aunt, four times over.[81] These images of happy and secure children amid the rising world tensions and her own professional insecurities gave rise to deep reflection:

> In the life of an artist there is no contentment and no security, a game of chance and gamble, and a game with odds well against me. Now, more than ever, the outlook for artists is pretty hopeless.
>
> It becomes daily more difficult to concentrate on any work, and quite impossible to shut out that daily millions are being slaughtered, and millions suffering the loss of all they possess. Today is a glorious Autumn day with the harbour sparkling in the sun—no wonder we out here find it difficult to realise the horror in Europe.[82]

Nora and Evie decided to move house once more. Evie's baby Meredith had arrived and Nora wrote that the new flat caught the morning sun, which was good for the baby.[83] Meredith Stokes says the two women didn't know how to cope with a small baby, and a nanny was called in to 'wheel me around and keep me quiet'.[84] Nora's aim had been to find an apartment that had a larger room for her to work in and she seized the opportunity to rent the four-roomed flat with a big kitchen and bathroom, despite hot water not being 'laid on'. This was a minor inconvenience for Nora as she had a large space to work in overlooking Rushcutters Bay, but the war and the impact it was now having on those around her worried her the most. Ure Smith's publishing enterprise entered a precarious phase (though it ulitmately survived):

> Over here everyone is gloomy, and the one topic is war news—it is hard to combat the depression, and work on, when the whole world seem [sic] to be toppling round our heads ... It is hard on people who have spent their lives building things up, only to see them crash round their ears, just when they are ready to sit back and reap some of the rewards. I was sorry to hear Ure Smith has had to give up. This is no age for art of any description.[85]

The war became personal for Nora when she heard that her two brothers Stefan and Michael had joined up: 'it is sickening to see the great liners storm out with their cargo of youth for the slaughter yard—it fills one with bitter resentment against the futility and horror of war'.[86] It was during this period of reflection in 1941 that Nora painted what she refers to as her Murray Madonnas, including *Dedication* (HAG) and *Motherhood*—a cycle of paintings of women holding children. *The Age* art critic Robert Nelson commented in 2009 that these two works:

> ... still have a sober gravity that makes the touching mother-and-child image rise above the merely sentimental. With optimal detail, both pictures express the institutional charge of parenting, as well as tenderness, which gives them a philosophical balance, the very genius of her tradition.[87]

Jane Hylton writes that Nora was deeply fond of children and that these paintings 'on the subject of motherhood are among her strongest and most poignant'.[88] *Dedication* was gifted to the Hamilton Art Gallery in Victoria in 1963 by Mr and Mrs S. Fitzpatrick and is held in its Australian Collection. The gallery's online collection catalogue quotes Nora:

> I still consider *Dedication* is one of my best paintings. I wanted to paint the people who worked on the land. I wanted to capture a working woman's dedication to her child. At the time, I chose the title 'Murray Madonna' but my mother persuaded me to change the name to 'Dedication'. I still wish I hadn't.[89]

The portrait is of Eileen Bellman and her son Malcolm, who was three. Bellman worked at The Cedars as a kitchen maid in 1941 when Nora painted her during a short holiday at her parents' home in March that year. It is interesting to note that in 2004, when looking to reframe the painting, Hamilton Art Gallery director Daniel McOwan found an unfinished self portrait of the artist on the back of the canvas.[90] Hylton suggests that these works were a continuation of Nora's theme of representing strong, capable women connected to the landscape as seen in her *Ruth* series.[91] It was certainly something she would pursue in the coming years. Nora entered and won the Art Gallery of South Australia's Melrose Prize for *Dedication*.

On 16 March 1942 Nora wrote to her parents that she was preparing to leave Sydney and was looking for a safer place in the country, possibly Canberra, citing four or five air raid scares over Sydney. Evie Stokes, with baby Meredith and her husband Henry, had moved to Canberra where he was a diplomat after he had evacuated from Singapore before it fell to the Japanese. The artistic world in Sydney that seemed so vibrant just three years before had vanished, despite valiant attempts by artists like Dobell and Margaret Preston who continued to exhibit.[92] Was it Nora's acute assessment of the trials facing an artist in wartime that helped her make a calculated decision to apply for a war artist's commission? There is no doubt that her desire to serve her country was a driving force, her empathy for all those affected was real, and the fact that her brothers were serving was perhaps also another factor. How could she continue her life as an artist while the country was at war? She chose to participate. She was an artist. She needed to earn a living and in her quest to find 'good subject matter'[93] as a war artist she could make a contribution to her country while honing her skills, earning a wage and continuing to do the one thing that meant everything to her.

EIGHT: WAR AND LOVE

Father didn't approve of me going to war. He said I would see terrible things I would never forget. –Nora Heysen[1]

In September 1943 Australian and American forces launched a major offensive in New Guinea against the Japanese in an attempt to halt its army's rapid southern advance and the imminent threat it posed to Australia.[2] After World War I, the League of Nations under the Treaty of Versailles allocated German territories in the region to the victorious Allies. By 1921 Australia had received a formal mandate from the British government to administer the country as a territory of Australia, including the north-east corner of the island formerly German New Guinea. The suspension of this mandate occurred when the Japanese invasion of New Guinea took place in December 1941. By this time Australians were facing the real possibility of the Japanese on their own shores. The proximity of New Guinea to Australia's northern coast made the unthinkable feasible. In 1942, prior to the combined forces' arrival, young and undertrained Australian units[3] had struggled against the Japanese and the diabolical impact of tropical diseases, most detrimentally malaria, and dengue fever and scrub typhus. The deployment of the joint forces numbering tens of thousands led by US General Douglas MacArthur and Australia's General Thomas Blamey eventually won back large tracts of territory from the Japanese. According to Australian War Memorial records this was the 'springboard'[4] for MacArthur's successful advance into the Netherlands East Indies and the Philippines. The Japanese sustained enormous losses against the comparatively well-equipped and resupplied Allied forces supported by air and sea drops:

> Between March 1943 and April 1944, some 1,200 Australians were killed, and an estimated 35,000 Japanese died. That the

> Australian fatalities were so comparatively low is a testament to the army's professionalism and its mastery of jungle warfare, as well as to the strong material advantage the Allies enjoyed over the increasingly desperate Japanese … People may never become familiar with exotic-sounding locations like Bobdubi Ridge, Komiatum, Finschhafen, Satelberg, Kaiapit or Shaggy Ridge. But each was a hard-fought battle honour; each was a bitter struggle in the liberation of New Guinea; each was a stepping stone on the long path to the Allied victory that finally came in 1945.[5]

While Kokoda is often the first location associated with the Pacific conflict, these locations listed above would become very familiar to Captain Nora Heysen. By 8 April 1944 she was en route to Finschhafen five months after its successful liberation. The assault against the Japanese had begun in September eight months before. By drawing the Japanese garrison out of their major base in Lae, the former administrative centre for Australia's mandated territory, the Allies conducted a 'slow, grinding campaign' in nearby rugged terrain, weakening the Japanese hold on the strategic centre of Lae on the east coast. Following this conflict, Australian forces made an amphibious landing east of Lae while more Australian troops were flown into Nadzab to the north-west. After a large-scale pincer movement by advancing forces, Lae was back in Australian hands. While the casualties for the push by the Allies between September and April have already been noted, it is sobering that the total casualties that are recorded for the New Guinea conflict were over 200,000 for the Japanese and 7000 each for the Americans and the Australians.[6]

This was the arena that Nora would participate in, recording the terrors of war and attempting to bear witness to the humanity within the horror. But first she would have to pressure the authorities to let her travel to the theatre of war. The idea of a woman war artist was anathema for some, and painting in the proximity of a war zone unthinkable.

In Australia during World War I, Hans Heysen and his family's allegiance had come into question, like that of all the residents of the German settlement in Hahndorf. They suffered the indignity of having their town, its name place and streets anglicised, as well as it being suspected of harbouring a Nazi spy radio base.[7] Though Heysen was born in Hamburg, he had lived in Australia from the age of six and was a naturalised British citizen. His love of the Australian landscape was 'as a part of his own spirit'[8] according to Thiele, and his birthplace left him open to ignorant behaviour. The art establishment embarrassed themselves by their prejudices, in particular the refusal in March 1915 by the Melbourne Art Gallery to follow through with the purchase of the large oil *In sunset haze*. It had been identified for purchase by the gallery at the Heysen show opened by Dame Nellie Melba at Melbourne's Athenaeum Hall, but it was not subsequently acquired. His accident of birth was the central issue for the gallery's trustees. Heysen told Thiele that it was the questioning of his loyalty and personal integrity that left him 'shocked and hurt'. Melba responded, 'I think the Melbourne Art Gallery has behaved very badly … It is a great shame, but it is their loss'.[9] The painting was returned to his studio where Heysen reworked it after realising there was a flaw in its design. He added a large red gum, 'which helped to bind the two sides of the composition'.[10] Renamed *Droving into the light* 1914–21, it was purchased in 1922 by Perth businessman W.H. Vincent and is an important painting in the Art Gallery of Western Australia's collection. Further insult came from the Australian Art Association, just two years after inviting Hans Heysen to become a member and to contribute to its first exhibition in 1913. Acting on rumours that Heysen 'lacked sympathy with the British cause',[11] the Association wrote to Hans asking him to declare his position in mid 1915. Heysen promptly resigned his membership. In 1917 the National Gallery of New South Wales also demanded Heysen 'definitely and satisfactorily declares whether his allegiances and sympathies are with the British Nation' otherwise the Gallery Board would not include his paintings in their Loan Exhibition of Australian Art. He wrote to his friend and fellow artist Elioth Gruner:

> I am sorry at not being represented, but as I disliked the approach of the Gallery Board on the question of nationality, I must take the consequences of what I thought right to stick up for—if a man's feeling for Australia cannot be judged by

> the work he has done—then no explanation on his part would dispel the mistrust ... I cannot give any explanation—it would not be understood in the present circumstances.[12]

The insults did not end there. The South Australian Society repeated what Hans considered an attack on his integrity and he resigned another membership. Family members, German speakers, were also vilified and an uncle of Sallie Heysen spent five years interned in Liverpool, Sydney.[13] In March 2017 the Australian Broadcasting Corporation reported that a PhD student at the University of Adelaide had found a cache of letters dated from 1914 to 1917 from a senior commissioner of police in Adelaide to the police officer stationed at Mount Barker. According to the student, Ralph Body, the letters described Heysen as 'being of a highly doubtful character and they request his home be put under surveillance based on little more than anonymous stories the commissioner had heard, and the fact Heysen was German-born'. Until this report in 2017, the Heysen family had not known that Hans Heysen had been under surveillance, though in 1982 a University of Adelaide History honours student, Trevor Schaefer, wrote 'The Treatment of Germans in South Australia 1914–1924' citing a litany of slurs against law-abiding loyal Australian citizens of German descent. It included the material cited by Body:

> One day when one of my informants passed Mr Heysen working, he called out, 'the war situation looks better, the British are too good for the Germans and are giving them hell'. From this it will be seen that although Heysen's sympathy may be with the Germans, he is too clever and cunning to show any sign of disloyalty ... The police for not one moment believe he is loyal [to the British Empire] ...[14]

Schaefer writes that the local police 'as early as October 1914' had Heysen under observation 'for weeks at a time, without any suspicious action being seen':

> But the local Britisher did not let the military forget Heysen 'the spy', and three years later they advised the Constable [Birt] to again have him watched. So Birt, with the assistance

> of 'reliable residents of the locality' carefully watched his movements and residence for a month, again with no result.
>
> Heysen is a very clever, shrewd man and would be particularly careful of his utterances and actions ... he always attends patriotic gatherings in the district ...[15]

Allan Campbell rejected the notion of Hans Heysen being disloyal: 'I mean calling Heysen shrewd and cunning, it's ridiculous. He was one of life's great gentlemen and a pacifist to boot'.[16] In his biography Thiele commented: 'Poor Hans, the gentlest and most peaceful of men ... who hated all forms of killing so deeply that he wouldn't even suffer his own turkeys to be sacrificed for the Christmas dinner, was being envisaged in the role of spy and desperado. It was ludicrous but also very sad'.[17] There were other insults, after the war, but Hans Heysen did not hold grudges, referring to it as 'one of those things ... Circumstance ... But of no consequence in the long run—not compared with the things that matter'.[18] Heysen had enjoyed widespread support during the attacks on his character. He received a number of personal letters from artists including John Shirlow, Norman Lindsay and W.B. McInnes. Shirlow wrote: 'I, for one, do not in the least share the quaint opinions of ... certain very remarkable loyalists ... I have always known you as a very honourable and upright gentleman and an exceedingly fine artist, and for these qualities I admire you and shall continue to admire you'.[19] For Heysen the important aspects of his life were in order—his family was safe, peace was restored and he continued with his work, developing his representation of light and introducing the human figure into his now famous ploughing pictures including *Turning the plough* 1920 (AGSA), *The toilers* 1920 and *Ploughing the field* 1920.[20]

By 1936, good sense prevailed. In the centenary year of South Australia, the German names of the Hahndorf and surrounding settlements were reinstated. In 1940 Hans Heysen was appointed a trustee of the South Australian Art Gallery, a position he held for twenty-eight years until his death in 1968. By World War II any question surrounding allegiances was gone, with two of Heysen's sons, Michael and Stefan, flying for the RAAF. Nora was keen to make her contribution to the Australian war effort alongside them. Her appointment as an official war artist came after she first tried to work as a volunteer in Sydney. Craig Dubery remarks that she had trouble keeping to the prescribed portions making sandwiches at a navy canteen: 'they disliked her because she was putting in way too much filling'.[21] Her desire to make a concrete contribution to the war effort was an increasing frustration. Her generosity learned in the kitchen at The Cedars was not well received in a time of rations and rules. Nora told researcher Phyllis McKillup that 'she was quite disillusioned by this censure for she felt these men should be given the very best treatment possible'.[22] As a war artist she would continue to push boundaries, well beyond the over-filling of sandwiches.

Sydney Ure Smith had been appointed War Art Council chairman and was arguing in favour of Australia to have a greater breadth of war artists recording the war, including women artists. Catherine Speck writes that Peter Bellew, editor of *Art in Australia*, was critical of the late arrival of Australian war artists on the international fronts. None were deployed until late 1941. Bellew felt Australia should look to the British scheme of appointing high-profile artists and of showing the work widely during the conflict rather than solely as postwar memorial records. His mid 1942 editorial reads:

> Australia has been at war for almost three years. Her troops have been at battle stations in Britain, Crete, Greece, the Middle East, and within the Commonwealth itself … but there is little evidence when it is all over that Australia's artists were at all concerned with the struggle. It is as if Art could serve no purpose in a total war, neither for the record, nor for the nation's enrichment, nor for morale.[23]

While Ure Smith was working to broaden the war art scheme, Nora Heysen sought advice from him and James McGregor, both trustees at the Art Gallery of New South Wales, on how to arrange a commission.[24] Using the influential connections that came with being a Heysen, Nora secured her appointment on 18 October 1943 with the help of Louis McCubbin,[25] who was the director of the National Gallery of South Australia (as it was then) from 1936 until 1950 and also a board member of the Australian War Memorial and a member of its art committee.[26] McCubbin wrote to the appointments committee: 'Nora Heysen is one of the most accomplished women artists, and represented in most Australian galleries ... She could be used in a variety of ways, painting portraits and covering the activities of the women's services'. Her appointment was approved along with Russell Drysdale and Arnold Shore 'to cover the industrial war effort and the Women's Service organisations'—the latter apparently a hastily defined job description added to accommodate Nora's gender and very particular role in the armed forces.[27] Like Nora, Louis McCubbin was an artist who lived under the shadow of a famous father. Frederick McCubbin, a founding member of the Heidelberg School, a major figure along with Arthur Streeton and Tom Roberts, is an Australian impressionist whose work portrays the Australian landscape and his view of the quietly heroic lives of the country's pioneers.[28] While Louis McCubbin did continue to paint, his role in arts administration was dominant.[29] As Nora's commission progressed, McCubbin would prove to be a strong advocate for this young woman navigating new territory. He also supported Stella Bowen's commission who was living in London. She would later join Nora as an official war artist along with forty-three male artists. It was not until March 1945 that another woman artist, Sybil Craig, was appointed along with a further six male artists. A fourth woman was appointed, Jacqueline Hick, along with fellow artist Jeffrey Smart, but by then the war had ended.[30] Craig remained in Melbourne and documented the work of women munitions workers and the trials of war on the home front.

It is significant that when the AWM decided to appoint Nora to represent women in the services, it precipitated the granting of military status with honorary commissions for both men and women artists.[31] Until World War II war artists operated under the same terms as war correspondents and were not under the command of the armed forces.

The army officer responsible for Nora's orders was Lieutenant Colonel John Treloar, head of the Military History Section at Army Headquarters in Melbourne and the officer in charge of the welfare of official war artists.[32] Those involved in deciding the details of her commission—the Army Finance Board, Treloar in the Military History Section, and the Australian War Memorial acting director Arthur Bazley—agreed on the rank of captain. Treloar and Bazley believed she was entitled to the same rate of pay as her male counterparts. The minister responsible concurred with Bazley, advising 'that artists were specialists and women should receive equal salaries to male artists ... women artists should be treated in the same way as women medical officers who received the same rate of pay as men'. It was not a straightforward process, however, with the Army Finance Board refusing to pay her at the same rate as male artists as it was not 'policy', insisting that if Treloar and Bazley wanted Nora to receive equal pay, the Australian War Memorial that had decided on her appointment would need to make up the shortfall. The two agreed that the AWM would pay the difference for the duration of Nora's commission as they firmly believed it to be the correct course of action. Nora was appropriately well paid as a result, receiving a male army captain's professional wage of £14.14.0 compared to female arms and munitions workers' weekly pay of £3.14.0.[33]

Aside from her patriotism, Nora was an artist looking for subject matter. Speck writes: 'Nora actually sought the appointment. Inspired by the photographic work of Damien Parer and George Silk which was reproduced in the daily press, she decided "I might as well use what I can do in some capacity"':[34]

> There were wonderful photographs of bringing down the wounded and the blinded men being led, and the comradeship amongst the men. I thought there would be subject matter there that I'd be interested in. I was a good draughtsman. I could draw, and that would be a contribution.[35]

Margaret Woodward offers an insight to Nora's actions: 'she was very determined to do things by herself, possibly because of her association with her family. She just wanted to be her own person. She had great courage'.[36] Nora's courage would be tested in many personally challenging events over the course of her life. But for now it was the war. Nora said: 'There was a lot of intolerance towards women artists especially flower painters. When I was commissioned ... the huge laugh went around—flower painter turned war artist—they thought that was very funny. I let them laugh and I went on with my drawing'.[37] By the end of the war the 'flower painter' had produced a portfolio of over two hundred and fifty works covering an extensive range of subject matter that holds a prominent place in the recording of Australian involvement in World War II at the Australian War Memorial in Canberra. Held in the Nora Heysen Papers, the NLA carries two boxes of newspaper clippings that Nora had collected, starting with a yellowed square of newsprint heralding her Archibald win in 1938. In another clipping of an interview dated March 1989, Nora responds to earlier news that van Gogh's *Irises* had changed hands for seventy-five million dollars: 'That'll teach them to laugh at flower painters'.[38] At the time it was the highest price ever paid for a painting at auction, and no doubt the news delivered her enormous satisfaction.

Nora was not impressed with her army uniform and said that though 'this field battle dress was comfortable, it was also extremely ugly, for it was loose, baggy and ill fitting'; she also saw the dress uniform as 'unimaginative and old fashioned'. In conversation with Phyllis McKillup in the mid 1990s, Nora revealed that there were issues with Lieutenant Colonel Treloar from the outset. McKillup suggests from these conversations that Treloar was an army man and she observes:

> ... he was proud of his uniform, the outward manifestation of his military success and power ... He did not realise that Nora saw the uniform as a problem ... Treloar appears to have had an unrealsitic perception of Nora's feelings, and his anxiety to get Nora 'militarised', shows the difference between his ideas and Nora's understanding of Army protocol.[39]

The uniform would not be the only matter of contention during her time of service. With no formal basic training, it is easy to understand Nora's lack of identification with army mentality and the fundamentals of a soldier's life. At first she was uncomfortable with army procedure, having private tuition rather than Officer's Training School 'until I can at least salute'.[40] She wrote to her parents about the mood surrounding her appointment:

> My position is a curious one and seems to cause worry and confusion all round. I am looked upon as some queer specimen that doesn't quite belong anywhere. What seems to disturb them the most is that I have no number. A number, it would seem, is one's identity. Without it, I am dust.[41]

Nora was conscious of her civilian status and that soon she would be a captain with a number, having done nothing in the army's eyes to earn her rank. She wrote of embarrassment at the idea of a lower ranking soldier saluting her. When Nora had first met with Treloar to discuss the possibility of a war artist's commission, it was somehow leaked to the press and an article carrying the news ran on 11 August 1943 in the Melbourne *Sun.* Treloar was approached by the Sydney *Sun* and the Melbourne *Herald* to confirm the report and he responded that it was premature 'and it would be in the interests of Miss Heysen to let the matter drop'; Treloar felt that the attention in the press may act as an impediment to Nora's appointment progressing smoothly.[42] The army and Treloar refused to comment. It was thought that perhaps McCubbin had been the source

22. Nora in dress uniform, Melbourne 1944.
Collection of the Australian War Memorial. 062802.

of the leak. McCubbin denied this and suggested it was Nora's father. The source was not discovered. Eventually the authorities determined how the first woman war artist would be integrated into the defence force's complex systems of appointments. The army made its official announcement on 13 August 1943 in the *Sydney Morning Herald*, which ran the story with a photo of Nora captioned 'Miss Nora Heysen, daughter of the well known South Australian artist Hans Heysen, who has been appointed an Official War Artist'.[43] When she was given her uniform and her appointment was publicly confirmed she wrote again to her parents:

> I ... have been caught up in a whirl of activity which has ended in my finally being cast into khaki—it took me two hours on Sunday to dress myself for my first rehearsal ... [I] was expected to be regimentally correct in every detail. Finally I walked stiffly out feeling very compressed and awkward, and rather damp from exertion. The high stiff collar is very hard to get used to, and my feet are blistered and sore in army shoes, but I dare say I'll get used to it in due course. At the moment I feel rather as if I was minus my identity and playing a part on the stage. When someone saluted me in the street the other day, I looked around to see whom it was they were saluting, then suddenly realised it was myself. These days I dodge everything with red on its uniform and I don't know which embarrasses me more, having to salute or being saluted.[44]

Nora's commission began with orders to paint the heads of the Australian Women's Army Service, and to execute these she was assigned to the artists' studios at the Victoria Barracks in Melbourne. Her quarters were at the Menzies Hotel. She found the khaki of the women's uniforms particularly unforgiving in her attempts to render an aesthetically pleasing scheme and it was a constant aggravation in her life as a war artist, but one that could hardly be avoided. She was also frustrated about being assigned to a barracks studio rather than being where the forces were actively engaged and where she would find more stimulating subjects. There was no lack of regard on Nora's part for the heads of the services she was painting—she had enormous respect for these extraordinary leaders, but she had a vision of herself in the midst of action making a lasting record of Australian troops at war.

It was here at Victoria Barracks that Nora would paint Colonel Sybil Irving in a somewhat challenging process, as discussed in my introduction. Nora wrote home that she wished she were able to get to know her subjects before she painted them in order to capture a better likeness.[45] The brief sittings and the khaki scheme did not suit Nora. After her first attempt to paint Colonel Sybil Irving (AWM, *plate 36*), she was invited by Irving to dinner. After getting to know Irving, Nora decided she wanted to redo the portrait. The second attempt reveals an improved handling of the difficult colour and also Nora's capacity to use light to lift the overall effect. A stronger sense of Irving is also captured, her surer gaze with an overall vibrancy reflects Nora's own self-assurance (AWM, *plate 37*). The two women ultimately became friends.

Discussions with Treloar two months after she began her commission resulted in a more positive Nora writing to her parents to tell them that arrangements were being made for her to move up to New Guinea: 'I feel that to do the work they require of me that I must be right on the spot, and the further up north I can go, and the nearer the fighting areas, the better the atmosphere for war activities ... and now that they have pushed into Lae, there will be good pioneering work to be done'.[46] Catherine Speck contends that Matron Sage had taken a liking to Nora[47] when they met during portrait sessions and wanted her transferred to New Guinea 'as soon as possible to record the work of the AANS and the AAMWS in hospitals in forward areas before they are fully developed'. This move also came with less restrictive orders for her scope of work, still to represent the women's services, but not confined to them. It is notable that at this point Nora was, as Speck describes her, a 'trailblazer'[48] being the first of the women war artists to paint in an area close to the front. Treloar supported Sage's request by placing Nora on the Special Army List, a move that would smooth the way for her to travel outside of Australia as commissioned officers in the AWAS were restricted to service at home.[49]

Before leaving Melbourne for Brisbane and on to New Guinea, Nora writes that she struggled to prepare for the trip:

> I'm trying to juggle my luggage into 60lbs and what, with my painting gear and all my tropical equipment, I'm having a heart breaking time. It becomes a tube of paint or a jar of face cream. McGregor saw me off in Melbourne armed with a cocktail of three large packets of calsellettes [a brand of laxative]. I drove off in an army truck, gasmask, steel helmet and first aid and dixies and what-not strung on. All I lack is a rifle and swearing vocabulary to be completely war minded.[50]

Nora was the only woman and Australian to fly on the American Lockheed out of Brisbane for Port Moresby at dawn on 8 April 1944. She wrote home saying that she enjoyed her first experience of air travel describing it as 'exhilarating and beautiful':

> Flying these days seems as casual as catching a taxi. It amazed me taking off with so little fuss on such a long trip. Passengers and luggage were piled in haphazardly with rubber tyres, and jeeps and soldiers, all on top of each other. A young fellow with rolled-up shirt sleeves took his place at the engines, and off we went with a cheery call to hang on, as everything tipped down to the tail end.[51]

She arrived in Finschhafen on the Huon Peninsula which, retaken just months before her arrival, had quickly developed into a large base for Allied operations. It was the most forward area where nurses were stationed. Later she served in Lae, Morotai and Borneo. She was assigned to record the work of the medical teams—doctors and nurses, the wounded, and the environs. Nora was also inspired to capture images of the Papuan Infantry Battalion critical to the Allies' success in treacherous jungle conditions. With the lifting of the constraint of recording only the women's services, she produced some dramatic and accomplished portraits and scenes. Speck suggests that she was 'venturing into the issues of cultural diversity she was surrounded by in New Guinea. Her portraits of the Indigenous people convey her undoubted respect for them'. Speck continued: 'Although poorly articulated at that time, the "colonial" relationship between Australians and Papuans was in the process of being redefined, since negotiating the jungle could not have been done without Papuan assistance'.[52] Nora's male counterparts were sent to the front while she was kept away from the fighting, recording the work at the medical stations and the grind of war in the tropics: 'But it was a wonderful test for me. People were willing to sit and pose for me, and those [the wounded] that had no say in the matter'.[53]

Nora was constant in her quest to get as close to the front as possible, to record scenes of lasting historical value and to honour the soldiers, the Papuans, and the medical staff she held in high regard. It was to prove a difficult assignment but Nora persevered. 'Being the first woman war artist—it was difficult for them to accept me. And McCubbin … he put in a good [word] and my father of course, although Father didn't approve of me going to war, he said I would see horrible things I would never forget'.[54]

In a letter home to her parents in May 1944 after three weeks at the base, she describes a scene that confirms her father's worries about what his daughter might see in a war zone. Nora recounted an expedition to Satelberg, the site of a bombed-out German mission, with a butterfly enthusiast, a photographer and an amateur artist escorted by four soldiers (*Church ruins, Satelberg Mission* 1944, AWM). She writes after negotiating a 'hair-raising' track where they became stuck numerous times in 'feet of mud' that they 'trudged' the last mile to the top on foot:

> The views were magnificent and everything of interest … Everywhere live bombs were still lying around. One found a Chinese cabbage growing out of an old German bible, sewing machines and silver entrée dishes, bomb craters 20 feet deep and the place a warren of foxholes, trees stripped bare, gaunt and broken. Only the cross of the Church is still standing and the pulpit carved and painted by the natives. I found a very nice piece of board amongst the wreckage and put up my paint box on a piece of old school desk and I sat in a foxhole and proceeded to paint the view looking over the scene where our men fought and struggled the bitter way. After working away quietly for some time I became more and more aware of a horrid smell, and looking down found I was quartered on the remains of a dead Jap.[55]

Nora would also face matters of the heart, a peril that her father had perhaps not anticipated. This was to be a fateful journey in Nora's personal life. In Finschhafen she fell in love with a tropical medicine specialist, Dr Robert Black, a member of a team researching prevention and improved treatments of malaria, the cause of devastating casualties in tropical warfare in the Pacific. Malaria had previously been encountered by the Allied Imperial Forces in World War I in the Middle East. Volunteers at the Land Headquarters Medical Research Unit in Cairns were infected with the parasite and the researchers worked with 'the sole objective … to investigate malarial pathogenesis and chemoprophylaxis, using human "guinea pigs"'.[56] Nora wrote home about these brave volunteers:

> The work done here is interesting, six wards full of men or 'guinea pigs' as they are called used for experiments for malaria treatments. They are bitten with the mosquitoes which are bred here and are given the malaria by biting a patient with the fever. One sees a good bronzed Anzac go down to it and in a week he's lost 2 stone and looks at death's door, then when he's provided the pathologists with the right number of wogs and reactions, he's brought to again, fed up to health and then down to another attack.[57]

AWM history records that it was the skill and the efficient supply chain of the Allies that turned the tide of the war in the Pacific but the extraordinary treatments developed by the malaria researchers must be acknowledged as having played a significant role in that success. The debilitating effects of the tropical disease that immobilised or killed thousands were dramatically reversed:

> As an outcome of the findings with atebrin, the Australian army promulgated orders to ensure that the proper dosage was taken regularly, and that the responsibility for ensuring this procedure rested with the unit commander, not with the medical officer. The results were dramatic. Whereas early in the Papuan campaign the malaria rate had been as high as 2496 per thousand per annum, it fell to 740 per thousand in December 1943 and to 26 per thousand by November 1944. Earl Mountbatten, allied supreme commander, South-East Asia, adopted the Australian orders, with similar results among

> his forces. The control of malaria was a turning-point in the war in Burma and the Islands.[58]

An article that appeared in *The Australian Women's Weekly* in July 1944 describes in detail how the research at the Malaria Research Unit was run. The magazine opened with the lines: 'A little more than a year ago malaria was as dangerous an enemy to the forces in the Pacific as the Japanese'. Soldiers who were convalescing from minor operations in malaria-free zones volunteered to participate once their health was restored. The commanding officer was quoted: 'Many of them have not yet had an opportunity of meeting the enemy, and in the meantime feel this is an effective way of fighting him'.[59] The article went on to reassure the reader that the volunteers rarely contracted full-blown malaria due to the scientific rigour involved in extracting the necessary data and the prophylactic treatment the men were given as part of the research. The wholesome picture for the *Women's Weekly* reader at home perhaps did not reveal the realities the volunteers endured as Nora described.

Robert Black, under renowned tropical medical researcher Colonel Neil Fairley, played a key role receiving recognition for his technique that 'showed that anti-malarial drugs, as metabolised in the body, were active against cultured parasites'. Many of Black's letters to Nora describe the highs and lows of his attempts to breed the mosquitoes in vitro 'under very basic conditions'[60] while in New Guinea. It appears from one of his letters to Nora that Black was also an active participant in the research: 'My malaria is not yet upon me—the CO reckons we'll get it this time ...'[61] In July 1944 he left Nora in New Guinea when he was transferred back to the Blood and Serum Preparation Unit at Sydney Hospital to pursue his research before moving up to Cairns under Colonel Charles Ruthven Blackburn, also known for his work in association with Fairley and who headed the Cairns medical research unit. Nora described Blackburn whom she drew as 'a brilliant young man ... and has an amazing head on his shoulders somewhere between Beethoven and Byron'.[62] From her drawing, it is clear what she means (*Lieutenant Colonel Ruthven Blackburn* 1945, AWM). Her desire to find good material for her artistic development was being met, while at the same time she fulfilled her army obligations. By December 1944 Robert Black was in Cairns and within six months he and Nora would be reunited when she was posted to his location to document the Land

Headquarters Medical Research Unit in July 1945. It is possible the two saw each other again in December 1944 when Nora was posted briefly to the Blood and Serum Preparation Unit at Sydney Hospital.

Nora's relationship with Black was fraught with difficulty. Black was married and father to a young son. For her conservative family, this affair would later prove hard to accept, but Nora would not be swayed. Letters between the two track an intense love and deep commitment to find a way to be together. The timing of their first meeting is not exactly clear, though it was in the weeks she was in Finschhafen, between April and June 1944. To add to her emotional turmoil in the early days of her posting to New Guinea, it appears Nora was not a particularly welcome addition to the base. The nurses who served there had earned their rank and place in the armed forces through service in North Africa and the Middle East and they were often outranked by Nora who had arrived direct from the comfort of the Menzies Hotel in Melbourne with automatic captain's pips and the pay to go with them. She was ostracised within the compound:

> I'm living with the sisters [nurses] and have been allotted a tent to myself. One sleeps on a straw mattress and under a net, and everything creeps and crawls and smells of mildew …
>
> My tent looks out onto the Owen Stanleys and just outside are growing paw paws and bananas. Five months at the Menzies was not the best training for this life.[63]

She adds in a following letter: 'There are 14 women here … They do not accept me as one of themselves, and I live isolated in my little tent apart from their quarters, and they have built-in sheds with electric light, wardrobes and soft mattresses'.[64] After a month of being in the nurses' company Nora suggests that 'they are getting more or less used to me here now'.[65] The working conditions were difficult for Nora apart from any personal issues but she did not allow either to affect her work ethic. Within a week of arriving she had a number of works underway, writing home:

> There is subject matter in plenty, but how to tackle it? I feel like a raw beginner and at quite a loss. When I go out painting for the day, they pack me up whitebait and asparagus and tinned orange juice, and I sit and lunch on a blasted coconut stump or

> on the edge of a bomb crater, and I find myself wondering how many died on just this spot only 5 short months ago. Incredible to try and picture it.[66]

Her descriptions of working conditions include the effects of the constant wet and humidity 'everywhere mud ankle deep and the smell of mildew and rotting ... My paintings mildew overnight, they'll be old masters before I get them back'. She spent time in the operating theatre making preliminary sketches for paintings. Her respect for the surgeon is clear:

> Every time a patient comes in for an operation, the surgeon rings me up and I go and get my impressions in the theatre. Yesterday had a native with a badly crushed foot. The surgeon did a delicate skin graft over the wound when he'd sewn the tendons and joined the splintered bones. The skin graft is wonderful and horrifying to watch. It is only by going out from time to time, and coming at it again, that I can watch and draw these things, and I wish someone else had been detailed off to do this job. There's no doubt it's interesting, but I can't get the things I see out of my mind. This composition progresses slowly. The surgeon is an artist at his job and one watches him sew up a vein with the delicate touch of a woman.[67]

Nora met a number of soldiers in Finschhafen who made a deep impression on her and she represented them working and socialising in the harsh jungle environment. She distilled their individualism on her page, an attribute that in the tropics somehow managed to work within an organisation based on working as a homogeneous group that moves as one. At the end of May she had been introduced to the Mechanical Engineering Company, in particular Sapper 'Bashful'—she wrote home 'believe it or not that is his name' (it was in fact Private Sapper Bashforth and perhaps the soldiers were teasing Nora)—known as Bulldozer Bluey:

> Bluey is a character that one would meet only once in a lifetime. A lumber man from Queensland, a great hulking fellow 6 ft 4

and ginger, with pale blue eyes with that distant horizon look, red headed, red moustache and red hairs all over his brawny chest. It was Bluey who blazed the trail for the tanks to get up Satelberg, and who mowed down the jungle to make roads, all under Japanese fire. He and *Dearest*, as he calls his Bulldozer, were a law unto themselves. No one dared give Bluey orders and he and *Dearest* went their own dangerous way. He's up for a Military Cross. He has an enormous red moustache and beard. What a man and yet, sitting for his portrait, he was blushing like a schoolgirl.[68]

23. *Study for Bluey* 1944, charcoal, sanguine crayon on paper, 61.5 × 49.0 cm.
Portrait of Private Sapper Bashforth, Royal Australian Engineers.
Collection of the Australian War Memorial. ART22663.

Nora's processes and her personal view of the way she should represent the environment she experienced caused friction between her and Treloar in Melbourne. He wrote to her, two and a half months into her posting, unhappy with the work she had sent. He felt that with the latitude she had been given she was neglecting the nurses and the crucial role they played in the tropical arena. Speck refers to a 'tension between the military culture she [Nora] was working in and her own background as an artist'.[69] Nora was dealing with a climatically foreign environment that made working in her preferred medium of oils extremely difficult. The spontaneity that was often required did not lend itself to the discipline of oil painting. The preliminary drawings that she usually did for an oil study often represented a moment in the cut and thrust of the casualty ward and theatre. In conversation with Catherine Speck in 1989, Nora told her:

> You were working in the wet, and you had to be very quick in the wards; working with patients or anything pertaining to war had to be done rather quickly and getting out oil paints and all this business ... and I don't work very much from memory. I work direct. The drawings can say as much as paintings, but paintings mean more to the War Memorial.[70]

An exchange of letters between Nora and Treloar set the tone of their relationship for the duration of Nora's commission. It had been tense from the outset as Nora pushed back against the Victoria Barracks work, before leaving for New Guinea. Once there was some distance, and licence, between her and Treloar, she had endeavoured to work hard. What she delivered was not what he had envisaged and he wanted her to return immediately to Melbourne.[71] Treloar suggested that she was now familiar with the conditions in New Guinea and that she '... should return to Melbourne ... and summarise the impressions of your tour of duty. Therefore at the end of the month we shall ask you be returned, but I should like you to have the opportunity of commenting before sending the signal'.[72] Nora was affronted and responded by defending herself in strong terms. Treloar initiated the exchange:

> Now that we have received a number of your pictures from New Guinea I think that I should offer for your consideration

> the following comments from the standpoint of coverage.
>
> The first which suggests itself is that the work of the AANS and the AAMWS is practically uncovered. In the pictures we have received there are only three which deal with this subject. Two are 'social'—one shows a dance party and the other a tea party—and one is a ward with, I think a male orderly on duty.

Nora's watercolour of the nurses' mess showing a relaxed setting with tea cups out, a picturesque view and flowers on the table was not what her superior had in mind (AWM, *plate 40*). It appears that Treloar's desire for Nora to create works that demonstrated the heroic work, the sense of urgency, and the difficulties of war was not the narrative Nora was providing. Nora responded to the criticism vehemently defending her choices:

> It is my belief that these social functions given by the sisters to entertain the men are an important diversion and help moral [sic] of the men. Its aspect is, I suppose, more frivolous but it is surely a part of the pattern worth recording …

Her scope of duties was particularly broad and she had barely settled in to the job in challenging circumstances when she was requested to send work:

> I think it is hardly justified to judge the output of two and a half month's work as conclusive proof that I am incapable of covering the work expected of me here. I think also that for one woman to attempt to portray the activities of all the women's services is an impossibility and that it is rather unfair to expect it of me.[73]

Nora felt Treloar was unreasonable and she had no qualms in letting him know this, despite his status as her superior officer. Nora had not experienced military indoctrination. A trained soldier would not commit such insubordination. Her response appears to be emotional, situated in her artistic practice rather than a response that she might have explained within the framework of her working environment. However, Treloar appeared to be taken aback at her communication, with positive results.

He delayed making a decision about her orders. Her correspondence with her parents over the matter gives an insider view. She wrote that Treloar was 'disappointed and dissatisfied with my New Guinea work' but in fact Treloar was focused on subject matter, not Nora's execution, and she seems to have conflated the two:

> I feel it is a rather unjustified and hasty attack, considering that he has only seen part of the work done here in the first two and a half months while I was trying to work my way in through new and trying conditions. Still, it is very depressing having done one's best, and to put it mildly, I'm fed up. I wrote back in an angry mood giving my comment on his every accusation and insinuation, and now I'm hastily getting out to escape repercussions. But just how long it will be before his authority catches up with me, is a matter for conjecture. I fear that my short career as a War Artist is fast drawing to a stormy close.
>
> The gist of his criticism was that I had not immortalised the war work of the Florence Nightingales. In fact, had gone so far as to undermine their prestige by depicting them in social mood, dancing and holding a tea party, and crime of crimes, I drew them in the bath tub.[74]

Nora also confided in Black about Treloar's communiqué and she received solid support from him as a result. Black displayed all the loyalty that she might have expected from this quarter and he wrote as soon as his work day was finished. He also seemed to forget that Nora was now an officer in the army where taking orders was an absolute:

> I've been bubbling over all the afternoon since your two letters came ... That a man should be a critic and be in a position to make his ideas about your work into orders makes me want to say a few well-chosen words. Darling, do not take it to heart—each picture you make is part of you—it is the product of your perception, training and self-criticism—I like your pictures and so do many others more in a position to give an expert opinion. Oh that I could be with you to comfort you. Smile for me ... if there is anything constructive

> in his opinion you will see and heed, but if it is personal dislike influencing it—you will know that, too and treat it as such.[75]

It is obvious from Treloar's balanced and sincere letters that his concerns were far from personal and were based wholly on the limited works he had seen. The subject matter was not broad enough. Nora was surprised that her tour in New Guinea might end so abruptly and McKillup writes that Nora was conciliatory at the end of her letter, requesting time to travel further with the nurses who would be travelling to Madang 'to see a Casualty Clearing Station established, and so see the conditions under which the sisters work before any comforts are available'. Nora believed this would provide the subject matter Treloar expected. Her request was in effect granted by Treloar by his deliberate delay in responding to her letter until 7 September, nearly three months later. When he did reply he informed her that the initial letter he had sent her 'had not produced the result he expected' and his delay in responding was 'to let you have the further time in New Guinea'. In the letter of 7 September he also indicated that artists should be engaged for periods of four to six months or twelve months for overseas tours. This was a directive from the AWM Art Committee. She would be recalled to Australia: 'As a result of this decision it will be necessary for your appointment to be terminated about the end of October by when you will have been serving for a period of about 12 months'.[76] The correspondence between Nora and Treloar is held in the archive at the AWM and on close reading it is clear that Treloar was a fair and reasonable man trying to fulfil his army role while taking care of the welfare of the artists under his orders. It is imperative to remember that Nora was the first woman to take on this role for the armed forces and the issues that resulted were firsts on both sides. The opportunity to reward Treloar for his patience with Nora would come after she had spent three weeks designated as rest in Lae during July 1944. She moved from Lae to Alexishafen in order to travel to Madang to cover the work of the nurses setting up the Casualty Clearing Station and this provided subject material for Treloar's brief.

The sights that waited for Nora as she moved further north would have provided her with exhilarating opportunities to record the troops'

24. Strip sitter 1945, conté on paper, 44.9 × 39.6 cm. Collection of the Australian War Memorial. Sister Lucy Mackenzie N500358 is seated at an airstrip waiting for her flight to take off, surrounded by her bags and oxygen equipment, and wearing full uniform, Morobe Province, Lae. ART24282.

movements. A diary entry by a Royal Australian Air Force Nursing Service (RAAFNS) flying sister sets the stage for what Nora might also have witnessed on arrival at Nadzab en route to her assignment:

> We duly arrived at Nadzab after 10 hours flying. It was a hot, sticky day as we circled the airfield and I simply could not get over the number of aircraft of every description that were in the air, on the tarmac, or camouflaged in the revetments. There were operating in and out of Nadzab approximately a 1000 aircraft daily. The whole area was one great big bee-hive of activity.[77]

Before Nora left Finschhafen she created another ruction, when she refused the first movement order to Lae. She already had a questionable reputation, due to a number of hapless incidents while exploring outside the camp. One in particular involved a lost jeep, a potential mudslide and a rescue after a picnic, causing her to write home: 'I haven't lived it down yet and that incident earned me a reputation of a rebel. It is true, I have managed to break every rule peculiar to this place'.[78] She had been working on a substantial oil painting of tropical flowers. This is well outside the parameters of her brief. Yet she produced the stunning work *The flower ship* 1944 (Private collection, *plate 39*) and wrote to her parents that she feared a court martial after refusing the order to move south to Lae. Her lack of army 'awareness' is stunning. The fact that she hoped that her gender might help her is also intriguing:

> Had just begun on a large bunch of tropical flowers and was in the midst of it, when a movement order came through to return to Lae immediately and my plane seat was already booked. I dug my heels in … Last night I was told I had to move this morning, but told them it was impossible as I hadn't finished my flowers, and now I'm waiting repercussions, probably a court martial or I'll be shot at dawn, or else. Being a woman they may allow for whims. This has gone on for three days and through them I have painted from dawn to dusk interrupted by the telephone. The flowers are lovely here … Hibiscus, frangipani, lilies, cannas and coral flowers … Here I am at home and have enjoyed the escape from military subjects.[79]

She continued in her letter that she was called before the commanding officer and was relieved when he told her she had been granted a week's grace. The painting, which changed hands at auction in 2013 for $48,800, is described by Jane Hylton: '… the composition records a moment of joy in an otherwise difficult time, the two blooms echoing the two roses that sit similarly positioned in Heysen's *The lovebirds* of 1942'(Private collection).[80]

Is it possible that *The flower ship* oil she was finishing off at the end of June was a representation of Nora and Black together in the turmoil of war and love? Nora described it in terms of a ship sailing out adorned with streamers and she kept the work on her return to Australia; she did not hand it over to the War Memorial as she was required to do with all the work done while an official war artist: 'I painted the flower piece and it was one the war museum didn't get'.[81] Eugene Schlusser comments that: 'Sick of war and the wounded, full of love for Robert, she was inspired to paint *The flower ship*'.[82] During the period in Finschhafen before Nora 'moved out', it is clear that the relationship with Robert Black had become serious very quickly—in fact in just over three months the pair had declared their love for one another. A letter held in her personal archive at The Cedars postmarked Sydney 13 August 1944 addressed to VFX94085 Captain Nora Heysen, Att 111 Aust CCS [Casualty Clearing Station] AIF [Australian Imperial Force], was sent by Robert Black. He had left Finschhafen and returned to the Blood and Serum Preparation Unit in Sydney, often referred to as the Blood Bank, 'growing his malaria family'—mosquitoes—for his research. He writes to say that he is happy that she has arrived safely at her new posting in Alexishafen after finally leaving Lae:

> I shall not know until to-morrow [sic] if my new little malaria family will thrive—it is a very tough problem they have set me—it is.
>
> No letter to-day but I am happy to know that you have arrived safely—
>
> oh darling—I love you—I do, I do. Keep well and may you find happiness in your work—until those hopes and wishes find their fulfillment—as they will for us.
>
> I adore you. Sleep tight.
>
> Bob.[83]

From what he says it can be inferred that the couple are writing to each other daily, sometimes twice a day, and the archive supports this theory. The letters are romantic and heartfelt. Black may also have been a man in crisis in the midst of his infidelity, back at home in the city where his wife and son lived.

Black in Sydney writes about his love for Nora; he hopes there is help available for her skin ailments; and he alludes to a former state of emotional emptiness. He even sends her news of the art world. He appears to have sent Nora a photograph of himself from a time before they met and he is responding to her letter that contained a drawing of her Alexishafen landscape autographed with a lipstick kiss:

> Your mountain with its reflections is before me—I sit beside you and we watch the ripples causing the reflection to shimmer—we do not say much with our voices—there is that feeling of completeness—a fulfillment of destiny—my darling, I love you.
>
> I hope there is someone who can fix your hands for you—those firm little hands which can do so much—can I say firm tenderness in their touch for that is what I mean … The little photo is from a period when things were so simple, x = ed y, there was no happiness, no wonder—I slept—waiting to be awakened to the beauty of the world to an appreciation that there were mysteries and magic and the loveliness of you … I give a tiny little modulated sigh as I read your letters—there are tears and a smile—oh darling, darling … The Dobell show had lots of visitors—an article in the *Women's Weekly* and a small paragraph in the [*Sydney Morning*] *Herald*. The Archibald win[84] was not there…
>
> And now good-night my darling. My heart is yours and my thoughts ever with you. I love you, yes'm, I do. Sleep tight.
>
> Oh darling…
>
> Bob. [85]

Black was six years Nora's junior but her lack of romantic experience would not have put her in a commanding position. From Black's letters it appears that both of them were shy by nature and he is expressive in his love-struck wonder. The fact that Black was married is not mentioned in the surviving letters between the two but it informs much of what is written—often from Black with pages of lament of the trials to be endured before they can be together.

> My darling—at times the seas are rough—dark clouds obscure the way—but my star and guiding light reaffirm my hopes and the sun breaks through. I love you—I do. My heart and thoughts are with you. Good night darling. Sleep tight.[86]

25. Nora and Black regularly illustrated their letters to each other. The sketch above appears on the last page of a letter Black wrote to Nora while she was recuperating in Hahndorf after returning home with severe tropical skin disorders. Black described the yachts he was watching on Sydney Harbour and drew one that represented them together: 'Dear Nora I love you. Does my little ship tell you so?' Sketch by Robert Black, Papers of Nora Heysen, National Library of Australia.

Oblique references to the difficulties the couple face might not only have pertained to the separation dictated by the war. As a recently married man and a new father, he had much to consider.

Black had graduated from medical school at Sydney University in 1939 and was transferred to Innisfail as a senior registered medical officer in 1941 after working as a junior RMO the year prior at the Royal

Prince Alfred Hospital in Sydney. On 8 November 1941 he was made a captain in the Australian Army Medical Corps. He married Dorothy Rosemary Elsie Tandy on 9 December 1941 and after seven months of married life he transferred to the AIF on 22 July 1942 and served with the 19th Field Ambulance and the 117th Australian General Hospital in Toowoomba, Queensland. Within a year, in June 1943, he joined the 106th Casualty Clearing Station and two months later was posted to New Guinea. While Black was in the field assisting with the treatment of troops on the ground in the jungles of Lae, his son Robert Bruce Tandy Black was born on 1 December 1943 in North Sydney. With her husband away, Dorothy Tandy returned to her parents' home with her newborn to Roseville, a suburb of Sydney.[87]

There is no indication that Nora communicated any news of her new-found love in 1944 to her family back at The Cedars. That revelation would come later and the accompanying consternation of her parents was relentless. It is evident from Josephine's situation that appearances and adherence to social rules played an important role in the maintenance of Sallie Heysen's equilibrium. Her response to Everton Stokes' role in her daughter's life also underscores her concern with propriety. The reality of her daughter in the role of 'the other woman' with a married man must have been a disturbing challenge. The couple's longing for each other is palpable in Black's words:

> [Your letters] bring you along with them—and it is a happy day when I see one waiting in the morning—sometimes in the afternoon. I wish. I wish—I am at the wishing well again—where two shy people found one another—a magic well in a fairies' garden.
>
> I can understand your walks half way through a letter—I can … when the river threatens to flood—when words will not come at all—when I wish to tell you in every way that I can that I love you. I do.
>
> Good night my darling … Sleep tight. I caress you.
> Bob.[88]

Nora received these letters from Black in her new camp at Alexishafen before heading to Madang and perhaps his sweet words offered some comfort in the midst of the discomforts she was dealing with. Her exposure to the tropical climate, poor access to clean water, issues of prickly heat and a susceptibility to tropical skin conditions had resulted in Nora developing serious eczema, dermatitis and tinea. It would later be revealed to Nora by a specialist back in Australia that atebrin, the anti-malaria medication, was a large factor in her complaint.[89] She described the conditions to her parents:

> After having been so free of skin troubles, I have now developed every brand peculiar to these parts and one all my own. This latter unfortunately is all over my hands. The doctors say sitting out in the sun has caused it, and that I must wear gloves, keep them greased and not get heated or sit in the sun. All things which I'm unable to do, however they are so swollen and irritated that it is difficult to work …
>
> Worse than all this are the rats. There are millions here, every night one gets into my bed. They eat their way through everything, crawl all over everything and smell. If there is one thing I hate it is rats in my bed, and one lies awake watching for them. What they don't eat goes mildew and musty. Sometimes it just gets me down, and I wonder what the Hell—is anything worth it?[90]

Running parallel to these letters to her parents would have been her replies to Robert Black. Nora's fascination for Black is evidenced in a number of her paintings and sketches of him. They are sensual works and he is a handsome subject; she is clearly pleased to render his physical attraction on the page. The viewer senses a pride in the artist's impressions of her man. She was deeply committed to him, while facing serious impediments given the customs of the day. The letters written between the pair over the period they were lovers separated by the vagaries of war and then throughout their marriage indicate a deeply intense affair, punctuated with symbolism they found in everyday objects that came to represent secret rituals. As he was waiting to leave Finschhafen for the Blood Bank at Sydney Hospital he wrote to Nora in Lae on 11 July 1944:

> There is some work to do, but not enough to keep me sufficiently busy. They won't let me go to see you and yet I remain here

trying to find some way to pass the time. Should you not hear from me for a few days you will know that I am on my way—& I hope to lots of work. My darling ... you must have sleep—we cannot have those blue eyes rimmed with darkness. Remember—sleep tight. Those two little glasses are tucked away safely until the time comes for them to be used again. For that time will come—on that basis all our hopes rest ...

Though there are tears in my eyes and in yours—may I bid you again to be happy in that thought.

I love you. I love you dear Nora

Bob.[91]

26. Nora produced this penetrating portrait in the early days of her relationship.
Robert Black c.1944, pencil on paper, 35.0 × 27.0 cm.
Nora Heysen Foundation Collection.

Two whiskey tumblers consistently sketched in the corner of many of the letters were an identifier of the private times and conversations they shared over a glass of scotch when they were able to be in each other's physical presence. Throughout their correspondence the abbreviated phrase 'I do I do' would mark their signing off. The pair attempted to keep their relationship out of the public gaze and army life, even posting their letters when in Australia in regular postboxes and not through the army dispatch system 'otherwise most everyone knows to whom you write'. The shared secret of a newly declared love is expressed in intimate terms by Black when he tells Nora that a drawing she had done of him was on view at the 106 Casualty Clearing Station in Cairns:

> Your drawing was on view to-day & I wonder if anyone will know what was going on behind it—a whimsical smile when at last I was sure I loved you as you loved me—a feeling of awe

27. Nora Heysen drawing of Robert Black: *Male nude in moonlight* 1940s, charcoal, white chalk on blue paper, 30.0 × 43.1 cm.
Collection of the Art Gallery of New South Wales.

> that it should be I, and of happiness that it was, a whole jumble of thoughts reflected in my inability to stay still. What tired me most was the effort required to keep myself looking at you, while you tussled with your problem—which was not one of pencil and paper but one of mind. How I longed to say those few words—that day I saw doubt and wonder change to near-certainty—confirmed when next you drew me.
>
> What a beautiful picture you made sitting behind your board—a picture that I keep near me always. Oh, that I could describe it—I cannot draw it. The blue all-seeing eyes—the brows arching as you criticise each stroke—the frown when you are not satisfied with it—the smile when you have caught it and the smile for me.
>
> Dearest—I walk with you beside your sparkling river and look at the hills and the sky.
>
> I love you—I do, I do. Bob.[92]

Meanwhile both Nora and Black were committed to making their contribution to the war effort, despite Black's often failing experiments, and her skin conditions that made life miserable. Nora wrote again that she had become so inured to the presence of rats that one had eaten a biscuit under her pillow before she detected it, while another ate through her watch band. She suggested to her parents that her diet was also a cause of the skin troubles she experienced as she had seen no fresh vegetables or fruit for two months. There is a wistful tone in her letter of 12 August 1944:

> Most of the men look ill and we women all yellow and patchy… I look at my hands in revolt… You will be welcoming the first days of Spring. How remote all that sweet freshness seems from this. Here the air is permeated still with the smell of decayed Japanese food, and bodies and camp refuse.[93]

Nora often had to paint in her tent with her canvas set up in an ad hoc easel arrangement out of the rain. It constantly poured in Finschhafen. Conversely she writes from Alexishafen that she suffered out in the 'blazing heat and glare'[94]—not just from the sun but from passers-by. Nora did not like working in front of an audience and felt the running commentary was an unwelcome distraction: 'You couldn't paint anywhere, without a dozen or so people whooping encouragement behind you'.[95] She arranged with the surgeon to use the operating theatre when it was not in use: 'I was frowned on by the surgeon until I made a drawing of the theatre sister for him, and now he's co-operative and we take the use of the theatre turn and turn about'. She was getting ready to 'blast'[96] Treloar with his desired subject matter:

> I'm working on half a dozen subjects at once. A portrait of the theatre sister in cap and mask and gloves preparing the

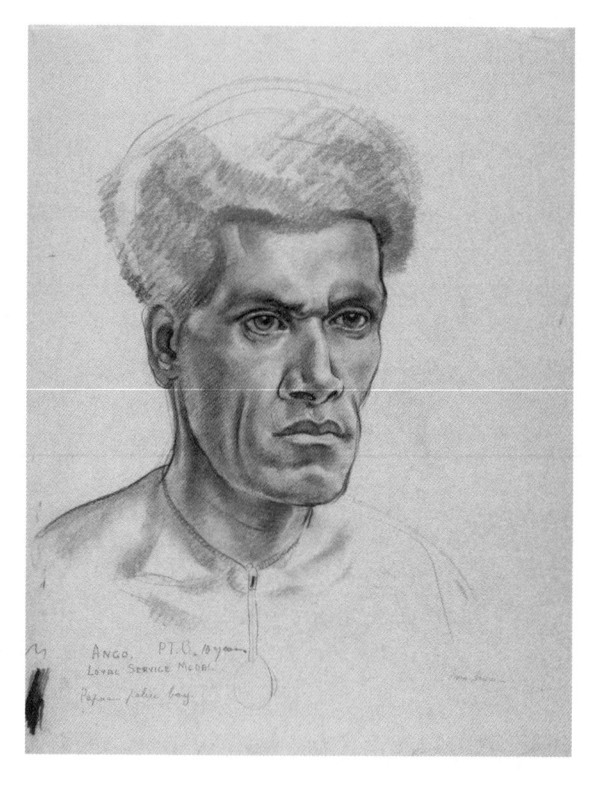

28. Nora drew this work in Finschhafen: *Ango, Papuan police boy* 1944, sanguine conté crayon, black crayon on paper, 52.3 × 39 cm.
Collection of the Australian War Memorial. ART22097.

> instruments of torture. As the theatre is the coolest place here, that subject is welcome. Also … painting a blood transfusion on a native, a scene of wounded being unloaded on stretchers off a barge, and a composition of men working amid the ruins constructing a picture theatre—the seats coconut logs, the screen a fantastic structure of bamboo stems. The men here are mahogany colour, they work just in jungle-green trousers and leggings, and make beautiful studies. One of these subjects alone could take months of study. I live and work in a daze of bewildered subject matter, and heat and mosquitoes and flies and smell.[97]

Nora said 'the operating theatre provided relief with its stone floors and white-washed walls'[98] and wrote home that the nursing sisters were friendly and inclusive.[99] She was particularly taken with the Papuans, describing them as 'marvellous models, unselfconscious, patient and understanding … [they] have such graceful movements that it is hard to look the other way towards subjects of military interest'.[100] Eventually she provided Treloar with more than he could have asked for, though it would take time for this to materialise.

By mid September Nora's skin conditions were so severe the specialist at Alexishafen advised her that she must return to Australia or be confined to her bed. On 18 September 1944 she advised her parents she would be leaving New Guinea on a flying boat, once arrangements had been made.[101] She arrived in Melbourne on 6 October. Officially attached to Keswick Barracks in South Australia,[102] she travelled to her parents at The Cedars the following day, where she stayed for four weeks to recover. During her respite from army life and the oppressive conditions of the tropics, Treloar had communicated his concerns about Nora's work to Louis McCubbin. He was clear with McCubbin that he was not assessing her on artistic merit but on the basis of subject matter and he asked McCubbin to visit Nora while she was at home to review her work and make a recommendation about whether to extend her commission.[103] At this stage Treloar's plan had been for Nora to recuperate and return to Melbourne to complete her New Guinea work, offering to try to arrange an extension should she require one. Treloar looked to McCubbin to help him decide what course of action he should take, and he sent McCubbin copies of his own letters and Nora's response:

> I am not an artist myself, and therefore not qualified to express an opinion, but I feel entitled to criticise the content of Heysen's painting … it will be apparent from the correspondence that Captain Heysen resented my comments.[104]

McCubbin visited Nora at The Cedars to review her work and he wrote to Treloar on 23 October 1944 in positive terms:

> … [the work] consists of drawings and paintings in oil and watercolour. The subjects of these are portrait heads of nurses, doctors and native personnel; sketches and studies of hospital wards, blood transfusions, sick and wounded diggers, natives and Japs, … I was greatly impressed by the amount and quality of the work … which is remarkable considering the very trying conditions in New Guinea, particularly for a woman. She feels … she had been dismissed because you were disappointed with her work and that she is the only one that has been singled out … I feel I have left her with less of a grievance. She is very anxious to do some more work … I have every confidence in recommending that her appointment should be extended for a further three months, and longer if necessary.[105]

It is easy to see when looking through the works done by Nora in the War Memorial archive that her methods could have been at the heart of the problem, as well as the time it took to communicate between artist and authority. The collection of her work shows a series of workbooks containing sketches and working drawings often heavily annotated regarding light conditions, reflections, and colours. She intended to use these as reference material for larger works back in Australia. She was clear about the practicalities of working in oils in the tropics during a war. This was an issue for a painter more at home in her studio with a cooperative sitter. As a result, Treloar did not receive many of the works in the early stages of Nora's commission that she planned to furnish to the army as a full representation of the women's services. This is clearly demonstrated in the studies for the picture *Theatre sister Margaret*

Sullivan 1944 (AWM, *plate 42*) at the Alexishafen Casualty Clearing Station and the completed oil painting done in Melbourne.

When she had recovered enough to continue painting, Nora arrived back in Melbourne, writing home on 7 December 1944 that she met with Treloar who had not received her letter about her movements. He was not expecting her in Melbourne nor did he know that she wanted to travel on to Sydney. It appears that Nora had decided that her next stop would be at the Australian Imperial Forces Blood Bank at Sydney Hospital, where Black was posted as part of the malaria research team on his return from Finschhafen. Letters at the NLA in Canberra between Nora and Black illustrate a level of planning as to how they might be stationed in some proximity to each other and how these orders might be brought about. In one letter Black writes from Cairns: 'So you told the Colonel [Treloar] you would like to see this part of the country—my darling—you know my answer but we must await the result of his thinking it over'.[106] Her time at the Blood Bank in Sydney was short, though she produced a number of works 'of nurses using the cumbersome machinery of the 1940s. As the *Weekly* reported in a feature story, she found it "most interesting … as there are AAMWS, VADs [Volunteer Aid Detachments] and Sisters all doing important jobs very efficiently"'.[107] Nora returned to The Cedars for Christmas after a request for leave was granted by Treloar. Thiele writes that it was the happiest Christmas at the family's home for eight years. Both Michael and Stefan had walked away from air crashes during their service, and Freya and her husband, Ted, joined Nora with Sallie and Hans around the tree in the studio with her brothers and their families. Young Josephine was seven and revelled in the festivities.[108]

Nora was back in Melbourne early January 1945 and again posted to the war artists' studios at Victoria Barracks. Here she worked on unfinished pictures from New Guinea, wrestling with the difficulties of reimagining the scenes she had witnessed. In March she wrote about her work and the other war artists at the studios:

> I am still working on New Guinea stuff, but I feel that I have almost finished what I can do with it. It is so difficult, I find

> to retain spirit and life working only from notes and memory.
>
> Seven new artists have been appointed. Donald Friend is already working here and has unfortunately the room next to mine. He giggles incessantly and entertains. I don't mind the racket of the trains and trams, but that giggling is an irritant. He wears heavy gold rings on his fingers, long hair and the work I've seen up to date repulses me. I'm convinced he is a fake, no doubt a very amusing and witty one with pretty camouflage, but my back bristles.
>
> There's another woman too, a Sybil Craig, elderly and a painter of flowers too so they tell me. Max Ragless and John Goodchild from Adelaide and Solomon Herman and James Flett from Sydney … for six months only and only 4 of them are to be official war artists.[109]

Nora always spoke her mind, and her personal response to Friend is not reflected in the AWM biographical notes on Friend's contribution to the war effort. He had enlisted in 1943. Perhaps if Nora had known that before he was commissioned as a war artist Friend was one of the soldiers who participated in anti-malaria drug trials in northern Queensland in 1943 she might have taken a different view of her flamboyant neighbour. Friend wrote: 'Nowadays we are being given about 30 grains of quinine a day. The result is that my ears ring, my skin is rapidly going yellow and I feel jumpy and rather weak'. Until his official commission as an artist in February 1945 Friend had consistently documented the soldier's life during his military service. Sydney Ure Smith had recommended Friend to McCubbin when there was pressure from the Contemporary Art Society and the media to appoint 'a diversity of modern artists'.[110] It appears that Sybil Craig's and Solomon (Sali) Herman's appointments were also a result of this push by the Moderns.[111]

Friend did not remain in Melbourne but travelled extensively, documenting some horrific aspects of the closing months of the war in Borneo and Balikpapan. He had planned to remain in the Pacific to record the surrender of the Japanese but he was forced to return to Australia and complete his work in Sydney due to a tropical rash which severely affected his hands. The AWM states at the end of Friend's biographical notes that it 'deplores his now known paedophile

29. Back in Australia between December 1944 and May 1945, Nora completed many of the oil paintings of her subjects in the army's Victoria Barracks studios in Melbourne using the studies she made under difficult conditions in New Guinea. After peace was declared, she continued to work in her own time to finish all her work to her own demanding standard finally delivering over 200 works to the AWM. Theatre sister Margaret Sullivan and Sapper Bashful portraits are being worked on, along with a portrait of nurse Private Gwynneth Patterson. Behind Nora is her work *Blood donor* 1944. Collection of the Australian War Memorial. 085075.

behaviour but acknowledges his works in conveying a unique insight into the Australian experience of war'.[112] Flett and Craig were both commissioned—Flett to Morotai and Brunei and Craig on the home front among the women of the arms and munitions factories. Nora's description of Craig as elderly is curious, as she was only ten years older than Nora. Herman was already an enlisted soldier and served in the Pacific as an official war artist.

Nora took leave in late April, the minimum three months extension McCubbin had recommended had passed. She briefly returned to

Hahndorf. In May 1945 Nora handed over eighty-six works in oil and watercolour to Treloar. He wrote to Nora: 'I myself would like to see your engagement extended indefinitely so that you can do with the WRNS (Women's Royal Naval Service) and the WAAAF (Women's Auxiliary Air Force) similar to which you have done with the Army Women's Service'.[113]

No doubt Nora felt vindicated. She would also have been secretly pleased as her plan to be nearer to Robert Black appeared feasible. In July 1945 she was given 'restricted approval to Land Headquarters Medical Research Unit in Cairns for the purpose of making pictorial records'.[114] While happy with Treloar's acceptance of her work and the extension to her commission, she was frustrated by Treloar's response to Sydney Ure Smith's request to publish some of her work when he visited her in Melbourne:

> Ure Smith was over for a week … and he came down to see my work—was enthusiastic and wants to publish some in his next volume on Australian Art—he says he wants to reproduce some of the war artists' work, but Treloar won't have it, as he thinks all proceeds should go to the Australian War Museum. It seems wrong that the work of the American artists has been given so much publicity, while ours is neglected and the artists, by being in this job, are out of circulation and the public eye.[115]

This could be considered another factor in Nora's gradual fall into obscurity after her Archibald win and her earlier successes. It would be almost eight years after the Archibald when she re-emerged into the public realm once again as independent artist. The early war years had been spent trying to make a contribution at a time when art was not a public priority, after the declaration of war. The rest of her time was spent in service to her country at a time when the focus was still not on art but on survival, victory and the quest for peace. She was certainly out of the public eye and some publicity for all the war artists would have helped in their transition back to civilian life.

Nora did not go straight to the army base in Cairns. Speck details that she was transferred from the army to the air force in May 1945 and appointed to the AIF Medical Air Evacuation Unit at the RAAF Base Townsville in Garbutt.[116] This led to confusion and concern for Treloar as a bureaucratic breakdown resulted in him not knowing where Captain Heysen was stationed. Nora was oblivious, thinking that the air force would have communicated her itinerary to Treloar. As a result, from August 1945 Treloar requested a weekly progress report from Nora.[117]

Early in 1944, fifteen nurses were recruited from the RAAFNS to the newly formed No. 1 Medical Air Evacuation Transport Unit (MAETU). 'The nurses' rigorous preparation included training in in-flight medicine and care, emergency jungle and ocean survival procedures, and weapons handling'.[118] Nora's time in Townsville produced some detailed and poignant drawings and oils that represented the flying sisters and their outstanding work, capturing, as Speck says, their 'elevation in status from ministering angels to members of the armed forces':

> As the war progressed the distinction between combatants and non-combatants in the army was becoming less obvious. Nurses died when their hospital ship the *Centaur* was bombed, they were executed at Banka Island, they were POWS and, late in the war they were issued with guns and given modified combat training. Fortunately Heysen was not in a position to document these events, but in an understated way she captured the transition to military nurse.[119]

Nora flew up and down the coastline of northern Queensland as she accompanied the nurses, known as the 'Flying Angels', who flew in and out of the Pacific combat zones delivering supplies and evacuating the wounded to base hospitals in Australia. Nora participated in medical evacuations from Lae and Morotai back to Townsville. She was focused about the kind of material she was after and eventually wrote home late in June that she was on the move from an undisclosed position in the Pacific later revealed as Morotai:

> The first night I spent at Higginsfield way up on the tip of Cape York, then Madang, Wewak, Hollandia and Biak, all round New Guinea and up … I move still further up, I'm going with a couple of the flying sisters to bring back the battle casualties.

> I'll be away three or four days, then will return here, I hope, with my subject matter. It will be difficult working on the plane full of stretcher cases over the eight hour flight, I don't know how it will go … The air is electric with rumours and every hour brings the peace nearer in talk … It will be bedlam here if news comes through. Everyone is hanging over the wireless waiting, the guns are ready to go off in the blast of victory. The island will tremble.[120]

Peace might have been in the air but there was tragedy still to come. Nora was sharing quarters with some of the sisters, and a memoir held at the AWM written by one of these nurses, Flying Sister Beryl Chandler, RAAFNS 502237 No. 1 MAETU, records the interaction her unit had with Nora, and the death of one of her fellow nurses, Flying Sister Marie Craig. Nora drew Craig three days before peace was declared in the Pacific on 15 August 1945 after the Japanese surrendered to the Allies:

> Miss Nora Heysen … was to spend a fortnight with us at Morotai painting us at work. Writing of these days brings to mind Nora's painting of Marie and how it came about.
>
> Nora had approached me many times to sit for her and for one reason or another I did not want to. One day there was only Marie, Nora and myself in the Officer's Mess when once again Nora asked me to allow her to paint me. Again I wasn't keen and dithered whereupon Marie said to Nora, 'Look Nora, you might as well paint me, I'll pose for you. This job is going to kill me anyway and at least people will know what Marie Craig looked like'. I was aghast at this statement, because she seemed to mean it. I remember saying to her, 'Marie, it is a volunteer job and no one would mind if you transferred to ground duties' … but she was adamant, she was going to fly on and she was just as sure she was not going to make it home to Australia. 'No Chan, the writing is on the wall. I am just not going to come through'. She loved the work, it gave her immense satisfaction, but she had this strong premonition that she would be killed.[121]

Craig sat for Nora one month before she was lost along with captain, crew and all on board in September 1945 when her plane disappeared. It was found twenty-five years later on the side of a mountain 14,000 feet above sea level in the Carstenz Ranges in Indonesian Papua.[122] In conversation with Michael Cathcart in 2001 for ABC Radio, Nora recalled the event:

> NH: I was detailed off for bringing the wounded down from New Guinea and there was always a nursing sister in attendance and I [drew] her. On two accounts they came down and were killed—and I thought well those portraits that I had done of them should go to their families and I sent them to their mothers,

30. Sister Marie Craig 1945, sepia conté crayon, charcoal, blue and sanguine crayon on paper, 47.6 × 32.7 cm, RAAFNS, No. 2 MAETU, killed in 1945 in a plane crash on a flight from Biak. Collection of the Australian War Memorial. ART24278.

31. Sister Sheah 1945, pencil with black conté crayon on paper, 39.6 × 29.0 cm. Sister Verdun 'Chic' Sheah RAAFNS was killed when the transport plane she was aboard crashed during a short flight between Jacquinot Bay and Rabaul. Collection of the Australian War Memorial. ART24305.

> I don't know if for better or for worse, I don't know, but I did that. The war museum could have objected to that, couldn't they?
> MC: I think in theory, but not morally.
> NH: Oh no, it was very sad, because they really didn't get any recognition.[123]

The lack of recognition for these nurses referred to by Nora, Marie Craig and Verdun 'Chic' Sheah has shifted over the years, with their work celebrated and remembered by the Australian War Memorial and the

32. Nora's work practice involved making studies in situ and annotating the drawings with various aspects for reference later in the studio where she produced fully worked oil paintings. Drawings are from her sketchbook and all inform the work *Ambulance plane carrying casualties from Morotai to Townsville* 1945. Collection of the Australian War Memorial. Sketchbook ART291199.

33. *Ambulance plane carrying casualties from Morotai to Townsville* 1945, oil on canvas, 38.7 × 45.1 cm. The plane is from No. 2 MAETU, RAAF, and a flying sister of the RAAFNS can be seen in the centre of the picture, Townsville, Queensland. Collection of the Australian War Memorial. ART24375.

RAAFNS and by authors such as Catherine Speck and Scott Bevan. The pictures delivered by Nora Heysen as official war artist recording their activities have been instrumental in remembering them and their sacrifice and underscore the valuable role of the war artist in preserving these memories. Speck describes the Craig portrait: 'Heysen's study of a serious, almost grim RAAF Flying Sister ... shows Craig in a peaked cap, collared shirt and jacket; an image in which her femininity co-exists naturally with her air force uniform'.[124] Flying Sister Beryl Chandler wrote that Sister 'Chic' Sheah earned her nickname for 'her immaculate appearance under any circumstances, even after alighting after a long and difficult flight'.[125] Well after peace was declared, operations to locate and repatriate POWs and the wounded continued, and Sheah's plane crashed on one of these missions. She was twenty-nine when she died on 15 November 1945. The two women are immortalised in Nora's work.

After her flying missions with the air force, Nora returned to Cairns. She was relocated to duties with the army at the Land Headquarters Medical Research Unit. She was also reunited with Black and she recorded the work of his research team. She produced a collection of work that documented the life-saving research by the scientists, and of the volunteers—she wrote to Treloar describing them as 'patients who suffer as "guinea pigs" with malaria for the progress of science: these volunteers do a good job, I think, and deserve recording'.[126] The AWM holds the series of artworks by Nora that record the diligence of the researchers and the sacrifice of the volunteers that contributed to research that would be crucial in later conflicts, including the Vietnam War.[127] Robert Black ultimately took up a position as professor of tropical medicine at Sydney University, a position he would hold for twenty years, and from 1955 served on the World Health Organisation expert advisory panel on malaria. In 1984, director of the Commonwealth Institute of Health, David Ferguson, wrote a tribute to Black on his retirement in *The Medical Journal of Australia*:

> He could be credited in large measure with the eradication of endemic malaria from Australia in 1962 (formally announced in 1981) and has fought persistently and tenaciously to keep the disease out, through the medium of his Malaria Case Register, national committees, clinical consultation, advocacy in medical and other press, meticulous correspondence, untiring advice to travellers and others, and teaching of generations of undergraduate and postgraduate students.[128]

But it was still early days in Robert Black's career. After the war, he and Nora would find a way to be together.

Some of Nora's most significant works representing the women's services were created in the last months of her commission. These non-commissioned portraits of women Nora selected herself display the power and capability of her subjects. Nora has cast these women as heroes in the fields that they were assigned, removing stereotypical representations and introducing the viewer to the new militarised woman. Two portraits central to this collection are *WAAAF cook Corporal Joan Whipp* 1945 (AWM, *plate 41*) and *Transport driver (Aircraftwoman Florence Miles)* 1945 (AWM, *plate 34*). Though the kitchen is traditionally seen as domestic, in this setting with her arms crossed over her strong body in uniform, army cook Joan Whipp is a commanding figure, ready to produce the sustenance necessary to literally feed an army.

Nora also painted the only female entomologist at the Land Headquarters Medical Research Unit in Cairns, Major Josephine Mackerras. Nora described Mackerras as 'another Madame Curie in her own field' and in Nora's typically frank style continued, 'an odd looking little person, ugly and interesting, bright intelligent eyes behind glasses and a lined and pitted yellow face and grey wispy hair'.[129] Despite Nora's unflattering description of Mackerras, she has rendered a strong and serious scientist situated in her professional capacity working in a vital area of research that significantly altered the rate of survival of forces in the tropics (AWM, *plate 38*). By now Nora had developed her technique in successfully rendering khaki in her strong representations of women in the forces. Her treatment of light on the subject's face, her hands, and her workbench suggests clarity along with the glowing edges of the microscope as an instrument of precision.

Aircraftwoman Florence Miles driving her truck is the antithesis of any notion of the tangled identity observed by Schlusser in Nora's 1937 self portrait *Down and out in London*. When the work was painted, towards the end of 1945, Nora was seven years into living as an independent woman, well away from her family and her father's direct influence. In this work, the shackles of the domestic sphere and the traditional role of soldier have been upended. Nora was also in uniform, the academicians that had thwarted her had passed on, London had been bombed and the threat of a Japanese invasion of Australia had presented as a real possibility and the women of Australia were on board, pivotal to a successful Allied effort. In ignoring her father's concerns for her wellbeing, by enlisting and taking independent control of her life, Nora had succeeded as the nation's first woman war artist. The National Gallery's assessment might suggest a description of the artist herself, not just in her supporting her country but in progressing her personal beliefs and goals to live her life as an artist:

> In this portrait Heysen combines the heroic with the everyday stoicism of women who just get on with the job. Getting on with the job in 1945 meant that women assumed the roles and responsibilities, which before the Second World War had been the preserve of men.
>
> Florence Miles inspires confidence; she is feminine and strong. Her committed gaze through the windscreen together with the RAAF flag, visible through her window, play like a confident anthem on the road to the allies' victory.[130]

Nora's own character mirrors the attributes the NGA applies to the work. This strength of character, her 'committed gaze' and determination is a testament to the upbringing that she received. She learned by example that through thorough application to a task a result could be achieved. That result could be measured in terms of how the job had been approached and this appeared to involve a profound sincerity.

In November 1945 Nora left Cairns and, reluctantly, Robert Black. She was required to return to Victoria Barracks to complete her folio of work for final submission to Treloar. The parting was difficult. Their relationship had been framed by the controlled environment of the armed forces, the constraints of that existence acting as a buffer from what society outside would impose on a single woman's and a married man's social transgression. Previously Black had written to Nora concerned about what his civilian career would be and whether or not there would be a job for him. His successes in the Army Medical Research Unit laboratory would see him put forward as a Fellow of the Royal Society of Tropical Medicine and Hygiene by Brigadier Fairley days after peace is declared.[131] His life as a research scientist was secured. Exacerbating his professional concerns and state of mind is the anguish attached to his personal life. It is potent in Black's letter after he and Nora parted at the end of the war:

> Oh my darling
>
> It has been a bad week—I could not write when so bewildered, never before has our parting been like this—I have just been existing… Please forgive my weakness—I love you, yes' m I do… It is hard to be left in the place which is so full of memories and is now so lonely… oh darling my feet took me over the road which you have painted for me… The heat and smoke haze made the mountains dance in the sun. It was there that I knew you were really with me. … I sat and listened and felt you there. Perhaps that is the only thing which makes staying behind bearable…
>
> Good night Miss Nora, I love you—perhaps more than ever—if that be possible—the ship has been through a storm & now rides before the breeze—sleep tight in that hollow which is yours. I caress you—please I do wish to hear from you.
> Robert.[132]

Nora's departure from Cairns and protracted trip to Melbourne must have been challenging if her emotional state could be compared to Black's. The logistics of travel were taxing, with armed forces personnel on the move around the country. Nora had a job to finish that would take some months but the personal hurdles that she was to face must also have weighed on her. How did she think this relationship was going to move forward? There was no mention of Black to her family and there appears to be a gap between her leaving Cairns and her writing to inform them she is in Melbourne suggesting she made a stop in Sydney to see Black.

Nora wrote to her parents after her arrival in Melbourne from Cairns:

> The trip from Cairns took me nearly a week instead of a couple of days. I arrived yesterday feeling utterly exhausted and today am still in bed… Arriving at the Menzies more dead than alive, only to find they had no rooms, absolutely crowded out as was every other place I tried in Melbourne. At last I rang Sybil Irving and she has put me up, so here I am. I've had air

> travel once and for all. Of course I had 350 lbs of luggage, most of it in brown paper parcels, eleven separate ones to look after and lug on and out of trucks, and planes, and transient camps.
>
> Written in haste and tiredness. I'll write again as soon as I straighten myself out. My love to all and hope it will be the Adelaide Express soon,
> Nora.[133]

Her official discharge from the army took effect on 8 February 1946 but Nora remained in Melbourne until she completed her work. It appears there was a visit home to The Cedars as she wrote in March to her parents asking them to send her some papers she left on the top of the linen press: 'preliminary notes for the cataloguing of my war work and I can't get on without them as I cannot remember numbers or details'.[134] McKillup writes that Nora requested further art supplies from Treloar, advising him that her work was progressing slowly:

> He was very concerned and asked Nora to tell him if she was working exclusively on her War Memorial paintings because if so he felt she must be paid. However there was no record of further payment to Nora. Her completed paintings were handed to Treloar on 22 September 1946.[135]

Nora had been tasked with the daunting role of sole official war artist to document the women's services in the Pacific arena. They are well represented in sixty-two paintings, 102 drawings and five sketchbooks holding eighty-eight works.[136]

NINE: RATIONS AND REVISITATIONS

> [*W*]*hat to come all the way to England, to sit in Liverpool, to paint flowers when the place was teaming* [sic] *with cracker slums* ... – Jeffrey Smart[1]

The Sydney Nora returned to after completing her official war artist commission was in the grip of the Engineer's strike, an action by all New South Wales metal trade unions seeking to guarantee a reduction in working hours and increased wages frozen during the war.[2] At the same time in October 1946, over six thousand waterside workers, striking in support of suspended fellow workers, and their own claims for improved conditions, immobilised fifty-seven ships holding sixty thousand tons of import and export cargo.[3] Twenty thousand tons of inward bound goods in short supply were held up, including fruit and potatoes from Tasmania and sugar from Queensland. The Engineers' strike lasted for six months and followed a series of strikes by the unions during the war years as they fought to protect their right to organise, to bargain collectively and to strike, even in war time.[4] These strikes were viewed by government and others as treacherous:

> one trooper declared that 'waterside workers were responsible for more hardships, shortages and deaths than the Japs'. He slammed them as 'gutless traitors', an assessment which was common among those who went off to war to defend the nation.[5]

These ongoing strikes included the coal miners' strike of 1940 that lasted sixty-seven days and resulted in 750,000 'lost' days that had a disastrous effect on electricity supplies,[6] on homes for heating and cooking, the rail system, tram services, shipping and ship building.[7] Only the advance of the Japanese towards Australia convinced the union to resume work.[8] The Sydney Nora returned to did not see the end of the full-scale strike by the

Amalgamated Engineering Union, and the nine other unions involved, until early 1947 when a favourable decision to the unions was handed down by the Arbitration Court.[9] Household supplies were seriously affected, and shipping and transport severely hampered during the unions' campaign for a £1 a week pay rise at a time when a male worker's average income was not quite £7 per week.[10]

Russia entered the war in June 1941 after Hitler invaded Soviet territory. In Australia this had the effect of helping to mobilise union workers politically opposed to the war who saw it as an 'imperialist conflict'. When Russia entered the war after its pact with Hitler had failed, the Communist Party of Australia (CPA) changed its stance, though its members had trouble with the shift despite their alignment with the CPA and therefore with the Soviet position. The CPA called on all workers to participate 'on the battlefield and on the home front' to support the Soviets now allied with the Americans, and as a result Australia. This sympathy with the Soviet cause resulted in the union workers' contributing to the war effort, but in 1946 working hours and wage negotiations were taking place under new peacetime conditions and the strikes had far-reaching implications for the person on the street. After relinquishing ground due to government and union leader intervention during the years they were urged to support the war effort,[11] the union rank and file was reapplying pressure to the Chifley government to meet demands for an increased basic wage and forty-hour working week.[12] During the war Nora was fortunate to receive equal pay for equal work but she was in a distinct minority. Women who had entered the wartime workforce doing men's work also campaigned when rates of pay that had been agreed upon were not forthcoming. While she was successful in 1943 due to Colonel Treloar's intervention negotiating equal pay, in the same year women metalworkers at the Richard Hughes canning factory in Sydney went on strike when the award the Women's Employment Board had granted them—still only ninety percent of the male pay rate—was ignored by their employer. Most women in the wartime workforce received around sixty percent of the male rate when working in areas such as clothing, textiles, and food processing.[13] Those working in roles usually performed by men were paid more, with some work-based child-care facilities provided, but it was not until the strike of the Hughes factory women that a ninety percent pay rate was achieved:

> The union secretary urged them to return to work by invoking 'the boys in the trenches'. The women angrily retorted, 'We know all about our boys in the trenches ... they're our husbands and sons'.[14]

While parity was not the result, it was a major advancement in the push for equal pay as well as an acknowledgement of the contribution women were making at the time. However, there was an understanding among government and employee groups that once the war was over the returning men would reclaim their positions and women would 'voluntarily resign'. Married women returned to their socially sanctioned places as homemakers and child bearers while those who were not married were expected to perform secretarial, nursing or teaching roles, customary positions in prewar Australia for single women. After a protracted campaign, in 1950 women's official rate of pay was lifted from fifty-four percent of the male wage to a mere seventy-five percent.[15] After World War II a returning single service woman reflects on being forced to take the retrograde step:

> We had to have a job and they took us on again, so well and good. But it was very difficult to settle down to the routine of office work ... It was back to what we were before, nothing had changed, and yet we had changed so much.[16]

As late as November 1966 women employed by the Commonwealth in the Australian Public Service could not marry and remain in full employment; once married they 'were obliged to accept temporary positions with poor career prospects and no entitlements'.[17] In Nora's home state of South Australia it was not until 1972 that a married woman could be permanently employed in a state public service position.[18] Some women kept their marriages secret in order to keep their jobs. Physicist Ruby Payne-Scott entered the workforce due to the manpower shortage in 1941. Prior to this there were few openings for Payne-Scott to work in her field as a scientist and once employed she was not about to go quietly. She had been instrumental in the defence of the Pacific region through her work with colleague Joan Freeman[19] as the first women to be employed in the Radiophysics Laboratory of the then Council for Scientific and Industrial Research at the University of Sydney:

> Their work was classified 'top secret' and would be instrumental in forcing the Japanese out of the Pacific. War demanded practical as well as scientific resourcefulness—Australia's coastline was protected by radars developed out of 'coathangers and sticky tape' by Ruby and her colleagues ...
>
> When her six-year secret was finally exposed in 1950, she was forced to retire as a permanent staffer and was reinstated on a temporary basis. Never one to mince words, Ruby told the CSIRO:
>
> 'Personally I feel no legal or moral obligation to have taken any other action than I have in making my marriage known ... the present procedure with regard to married women ... seems to go far beyond the simple statement in the [Public Service] Act ... [it] is ridiculous and can lead to ridiculous results ...'[20]

Nora had made her unintentional personal contribution to establishing new opportunities for women with her Archibald win and as the country's first female official war artist on equal pay. She enlisted to make a contribution to the war using her talent; her remuneration had not been part of her agenda, her art was always her focus. It was her pioneering of a new position for women that forced the question. She returned from her army commission to a postwar environment where women were left in a state of flux—the momentary opening of equality and opportunity vanishing in front of their eyes as they watched like late arrivals at a closing elevator. Nora's chosen profession and its solitary work environment resulted in her being insulated from the regulations that affected women attempting to enter the regulated workforce but it did not protect her from the ongoing prejudices and assumptions attached to being an artist 'disadvantaged by the dominance of a sexist hegemony'.[21] However, Nora was prepared for the task after fending off the complaints of unsuccessful Archibald entrants, and having to stand her ground in the army. She was aware of the pitfalls for women particularly after her experiences as a student in London but her dedication to her art banished any trepidation she might have felt. She had the support of her mother and father in her decision to make art her career, and that support remained constant.

The atmosphere in Sydney resulting from the ongoing strikes did not deter Nora, nor did the diminished prospects of her fellow women see her falter in her move to re-establish herself in the Sydney art world. Dealing with obstacles required Nora's calm negotiation, whether the obstacles took the form of out of touch teachers, jealous contemporaries, financial constraints, personal relationships, or family. All Nora's negotiations took place in a period of modernisation during and after a war fought with weaponry developed with 'incredible advancements in technology—necessitated by the advancements of the enemy';[22] where women played active roles in the armed forces for the first time other than nursing; where at home women had taken on roles traditionally the provinces of men in science, industry and manufacturing for the war; and where the art world in Australia and beyond was witnessing rapid change in what was considered an acceptable visual language in response to a rapidly shifting industrialised landscape. Yet post World War II, an atmosphere of conservatism set in as women were expected to return to their homes and procreate in the same way they were after World War I:

> Certain norms of Western middle-class femininity all but disappeared, and women's visible appearance before 1914 and after 1918 markedly differed—with many women having shorter hair and wearing shorter skirts or even trousers. New forms of social interaction between the sexes and across class lines became possible, but expectations about family and domestic life as the main concern of women remained unaltered.[23]

This was the cultural climate in the 1920s in which Nora transitioned from teenager to young woman, and in the early 1930s travelling overseas and living independently. New opportunities were open to her with the shifts that occurred post World War I but she was still bound by the conservative expectations of her parents and by societal constraints though change was taking place around her, not just in art, but also in the role of women and the rules that had been so stringent regarding the protection of a young woman's reputation.

In the late 1920s Josephine's letters to her friend Jacqueline Whyte record the tension between mother and daughter. Permission that was revoked for travel due to the lack of availability of a chaperone was just one of the many issues causing frustration for Josephine in a world of new freedoms not embraced by her mother.[24] Josephine enjoyed the changes that resulted from a post–World War I world that could condone women in trousers. Thiele comments on the family trip to London in 1934: 'it was a wonderful voyage—informal, unhurried, friendly—with the days largely their own, and the girls able to wear slacks and shirts without appearing forward or ill-mannered'[25] while he also reports that Sallie was aghast in Hyde Park 'watching with disbelief the open love-making of young couples'.[26] Witnessing the tension between her sister and mother, Nora can be imagined learning a way to approach change and modernity, avoiding head-on clashes with her elders while formulating her own values that would stay with her throughout the challenges of her life. Barry Pearce asks the question:

> How did her innocence come through unscathed in that city [London], not always the most forgiving for Australian artists trying to eke out an existence there during the years of the Depression? How did she evolve at all from the self-effacing girl living in the shadow of one of Australia's most famous artists into the great survivor she eventually became?
>
> The answer is simple: her stubborn devotion to the vocation of painting. Painting to Nora had the significance that prayer holds for the devoutly religious. Being a painter was all that mattered, was all she could be, beyond the dogged sequence of art schools, beyond even the prospect of fame itself. That sense of preserving the inner self, hard-wired in childhood, served her well.[27]

Pearce refers to the formative period of Nora's study in the art schools where the men around her, whether intentionally or not, subverted her sense of self. Nora was oblivious to this interference, seeing it as valid criticism at times, and rationalising it at others. She respected the positions they held and the fact they were recommended to her by her father whose judgement she trusted implicitly. Although she was deeply affected by that experience, the stubbornness that Pearce highlights prevailed. Demobbed, back in Sydney and ready to reclaim her civilian life, Nora was far from the naive girl who arrived in 1930s London, nor was she the idealistic woman who wanted to make a difference for her country. She had endured the hardships and the shocking realities of war and now she was a woman in love, committed to a married man. This romance was as undeniable for Nora as it was difficult for her conservative parents. Somehow Nora had managed to negotiate another challenge. Quietly and efficiently, her parents were delivered a fait accompli. She had left The Cedars eight years earlier, established her career as a painter, entered the army against her father's better judgement and was a grown woman with no need for parental consultation. Her relationship with Black had flourished in wartime, in a set of circumstances that would not have fitted into the prescribed acceptable framework had it been peacetime in suburban Adelaide. The threat of invasion, the extreme remoteness of the New Guinea jungles from The Cedars, and quite possibly the observations she was forced to make with young soldiers and nurses losing their lives, their minds, or their limbs, all combined to create an alternative landscape; a reality so far removed from life in the Adelaide Hills that the same rules no longer applied. Perhaps, also, she was conscious of the loss of Josephine, a loss that was compounded by her parents' disapproval of her choice of man. Nora's choices were hers alone and she would allow no interference.

One of Nora's first communiqués once back in Sydney was written from Usher's Hotel to her parents after visiting the Society of Arts exhibition of drawings at David Jones. She reported briefly about the show, including a mention her father received and that she and her brother Stefan had caught up with friends including Bill and Ursula Hayward. Headlines in Sydney newspapers on 6 October 1946 heralded the imminent strike chaos that Nora wrote about to her parents: '50,000 involved in disputes—NSW strike threats':

> Nearly 50,000 workers in New South Wales will either be involved in strike threats or in actual strikes in the next few weeks.
>
> The industrial situation in the case of the largest unions

> involved in this wide unrest is:—
>
> 22,000 railwaymen will consider strike action to force a demand for wage increases and improved conditions; 200 key railway electricians will discuss a stoppage at a meeting on October 17.
>
> 4,500 moulders and assistants in all foundries in Sydney and Newcastle will receive a week's notice of dismissal on Friday unless moulders at Mort's Dock, Babcock and Wilcox, and Purcell Engineering Company return to work.
>
> 20,000 engineers in 200 shops in Sydney will hold a mass meeting next Wednesday to discuss claims for an increase of £1 a week.
>
> 1,200 employees of the Riverstone Meatworks will hold a mass meeting this morning to decide whether to declare a general strike in support of 12 dismissed engineers.[28]

Nora was now feeling 'marooned' in Sydney as transport was severely limited, including the trains that could have carried her to Hahndorf. She refers to a small room she had rented overlooking the harbour at Potts Point and to the flower pieces she has enjoyed working on.[29] In June 1946 Black had been placed on the Reserve of Officers after returning to his civilian life—and, it would appear, his family—and he resumed his work as a bacteriologist at the Institute of Medical Research at the Royal North Shore Hospital in Sydney.[30] Late in 1946 he travelled as ship's surgeon to England to take up a position as a research fellow at the United Kingdom Research Council at the Liverpool School of Tropical Medicine where he stayed until August 1948.[31] His wife and son joined him in his new post. For just over a year, while they were in different hemispheres, Black and Nora maintained close contact through their prolific letter writing, reporting to each other the minutiae of their daily activities. Nora eventually followed Black to Liverpool, intent on maintaining close contact. Meredith Stokes stated, 'She went specifically to get him back because she loved him so much and was trying not to lose him'.[32]

Nora spent part of 1947 in Hahndorf while she made plans to join Black. The housing shortage in Sydney meant that occupancy at hotels was only allowed short term and Nora was obliged to move frequently.[33] It appears Nora returned home in preparation for leaving the country.

She painted her father's portrait during this time and entered it in the 1947 Archibald Prize. In April that year Black wrote to her of his lack of confidence about his work, worrying about himself as the newly graduated researcher, of issues about his workload increased by taking on the duties of his supervising researcher due to a sick wife and child, of cultures that fail, and of chickens injected with malaria. He writes of feeling depressed and concerned at the responsibility he feels for the taxpayer funds that have financed his research abroad,[34] but he always returns to a buoyant tone when he writes of his love for Nora. His rhetorical plea for the patience that they both need to find is often how he signs off, a call to be calm as they wait for the moment when they can be together—'Good night dear, sleep tight. I hold you close and kiss you. I love you. Yes'm. Miss Nora. Oh give us patience Miss Nora. Robert'.[35] And he follows the next day in another letter—writing daily was their ritual—'Did I remember to tell you I love you—you are lying on your left side. I hold you very close and kiss you. Sleep tight my dear Miss Nora. I do. Robert'.[36] The endearment 'I do' remained a fixture throughout the years of their letter writing.

In late January 1948 she sailed for England, the country she had left ten years before. It was a very different place. Once again she would take up solo lodgings, this time at 47 Croxteth Road, two miles from Black's work at the School of Tropical Medicine. Her flat was a forty-minute walk from the school, passing by the Princes and Sefton parks that might occasionally have provided her with blooms for her work. While the location was suitable, there were other issues to contend with that Nora wrote home about in her pragmatic manner:

> Although I have but a room it is fairly large, and the windows being big and high, the light will be good for painting. The lack of bathroom is the chief drawback, the kitchen-in-a-cupboard is amusing ... I'm learning to adapt myself to cooking in a frying pan, washing and laundering in a fire bucket ... Food and the shopping for it, is the biggest problem and time waster ... One queues up for everything and even to buy one's handful of rations takes hours.
>
> I miss flowers they are too expensive to buy. How I'm ever going to get enough to paint God only knows, I'll have to resort to pinching them out of the Gardens.[37]

34. *Transport driver (Aircraftwoman Florence Miles)* 1945, oil on canvas, 66.6 × 81.8 cm. Collection of the Australian War Memorial. ART24393.

ABOVE: *35. Matron Annie Sage* 1944, oil on canvas, 76.6 × 56.4 cm. ART22218.
OPPOSITE TOP: *36. Colonel Sybil Irving* 1943, oil on canvas on paper, 76.5 × 56.4 cm. ART22214. OPPOSITE BELOW: *37. Colonel Sybil H. Irving, Controller AWAS* 1943, oil on canvas, 76.4 × 56 cm. ART22220.
Collection of the Australian War Memorial.

ABOVE : *38. Major Josephine Mackerras* 1945, 82.8 × 66.0 cm, oil on canvas.
Collection of the Australian War Memorial. ART24395.
OPPOSITE TOP: *39. The flower ship* 1944, oil on canvas, 56.5 × 66 cm, Private collection.
OPPOSITE BELOW: *40. View from sisters' mess, Finschhafen* 1944, oil on canvas,
39.0 cm × 44.4 cm. Collection of the Australian War Memorial. ART22392.

41. WAAAF cook Corporal Joan Whipp 1945, oil on canvas, 82.4 × 64.4 cm.
Collection of the Australian War Memorial. ART24394.

42. *Theatre sister Margaret Sullivan* 1944, oil on canvas, 91.8 × 66.0 cm.
Collection of the Australian War Memorial. ART22234.

43. *Robert H. Black MD* c.1950, oil on canvas laid on composition board, 78.0 cm × 59.0 cm. Collection of the National Portrait Gallery.

Early postwar Britain was struggling. The rationing of goods that had not been rationed during wartime was introduced and the country was suffering not only the physical ravages of war but also the burdens of a nation that had exhausted its financial reserves. Rationing ended in 1954. Had it not been for loans from America the British economy would have been at grave risk: '... it is certain that the America loans were vital to keep the UK economy afloat—especially in that awful winter of Britain in 1947, where secret government records show they drew up contingency plans for mass starvation'.[38] This was a period of austerity and deprivation. Australia played its role by growing food for the struggling UK, announced in the Launceston *Examiner* in October 1947:

> AUST. TO GROW MORE FOOD FOR BRITAIN
>
> LONDON (A.A.P.).—Far-reaching measures to increase food production in Australia to provide larger quantities for Britain have been agreed upon by the Minister for Food (Mr. Strachey) and the Australian Resident Minister in London (Mr. Beasley).[39]

Nora's father writes with concern about the England that Nora had returned to:

> It makes us sad and apprehensive when you describe the children of your surroundings, it sounds unbelievable in this land of plenty. Here there is endless talk of growing and sending food to Britain, but with this everlasting string of strikes going on, I can't see how we can produce more than we actually consume.[40]

Nora had arrived in a country undergoing massive reconstruction. There was a housing crisis since housing was under pressure from returning evacuees. Women who were now widows were struggling to support their families, and many of the evacuees were orphaned children. During this time Nora painted 'a deeply sensitive image of a young orphan named Margaret'.[41] Hylton writes that it remained one of Nora's favourites. She had inscribed a discreet dedication in the bottom left corner, '*Margaret* for Robert', and it was marked 'not for sale' in a later exhibition.[42] Mary Eagle noted that *Margaret* 1948 was at The Chalet in 1996 (it is now in a private collection) and, as was characteristic of Nora's attention to detail, framed in an elaborate Italian hand-carved wood. The head and shoulders portrait is a poignant work and in conversation Nora told Eagle that she had wanted to adopt the girl.[43] One assumes that the obvious barrier to this desire was her personal situation.

It was now four years since Nora began a relationship with Black and some level of acceptance appears to have been adopted by Hans Heysen, evidenced in his letter to her on 19 April 1948: 'You do not mention Robert and in what spirits and health you found him. I do sincerely hope all is well, and please convey my good wishes to him'.[44] In fact, Black's health was not good. From exchanges in the letters it is clear that the Liverpool climate and possibly poor nutrition issues were plaguing him.[45] Nora later writes that 'I am constantly reminded here that "things are not what they used to be" and it is sad to see and feel the damage, and sadder to realise that there is little hope of any quick recuperations'. Art supplies were impossible to procure: 'no brushes, no turps, no paper, no canvas, no stretcher, a few restricted colours in stupidly small tubes … one is curtailed as linen is couponed and the ingredients for priming are nearly unprocurable'. Nora voiced her frustration to her parents. She regretted not bringing an artist's necessities with her from Australia.[46]

Apart from being her father's good friend, James McGregor was a consistent advocate for Nora and a great supporter of her career. Before she departed for Liverpool he wrote from his Darling Point home in Sydney sending good wishes and saying that he would be in Adelaide soon but not in time to see her off. He added that he was looking forward to seeing a portrait of Hans Heysen Nora was submitting for the Archibald Prize. He wrote to her in May offering to send food parcels weekly from Sydney through the Lord Mayor's Fund if she had not made arrangements before she left. Nora had underestimated her need for art supplies and it appears she had not prioritised food, something she might also have later regretted. It is apparent in McGregor's next letter that, despite how much he supported her, he was not enamoured with her latest work and pointedly sent encouragement to remain true to her own style:

> You badly needed to get away from Hahndorf Nora dear—more than you realised—I saw that when I saw your portrait

> of Hans—I want you to get back to the high clean painting standard you had previously—and which you lost in the Adelaide Hills.[47]

Other news from home at this time included the passing of Howard Hinton,[48] the wealthy shipping agent and art patron in Sydney who had shown interest in Nora's career, buying her work among the many pictures he amassed for the AGNSW, including important works by E. Phillips Fox and George Lambert. Hinton donated 122 works to the AGNSW, where he was trustee for twenty-nine years until his death. He also endowed the regional art collection at Armidale Teachers' College. He had been a supporter of Hans Heysen, Arthur Streeton, Tom Roberts, Elioth Gruner and the Lindsay artists along with many others who had represented the Australian landscape in their work, donating over a thousand works and a significant collection of art books to the College's library at Armidale, now known as NERAM. Hinton supported Nora's contemporaries Dobell and Feint.[49] At the time of his death, another stalwart was fading. Hans Heysen wrote to Nora in the same letter that Sydney Ure Smith was in hospital: '... he is very ill and has resigned from the Presidency of the Society of Artists. I am afraid that he is not much longer for this world'.[50] Ure Smith died in October 1949, aged sixty-two.

These losses were significant, and particularly personal for the two Heysen artists who had enjoyed the benefaction but also significant and enduring friendship from both men. The world was changing, and familiar voices that had been central to Nora's and her father's artistic conversations were also diminishing. Yet for Nora there was new territory to cover and a trip to Edinburgh to meet once again with her father's friend Shirley Jones, a trustee of the charitable Liverpool Blue Coat School. Jones commissioned Nora to paint the orphaned girls in Liverpool on their way out of chapel. Nora met the young Margaret there and painted her portrait. The trip to Edinburgh allowed for new subject matter and the opportunity to buy paints and canvas. The food situation at the Joneses though was not much better than in Liverpool:

> It was odd amid all that opulence and wealth to sit in the evenings before a fireless grate, because there was no wood to burn and at meal times to be ushered in in evening dress to a

> polished table and all the do-dahs, butler and servants to wait on one, to be served a slice of bacon on a piece of toast, or a piece of lettuce and a carrot, and then to get up with an empty tummy.[51]

In June 1948, a month before Nora wrote home about her Edinburgh trip, she was witnessing the alarm felt close at hand with the first heightening of Cold War tensions—the blockade of West Berlin by the Russians and the United Kingdom's and the American's airlift of supplies from Allied airbases.[52] She enquired about sending food parcels to Germany but writes home that this avenue was now closed with the passing of a new law.[53] Food items from home were appreciated, including what appear from her descriptions to be pickled eggs:

> … the eggs are excellent for salads and currying, and the bacon is a wonderful acquisition. The rations don't improve here. There's been another cut in butter which leaves 2 oz a week and meat is almost negligible.[54]

During her time away, as throughout her life, Nora remained in conversation with her father about art. In one letter she enquired about the Henry Moore exhibition that toured Australia during 1947 and 1948. He mourned the depressing effect of Moore while he remained buoyed and inspired by the Tom Roberts touring exhibition of 1948. Though he conceded that Moore was 'utterly sincere and honest with his art and definitely has something to say', Heysen wrote to Nora on 1 June 1948:

> The Henry Moore sculptures and drawings have come and gone—it left me with a feeling of hopelessness. There was no joy in his life. He seemed obsessed with one type of form or shape which he repeats in nearly everything he touches, just as if his mind had been 'twisted' out of the normal by what he had seen, felt and experienced during the war years …
>
> In every way what a contrast to the outlook on life of Tom Roberts who loves the sun, the trees, and morning clouds in the sky … Altogether it is a delightful exhibition, full of good taste, charm and honesty of purpose, and also always searching.[55]

Later in 1952, two years after Sydney Ure Smith's death, Nora echoed a similar sentiment to her father. Her views remained constant. She described the Society of Artists show as 'derivative'. She wrote to her father that the new director of the National Gallery of South Australia, Robert Campbell, had opened the show with the remark that 'it was a pity the artists were not directing their talents towards seeing and feeling their own country, rather than becoming slaves to European trends and cults' and this comment pleased her. Nora reported that *The Sydney Morning Herald* critic Paul Haefliger and his wife, artist Jean Bellette, along with John Passmore, Michael Kmit, Russell Drysdale, Desiderius Orban, and others had taken over the Society of Artists in a dictatorial manner:

> ... the movement which has been infiltrating Australian art and angling for supremacy is now in complete command, and like the dictatorship powers have announced their victory with a purge of all their enemies. Haefliger sits enthroned on the dais with three huge canvases of Jesus Christ and his apostles around him—Passmore, Kmit, Orban, Drysdale, Jean Bellette and his other friends of today ... Only a few canvases, which owing to the laws of the Society that one picture from each member's entries must be hung, are tucked away in corners where they don't interfere and ruin the great advancement of the new and exciting modern group.
>
> As you can imagine no gum trees or blue skies were to be seen in this show. I liked the Lloyd Rees canvases more than anything. At least I can find depth and sincerity there that are not borrowed.[56]

Nora and Haefliger were born just three years apart, both to German parents. Haefliger also studied under Bernard Meninsky in London in 1936, two years after Nora. Nora was born and raised in the conservative art world of Hans Heysen's Australia; Haefliger in contrast was born in Hamburg in 1914 and grew up influenced by Europe's nascent modernism movement with an artist mother and diplomat father in Bern. Their childhood environments perhaps reflect their differences in their approach to art. In retrospect, observing the Heysen resistance to changing trends only heightens the futility of resisting innovation, especially visual innovation that is arguably so closely connected with experience of war, industrialisation and social change. Not all households were as stable as The Cedars. The Heysens continually searched for more clarity in what they hoped to represent, searching for their truth, but there were other ideas about visual truth. Nora's disdain for visual experimentation is clear and her analogy to dictators, so soon after the war has ended, is potent.

By August 1948 Robert Black was forced to return by ship to Sydney due to his ill health. Nora hoped that the Australian sunshine and fresh produce would restore him.[57] Black's son and wife also returned to Sydney in 1948 a month after Black, but not to their nuclear family arrangement. As a sole parent, Dorothy Black pursued work as a locum general practitioner and eventually secured a position as a physician at a private hospital while her mother cared for her young child. In 1952, the year he turned nine, Robert junior commenced at boarding school. In the same year on 21 August, his mother as petitioner was granted a Decree Absolute, ending her marriage to Black and granting her sole and permanent custody of their son, with Black providing financial support. Young Robert's first memory of his father was when he came to visit him at boarding school when he was eleven. Over the ensuing years Black sent his son postcards 'from each of his trips—always in his very neat handwriting—and I would visit him … perhaps two or three times a year'. These meetings took place at the house in Hunters Hill where Nora and Black eventually lived, and Robert remembers Nora as kind, in a house with 'a flock of white cats' and possums in the attic. His father tried to interest him in ham radio but as the school did not allow radios it was not a hobby he could pursue: 'My father would take me into his den, talk to other ham radio operators—his call sign was VK2QZ and his contact card had an anopheles mosquito on it…I was aware that Nora painted, but only much later did I come to appreciate her stature'. Robert would spend more time with his father as an adult as he pursued his studies in applied maths at his father's work place, Sydney University. In 1972 when Nora was in London, she met up with her stepson and his new wife. They enjoyed dinner and the theatre, but this would be the last time they met.[58]

In 1948, Nora had travelled a long way to be near Black but she also returned to Britain to revisit the collections that had been central to her student days. With Black back in Australia, Nora reconnected with friends, including artists Jeffrey Smart and Jacqueline 'Jac' Hick, and Adelaide art patrons Ursula and Bill Hayward. She spent her time socialising, viewing the works that inspired her and also noted to her parents that there were 'a few commissions floating around here [Liverpool]' and that she intended to spend time in London before attempting to travel home. Passages on ships to Australia could take up to three to four years to secure, though Nora reported that as an Australian returning home she would be given priority.[59] It would be January 1949 before Nora was back in Sydney.

Nora's lifelong friendship with Jeffrey Smart began in Adelaide when they were both members of the Art Society in the 1930s. I discovered how deep the friendship was between Smart and Nora when I first started my research at the Nora Heysen Foundation archive held at The Cedars. A neatly catalogued small cache of aerogram letters in one of the files caught my attention. The list written in the archivist's careful hand in the obligatory pencil startled me when I saw Jeffrey Smart's name. I had long admired his work, and reading the letters was a memorable discovery for me as a researcher. I explored the connection between the two as Smart's words brought postwar London to life. He occasionally omitted writing his name on the envelope or a return address—instead he simply drew an artist's palette dotted with puddles of paint.

Nora wrote to her parents that her friend surprised her when she was in Liverpool:

> I've been busy painting a couple of flower pieces—right in the middle of them who should walk in but Jeff Smart. I was staggered by surprise. His ship had docked in Liverpool, and having my address, along he bounced. There was I sitting painting a little bunch of flowers. Jeff couldn't believe his eyes—'what to come all the way to England, to sit in Liverpool, to paint flowers when the place was teaming [sic] with cracker slums'. For him the place was an artist's or rather a Smart paradise with subjects big, black and beautifully worded in all directions.

> Well we talked non-stop for ten hours or more, went to the opera, dined out at the Adelphi, did the Cathedral and went into ecstasies over the slums. That latter I didn't participate in. He can have all the slums in Liverpool for one white rose.[60]

Nora spoke to Kate Nockels about the day Jeffrey Smart came calling:

> She [Nora] laughed about it, she was fond of him and respected him as an artist but didn't want to paint what he was painting. She loved her flowers and loved nothing better than having a basket full. I would visit [in the mid 1990s] and there'd be a basket of tomatoes, a basket of apples, pears or something—she'd be working on a pastel, she loved colour, flowers, fruit—that was who she was because that was the environment from which she had come.[61]

These were early days in Liverpool but Jeffrey Smart was already developing his unique style. In his obituary for Smart published 21 June 2013, a day after the artist's death, his friend, art historian, curator, critic and Emeritus Professor at ANU, Sasha Grishin wrote:

> His pictures are unmistakably and unforgettably his, they do not remind you of someone else's work, they maintain a certain autonomy within our imagination.
>
> Smart's art champions a modern urban iconography—the autostradas, road signs, factory facades, deserted airports and taxis ranks—these are the motifs which recur throughout his oeuvre …
>
> One could argue that Smart invented a new iconography of urban decay through which to convey, in an effective and subtle manner, his commentary on the human condition.[62]

In his memoir *Not quite straight*, Smart refers to Bill and Ursula Hayward's arrival in London and their 'handsome apartment in Berkeley Street' in Mayfair, and also to Nora's arrival from Liverpool and the large portrait commission she had to complete: 'a whole choir … She had fifteen likenesses, and she brought them all off'.[63] He also writes that until the Haywards' first invitation to the theatre he and Jacqueline Hick could only afford seats with limited views of the stage, while Nora would later opt for standing-only tickets to conserve funds:

> Although Jac and I had been going to the theatre a lot, we complained that we never saw the sets of any production. All we usually saw was a tiny illuminated square of stage, way down there below us. We were always in the Gods, and if an actor went up-stage he disappeared ... Our first night out with the Haywards was unforgettable. We had drinks at Berkeley Street and then went to a performance of *The Beggar's Opera*, arranged and conducted by Benjamin Britten ... We sat in the centre stalls two rows from the front ... Afterwards Bill and Ursula took us to a glamorous theatre club where we had a wonderful supper and lots to drink.[64]

Before relocating to London from Liverpool, Nora visited the Haywards as a guest at their Berkeley Street townhouse, prior to their departure for Australia in October 1948: 'Nights turned into days, and no-one went to bed before 4 or 5 in the morning'. She slept on a sofa—'every bed, couch

44. Nora Heysen and Jeffrey Smart at The Cedars c.1940s.
Papers of the Nora Heysen Foundation Collection.

and table had someone sleeping on it'—in between visits to concerts, parties, plays and nightclubs. Nora told her parents that 'the hospitality of those people [the Haywards] knows no limits' and that 'a great number of people are going to find life very flat now that they have gone'.[65] The Haywards' marriage was the joining of two of Adelaide's most prosperous families. Bill Hayward was the son of a wealthy merchant family that owned John Martin's department stores. It traded in Adelaide for over 130 years and was colloquially known as 'Johnnies'.[66] Ursula Barr Smith was the daughter of 'an even wealthier family of Scottish descent whose involvement in mining and pastoral activities was vital to the development of South Australia'.[67] She was a product of 'landed gentry' and he was 'trade'. When they married, the local newspapers carried the headline 'Heiress Marries Shopkeeper':

> The match was unconventional and set the tone of their marriage ... They took no notice of the conventions of behaviour and taste in conservative Adelaide. Both had travelled extensively before their marriage and brought sophistication to the style of their home and the hospitality they provided for their house guests and visitors.[68]

The couple shared a lifelong interest in art. Ursula Hayward would become the first woman to sit on the board of a public art gallery as a trustee of the National Gallery of South Australia in 1953, and Bill Hayward was a founding director of the Adelaide Arts Festival in 1960—the first of its kind in Australia. His community work and philanthropy was financially supported by his entrepreneurial capacity: 'During the war he had noticed that American soldiers were willing to swap a bottle of whisky for three bottles of Coca-Cola; recognising that it was a profitable product he acquired the franchise and in 1950 founded Coca-Cola Bottlers (Adelaide) Pty Ltd, with the help of other local businessmen'. Bill remained chair of this company until 1983.[69]

Ursula was also a painter and her work is in the couple's collection, which is an eclectic mix featuring both traditional and avant-garde painters, sculptors and crafts. The prominent European artists they collected included Spencer, Epstein, Renoir, and Gauguin; and Ursula had inherited earlier period works including some by Henri Fantin-Latour, the favoured flower painter of both Heysen artists. The Haywards were also committed patrons of Australian painters and collected, among others, William Dobell, Russell Drysdale, Donald Friend, Ray Crooke, Kathleen Sauerbier, Ivor Hele, Hans Heysen, and their good friends Jacqueline Hick, Jeffrey Smart and Nora. They kept four homes, the Mayfair townhouse and three in Australia including Carrick Hill, a version of a seventeenth-century English manor house they completed building in 1939.[70] Carrick Hill houses their art collection and was a bequest to the people of South Australia in 1983.[71] The Hayward London hospitality Nora wrote of came to an end, but not before Nora toured the galleries with Bill Hayward; she reported that Hayward had spent most of his time in London adding to his art collection.[72]

Nora wrote again in November to tell her parents that with the help of Jeffrey Smart she was settled in a bedsit in Notting Hill Gate.[73] Despite the Haywards' departure, Nora was actively engaged in the London scene, including getting in touch with her father's friend James Bateman who had given her particularly harsh criticism in her student days in London. Nora was a mature woman and clear about her direction and in stark contrast she found Bateman a shadow of the Royal Academician of twelve years before. When Nora called at his studio she saw a painting that he had been working on over a period of years—'a large intricate figure composition at Elephant and Castle (the only horse sale still operating in London)'.[74] He appeared aged both physically and mentally and Nora reported home that he was embittered over his relegation to the sidelines of the art world, not having sold a work in three years: 'He complains that the only people who are recognized and sell here are Sutherland, Moore, Piper and Picasso … that good work is no longer recognized. He blames Sir Kenneth Clark (director of the National Gallery in London 1933–1945)[75] for extolling these few men at the expense of everyone else'.[76] This scenario would have its own version in Australia as the moderns encroached on the provinces of established painters such as Hans Heysen, Lionel Lindsay and others. Nora notes in her letter that she believes the Australian critics of 1948 were favouring Dobell, Drysdale, Friend and Jean Bellette (though Haefliger never wrote a word about his wife Bellette it could be assumed his influence went beyond the pen[77]). This was the time of the ascendency of the Reeds, Max Harris and the Angry Penguins, a time of change and shifting tastes, when Tucker, Boyd, Perceval, Vassilieff,

Hester, Nolan, and Blackman were attracting considerable attention and sales.

Nora was pleased that Jeffrey Smart and Jacqueline Hick had a flat just doors away (she at number seven, and they at number twenty-seven Stanley Crescent), and they shared their cooking arrangements—Smart and Hick had a kitchen, while Nora had limited facilities.[78] She attended the opera when she found she could buy standing-only seats cheaply and told her parents, 'I've managed to see *Tristan and Isolde* and the four operas of *The Ring*—all of which last four hours apiece. So you can imagine how weary one's feet get'.[79] Nora also attended parties at expatriate Australians' homes with Smart and Hick, including one at the home of a Melbourne cellist who was then with the BBC Orchestra. At this party, the degree of separation between Hahndorf, the reach of her parents, and London was negligible, with one guest introduced to Nora exclaiming: 'Oh yes, of course I remember, your Mother is the best cake maker in the world! And he went on to tell me in detail what he'd eaten on his last visit to the Cedars'. Despite the happy days with her friends, she had concerns for Black's health, telling her parents that the beneficial effects of his passage home had evaporated: 'News from Robert is disquieting... He has too much worry and strain on his shoulders, and as the cause of it is also my concern, I feel I must be with him to stand by'.[80] It is possible that Nora may have felt she had played a role in the strain that Black was now under, though she does not expand on this in her letters home. A pattern begins to emerge where Nora subjugates her goals to the needs of Robert Black. Her support for him for the duration of the relationship resulted in her subordinating her life as an artist to his life as medical researcher, a fact that she would later reflect on.

Only weeks after settling in London, Nora secured a passage home on the Peninsular and Oriental Shipping Company's SS *Mooltan*. The London office of the Australian Elder Smith and Co. Limited wrote to her the same day of her enquiry on 1 December 1948 offering tourist class accommodation in a four-berth outside cabin, number 547 on 'B' Deck, for £88.[81] Nora sailed two days before Christmas. She was thirty-seven years old and heavily emotionally invested in her relationship with Black. In terms of artistic development, the impact of her early departure from London can never be measured.

TEN: LETTERS FROM A FRIEND

We have just returned from a weekend at a very Noel Coward sort of country house. Wonderful collection, 3 Cezanne oils, 8 watercolours, 4 Renoir, a cracker large Manet, 2 beaut Derain, 2 magnificent Picassos, Matisse, Degas ... We could hardly believe it all.–Jeffrey Smart[1]

The letters written by Jeffrey Smart to Nora provide a unique, first-hand account of the life of an Australian artist abroad. Written from one artist to another, the subject matter is particular, it speaks to what was at the heart of their joint interests, what sustained them, and also their personal views on other artists. I have taken the liberty of reproducing a selection of these letters as they tell a story that does not benefit from paraphrasing or retelling. The colour of the narrative is his alone. It takes the reader into a world rarely accessible when the original intention was to communicate with an audience of one. Nora's lifelong habit of retaining her correspondence has made this legacy available to share. When Nora left London, she asked Jeffrey Smart to complete a few final housekeeping tasks. After he had finished, he had time to pen a quick letter and let her know how much he valued her friendship:

25 Stanley Crescent
Nottinghill Gate
W11
29th Dec 1948

Well, dear Nora

Your large letter you left us to post on to you is going off very shortly, by 6, & I'm getting this down, by the fire, to go with it. Thanks ever so much for sending that post-card—the sort of thing I think makes the world go round. I got it Xmas Day, & they didn't come to light with my cheques, etc, at all, at Airedale (after me spending £3 on the cows)* was feeling a bit mournful, and lo! your card turned up. Read it through at least 10 times and felt beaut. I'm so sorry you have a child in the cabin, that's awful, but I dare say they think you're awful, too, with all your luggage. I arrived at Airedale just as you left Tilbury, and my thoughts have been with you, wondering where you are now, how you are sea-faring, and if you're lonely—but you wouldn't be bothered with that, I think.

Don't forget: if there's anything I can do here for you, you only have to ask, and it will be a real pleasure. Went over to your room today & collected an air form, the baking dish, & the shelf. I'm a sentimental bloke, & looked at the room—empty, all the life gone out of it, & a lump came to my throat, & I got out for the nick of my life. I do miss you very much Nora, & can't seem to realise you have really gone. You only hurt my feelings once—when you said 'ships that pass in the night'. Well that's all BALLS. And please remember that. There's a great deal more in human relationships than that. Not most associations, but I presume to think that we went a little deeper than everyday 'how d'ye does' and 'see you later'. Even in my few years I can see a pattern, a mosaic of threads that weave to make not a background, but the very pattern that makes up one'self [sic]. And no person, as Donne remarked, 'is a person of himself contained'; 'no man is an island', he is a promontory of the continent of man. If the ships do pass in the night, they were drawn together by gentle threads which are in their patterns, and those threads do not break. They are still there, and will always be there, to draw those ships together in another sea.

No more of that! …

I've written to John Rogers, and although he's a bit out of Colombo, I know if he can, he will be on the look-out for you. Young in years, but not in painting—at any rate after a couple of weeks in the camps of the Philistines you may appreciate a natter. He's tall and dark, and rather Oriental in features, slanty eyes & thick lips—you'll want to draw him on the spot. Bill & Urs sent us a cable for Xmas, very nice of them don't you think? Now I'll start making you want to come back again—last night we saw 'The Magic Flute'. Sets by Oliver Messel. The tenor was an Aussie, the baritone an Aussie, the soprano a Yank. So Covent Garden is getting full injections of the New World. It's now 5.45, and I'd better get this to the post pillar. You can imagine us sitting here by the fire & Jac (of course) sitting on the floor and Stanley Crescent outside. It's very cold now, but I wouldn't change it for the heat, no thank you!! Well dear, much love, and hope to hear from you soon, and all the good things you deserve.

God Bless,

Jeff.

*Jeffrey Smart had gone to stay in Airedale in Yorkshire and this reference suggests that he had paid the money to the Post Office for a mail redirection order.

Nora wrote to her parents on 11 January 1949, a day before arriving in Colombo. She refers to overcrowding on the ship: 'four are squeezed into a two-berth cabin and six into a four-berth cabin. At night most of the people, to get out of their stuffy cabins, sleep on the deck'.[2] When she disembarked in Sydney, Nora had difficulty finding permanent accommodation. She wrote that she has returned to her old Potts Point flat where she was given a bed for a few days.[3] Robert Black did not feature in her letters to her parents and it is unclear where he was situated. Postwar rent controls were still imposed on the city and finding permanent accommodation was almost impossible as investors refused to build new blocks of flats at prewar rental rates. After weeks of moving from one temporary residence to another (rules stipulated that three days was the maximum stay allowed) Nora took a studio flat at 36 College Street, the former address of the artist Elaine Haxton, a mutual acquaintance of Nora and Smart.[4] Nora described it as having 'good light (on bright days) for working—a pleasant liveable room with divans round the fire and bookshelves piled with books, simple nice furniture, and a little balcony … which catches all the sun that's going and overlooks the park'.[5] Black moved into the College Street flat and it would remain their home until 1953.[6]

As I read through the letters from Jeffrey to Nora, the London they enjoyed together comes to life. In straight lines, in particularly neat and small handwriting, Smart managed to record a large amount of information on the regulation blue aerogram forms. He kept her up to date with all of his and Hick's activities. He shared his feelings about his own work and his views about the state of art in general, and earnestly reported about a technique he presented as all the rage and that he has adopted himself, a description of which follows below. He mentioned his own visit to James Bateman and offered some brighter news of the aging painter. Just over a month after Nora had returned home he wrote:

25 Stanley Crescent
Notting Hill Gate
15 March 1949

My dear Nora
I do hope by the time this reaches you, you are comfortably settled in somewhere decent ... Thanks ever so much for your letter it was a real tonic—just to hear from you was enough! I thought of you very much the other night, we all went mad & got a box at Covent G., 17/6 each (no other seats) & heard that divine 'Marriage of Figaro'. It was 'quite out of this world' & when we came out, it was London's first snowfall of the winter & everything looked so beautiful. I felt madly hilarious. Sending in day for the R.A. [Royal Academy] is on Monday & both Jac and I are having a crack at it. Just at the moment I'm less displeased than usual with my work—having been going at it fairly hard to forget the cares and tribulations of this world. Braved the snowstorm on Bayswater Road and painted like a mad thing. It's still the same old dreary stuff—but a little better painted I hope. The art shows, are, as usual, quite crazy. The crazier they become, the more determined I become to paint in the best traditions.

The new director of the National Gallery, Phillip Hendy, who has been the arch-priest of modernity gave a lecture to the exclusive longhairs in London, and I hear that he said that contemporary painting is going to become more academic. Not that it makes any difference to you and me what he says, but it is heartening to see signs that the whole experimentation era is coming to an end. Jac & I have been out to Bateman's where we talked about how much we missed you, & since then Jac & I have been out to his studio. I like the 'Horse Market' very much [the same work Nora referred to in her letter home] but he can work his Leda and Europa etc with his rubber gloves. Their financial affairs seemed to have improved as he is buying a very nice little place on the embankment at Chelsea, and they both seemed much, much brighter.

Mrs. Zander* came here one evening & then we went to a very swish 'do' at her place. A Marquis kissed Hick's hand & she nearly offered her foot! As you said, I don't think you would get to know her [Mrs. Zander], ever, very well. We have just returned from a weekend at a very Noel Coward sort of country house. Wonderful collection, 3 Cezanne oils, 8 watercolours, 4 Renoir, a cracker large Manet, 2 beaut Derain, 2 <u>magnificent</u> Picassos, Matisse, Degas, etc etc. We could hardly believe it all. I found through very close inspection that most of them, Nora, paint on a white base, burnt sienna washed in, & then pigment. Of course, I knew of it, but it comes as a shock to find the method used so very consistently. I'm at it myself now. Even Picasso, Nora, does it. I've been in London now for seven months, & at the end of this month I whizz off to Italy.

*Australian-born painter and the manager of the Redfern Galleries in London in the 1930s.

Smart asked Nora's opinion on his next move. He clearly valued her advice. Should he stay in London and see everything and stop painting for one year? Or should he teach, presumably to stretch his money further, paint and stay for two years then have a show—'What do you think? Now your opinion really will help me'. He then comments about a brief sentence in Nora's last letter to him. It appears that Nora had shared little with Smart about her relationship with Robert Black, and waited until she was back in Sydney before broaching the matter. Smart was full of heartfelt advice:

In your letter you say you found 'your man' in hospital. Whether you put it in deliberately to pique my interest I don't know—but I shall not inquire. But I will say he is about the luckiest bugger in the world and surely must realize it. I'd go for you myself if I thought I even had half a chance!!!! Whatever decisions you make, make yourself; even though in those things I'm afraid I say 'don't let anybody mean too, too much to you' … All the very best to you dear, and good painting and God bless you.
Love Jeff.[7]

It was advice that in hindsight she would have done well to heed.

Albergo Rex
Via Torina, Rome
15 May 1949

My dear Nora

I'll write very small as I have such a lot to say to you. Thanks ever so much dear for your cracker letter which arrived in Paris in 3 bits over a period of a week—it was like a serial in the papers! And all the news of Sydney doings was water to my parched lips. This letter is from Rome but posted in an envelope to Hickie who sends it on because airmail on the Continent is very expensive. Is this small writing boring you? I do hope not. Thanks for your advice on staying on here—you said just what I really thought myself I now realise, & will hang on here as long as I can. Ursy [Ursula Hayward] wrote to me in Paris—I was there for 6 weeks & said that you have [Elaine] Haxton's studio—I'm so glad dear that you are fixed for a while at any rate—nothing is too good for you, you know what I think! I'm often thinking of you—and do hope this finds you in the midst of Heysen flower pieces & hard at it—it's dreadful when you don't work isn't it? you feel so useless and wandering. Judy left on Monday so by the time you get this will almost be in England. I intend roaming thru Italy until end of May, June in Paris and return to dreary old London end of that month.

As I told you Hick and I sent all together 6 pictures to the Acad, [Royal Academy], & my dear every one of them was chucked out! It really is funny—here we are landed with them all again after our high hopes! Something very odd happened to me when I first arrived in France—I sort of came alive—I can't stay in bed in the mornings, I wake before it's a respectable time—I rush around like a mad thing and am full & overflowing with ideas for pictures so much I haven't got time to paint them all. This is the place! There is something so dull, puritan, stern and Roman about England & particularly London. I love it here Nora & am very happy. Hick is still back there, waiting for Shirley [Adams] to recover from an ear operation; & Mike Shannon* & I are going to Florence next week—poor old things! I'm nearly flat broke but somehow it doesn't worry me, suppose I'll come to earth with a thud soon! I shan't start on Paris—to sit on a bouvelard [sic] & drink coffee in the sun! to see the Musée de Paume & Musée de 'lArt [sic] Moderne, what joy! and the slums are wonderful, I'm torn between painting the Tuileries & the slums all the time. Went to an Academie called Grand Chaumière [an art school in Montparnasse] but got all bound up & wasn't happy. My French was quite adequate, amazingly enough, & in Paris felt so much at home it just wasn't true!

Then we went to Avignon which I thought was like Victor Harbour with its tourist trade, then Aix-en-Provence—how truly Cezanne got the character of that country side—then the Côte d'Azure, & stayed at an incredible place in the mountains called St Paul, near Vence. Saw the Picasso Museum at Antibes which I thought was ridiculous—he may be gifted but I resent the way he despises his paint—but his pottery & ceramics are really really lovely, sometimes severe & sometimes amusing—but good I thought. There isn't much painting to see in Rome apart from the Vatican, which has been closed for two days but opens tomorrow and you can imagine me right on the doorstep in the morning, tomorrow, waiting to see the SISTINA—whacko!! Get absolutely lost in Rome—not a word of Italian, it's ridiculous. Things are so cheap here it just isn't true! —cup of coffee with a huge pile of cream as big again as the cup, for 6d!! And what coffee! Good 3 course meals for 1/9 or 2/- !!! But Rome is full of pitiful beggars with no arms, or eyes, or rickety legs, spivs selling fountain pens, I carry mine with me & try to sell mine to them, which is the only way to shut them up!! Rome in the evenings is magic isn't it? Hope this doesn't make you feel unsettled with my rapturous extolling of the Continent.

All the best dear, & much love,
Jeff.

*Shirley Adams and Mike Shannon were South Australian artists and lived with Smart and Hick during part of 1948 in Notting Hill.[8]

By now Nora had settled into the rhythm of life back in Sydney, visiting Sydney Ure Smith whose health was fading and writing once more to her parents about the annual Society of Artists show at David Jones.[9] Her father responded to her that Sir Kenneth Clark and Professor Burke (the first Herald professor of fine arts at Melbourne University)—'both of whom I found most agreeably catholic in ideas about art, and both are "livewires" and most enthusiastic'[10]—had come to visit him at The Cedars. Nora was now writing openly about Black, his work, and his movements, indicating when his travels for his malaria research would take him to the Northern Territory via Adelaide and when her parents could expect a visit from him. She reported on the works she has painted for the Society of Artists show including a portrait of Black. She noted that the three big 'D's will not be in the show: Dobell, Drysdale, 'Donald'[11]—Donald Friend was in Italy as Jeffrey Smart later tells her:

Casa Antica
Testaccio-Barano
Isola d'Ischia Napoli
10 November 1949

My dear Nora

I've carted your letter with me all over the place: it got to me where I was staying at West Minster, went to Norway with me AND Denmark, Amsterdam (it's been to Germany too!) & thence to Paris where it stayed a week (it got lost in Denmark incidentally for a week in my luggage!) and now it is on this divine island in the Mediterranean. More of that later. You can see I've been travelling: and forgive me for not writing before, and also forgive me when I tell you I hope for a letter from you very soon, despite my long break. Now, I'll have time to think & write, & I'll need to hear from you soon as I've often thought of you and hoped all is well with you. Thanks for your description of the Soc. of Artists show—you know how interesting it all is when you are away, & I was glad to know you found a temporary rest at least. Ursula wrote recently & said she was very much afraid she'd miss you in Sydney as you were dropping in on Adelaide. Met Elaine Haxton a few times in London & like her very much. Clarice Zander & I became good friends I think, after a row when I called her 'an old bag' & she took offence (you always disliked that phrase too). At any rate I saw much of her. A good person—& not nearly as brittle as I first thought. When I got back to London after 3 months on the Continent I worked fairly hard, but was VERY VERY unsettled, & just before I left for Norway got 3 galleries to look at my work.

This is confidential Nora. The result was no show! Not at present. The Leicester definitely promised me a show, they thought I was O.K. but too diverse in style, no consistency—which is true, & said, in a year's time perhaps I will settle. They all said much the same. SO I'm not discouraged, just determined to work. Seeing you know so much of my affair with Judy Anne you may as well hear the end of this funny story. During the year I was away from her I was constant physically and even mentally. When she arrived in London we both found that everything was as it ever was—all was well—and we were both terribly happy. You can imagine how relieved & happy I felt. We had a wonderful month in London, & 3 days before she left for Scotland, I met someone else!!! It was all over with me, Nora, in 5 seconds! All my year's hopes for nothing. Someone just walked into the flat one night and that was that! So don't talk to me about LERV any more! If I read of it in a book I'd never believe it, but there it is. I'm not a butterfly by nature, I hope—it was just inevitable I suppose—I did have a most peculiar premonition 3 days before it all …

Well here we are, Jac & I, and Mike Shannon from Adelaide, installed in this beaut villa on the Isle of Ischia near Naples. We arrived 1st Nov, and stay here for 5 or 6 months. The idea is generally (1) to escape the London winter, (2) paint like mad, away from ALL influences, after having absorbed many (3) save money, as rent and living is cheap here (4) make trips to the mainland, Rome is only 14/- away, & Naples 2/-. Florence 25/- away. We have a really beautiful villa, huge rooms, each one with French windows opening onto a terrace, which looks out, south, into the sun & the blue Med. Beneath us, between us & the sea, the land slopes steeply, covered with olives, orange trees, mimosa, geraniums—oh it's a lovely sight! There's a lovely beach straight beneath (Capri is just opposite) & I went for a swim this morn, & this afternoon got a letter from London telling of fogs.

It was about this time last year, my dear, we went to the Albert Hall, & then to the Vic & Al Museum, & then that mad walk through Kensington Gardens. Remember!? For all this splendour we pay £2.10 rent a week between the 3 of us, & 6 rooms! Mrs. Simpson & Prince of W once lived here and we have a girl who does everything except kiss your foot for £5 a month! As meat is costly, we live on beaut fruit & macaroni cheese & tomatoes. But oh! the wine! Nora, & the vermouth, it is 6d a litre, & 1st class! How you would love this! I don't want to make you jealous, so will stop! Have only been here a week, & have been for walks to get the feel of the place, but started a thing this afternoon. Will have more news of work later. Do write soon, I look forward to hearing from you very much …
Love Jeff.

The two friends shared their personal business. Smart was in a relationship with a woman, Judith Anne Ingoldby, the Judy Anne referred to in the letter above. He had decided to remain loyal to her when she went back to Australia, anticipating her return to London. The relationship foundered. I asked him about this, and about the fact that he wrote to Nora telling her that he had succeeded in his goal of being in a relationship with a woman only for it to disintegrate. He told me that it was not easy being gay in the 1940s and he thought he would try to be straight.[12] Judith Anne ended up marrying Smart's friend Basil Lott, who had posed for his seminal work *Wallaroo* 1951. Writing in early 1950, when he travelled to France and Italy, Jeffrey reported that there had been a flow of visitors to the villa he had rented on the island of Ischia including Donald Friend and Margaret Cilento. Cilento, a close contemporary of Margaret Olley, with whom she shared her Sydney student days, was two years younger than Smart and is credited, along with Jon Molvig, with bringing abstract expressionism to Brisbane in 1951. Her father, Sir Raphael Cilento, the distinguished medical practitioner and public servant[13] had been seconded to the United Nations in New York in 1947. Margaret was an emerging artist and studied at Stanley William Hayter's Atelier 17 printmaking studio and also at the Subjects of the Artist school, which promoted avant-garde art in New York.[14] In 1949 her father's secondment ended, and the family left for Australia while Margaret returned home, taking the long route via London and France with a side trip to Ischia.[15] It appears that Jeffrey did not find significance in her abstraction. Sasha Grishin stated that 'Smart was a staunchly figurative artist who viewed the path to abstraction as a path to artistic suicide'.[16] Perhaps that is one of the reasons why he and Nora were *simpatico*. Smart also expresses great interest in the Haywards' purchase of Dobell's 1943 Archibald Prize winner, *Portrait of an artist (Joshua Smith)*, the painting at the centre of the court challenge controversy.[17] Nine years later it was virtually destroyed by fire at Carrick Hill and though Bill Hayward approached Dobell to restore it, he refused.[18] Years later, Hayward sent it to London for restoration but it was not successful:

Casa Antica, Testaccio
Isola d'Ischia
Napoli
16 Febuary 1950

My dear Nora

Many thanks for your letter and news of all the doings.

Am particularly glad to know you may not have to shift from where you've more or less settled in. And since then I've heard from other sources that Elaine H is shifting so I immediately thought of you! 'The source' was Donald Friend, who has been staying here for about a month now. At first he was in a tiny little fishing village but got lonely & so is here. His work is changing a lot I think, and he says he's going to have a Sydney Show soon so you will be able to get the atmosphere of this place, if not the appearance! Unfortunately he leaves end of this month, and as Jackie has already gone I should be left in this huge house alone and so must shift again! O Hell! Don't relish the prospect of seeing London again even a little bit and only wish to stay here in Italy. Have no plans at all, and feel like a floating something. Am glad to tell you that in the last two months the old brush has at last come good—a little—I did hope the peace & isolation of Ischia would work the oracle and apparently is has to some extent. I shall be able one day, I hope, to show you photos of the place & then you'll see how divine it all has been. Nora, I've definitely decided that there are only two places where one can live, Italy or Aussie, do you think perhaps my being a long distance from all the galvanised iron gives it all a rosier hue? Hope not, or I shall have a rude awakening about November of this year!

Apparently simply everybody has gone to London, & I'm beginning to think that the most fashionable thing now may well be to be in Australia. By the sound of all the names there must only be a handful left in Aus! There's one thing I'm becoming to see more & more clearly. One must have a settled abode. All this rooting up from one place to the next is no good, and now I've been in Utopia for four months of course I hate to leave.

We had Margaret Cilento here for a few weeks, but didn't like her work much. Jackie came good with some really interesting & different canvases here. Haven't heard from Ursula for ages, but expect she'll be in London soon. Fancy them buying Dobell's 'Joshua', I heard the price was terrific. Would love to know what Ivor Hele thinks about all that! I've shoved an

> Ischian canvas in for the Crouch* in an attempt to raise some money—but like all my attempts I suppose it'll be doomed to another 'honorable mention' such as I've had before, twice now. Isn't it irritatingly near yet far?! Well my dear Nora this has been a shocker of a letter to you, but it takes with it my thoughts & best wishes & love to you. May all the colours on your palette be the right ones! (Damned if mine are!)
> Love, Jeff.

*A prestigious regional art prize in Ballarat.

This is the last letter that survived Nora's travels. When I finished reading it, I realised I had found an intense connection between two very different characters who shared such conviction in their lives as artists. I had a strong desire to interview Jeffrey Smart, to know more about the bond between Nora and Smart as well as the experiences he and Nora shared, and it was difficult to contain. I had been working at The Cedars archive, which holds Nora's personal collection including the Smart letters not deposited at the National Library in Canberra. It was October 2012 and I attended the retrospective exhibition *Master of stillness: Jeffrey Smart 1940–2011* at the Samstag Museum of Art at the University of South Australia, a survey that was complemented by a selection of Smart's work held in the Hayward collection at Carrick Hill. It was a year after the university had conferred Jeffrey Smart's honorary doctorate. After re-reading the letters from Smart to Nora, I contacted the exhibition curator Barry Pearce and asked if he thought it might be appropriate or even possible to speak with Smart. He kindly forwarded me the email address of Dr Smart's partner of thirty years, Ermes De Zan, who by now was shielding the artist from the intrusion of people like me.

Jeffrey Smart had been extremely unwell and had suffered recurring bouts of pneumonia. At ninety-one he was wheelchair bound, with oxygen on standby. At the time I wrote with my request for an interview he had just returned home from being hospitalised in nearby Arezzo and was 'only seeing people in small doses', replied Ermes. Nevertheless the tenderness he had held for his friend Nora was still present, and his willingness to add to our understanding of her was moving. Ermes communicated that Jeffrey 'would like to do as much as possible concerning any scholarship to do with Nora Heysen … When you arrive in Italy call to see how Jeffrey's health is. You could then come for a chat in the afternoon'.[19] And that was what I did.

When I arrived at La Posticcia Nuova, Jeffrey Smart's villa, I walked up the staircase behind Ermes to the first floor. I didn't realise that the door opening into the loggia also led to the darkened bedroom of Jeffrey Smart. Ermes called to ask him if he was he ready to speak to me? A deep and resonant voice came from inside the darkened space; it was an emphatic 'not yet'. It was suggested that I make myself comfortable and wait. I decided to take a minute and reflect on my surroundings while I waited for my interviewee to emerge. These are the notes I made at that time:

> I arrived in Arezzo yesterday afternoon. I was facing the possibility of not being able to reach Pieve a Presciano, forty minutes south east of Arezzo, because of the flooding that had surged between the Arno and Tevere Rivers after Venice was flooded. Four days ago the roads I needed to take to reach the artist's villa were impassable. And then yesterday Jeffrey Smart's partner of thirty years, Ermes De Zan (Australian), was dubious about Dr Smart's health and whether he would be able to talk at all. He has been struggling with pneumonia. But he insisted I come today even if for only a thirty-minute chat. It is quite possible, and I can say this because I am now at La Posticcia Nuova, that this may be his last interview.
>
> I am in Jeffrey Smart's beautiful villa. He is awake but not ready to talk yet. Only metres away I can see just his ugg boots through his open door. The villa is just what you would imagine out in the countryside of Tuscany and is exquisite. The decor is in a setting of rich, aged terracotta floors and Persian rugs, rustic and fine antique furniture, two or three sensational Smarts on the wall of the dining room which is painted a dark ocean blue. Gilt frames, candlesticks, mirrors, and bottles of spirits

> are sitting on a golden honey-coloured sideboard. In the main sitting room there are inviting overly-down-filled classical couches, adjacent is a baby grand piano and sheet music and just two carefully chosen artworks—not Smart's. Ermes, after attending to some work matters, is putting the finishing touches to some lunch prepared by one of the housekeepers in the upstairs kitchen that I can just see beyond a set luncheon table. Vintage beautifully starched linen napkins are rolled in antique silver rings, water and wine glasses and white plates and bowls are laid out clearly indicating three courses are ahead. The weather is gorgeous, warm, and sunny and I am sitting in the upstairs loggia with birds, cyclamens and ficus loving the warm glazed space. There are five pugs, six peacocks and a pheasant in the garden. The glazed loggia windows face toward one of the hundreds of rolling Tuscan hills, the view is completed by the dozens of pencil pines planted around the boundaries of the villa and its winding driveway. Going to talk now.

When Jeffrey Smart was ready to speak with me, he entered the loggia in his wheelchair, helped by Ermes. He was impeccably and elegantly dressed in a blue and white pinstripe shirt, a navy cashmere sleeveless V-neck vest and camel trousers. His white hair was smoothly swept back at the sides and his moustache and goatee were meticulously trimmed. He was gracious and welcoming, immediately putting me at ease. When I told him that Nora had kept his letters, he was moved. We started at the beginning:

> We first met in Adelaide at the Royal Society of Art … we'd meet at mutual friends' houses. I liked her immensely immediately. She was so good looking, so terribly good looking … very private. Dignified, withdrawn, but I liked her immediately. We became close friends … [Hers] was the only house I went to that they talked about the food. And how they were going to cook it. It was a true German interest in good living. And sausage. And wine. Completely different from the English where you never talked food.[20]

He recalled the early days of their friendship in Adelaide; how he called in on her in Liverpool; and how their mutual friends the Haywards brought them together again after the War. He said that when she took the room nearby to him in Notting Hill Gate she didn't want to get 'too chummy' but matter-of-factly states that 'she had to because we had great friends in common, the Haywards, we'd meet at the Haywards''.[21] He made a point of telling me he never saw Robert Black in that time.

Our conversation covered a broad range of topics including Nora's disdain for Picasso. I told Jeffrey Smart that in a letter to her father Nora wrote that she thought Picasso was a fraud, though she liked his earlier work. He left her feeling confused.[22] Smart had written to Nora about a discovery he had made about Picasso's technique and they exchanged their thoughts about the progression of Picasso's work:

> We [Nora and I] had something in common, that we wanted to be realists, realist painters, figurative ... well, she was right. Picasso was a disaster, a real disaster ... so gifted and so perverse ... the late Picassos, those female nudes they're horrible ... The captain of our ship, of art, and he lost direction, and we all lost direction, I didn't and Nora didn't, but we were able to know that it was not right.

Ermes commented that Picasso's last great work was *Night fishing at Antibes* 1939 (MoMA) and Smart concurred, 'That was true'.[23] Ironically this painting was one of Picasso's few attempts at combining figure and landscape,[24] fruitful subject matter that both Nora and Smart each contemplated and delivered.

Smart discussed Hans Heysen's parting words to Nora in 1934 in London, that her innocence would protect her. Smart believed in a way it had protected her: 'because she was pure, not stupid, but pure'. He had quizzed Nora on why she continued to look at the man who insisted on exposing himself when she arrived in London that first trip. Smart said, 'Nora felt he was doing it for her so she drew up a chair and I said no you shouldn't have let him see you and she said he wanted me to see him, and I said why didn't you draw the curtains ... good manners gone a bit too far!' He also shared the story of when Nora smuggled a painting into Australia for the Haywards. One of the works that the Haywards purchased during their 1948 visit to London, a painting by Stanley Spencer, might not have passed the Australian censors' scrutiny. Rather than risk trying to import the painting with their other purchases, the Haywards enlisted Nora to carry the work into the country for them, concealed among her own work.[25] Nora did not mention this to her parents, but perhaps it was implicit as in a later letter it is clear that her father was familiar with Spencer's subject matter and approach though Nora clearly downplayed the substance of this work. Her father responded to the news of Hayward's acquisition by saying with 'your description of his Spencer makes me most eager to see it':[26]

> The best thing Bill bought was a Stanley Spencer figure, I'm going to bring it out for them. It's a nude of his wife getting out of a voluminous pair of combinations [a chemise and drawers combined in one garment] with a caricature of himself to set off the picture.[27]

Jeffrey Smart recounted this story to me over our lunch. In his memoir *Not quite straight* he also discusses the work in detail. He describes the 1930s Spencer series *The beatitudes of love* as 'all wildly indecent' and 'based on the senses, *Seeing, Hearing, Tasting, Smelling*'. Ursula Hayward had become friends with Stanley Spencer and bought *Seeing* from him. Smart described the work and the concerns the Haywards had about importing it into Australia:

> This [*Seeing*] showed a huge Hilda [Spencer's first wife] standing up on a bed which was covered with a patchwork quilt. She had pulled apart her combination underwear to display two enormous breasts—one was cancerous and larger than the other—and a huge hairy vagina. She had a terrifyingly challenging look on her face. Down in the right-hand corner little Stanley was pulling down his pants to gamely tackle the monstrous Hilda.
>
> Ursula brought it back to Berkeley Street and it looked handsome and arresting. When they were packing up, they felt very apprehensive about customs in Adelaide. A painting of a female nude by Charles Camoin, a good French Fauve, had

> just been banned from exhibition in Brisbane on the grounds that it showed pubic hair. Nora said that she was going back to Adelaide shortly with a lot of flower paintings; why not include the Spencer with her work? They decided this was the best solution.

From Smart's description it is clear why Nora kept her communication about the work to her parents to a bare minimum. Nora's education in art and life had expanded since she left the shelter of the Adelaide Hills, and she was unperturbed by the subject matter of the painting:

> The painting came to [Nora's flat in] Stanley Crescent and Nora put it up on the mantel shelf so she could see it every day. When the landlady came to collect her rent, she was riveted by the painting and couldn't speak. Nora liked it because she said the patchwork quilt was so exquisitely painted.[28]

Her passage home on the SS *Mooltan* was uneventful. The bulk of her luggage she had booked through to Sydney while she disembarked in Adelaide in order to visit her parents. She was also able to deliver the painting to the Haywards under the authorities' radar. By the time the ship had sailed on to Sydney, the train delivered her in good time to collect her luggage and pass through Customs. Soon she would be reunited with Robert Black.

In the afternoon Jeffrey Smart was awake but he didn't want to get up. He asked me to sit with him in his room. The light was dim in the room as the sun was dropping in the afternoon sky and the door that opened out into the loggia's light source was only slightly ajar. He began to talk about his father, who believed that he was the reincarnation of the minor nineteenth-century poet Arthur Hugh Clough. He took his son Jeffrey to Italy when he was nine to find 'his' (that is Smart's father's) grave in Florence. This was the trip that introduced Jeffrey Smart to Italy and started his passion for the country that he would eventually call home.

It occurred to me as I sat in this beautiful villa, and while I walked in its grounds, looking across the valley to the ubiquitous Tuscan pines on the other side of the hill, that Nora would have been very taken with her friend's home. What might have been in store for this woman had she not cut her time in England short in 1949 to follow Black back to Sydney; if she hadn't abandoned the idea of painting landscapes in order for the other Heysen to cover that artistic territory? What might she have made of European subject matter had she chosen to retain her liberty? It was not too long after Nora returned to Australia that Smart also made his way back in 1950 at the insistence of his parents, who arranged for his passage home.[29] He was impecunious but he had prepared enough paintings during his time away to stage an exhibition in Adelaide that sold well. Like Nora, he decided he could not stay in Adelaide and in 1951 he made his way to Sydney. He wrote in his memoir about his arrival:

> One of the first people I looked up in Sydney was Nora Heysen. She was installed in Elaine Haxton's old studio in College Street. It was in a beautiful row of old three-storey terrace houses facing Hyde Park… Nora and her husband Robert Black [they were not yet married as Robert's divorce was not finalised] invited me to supper. Nora was cooking jugged hare she said, her mother's German recipe. I put on a tie and my old pin striped suit to pay her a compliment. The other guest was John Passmore, an old fellow student of Nora's from London Westminster Art School days… that evening at Nora's was interrupted by a phone call from my sister Dawn. She had a telegram telling me I had won the Commonwealth Jubilee Art Prize. I had 500 pounds![30]

The prize was awarded for his painting *Wallaroo* 1951, which is now in the collection of the National Gallery of Australia. He had come home to earn a living as an artist. He taught art in high schools and at the East Sydney Technical College, was an art critic for Frank Packer's *The Daily Telegraph*, and was a cast member of the Argonauts Club show, an ABC radio program in 'The Children's Hour'. Every week he gave a talk about art to his listeners and encouraged them to send in paintings to 'The Art Gallery of the Air'.[31] By 1964 he had established himself as a painter and had accumulated four small rental properties in Sydney and put them under management. These investment properties provided him with an income that enabled him to return to Italy to paint without the pressure of having to sell his art to live. He could live to paint.[32] Though he regularly visited he would never live in Australia again. Nora remained dear to him.

It was time for me to leave. The pines casting long shadows in the late, low rays of an autumn sun were beautiful. I thought about the years Jeffrey Smart and Ermes De Zan had lived in the villa, and of the extraordinary array of visitors that had walked up La Posticcia Nuova's driveway.

Six months after my visit, on 20 June 2013, Jeffrey Smart died in hospital at Montevarchi near his home, with Ermes by his side. He was ninety-one. I felt fortunate to have met him and to hear about his friendship with Nora and of the high esteem in which he held her.

ELEVEN: MARRIAGE, HOME AND ANOTHER WOMAN

> *There are so many things about the old place that remind me of home ... many odd things that bring a smile of remembrance ... there's a beautiful big room with the right light for a studio ... you can imagine how thrilled I am.* –Nora Heysen[1]

> *When Robert left her, she said he was the love of her life, that there would be no-one else and that she would die loving him—'that is how I want it known because that is how I feel'.*–Meredith Stokes[2]

During the immediate postwar years, Nora and Robert Black were able to maintain some sense of stability in the College Street flat, and both spent time consolidating their professional lives. After his return from Liverpool, Black was appointed medical officer in 1949 to the School of Public Health and Tropical Medicine at the University of Sydney and later became a lecturer in 1951, progressing to senior lecturer in 1956 and professor in 1963. The couple had settled into living together and in August 1949 Black left for the Northern Territory for some months to participate in a government malarial survey scheme. Meanwhile, Nora was busy finishing three flower pieces and a portrait study of Black for the Society of Artists Show that year.[3] In February 1950 Nora wrote positively to her parents that she had sold two flower pieces in the David Jones Gallery and that another gallerist was asking for her work: 'Wal Taylor seems to be sitting up and asking for flower pieces so that I feel that I'm beginning to re-establish myself here'.[4] Domesticity, however, had its downside:

> I feel like getting down to painting again, or rather I should say I feel as if I can cope with the chores so as to get to my painting. There is always such paraphernalia of tiresome

> necessary jobs which stand between a woman and any work she wants to do, apart from the demands of the home.[5]

Nora had adopted the stereotypical role that she seemed to have escaped when she broke with custom by living with a married man. Her conditioning and sense of duty appear to have overridden her initial impulse to claim domestic freedom for herself. Jeffrey Smart discussed what he believed was Robert Black's irksome ham radio hobby that encroached on Nora's physical space:

> ... he became besotted with this ham radio thing and where they lived in College Street she was cooking and looking after him and it was her studio and he filled it with gadgets and was always chatting away to people on the ham. I think she felt quite rejected a lot of the time and she didn't have her own space to work which frustrated her enormously ... he'd fill the place with aerials and wires stretched across the floor and he was always talking to his other ham radio people—conversations like over to you 3-3-6, I think you need 2GGV installed ... all this talk would go on ... it was very crazy, she let him go ahead with it of course, what could you do?[6]

She did find space and time to paint and entered the Archibald with a portrait titled *Robert H. Black MD* c.1950 (*plate 43*). She was not successful, and in 1952 she renamed the painting *Portrait of a young man* and entered it in the Melrose Prize at the National Gallery of South Australia. She was disappointed again with a close second yet pleased to hear her work 'stood up to the other entries'.[7] In 1999 Nora gifted the work to the National Portrait Gallery in Canberra. It currently hangs on the wall adjacent to Nora's *Self portrait* 1934 (*plate 9*), Black's gaze ironically angled, seeking Nora's as she looks straight ahead.

In 2007 she reflected: 'Robert Black was one of my subjects, he was a pathologist. I got very interested in drawing him as a subject. That was my first love affair in my life—so it really was a very strong emotional upset'.[8] Black was her only acknowledged love. As they were unable to marry, the social difficulties for her parents were perhaps ameliorated by the geographical distance between the parties involved—Nora in Sydney, Black travelling for his research in tropical medicine, and Hans and Sallie in Adelaide. Though she had lived away from The Cedars for some years, Nora was not out of mind for her parents. According to Kate Nockels, 'reading between the lines', it was very difficult for Sallie Heysen to cope with the fact that her daughter was living with a married man. Nockels comments, 'the relationship between her [Nora] and her mother was an interesting one'.[9] This is quite an understatement. When the pair finally married at a Sydney Registry Office with two witnesses, 'only taking fifteen minutes or less', Nora wrote to her parents:

> After all these years, I can scarce believe that our wish of ten years standing is now fulfilled. If anyone had told me that this is how I'd eventually do it, I wouldn't have believed them. After endless delays, Robert eventually received his clearance papers on Saturday then had to wait till Monday to fix a time and someone to marry us. So it was all rather hurried in the end. Robert took half a day off, we lunched on a couple of pies and walked down to the Registry Office … I had a few quiet chuckles at the disparity of my youthful vision and the actual matter of fact event and yet it is a miracle how the real thing can transform such factually unromantic surroundings into something significant and moving.[10]

Nora had waited eight years to marry in a time when living out of wedlock was largely unacceptable. Josephine Heysen Wittenburg recalls her aunt telling her that Robert's wife was uncooperative: 'I remember talking with her and she said that Robert's wife did not give him a divorce until she, Nora, was too old to have children, and she was resentful about that … she expressed a real sadness at not having had children'.[11] The last months were difficult. Nora had expected the final divorce papers in June 1952, but the marriage took place in early 1953 when she was forty-two. Her father's response to the news of her marriage was pointed. Catherine Speck referred to it as 'tough' and 'censorial':[12]

> … it seems strange to congratulate you now when in your own conscience you had found your life's mate some years

> ago. And congratulations can only come on the legal binding and so I am glad this has been accomplished (to everyone's satisfaction).

After a brief wish for a happy second honeymoon, Nora's father was swift to return to the preferred subject of art, Dobell's Archibald portrait for that year and its potential purchase for the Adelaide gallery, and the successful acquisition of a Wilson Steer also for the gallery.[13] The subject of her hard-won marriage was closed.

In 1953 the first of Nora's trips accompanying Black to the tropics for research took place, with the newlyweds travelling to the Trobriand Islands. Hans and Sallie Heysen acknowledged the union, sending much needed funds to Nora as a wedding gift, which she acknowledged as making all the difference: 'I was just wondering how I was going to manage to get the necessary materials together and meet the fare with what I had saved up ... I can't express my thanks for such a timely and generous gesture'.[14] Hans Heysen was a generous man and often sensed when his daughter could do with assistance, aware that life as an artist was never easy. This awareness might also have prompted his offer later that year to buy the first of Nora's *Ruth* portraits for sixty guineas for Sallie Heysen's birthday. It had hung at The Cedars since the early 1930s and more than twenty years later the offer to purchase perhaps concealed an altruistic attempt of support for his daughter. The letter by return mail from Nora reveals a deeper issue. Nora and Black unexpectedly vacated the College Street flat when they returned from the Trobriand Islands, as tenants were being evicted from the building.[15] Nora was again living in shared rental accommodation in Longueville on the Lower North Shore of Sydney, where the couple had taken rooms at the old Kingsford Smith home: 'a rambling uncared-for garden and a little wooden house'.[16] Despite initially sounding happy with her more peaceful surroundings, she shared the space with artist Tom O'Dea and Black, and she was preoccupied with the search for her own home. She found the realities of her choices had impacted the way she preferred to work and when her father offered to purchase *Ruth* it highlighted what she had relinquished:

My Dear Daddy

Many thanks for your letter and the cheque anticipating my 'yes' to your proposal to buy the Ronda portrait study for Mother. I willingly accept the 60 guineas and am glad to think that the portrait will remain in the home. Also it seems appropriate that Mother should own that first painting of 'Ruth', as she was instrumental in my getting her as a model. When I look back upon the quiet days in the studio with Ronda patiently and serenely posing and with refreshments brought to us, the more I appreciate the 'atmosphere' (for want of a better word) that made painting like that possible, and I realise that I have never since found a set of circumstances—a studio with freedom from financial and domestic worries. Painting requiring contemplation demands some stability in one's way of life. I find I can't really settle down to doing what I want to do until I find some permanent home. That said home still seems as remote as ever.

We are both looking forward to being with you for Christmas Eve.

Love to all,

Nora[17]

The atmosphere Nora refers to had been provided by a financially buoyant artist father and a supportive mother, as well as a system of running a house that was more appropriate to a past era, where a gentleman's family could enjoy the benefits of home help, the niceties of life could be observed, and time was immaterial. She had also forsaken her single status and there was someone else to consider on a daily basis, which was not always easy. The fact that she must accommodate this person in different ways than he had to accommodate her was at the heart of the matter. Despite the longing and sense of loss that are apparent in Nora's letter, she maintained her work ethic and in September 1953 held a solo exhibition in Brisbane at the Moreton Galleries. Her letters tell of the show's success and of her house-hunting progress. During this time her mother was not well. The health of her aging parents became a recurring topic. Sallie Heysen underwent emergency surgery in October 1953 and her father reported good progress and much relief.[18] Nora responded in November, pleased her mother had improved but could not say the same for the search for a home of her own or her attempts to find the equilibrium required to work. Her favourite flowers could not salvage the situation:

> The so-called modern new places we've been offered give me the cold shudders—with their gimcrack foundations, box rooms, suburban gardens and lack of space or privacy. My idea is to find an old place solidly built that we could add to and make to our requirements, but so far nothing approaching it has come along.
>
> I don't find much time for painting and even if I did make the time, somehow I feel too unsettled and disorientated to find the state of mind to concentrate. I've begun on a couple of flower pieces, but they've remained unfinished.[19]

By January 1954, Nora had moved to Baulkham Hills, to the home of Black's parents. She had packed their belongings and was preparing to join her husband who had travelled ahead on another of his research trips, again to the Trobriand Islands via Port Moresby and the remote settlements of Esa'ala, Samaria and Minj. Before her departure she enjoyed the spectacle of Queen Elizabeth II and the Duke of Edinburgh's arrival in Sydney during their royal tour, and she noted from her perch on Wal Taylor's city balcony that 'The Royal couple looked very youthful and gracious and slightly bored, but the enthusiasm of the crowds was infectious'.[20] She packed enough art supplies to last her three or four months but her enthusiasm appears to have dwindled from the first time she arrived in Port Moresby when she wrote about the local women, 'their natural grace and dignity … I itch to get out my chalks and begin',[21] to the second time, reporting with reluctance to her father: 'Well, here we are once again sweating in the tropics … I have no liking for the tropics and wonder how I'm going to get rallied into working again … only the energy to begin is required'.[22] It appears her loyalty to Black is boundless. Despite her apathy, the collection of her works done during her visits to the islands delivers a series of images that holds a significant place in her oeuvre.

Nora accompanied Black to the Pacific between 1953 and 1961 and included stays in New Guinea, the Solomon and Trobriand Islands and

New Hebrides. Her great-niece Rosemary Heysen discusses Nora's work in her master's thesis and describes Nora's experiences as fluctuating between 'suffocation to complete isolation ... often alone while her husband was away conducting research on nearby islands':

> Heysen felt restricted both in terms of her movements and in her work. Her misconception that subjects would be readily available saw Heysen forced to journey great distances and establish relations with local people in order to convince them and their families to come and sit for her in her makeshift studio ...
>
> Heysen continued drawing whatever and whoever was available to her including the local men employed in her service to help with domestic duties. She also took ramshackle boats to surrounding islands where she captured images of Melanesian and Tikopian people.
>
> Heysen was working in an isolated region requiring intrepid travelling and cross-cultural exchange.

Rosemary Heysen writes that these works were closely held by Nora and were largely unseen until after her death. She says they were 'a labour of love for the artist and grew from her passion and the circumstances she found herself in'.[23] Her thesis also underlines the fact that these works differ significantly from the work widely associated with Nora and, as curator Hendrik Kolenberg noted, are some of her most sensitive and beautiful.[24] Nora wrote of the effort involved in producing her portrait of King Mitakata in Losuia; the language barrier made it 'frightfully awkward' but the great chief arrived, she said:

> ... in full regalia, necklaces of pig tusks, beads, bangles and strings of shells dangling in festoons round ankles, wrists and calves and forehead ... two attendants with him carrying his royal carpet, lime, gourd, betel nut and other appendages ... He's a wonderful subject really, but quite beyond me.

The portrait shows a nobility that Nora referred to in her letter. That he was the 'last of his blood'[25] adds poignancy to the work. As the recipient of a bequest by the artist, the Art Gallery of New South Wales has held part of this collection since 2006, including the Mitikata drawing gifted in 2003. In a move that surprised Nora at the time, *Moulasi* 1954 was purchased by the AGNSW at the Society of Artists Show in Sydney when it was shown in 1956.[26]

In late May 1954, the couple returned from New Guinea to Baulkham Hills. Nora had grown despondent in her search for an acceptable house when she saw an advertisement in *The Sydney Morning Herald*. When she found her home that June, The Chalet in Hunters Hill, Nora had been in a relationship with Black for ten years and married to him for one. She announced to her parents that she had found the house of her dreams, and that she and Black had purchased the property—'an old Colonial type house overlooking the water in a peaceful spot'.[27] Nora had been clear about what kind of house she wanted and her unwillingness to compromise, coupled with her characteristic patience, delivered her The Chalet. Built in 1854 and offered for sale the following year, the house was one of four prefabricated structures imported from Germany and erected in Hunters Hill by entrepreneurial Swiss immigrant Leonard Etienne Bordier. The selling document offered an attractive version of a kit home:

> ... spacious houses with verandahs nearly all round, built in the most substantial manner of wood, well and strongly framed together, erected on high stone foundations and covered with slates, well ventilated, painted and papered all through in suitable and handsome patterns.[28]

It reminded her of The Cedars with its European touches and century-old charm in stark contrast to the modern suburban Australian home of the 1950s, which held so little appeal for her.[29] She wrote to her parents in July 1954:

> There are so many things about the old place that remind me of home. The heavy cedar curtain rods with the big rings, the big rooms with the French windows, the stable doors opening onto the back courtyard, the old black iron, the jam making pan lined with white, the hand painted porcelain pieces on the doors, and many odd things that bring a smile of remembrance.

> It has a quaint staircase leading up into a huge attic, and a lovely little lemon tree loaded with fruit outside the kitchen. There's a beautiful big room with the right light for a studio—about 10 rooms in all, and after the congested living I've had for 10 years or more, it's going to be heaven to be able to move around in space. You can imagine how thrilled I am.[30]

Aside from the architecture and European heritage of the house, the large garden was central to the attraction the property held for Nora. She was able to pick her own flowers rather than relying on friends, having to buy what was on offer, or pilfering from parks in order to create a bunch to paint.[31] She looked forward to spring when she anticipated the garden would reveal itself further. She described it as 'packed tight with all sorts of shrubs and bulbs' but not one rose. She requested that her father send a cutting of her favourite rose, the Souvenir de la Malmaison, from The Cedars garden: 'This house is just the right setting for its simplicity, graciousness and its quiet tones of white and greys'.[32] It was a bourbon rose both father and daughter painted many times. After settling in at The Chalet, Nora wrote to her parents:

> … the lovely incomparable Souvenirs … I can just see them in this setting. I plan to have the one Daddy has struck for me by the entrance door. 'Souvenir de Mal Maison' [sic], not so appropriate by name I suppose, but I chose it as my emblem and would like one planted on my grave when I die.[33]

It is not surprising that Nora would wish to recreate the best of life at The Cedars. Nora emulated her father's practice of creating a haven in the garden, shut off from the outside world at The Chalet. The garden became a life's work almost as consuming as her art, each feeding the other. Her father's generosity surfaced again when he sent a cheque for £100 to cover the purchase of some of the home's furnishings that appealed to Nora. She bought an oak dresser, cedar wardrobe, a leather chair for her husband's study and 'a very charming little walnut sewing table for still life studies',[34] along with two Windsor chairs, a cedar lounge, copper saucepans and the jam pan that reminded her of home. Nora told her parents of the neighbours she had met including a Dr Reid who had lived at Mount

45. Wes (Wesley) Stacey, *Verandah and garden at The Chalet at Hunters Hill, New South Wales, c.1968*. Papers of Nora Heysen, National Library of Australia.

Lofty in Adelaide and who had met Nora as a child on a visit to The Cedars.[35] She felt comfortable in her new surroundings and wrote in July 1954 that they would be in within the week and 'there will be some folk around with my interests'. Her other neighbours included John Amory, a former director of the David Jones Art Gallery; Hal Missingham, the director of the National Art Gallery of New South Wales and president of the Australian Watercolour Institute, was a few minutes' walk away; and Norman Lindsay was in the process of moving to an old house nearby.[36]

Nora's happiness was evident in her correspondence: 'I cannot yet fully grasp that it is my home—I'm afraid it will vanish like a dream and I keep wandering round and round it to substantiate reality'. To consolidate her sense of ownership, the hanging of her small art collection that included treasured works by her father was a priority. She described the house as being full of charm and 'delightful interiors', adding, 'I'm going to find many new settings for my still lifes'.[37] It is understandable why Nora felt this moment might evaporate. She was a woman who had spent her youth in a bountiful environment, submersed in the arts, living a life circumscribed by society's dictates. She had extricated herself from the scaffolding of parental approval, taken on her war artist's commission, and found herself on the wrong side of the opinion of those close to her when her professional path crossed with the personal. She had remained discreet and fixed in her love for Black. Now she had been rewarded. She was married to her only love and had found a house that held all that resonated for her. It had been a long time coming.

Nora was quickly absorbed into the art scene that same year when she was invited to join the committee for the inaugural Hunters Hill Art Exhibition of 1955, featuring paintings loaned from the residents' private collections.[38] Nora joined Hal Missingham, John Amory and cartoonist Hardtmuth 'Hottie' Lahm on visits to what she described as the 'old homes' of Hunters Hill to make their selections.[39] Hunters Hill was affluent and there was the opportunity for portrait commissions. Despite Nora being invited in to select paintings for an exhibition, Meredith Stokes recalls a different scenario when Nora delivered commissioned portraits of the children in the neighbourhood:

> In the lean years she survived in Hunters Hill with commissions she got from people wanting their children drawn—photography was not such a big thing then so they wanted an artist to draw them. She got very little—£35 for one drawing of a child … and, being Hunters Hill, she was not allowed to go to the front door with the picture or painting to deliver it and be paid—she had to go to the tradesman's entrance at the back. That was the attitude to artists. She really was quite humiliated.[40]

Nora reported a slump in picture sales in May 1956 and the children's portraits supplemented her earnings. She wrote about the practical difficulties of dealing with children who did not want to sit still to be drawn, and she described one as 'a perfect little devil'.[41] It also appears that the parents could also be less than accommodating, which perturbed her more:

> The neighbour for whom I painted the child commission has just called down to say her husband doesn't like it, and will I do something to alter it so that he'll be pleased! As I haven't been paid I suppose I'll have to do something or take it back, and I know which I'd prefer.
>
> All those weeks of exasperating work! I'd best stop before I vent my spleen on the givers of portrait commissions.[42]

In October the same year, Nora arranged for a solo show in Adelaide where she exhibited twenty-six works and sold twenty at the John Martin's Art Gallery, the store owned by her friend Bill Hayward. It was at this show that her well-known work *Spring flowers* 1956 was purchased by the National Gallery of South Australia. She arrived in Adelaide exhausted from the pressure of completing the works, running her home and seeing to her husband's needs. She stayed with her parents for two weeks:

> It seems I need to return to the place and atmosphere of my youth for that renewal of the spirit. Nothing else will work the cure, it's my 'magic adrenalin'. After going thoroughly tired physically and mentally, I've come back with a fresh zest ready to begin again.[43]

Life settled into a pattern at The Chalet, with Black regularly travelling for research purposes and to deliver papers at conferences to destinations that included Malaysia, the Philippines, Africa, India, and, in later years, Europe. Nora painted and continued with her projects to improve the property. The family correspondence tracks the health of her parents and the decline, in particular, of her mother. Throughout these years her elderly parents had cared for Josephine, who was now almost twenty. For Josephine, Nora was 'Aunt Nora' who lived away in Sydney and occasionally visited. Within a few years she would come to mean much more to Josephine. Letters refer to Sallie's nervous state, to operations, headaches and 'Cerebral Fibrositis',[44] or fibromyalgia. At this time Nora received some significant portrait commissions including Professor Charles George Lambie, the retiring head of Medicine at Sydney University. This work was unsuccessfully entered in the Archibald. Late in 1957 she wrote to her parents that she was trying to finish some flower pieces for the Society of Artists show but was not inspired:

> I must admit I have no interest in sending in now, and would just as soon pull out of it altogether. That Society died with Ure Smith. There are no meetings at all now, and no unity or cooperation between the members, and it's so divided in interests and aims it ceases to function.[45]

Between the many discussions about art and various exhibitions, the Heysen artists corresponded on a variety of issues including the appointment of Ivor Hele to paint Hans Heysen's portrait. At the time this work was finished, the announcement of Heysen's knighthood was made in July 1959 and Nora later joined her family members, except for her mother who was too ill to attend, at Government House in Adelaide for his investiture in October.[46] Despite the excitement around him it appears the man maintained his characteristic humility, though doubtlessly quietly pleased. Ivor Hele wrote to Nora suggesting that her father 'could care less'.[47] At the time of the announcement Nora was dealing with the more mundane and troubling issues of two new children's portraits. A few weeks later she was happy to hear that her friend Jacqueline Hick had won the Melrose Prize with a self portrait, despite having entered with her own self portrait. Nora was philosophical about her relegation, admitting that merely entering did keep an artist in the public eye and helped with receiving commissions.[48] This was a policy she maintained as part of her continuing art practice. Catherine Speck believes that it is Nora's lifelong production of work that sets her apart from many artists and considers Nora's portrait work as the defining aspect of her oeuvre despite her reputation as a flower painter.[49] In 1960 she produced the beautiful *Mother and child* (Private collection). It was not a commission but a studio work Nora created by painting the cleaning woman of a Hunters Hill neighbour.

Nora was always looking for subject material that she found inspiring and described her in admiring terms: 'Dark olive skinned of Greek Egyptian Belgian extraction, fine eyes and a great dignity of bearing'.[50] That she was consistently producing work and entering the Archibald through the 1970s and into the 1980s is significant for an artist who sold her first painting in 1926. In 1988 she was a finalist in the Doug Moran National Portraiture Prize with a self portrait. While she might have been out of the wider public view, those in art circles were aware of her consistent output. Her father was also still prolific, receiving commissions and producing studio paintings. In 1960 the Hahndorf Academy held a highly successful show, *An exhibition of work by Sir Hans Heysen*.[51] In a two-week period seventeen thousand people visited the village in the Adelaide Hills to see his work during the inaugural Adelaide Festival of the Arts. In the same year, after twenty-nine years as a member of the Society of Artists in Sydney, Nora was voted on to the selection committee for the first time, the sole woman, twenty years younger than the five other members.[52]

In 1959 it was twenty years since Nora and Evie had shared a flat in Elizabeth Bay and their now long-distance relationship had gone in a direction that might have surprised Nora. Certainly her parents would not have expected the shift that occurred. When Evie joined Nora in Sydney in 1939 she was married and expecting a child. She had lived life committed to her art as Nora had in London, but her marital status changed how she viewed herself. Everton Stokes the sculptor and artist was self-relegated to a subordinate role. Meredith Stokes recalls how her mother told her that when she arrived in Sydney she was offered a significant public art commission, a large sculpture in Hyde Park. Meredith says her mother turned down the commission: 'She said, "No, married women didn't work" and certainly not with a baby. It was a common attitude for the day'. This move away from her art and towards a mainstream family life in Canberra, married to a travelling diplomat, raising two children often alone, led to a gradual bitterness, perceived by Meredith, in the relationship between her godmother Nora and Evie. Nora never wavered from her artistic path. Evie did not sculpt again after Meredith was born. Meredith spoke about her mother's withdrawal from her first artistic occupation that had been inspired by her sculptor idols Barbara Hepworth, Jacob Epstein and Henry Moore:

> She took up flower painting—she was bored, she didn't know what to do, she was a girl with two children on her own because Henry was always in another country. The work [was] sentimental, decorative, like screen fabric—she did design and sell wallpaper designs to London to make money—she was very, very good at design but not a good flower painter. She did it to keep her sanity because she said she couldn't sculpt because it hurt her chest, she was such a bad asthmatic, she couldn't do the chiselling for the dust.

The two women stayed in touch through letters and through the relationship they shared with Meredith: 'Nora used to write to me regularly and she always put little sepia ink drawings on the top of the letter'. She visited Nora at The Chalet from a young age and has vivid memories:

> We walked for miles—she was a great walker—long walks and long talks, always about the past and her memories of England, days with my mother, their student days. It was a very productive time for both of them. My mother did quite a few sculptures of Nora, and Nora painted my mother. [53]

Meredith said she felt closer to Nora than to her own mother. When she had her children, married and living in Canberra, she and Nora regularly exchanged visits. She says she routinely saw her mother just twice a year. Evie and Henry Stokes had divorced when Meredith was a child: 'He was just never there. As children, we saw him off and on between countries—we got exotic presents, they argued like mad, then off he went again to another post. I didn't know him very well'. Stokes left his life as a diplomat and his family in Canberra for London to work as a Fleet Street journalist. Evie took her children home to Adelaide: 'Nora always said my father was away too much. She [my mother] preferred Nora's company and doing art and being an artist'. From Evie's viewpoint, Nora had the benefit of enjoying her daughter without the responsibilities of motherhood. Meredith suggests that though her mother and Nora remained friends, over the years her mother saw her own more constrained circumstances in stark contrast to Nora's in Sydney:

> It was a bit strained towards the end. Nora had led a different life, had kept up her career, was up to date with everything in Sydney, whereas my mother retired by the sea and … led a very quiet life. Nora was very involved with the arts, friends and paintings and exhibitions—very different from the days when they were so close—she [Evie] was ill and I think she did regret not going on with her art and having to bring up kids on her own … [there was] a lot of bitterness about giving up her career.[54]

Evie Stokes died at home aged eighty, from a fatal fall, in 1986.

During my conversation with Meredith, she regularly returned to what she called Nora's broad-mindedness. She recalled her own days as a student and activist describing herself as radical and how accepting Nora was, even if she was opposed to a particular view. In the 1960s Meredith's activism was related to women's rights and left-wing politics. Nora was firmly positioned on the right.[55] Once when she was visiting Nora, a bullet shattered a pane of leadlight in The Chalet's front door. Meredith suspected it had something to do with her activities:

> Nora accepted all that—she knew I was … very, very radical. She let me take my boyfriends there to stay. They were often diametrically opposed to her politically—and she let me go with them, and they stayed with me there. She was extremely broad-minded, tolerant. She loved my Papuan boyfriend … they sat on the verandah, he played the guitar for her, it took her back, of course.
>
> Her attitude was the same for all artists, also the views of young people and books she read, like Patrick White; she always followed all the plays. Some of my theatre friends were friends with her. Dorothy Hewett—I introduced them—they were friends for life. Yes, she was broad-minded about all theatre and movies we went to, and the latest and most modern art … Long before others were open [to things] she was very open-minded.[56]

Describing The Chalet in an interview in 1965, Nora reveals a personal perspective on her approach to her art, but it is also relevant to the wider aspects of her life:

> This peaceful spot is not so remote that I'm not all too aware of what is going on in the art world, and the disturbing trends. It is very hard to find what is true to oneself. There are all these new trends, and it is a very exciting experimental age to be working in, but after all one's own individual way of saying something is the important thing.[57]

Nora did not require outside approval and her comment could also relate to the world outside of art and possibly speaks to the broad-mindedness Meredith Stokes admired. Nora's artistic expression was a mixture of innate talent, her enculturation at her father's side, the ensuing criticisms and her ultimate independent choices. She lived with her choices in full view. From living with her best friend in London, to falling in love with a married man, to sharing her home with her 'adopted' homosexual 'son' who would eventually succumb to AIDS, Nora lived unconventionally, honestly and openly. Her feelings about art spilled in to her philosophy about life.

Between September 1961 and February 1962 Nora and Robert Black made a third trip to the Pacific, this time to the Solomon Islands. Josephine, now twenty-three, had left The Cedars to travel and work for a year as an au pair in Europe. Before Nora and Black's departure, both Nora's parents were experiencing health issues. Her mother's problems were ongoing and her father was recovering from a painful fall. Hans Heysen was also dealing with the death of his friend Lionel Lindsay, whom Colin Thiele describes: 'Mentor, friend companion, critic, champion, he had done far more than anyone else to give acclaim and recognition to Hans ... For half a century, rightly or wrongly, he had been Australia's interpreter of Hans Heysen'.[58] Sallie Heysen suffered a heart attack in October 1961 and Nora wrote from Yandina in the British Solomons concerned but relieved that she was recovering. Sallie Heysen's health continued to decline due to an inflammatory condition of her arteries. Treatment involved a new drug—cortisone—but her impaired circulation was affecting her heart and she suffered muscle fatigue. By the end of the year it was evident that the matriarch would not recover and she succumbed in May the following year. Josephine returned home to her grandparents to help the live-in nurse as Sallie Heysen spent her final months in her bedroom at The Cedars. Thiele writes:

> From here she had seen the morning mist as only Hans had painted it, the rime of spring frost on the grass when the air was pure as ice … From this room she had heard the rain of fifty winters, the wild winds in the pines … She had heard the movement of children, the whimper of childhood sickness, the laughter of youth, the hush of grief, and the long silence of loneliness breathing through the empty house.
>
> The dream she had written down in the earliest days of her courtship for a house in the Hills with trees and an orchard and children playing in the grass had all been brought to life magnificently. That, and more: the grace of books and the integrity of her husband's art, the graciousness of their table and the respect of their friends. And now, consummately, even a title. Lady Heysen! It provided a peculiar little pleasure, a personal satisfaction, by banishing the familiarity of 'Sallie' for ever. She had never liked it. Her natural dignity demanded the correctness of 'Selma' yet her own circle rarely used it.[59]

Sallie Heysen was buried in the Hahndorf cemetery alongside Lilian and Josephine. This strong woman lived a life committed to her husband and the perpetuation of the Heysen name. She had relinquished her own artistic aspirations. Just before her death, David Heysen, who had established himself as an exceptional framer of his father's works as limited edition prints, framed some of his mother's early works done as a student before her marriage to her teacher. She remarked on seeing them: 'Perhaps I would have made an artist after all'.[60] If her attention had been divided and her dedication to her husband's career and her family diluted, it is likely Hans Heysen's story would have been different.

With life irrevocably altered after Sallie's death, Heysen's biographer observed that despite his loss he remained in his home: 'There he slowly took up his brushes and charcoal again, the resilience of his spirit no less astonishing than the strength of his body, and continued his daily round absorbed in the wonder of life rather than the gloom of death'.[61] For the next six years Hans Heysen continued to enjoy a revered position in the art world with Bernard Smith's 1962 publication *Australian painting* endorsing Heysen as the great draughtsman along with David Dridan's *The art of Hans Heysen* in 1966 also celebrating his reputation.[62] All-time-high prices of Hans Heysen originals were realised when they were offered at auction.[63] As the public demand grew and originals were not available to buy, they turned to the reproductions that David Heysen was producing in consultation with his father and a master printer.[64] In 1966 a successful retrospective, spanning sixty-five years of his work, was held during the Adelaide Festival of Arts at the John Martin's Art Gallery.

During the years immediately after Sallie's death, Josephine took care of her grandfather and the running of The Cedars: 'A beautiful young woman, with her mother's eyes and supple grace, she remained its hostess for more than three years'.[65] It was the beginning of a closer relationship between Nora and Josephine as correspondence between The Chalet and The Cedars was directly addressed to her father and her niece, and Josephine began to write directly to Nora sharing her thoughts and future plans. Josephine said the relationship shifted from 'Aunt Nora' to Nora, friend and mentor. The two women remained close. David and Lyly returned to live at The Cedars, leaving their south-east rural property Derrymore in the hands of a manager, allowing Josephine, then in her late twenties, an opportunity to travel. They wanted to give Josephine a holiday removed from the responsibilities she had borne since Sallie's death. It was during this period in 1963 that David supported Nora by arranging an exhibition of her work at Millicent in the south-east of South Australia. Twenty-eight flower pieces and still lifes, three landscapes, nine portraits and twelve drawings made up the show. Chris Heysen, David's son, said that it was 'a period of obscurity'[66] for Nora and she was grateful for her brother's effort.

Tim Heysen recalls he was ten when he sat in the front seat between his parents on the drive to Sydney from Kalangadoo to collect the works for the Millicent exhibition in the family Plymouth. The back seat had been removed to accommodate the cargo and David helped his sister with the hanging of her show which was a part of the South-East Festival of Arts. It was opened by then chairman of the Australian Broadcasting Commission, Sir James Darling, and Chris Heysen recalls Sir James giving him a lift back in the Commonwealth car to Derrymore after the opening, for afternoon tea.[67] The exhibition was held in March, and in April the same year Nora and her father held a joint exhibition at Hamilton in Victoria. Not only was David Heysen a facilitator of these shows but he provided transportation, as both Nora and Hans never learned to drive. Nora was the child who proved to be the artist among the offspring of Hans and Sallie but it was David with his practical skills and a deep appreciation and understanding of his father's aesthetic who became central to the painter's enterprise following Sallie's death. He had spent prolonged periods by his father's side in the early 1930s when he accompanied him on his early camping trips to the 'Far North'[68] as they referred to the Aroona environs of the Flinders Ranges. David was the driver and mechanic in charge of the car and camper trailer, as well as camp cook while his father painted.[69] Later, his skills as a trusted and sensitive restorer of Hans Heysen works established David Heysen as an expert when questions about copyright or provenance of a work arose. Alongside Nora with her expertise and intimate knowledge of Hans Heysen's oeuvre, David Heysen protected the integrity of the Heysen brand. Today, his four children, Peter, Chris, Robin and Tim continue to preserve and promote their grandfather's and aunt's legacy as a national interest. Nora's sensitive portrait of a young Tim Heysen, drawn during a visit she made with Robert Black to Derrymore, was gifted to David by the artist in appreciation for all he had done for her.[70] Tim's relationship with his aunt continues in his role as a trustee of her foundation. In 2014 he opened an exhibition curated from the Nora Heysen Foundation Collection, *One hundred drawings*, at the Riddoch Art Gallery in Mount Gambier.

David and Lyly Heysen cared for Hans Heysen until his death on 2 July 1968. Aged ninety, he suffered a mild stroke in mid June and deteriorated over the following weeks. Nora had travelled to Europe with her sister Deirdre and brother-in-law D'Arcy and was in Spain when her father died. Her last exchange with him by letter sent her impressions of the Prado with its Goyas and El Grecos, and the Velazquez work, *Les Meninas*, 'superb in a room all to itself'.[71] She did not arrive in time for the private burial at

Hahndorf cemetery two days after his death. Nora returned home to the task of sorting through his studio and Catherine Speck writes:

> Hans, with an eye for detail and believing that an artist's reputation beyond his lifetime rested on protecting the circulation of his completed works, had, in his will, entrusted Nora with this responsibility. For her, this included signing work her father had forgotten to sign, something each had done for the other over the years.[72]

Hans Heysen's will created some family tension in 1968 but his decision on how his estate would be shared among his six children has proven to be sound. His desire for The Cedars, the seminal works in the art collection, his and Nora's studios and the surrounding acreage, to remain intact rather than be sold and divided, is now secure. All are vested in

46. Nora and her brother David Heysen prepare to hang the 1963 Millicent exhibition. Nora Heysen Foundation Collection.

the Hans Heysen Foundation established in 2016. A multi-million dollar gallery planned for the historic site aims to develop an internationally recognised artistic and cultural centre in the Adelaide Hills.

In 1970 Nora oversaw the sale of many loved pictures from her father's collection in order to pay death duties, a tax that was abolished in 1978. The pictures chosen to go to auction, Speck writes, included 'works by Rembrandt, Augustus John and Louis Buvelot and by Hans himself'. Nora is reported to have said: '[I]t's a shame to sell father's paintings, these paintings have been like a family to me—I grew up with them all my life'.[73] The loss of her father with whom she had been so closely aligned, personally and artistically, was closely followed by another heartbreak. In 1972 Robert Black left Nora. Deirdre Cowell, Nora's sister, told Allan Campbell that when she was travelling with Nora in 1968, Nora told her that she suspected Black was getting ready to leave her. The death of Hans Heysen made this planned departure difficult and Black remained with Nora for just over three years during what has been described as tempestuous times for the marriage.[74] Craig Dubery says that Nora's almost fatalistic approach to the course nature can take meant that she understood the close affiliation Black had with his nurse, Gail Grimes, was undermining her own relationship with him: 'She could see the course of things happening, not so much that you couldn't do anything about it, but just understanding the situation'.[75] Nora's personal strength and dignity observed by Dubery were central to her survival.

In 1976 the couple divorced and Black, aged fifty-nine, married thirty-one year old Grimes at the registry office.[76] During her research while editing Nora's letters for her book, *Heysen to Heysen*, Speck suspected that Black's constant travel and research, away for months at a time in the company of his nurse, led to the estrangement.[77] When Black was terminally ill in 1988 he wanted to reconcile with Nora. He asked Gail Black to contact her. Some years later Gail Black contacted Hendrik Kolenberg after reading an obituary for Nora written by him. Kolenberg recalls that she wanted to tell him what had happened leading up to Robert Black's death:

> She told me that she dared to contact Nora when Robert Black was dying of lung cancer and wanted to reconcile, he had asked her to, so she went to see Nora. It was quite a brave thing for a younger woman who Nora would have seen as perhaps someone she would like to strangle. They [Robert and Nora] didn't meet up but they did come to some kind of reconciliation before he died.[78]

Meredith Stokes says that Nora and Gail Black remained 'on good terms'.[79] In his documentary, Eugene Schlusser observes 'she kept the house and threw him out of her heart'. Nora responded to Schlusser's comment during the interview with quiet resignation:

> Well I can't say I did it easily, but I survived. I think great emotional upheavals like that—well, people say they're good for your work. I think a person who doesn't go through depths of feeling doesn't have so much to give.[80]

Catherine Speck suspects that Nora might have known for some time during her marriage that Black was unfaithful.[81] Drusilla Modjeska, writing about Stella Bowen and the love triangle between her and writers Jean Rhys and Bowen's de facto husband and father of her child, Ford Madox Ford, notes 'the fate of a woman won't change until she can see herself as neither wife nor mistress'.[82] It was not until Black left Nora for another woman that she appeared finally free to paint as she wished. Speck comments that she felt Nora's work 'went downhill' during the years she was married: 'I had a feeling that getting married was just not the right thing ... once the marriage was over there was a kind of freedom of spirit [in her work] that was lacking in those middle years'.[83] In her memoir *Drawn from life*, Stella Bowen describes her own life with Ford:

> My painting had, of course, been hopelessly interfered with by the whole shape of my life, for I was learning the technique of quite a different role; that of consort to another and more important artist. So that although Ford was urging me to paint, I simply had not got any creative vitality to spare after I had played my role towards him ...[84]

Similarly, Nora subjugated her work as artist to that of wife—to the needs of her husband, his profession and interests, the running of a home, and the demands of a large garden. Only children were absent. Though she produced significant work during the course of her marriage, one wonders what her output and subject matter might have been had she been presented with the work conditions that her husband enjoyed. She prioritised him and applied herself to her art when his needs had been met. When Nora travelled with Black, she hoped that the trips would provide subject matter. However, compromise continued to stalk her. On one occasion, Nora wrote to her parents from Esa'ala and these few sentences communicate the imbalance and her raw frustration:

> Robert perhaps fared better than I, as he was away visiting the islands and doing field work. I found it practically impossible to settle to doing any work, as I had no retreat where I could work or get peace in which to collect my thoughts and impressions … In the end I shut myself in the small stifling hot bedroom we shared and painted a flower piece.[85]

Her correspondence suggests she did this willingly with respect for his work, and as a woman who loved her husband and who accepted the expectations of the day. From their meeting in 1943, it took ten years for Black to divorce and be free to marry Nora. It was another twenty when he divorced her.

Nora's young Hunters Hill neighbour Steven Coorey took art lessons with her in the late 1960s. He would become central to Nora's life. The pair met when a young Steven, around nine years old, according to Craig Dubery, was interested in getting a cat. He saw an advertisement in the local newspaper that led him to The Chalet and Mrs Black. Dubery says Nora was very taken with the young boy who had called on her for a kitten:

> After he had met Nora he continued to go there … after school for afternoon tea with her because he loved the garden

> and that was really the start because he had such a way with gardens, he just had this natural ability and interest … as soon as Nora saw this there was a great rapport.[86]

Steven corresponded for years with Nora, beginning in 1972 aged fifteen when he moved to Tasmania with his mother and stepfather, reluctantly leaving his neighbour and Hunters Hill. The letters written from Hobart by Steven reveal an earnest young man with intense interests that revolved around gardening, grafting roses from cuttings, sourcing rare bulbs and, in particular, unusual ranunculi. He was an avid coin collector and breeder of budgerigars. His letters are expansively informative, almost educational in tone—they read as if he knew the recipient was sincerely interested, that she cared and wanted to know it all. It appears her interest in him gave him a chance to speak. His deep thinking and passionate personality are evident in his writing along with a strong sense of his responsibilities reflected in the propriety with which he addressed Nora. These early letters are addressed to Mrs Black and in his signing off he writes his full name, Steven Coorey. Craig Dubery believes the letters show the deep level of communication between the two:

> The care for each other was unimaginable. If you can see that in the letters then you can see the essence of their relationship there … nothing was too good to be put into the letter because he knew that Nora's understanding of what he was saying would be appreciated. It was not superficial even though an outsider could think 'why would they write that to each other'. Because they both understood the appreciation of such things.[87]

Steven shared with her his precise budgeting of his wages after leaving school when he passed his leaving certificate, having decided against the extra matriculation year. He started his first job in March 1974 at FitzGerald's Department Store earning $30.30 a week and he wrote excitedly about purchasing an 1817 George III half crown for ten dollars. He augmented his income selling the birds he successfully bred and he detailed his spending to Nora as he allocated his earnings to the things he found beautiful and worthy.

In June 1975 he returned to Sydney after asking Nora if he could live with her. Meredith Stokes suggests that though Steven had caring parents his sexuality had become a difficulty between them.[88] Steven had witnessed the separation of Black and Nora before he went to Tasmania. His letters are a record of support and mutually beneficial conversation.[89] He understood the loss Nora had suffered and she welcomed his request to move to The Chalet after three years on her own. Peter Heysen's brother, Chris Heysen, acknowledged the deep connection between his aunt and Steven: 'You can't imagine anyone more appropriate to be there for her at that time—it was just amazing. How lucky. Theirs was a very special bond'.[90] When Steven travelled he kept Nora constantly updated. Her pastel drawing *Steven's bed* 1979 (Private collection) is a portrait of the absent occupant. It is a comfortable interior, intimately and warmly rendered in soft light. His made bed is like a 'missing persons' notice, yet the artist is privy to his movements. For Mother's Day he wrote to his mother, and also to Nora, often sending her a carefully selected card featuring a famous artwork and in 1988 he wrote: 'Dearest Nora, Happy Mother's Day for the 8th of May. Wish I was there—I'd bring you chrysanthemums'.[91] His regard for her was deep and he always sent warmest wishes to the menagerie of cats, birds, dogs and possums she fostered. He addressed postcards, 'To: The Angel Nora'.[92] In the early 1980s, he travelled to San Francisco, a place he thought that he could belong, without prejudices, and he shared his private thoughts with Nora.[93] Their connection lay in a mutual appreciation of beauty in the natural world and in art. Steven was serious about his own art and studied in San Francisco while training and working as a hairdresser. Just as she exchanged letters about art with her father as a student, she discussed figure drawing and art theory with Steven. His letters are full of understanding of what it meant to grow and love a garden, of the artistic process, and of a love for animals. In his apartment he cultivated flowers in pots and regularly reported their progress to Nora:

> The last of my ranunculi have just about collapsed … yours will be planted soon. I'd buy a new packet to add to your ranunculi collection, as it would be just too awful to miss out on a needed colour once Spring arrives and you're wanting certain colours to paint. I'm sure there must be room for some more.[94]

His handwriting was copperplate-like, considered and beautifully formed. The letters radiate respect for the woman he is writing to, as do his other-worldly turns of phrase. On 1 September 1986 he wrote to Nora:

> Today in Sydney is of course (officially) the first day of the Season of Spring and here I am away from The Chalet for the second Spring in a row—mostly away 'in body' not so much away 'in mind'. I wish for you a Spring filled with tempting colours and storms of inspiration, and an absence of intrusions.[95]

47. During the years he lived in San Francisco, Steven Coorey cultivated flowers in the window boxes of his apartment. They included some of his and Nora's favourites—ranunculi and tulips. When those were not in season, roses reigned. Photograph courtesy Craig Dubery.

In 1986 Black was long gone and Steven was abroad when he wrote to Nora from San Francisco with a protective tone when it was proposed that his friend Craig Dubery might stay with Nora: 'I have explained fully to him your need for solitude and space, and that you and I were able to co-habit well as we understood this fully with each other'. In the same letter where he insists Nora need not feel obligated to have Craig stay, Steven writes of the garden he helped nurture with Nora, learning the foibles of bulbs in coastal Sydney hostile to their cultivation, and the pruning needs of roses: 'You're in the middle of Winter (or just past the middle) and things are grey and bare. I imagine you're anticipating Spring though ... your Roman Hyacinths should be up by now'.[96]

Steven discussed with Nora the garden according to what he remembered should be flowering at any given time, the jobs she faced with the seasonal fluctuations, and the beauty that he remembered. He missed the familiar joy of the garden and what it represented. The ubiquitous arrangement on the round cedar pedestal table was a direct reflection of Nora's mood, her thoughts and her passion, and he understood this. Her attachment to Steven was now well into the catastrophic period of the eighties when AIDS and HIV were new and feared terms. He wrote: 'I miss you and our peaceful and productive co-existence. It all seems so stable and well balanced and secure in comparison to recent changes and events. Nothing to be done about it just now'.[97] His letters were filled with mysterious symptoms, reports of antibiotics for a 'flu' that does not respond, and odd treatments for parasites and fevers that his community whispered about in terms of a laboratory-bred conspiracy.[98]

The pair regularly exchanged photographs of the paintings they were working on. Nora offered constructive criticism and encouragement just as she had received from her benevolent father. Steven always responded with gratitude and reciprocated with open admiration for the works she shared with him: 'As far as needing encouragement goes (and indeed contact) I find that just thinking of you gives strength and encouragement. Here's to success for us both. I'm sure we're deserving, more than less'.[99] His staunch support of Nora is evident when he writes to congratulate her for making the final selection in what the letter suggests was the David Jones Sydney second *Annual survey exhibition* in 1987:

> … your fabulous Impressionist Self Portrait—I love it and obviously so do the judges! I'm sure it's given a lot of its reviewers something to think about —like—Why wasn't this artist given more exposure and due long ago![100]

Dubery believes that Steven and Nora shared a unique connection:

> Their relationship was a closeness that is hard to describe. They recognised the individual in each other and their love of nature, the seasons, and the garden … Nora and Steven could recognise their shared sensitivities. That really does encase their whole relationship because to be an artist you have to have a heightened sense of things, especially in Nora's case where she is painting from nature … her understanding, her way of looking was totally the same understanding that Steven had of things … it was like they were meant to be, the closeness of their friendship was based in that common understanding.

Dubery also says that Nora had no time for the petty inquisitions that some people around her thought were appropriate, remembering a time when Nora refused to engage with questions about the nature of her relationship with Steven from a number of guests at a party they attended together. Just as Meredith Stokes recalls, he says that one of the outstanding aspects of Nora's personality was that she never judged people for what they stood for, that 'she was very much an individual that thought it was perfectly alright to have your own ideas about things and to agree to disagree' though this did not go as far as dignifying a rude question with a response:

> She would impart her opinion but at the same time it was for you to decide whether her opinion counted for whatever it pertained to … she appreciated people from all walks of life whatever their orientation was … she appreciated that and didn't shun them or decide that they weren't good enough or up to scratch because of what or where they came from. She could easily have had prejudices because of her background

> of how to judge other things. But she didn't. She was very much her own person from that point of view.[101]

In 1994 Steven returned to Sydney and the world he and Nora shared, though he did not move back into The Chalet. He was also an artist who understood the necessity to separate in order to work originally and independently, but he succumbed to his illness just a few years later. Nora's relationship with Steven was as mother and son, and she had made extensive provision for him in her estate. His untimely death devastated her but Craig Dubery remembers her inner strength prevailing as it had with her father's death and Black's departure:

> When Steven passed it was very difficult ... She was upset but she was dealing with it. Again, her core strength was that when these things happen in life you still remain in the present ... getting on with things and maintaining some sort of dignity. Her dignity with a lot of things was heightened because to her that was something that was a strength. She took strength from the fact that the way you deal with things is a responsibility.[102]

Steven had lived to see Nora's work celebrated once more as Klepac reintroduced her to the Australian public. Steven died in 1997 and the depth of Nora's loss was immense.

The retrospective exhibition *Faces, flowers and friends* was organised for Nora by Lou Klepac at S.H. Ervin Gallery in 1989. Meredith Stokes recalls Nora's response to Klepac's work on her behalf:

> She said without Lou she would never have made the comeback as a woman artist because women artists weren't getting recognition until our women's movement in the 1970s. They started to get recognition in the Gough Whitlam years—before that, she said, there was no recognition ... or very little. 'But for Lou taking me on, there would have been

> nothing after my early recognition'. She said she was eternally grateful for him.[103]

In 1989 Catherine Speck met Nora for the first time and, along with curator and fellow historian Jane Hylton, has been pivotal in positioning Nora in Australian art. Some who knew her have suggested that Nora was a private person who shunned the idea of self-promotion and preferred her work to speak for her. My research suggests that she was not private in an attempt to exclude or withhold, but she was quiet, getting on with her art practice, tending her garden at The Chalet that provided her inspiration, and caring for her pets. Nora had opinions on many things, mostly art, and she was not reticent in letting them be known. In the years she had lived alone she had developed a reputation of being difficult to approach, perhaps even thorny, but that characterisation sat more within her unwillingness to waste time on issues or people that she felt were not relevant to her. People who knew her, and counted her as a friend, refer to her directness. Hendrik Kolenberg says:

> She was very direct and honest, of an old-fashioned school. If she liked something she said it as she saw it. Tact wouldn't have come into the story with her. She wasn't necessarily *tactless*, but she was very direct. I remember being with her at an exhibition on a number of occasions when she would make a comment about someone's art—if someone didn't like it [what she said] she would say why.

Kolenberg was introduced to Nora in 1986 by Lou Klepac when the two men visited her, along with Barry Pearce. He remembers the meeting. It was important as, at the time, Kolenberg was curator of art at the Tasmanian Museum and Art Gallery (TMAG). The meeting resulted in him buying Nora's self portrait that was later chosen for the prestigious cover of Frances Borzello's book *Seeing ourselves: women's self-portraits*:

> I liked her immediately. I liked the look of her. A very handsome, strong, good looking woman and [I felt] very comfortable in her company… she took out a lot of her

paintings and I responded to one in particular … a self-portrait with her in a white jumper. It was very expensive—she wanted more for that painting than any painting she had sold up to that time. It wasn't dear by today's standards, I think it was $9,000 … I actually think it is still her most exciting self-portrait. It has both her certainty and her cautiousness. It had a wonderful frame, one of her father's, and a piece of plate glass. I fell for the picture in a big way and I asked if we could buy it.

48. Hendrik Kolenberg arranged the purchase of *A portrait study* 1933 for the Tasmanian Museum and Art Gallery. Nora is pictured on the back verandah of The Chalet in Hunters Hill with the portrait behind her.
Papers of Nora Heysen, National Library of Australia.

> Hobart wasn't a place with a lot of money so I knew it would be a battle.

The TMAG agreed to purchase and Kolenberg explained that when the painting arrived in Hobart, as a curator, he was keen to see the back of the picture: 'to see what inscriptions or whatever might be behind the work':

> I noticed there was a big piece of canvas tucked up the back [of the frame] so it looked like it had been heavily cropped, and that she had put the work on a smaller stretcher … I dared to have it taken out of the frame and off its stretcher so we could see what was wrapped around it. It was cropped … it was still a good composition [but] there were a lot of very interesting things missing. She [had cropped] to fit the frame—and it was a marvellous frame with roses and snakes going around it, beautiful, in gold leaf rubbed back, and this piece of plate glass. I remember asking why plate glass. I didn't know at the time but all glasses used to have a bit of colour in it … mostly green. But plate glass is absolutely clear so you can use it. Heysen himself liked it for his paintings. So she actually had just listened to her father.[104]

In consultation with the TMAG conservator, Kolenberg had the work put on a new stretcher to show the complete image. Details that were revealed in the foreground of the work include the pottery jug to the left of the image, a tube of paint and a book. A new frame was made as close to the original as possible using gold leaf and similar carved detailing:

> Then I sent her a long letter with slides of before and after. There was a silence that lasted two months. I got very panicky. Eventually a letter did come from her and she started by saying that 'when I first received your letter I was so angry I closed the letter and didn't look at it for a while. Then I reread it, looked closely at the slides and said, you were actually right. I did crop it for the frame. You were right to show the rest of the painting'.

Kolenberg said they went on to form a 'terrific friendship' and that perhaps he should have been more tactful during the process. Nora asked him if she could have the frame and plate glass back and he was quick to comply with her request. During his friendship with Nora, Kolenberg was very aware of the importance of Nora's father to her. He said that she thought that 'he wasn't in any way a brake on her' or that she was 'under his elbow' though she was aware that 'his reputation was often in the way'. This can be read as a contradiction. Nora's love and respect for her father appears to mean that she was not willing to consider him in any negative light but this does not ameliorate her position. Kolenberg said he went to visit her whenever he could, and when he moved to Sydney for his role at the AGNSW he would take young curators to meet her:

> I used to like taking other curators there, particularly the younger ones who often don't have a chance to meet an older distinguished artist who is almost a part of history. I thought she was a remarkable, independent-thinking individual woman. But she didn't see herself in any way as a feminist … She disliked that and she got a lot of younger women historians who were coming to her in the last years seeing her as another example of feminism breaking through which she actually didn't like. They tended to come to her with questions about her father. I think she particularly disliked that because she didn't have any negative things about him. So that was interesting to hear that. She really wanted to be known as an artist in her own right. One of those people who, if you use the word, she was 'fantastic'. Her drawings are wonderful. An Australian term for someone who draws well is draughtsman and you wouldn't call her a draughtswoman. She wouldn't approve of it. She wouldn't want to be called a draughtswoman.[105]

Nora's rituals were known to those in her inner circle and each person I spoke with had the same recollection of her serving strong coffee in her brown Denby pottery mugs. Kolenberg describes her rituals as very specific:

> She loved strong coffee, loved butter, was a great drinker of whiskey ... she smoked heavily. You would come in and the first thing would be that you would sit at her round table in the very tiny dining room next to the kitchen ... there were flowers on the table and usually the most delicious cakes and biscuits and very, very strong coffee in great big mugs.
>
> She would smoke, and then the birds would come to the window so she went outside to feed them. She would throw great chunks of mince to butcher birds and magpies and pigeons. They were all equal. She was very democratic.
>
> You would spend a lot of time sitting there talking about this and that, and then sometimes she would take you into the little studio—off a small passage way, off the back verandah, there was a small room where she had her work. I loved going in there because you would see something you knew she was working on ... usually pastels of flowers or fruit ... and I really fell in love with them ... The late pastels are extraordinary, exciting. They are actually joyous, some of them, that they sparkle. There's no-one quite like her in Australian painting. That's more than just in [her] observation. That's something in her emotional spirit, I think. [106]

In the catalogue he prepared for her 2000 retrospective, curator Lou Klepac is equally captivated by Nora's pastels and in his observations of *Quinces* 1991 (Private collection, *plate 16*), which he describes as 'one of her loveliest works', he suggests that this is quintessential Nora at work. He alludes to the emotional spirit that links with joy:

> So much lies behind the seeming simplicity of this work. There is an allusion to Courbet and Cézanne, but if we look at it as deeply as it deserves, we find the certain, masterly gaze of an artist in complete control of the means of expression. It is a cautious gaze which conceals as much as it reveals. Only slowly does one realise that the artist has projected her own visual ecstasy onto this assemblage of quinces on a wicker tray casually placed on a stool. What may appear a simple still life is in fact a miraculous moment where the consciousness of the

> artist has reached a point of incandescent communion with the object of its gaze.[107]

Nora's emotional balance in her work and life was also directly connected with her affection for the living creatures that shared her life. This is illustrated by Craig Dubery as he describes the death of Bosie, Nora's border collie who adopted the artist after leaving its nearby home. It was not uncommon for pets in the surrounding streets to 'up and leave their owners' according to Dubery, to settle in with the artist who demonstrated an uncanny affinity with the animal world. Dubery was with Nora when Bosie died:

> It turned out to be a whole week of rain when Bosie passed away and she had him [lying] in the bedroom on an old army blanket. I kept saying to Nora, what are we going to do with Bosie? We must have looked like the oddest pair. I came in with the wheelbarrow to lift Bosie up—a dead dog is quite heavy. She was very upset, she was ninety or ninety-one and didn't want to bury him ... So she gets dressed like Widow Twanky with a big coat because it was pouring outside. I'm out in the pouring rain digging the hole in the garden and we had to devise some sort of agreement about where we were going to bury Bosie.
>
> 'No, it can't be there,' she says, 'Mink is there'. 'No, it can't be there because whatever [pet] is there'. She knew where they were all in the garden. Eventually a spot was decided on and I started to dig. I wheeled the dog out and Nora said [he] can't go in the hole with damp dirt in there ... it's pouring with rain. I said Nora he's going to get wet anyway. In the shed there was dry dirt in a bag, so I had to ... bring it out while she held the umbrella over the hole. I swear that the bluebells and jonquils around that spot just went berserk. She could torture herself with things like that because of her great love [for animals], the affinity and her deep empathy.[108]

Her nephew Tim Heysen says 'she was a very strong willed and independent person' agreeing that she was 'a bit of a law unto herself'.

Her love for cats was stuff of family legend and her white cats became part of The Cedars mythology and also later at The Chalet. Tim Heysen recalls, 'She smuggled a kitten onto the plane and brought it in her handbag from Sydney to Hahndorf. Nora always had cats, many, many cats [at The Chalet], and when she went shopping, just up the road, not very far, there'd be these cats following her'.[109] Her animals featured in many of her works, as did Robert Black, who one day 'walked out'[110] and never returned. Dubery suspects it was the loyalty that animals gave to their owners that appealed to Nora, 'she loved animals more than people I think', and he suggests that her affection for animals was even greater after Robert left her:

> She had some exceptional animals. Mink was a grey cat and after Mink came Cello. Cello was the most beautiful Siamese and absolutely adored Nora—I can't remember a time when he wasn't up on her shoulders. And there was Gustaf—he also wandered in from the neighbours and never went home ever again. Animals were attracted because there was a quietness and an appreciation of [them] … Nora would just adopt them. We just bought more chicken livers … Two had litters and at one stage there was something like thirty-two cats. That particular painting [*Morning Sun* 1965, Private collection] where she painted all those white cats in the back vestibule, that was the period in which she had all those.

Nora managed an unusual harmony between the wild and domesticated creatures that inhabited The Chalet. She provided mince for the magpies and butcherbirds, and Scotch fillet for fussy cats. Treats for possums that included buttered bread with jam resulted in rats nesting in the house's attic, competing with the possums for space. Nora considered them all part of the natural order. She was also unconcerned with keeping her house secure. Dubery says it wasn't until the 1980s when she was burgled that she started to lock her back door that had always been left open for the cats to move in and out as they pleased:

> Nora was of the belief that you are far better off to make things accessible than to get things broken. Lock it all up and you

> get smashed windows or a jimmied door. What is the point? she'd say. There's plenty of stuff inside for them to be satisfied to take—they'd be overwhelmed—well what do I take?

She planted what appeared to be a small Renoir portrait of a little girl just inside the back door to tempt would-be thieves into believing they had found a prize. Dubery says that she thought they would see her name on paintings and simply reject them while she cut her losses with whatever they decided had value:

> She was clever like that. She thought things through and it was that calmness … not getting paranoid about the situation but simply dealing with it. She accepted the likelihood of a robbery. She was extremely wise. She never did herself out of how she was to exist. It was true that when you went there you felt you had entered another world. A world that was set back from anxiety and the ridiculous speed of things. You would go down Yerton Avenue and into the yard—in there was just the embodiment of calmness, rational calmness, and nature.[111]

Nora could not attempt to stop inevitable progress as her father had. He was able to purchase surrounding fields to form a buffer zone when modernity encroached on his hillside sanctuary in Hahndorf. She could not buy the adjacent suburban blocks to protect her from overdeveloped building sites that eventually impacted on the peaceful haven she had created. Despite her protests to local council, unsympathetic developments towered over her back garden cutting the natural light she prized and stripped the privacy she cherished. She retreated further behind her garden wilderness. The streetscape around her changed, like so many desirable waterfront properties in Australia in the economic boom of the early 1980s. The slender timber house untouched was showing its years.

TWELVE: SACRED GROUND

> *Even at the age of eighty-odd I was thinking, God, she must have looked sensational when she was young. She had this distinct, still very good face, amazing, and with her hair pulled back—the fags and the whiskey—I thought what a character!*-Nat Williams[1]

> *She was a true philosopher of painting. For her, painting was about an exploration of the world, not about being famous or being hung in museums. To paint a flower was like a prayer.*-Barry Pearce[2]

When Robert and Steven had gone, Nora lived quietly at The Chalet. As her father had held an artistic court at The Chalet, Nora maintained a small, select group of friends that she was willing to engage with, artists, curators, writers and poets. A day after her ninetieth birthday in 2001 she told Michael Cathcart:

> I fell in love with the place when I saw it. I thought, I could live here and I could paint here and it would be my setting ... That's how it happened and I've never regretted it. I've made this my home and I never want to move and I feel happy here with my work.[3]

Occasionally one of her friends would ask if they might bring someone to meet her and this was often met with reluctance but once she was engaged she was a gracious host. When a visitor first met Nora they were fascinated by the elderly woman who knew her mind and smoked continuously. When Nora met Black, he introduced her to smoking. Chris Heysen remembers his aunt's comment:

> She had a wonderful expression for it—'all he left me with was an addiction for cigarettes'—she was the most rigorous

> chain smoker I've ever met! It certainly became something to do—it wasn't her character not to have a haze of smoke around her—it was quite beautiful actually.[4]

Robert left her with one other lifelong addiction. He gave her a gramophone for Christmas in 1959, something she said she had always wanted.[5] Music, like whiskey, cigarettes, and coffee, was one of Nora's few non-negotiable essentials. She told interviewer Heather Rusden about her affinity with Mozart:

> To get in the mood for painting I always play music. When I get into the painting I don't hear it anymore but it creates the right mood. Mostly Mozart—it's the lift that he gives me, the response that I get from Mozart is essential; especially for flower painting, the joy of Spring. He goes deeper than that of course ... particularly Mozart I go to, more than Beethoven or Mahler.[6]

In his capacity as curator at The Cedars and as Nora's friend and advisor, Allan Campbell kept a journal of his meetings with Nora at The Chalet. One entry reads:

> 5.00 pm Nora's expression: 'It's the hour'. Single Malt Whiskey, dash of rain water. Nora would sit on one whiskey for quite some time—Pringles (and one for Bosie). Music—always Mozart. 'Mozart—Oh yes, Mozart, the master. I love to listen to Mozart late at night when I have him all to myself'.[7]

Her friend and carer Craig Dubery says that until her death, while she was able, her daily rituals remained unchanged including the 'tweaking of the daily mixed bunch' on the sitting room table: 'the flowers that were spent were taken out, not that she disliked spent flowers, they were lovely as well, but because there was so much in the garden ... she would visit all the little enclaves, it was the most incredible thing'. He says that her mornings started consistently early at around six with a cup of tea:

49. In August 1991, just before her eightieth birthday, Fairfax Media photographer Tim Clayton photographed Nora at The Chalet. The decay that visitors witnessed was viewed entirely differently by Nora, who enjoyed the aging process of the things around her, the patina of time on natural materials, the character and integrity of something that had been allowed to age untouched. Photograph: Tim Clayton / Fairfax Media.

> She would sit and cogitate what sort of day was unfolding. It was fairly early for someone between the ages of eighty and ninety-two who never went to bed before midnight, sometimes one in the morning. She was fantastic, clear as a bell after her tea. Then she would get ready for the day, dress and come back for coffee and a cigarette.[8]

Chris Heysen recalls her coffee in a saucepan, Turkish style, with 'mud in the bottom so strong a spoon would stand up'.[9] Allan Campbell arrived for his morning visits after eleven and describes Nora receiving him in the small back sitting room, curling smoke surrounding her, a ribbon in her white hair and always with make-up on.

Each person I interviewed who knew Nora refers to her garden, her love of flowers, and how she held the natural world in a kind of spiritual reverence. Dubery says that whenever he was in the garden with Nora he would think of her saying: 'My prayers are drawn from nature not from bibles ... picking a bunch of flowers and painting them is a prayer'.[10] In conversation with Eugene Schlusser, Nora examined this sentiment that she held so deeply and that which constantly inspired her. She explained herself in relation to Cézanne:

> He wanted to make things permanent. He didn't like the impermanence of things, of everything going. He wanted to make them permanent. I wanted to preserve flowers in a way that captured the beauty of flowers, the fragility of flowers, and the ephemeral feeling of flowers—that they were only going to last a couple of days or a day—and yet give them quality and substance. It is not an easy thing to do. It has moments of *extreme* joy, exhilaration. And sometimes—when you feel you've really done something that you've wanted to do—it makes everything worthwhile. But it doesn't last very long until you are striving again for a 'feeling' that you hadn't gotten.[11]

Nora's life was unconventional and at times fragmented. The constant was flowers. Jane Hylton suggests that Nora's flower paintings and still lifes could be read as self portraits, an intimate view into her daily life.

Angus Trumble, the National Portrait Gallery director, agrees with Hylton and also with the proposition that Grace Cossington Smith's interiors are a form of self portraiture. Trumble makes his point in terms of gender and environment:

> It's not a stretch to say that part of the gendering of subject matter, in the sense that the domestic sphere and the domestic still life both in scale and composition, has a resonance with the way the life of a woman artist was circumscribed by social usage up to forty or fifty years ago.

To highlight his point about an artist's personal environment influencing treatment of subject matter, Trumble uses English painter Graham Sutherland's landscapes: 'rather surrealistic Welsh landscapes which are full of knots and boulders and crags and clefts' reflecting the same amount of 'nervous tension' as his later portrait works. Trumble suggests that these portraits say more about Sutherland than they do about the landscape or his sitter. He also points to John Brack's portrait of Joan Croll that hangs not far from Nora's self portrait in the National Portrait Gallery: 'It's enough to spend five minutes with Joan to know that the portrait tells you more about John Brack than it does about Joan Croll'. He continues: 'To Jane Hylton's point, Nora Heysen's still lifes probably contain an awful lot about Nora and not so much about vases of flowers'.[12] The event that perhaps foreshadows these floral 'self portraits' occurred while Nora was serving in New Guinea in 1943 when she met and fell in love with Robert Black. Black's situation, married and a father, would test Nora, casting her in the role of mistress and later wife, and both would ultimately prove unsatisfactory. The *Australian dictionary of biography* carries this description of Black: 'Frequent travel abroad, coupled with a reserved manner and introspective temperament, sometimes impeded his professional collaborations and placed a strain on his personal relationships',[13] suggesting that Black was not the easiest of men. It could be argued that Nora reveals herself in her still-life work through Klepac's reflection that her nature was 'probably best suited ... for her favourite subject of flowers'. He offers that this subject matter was deeply entrenched in her world as a child, content at home surrounded by nature:

> They have remained the means of keeping such a perfect and happy dream alive no matter what else has happened to her. She has always been able to surmount grief or disappointment by painting flowers ...[14]

Nora was pragmatic about her obsession with flower pieces:

> Oh, they have always attracted me very much, but I suppose, I fell in love during the war and then ... flower pieces ... we were busy getting a house and getting married, and all that, and flower pieces were something I could continue with.[15]

There was a point in Nora's early career where a position in the art world was open to her, if her scale of work had been less intimate, and if she had moved with modern trends. Former head of Art at the Australian War Memorial, Lola Wilkins, agrees with Nat Williams of the NLA that while Nora was committed to exploring her art on her own terms she was not good at pushing herself into the public eye. This absence of active marketing was not helped by what Wilkins says was Nora's lack of a dealer.[16] Nora relied on commissions, sales from group exhibitions, and entering competitions to remain in view. It could also be suggested that the benefit she derived from her association with the brigade of older male friends of her father's, who facilitated the circulation of many of Nora's early works and who secured her private commissions, gradually diminished as each of them passed away. They had, in effect, acted for her as proxy dealers. By the early 1960s gallerist Wal Taylor, Sydney Ure Smith, Louis McCubbin and Lionel Lindsay were all dead. For forty years after Ure Smith's death in 1949, Nora remained an independent operator without commercial guidance. Ursula Hayward died in 1970 and though the friendship with Bill Hayward remained until his death in 1983, the days of patronage were limited. James McGregor remained a part of Nora's life in Sydney but by the 1960s he was aging and died in 1973.[17] The rise in the influence of new private galleries focussing on modern art and the gradual devolution, and ultimate closure, of the Sydney Society of Artists in 1965 also had a significant impact on Nora's reach. It was not until Lou Klepac's exhibition of her work in 1989 that she once again experienced the power and benefits of outside support. Wilkins comments on Nora's passive practice:

> Though she was very devoted in terms of her art practice she wasn't a self-promoter, that was one of the biggest things with Nora. I think she was also an artist who was very much about her own work and not necessarily influenced by 'isms' ... She always said to me that she felt her drawings were her best work ... Her draughtsmanship was hugely important to her. For all the artists of her generation, drawing was such a foundation for them, and she certainly falls very much into that—she was certainly not in the modernist school at all, or an avant garde artist, she wasn't a Nolan for example, she was very content to explore through what she knew.[18]

This limited exploration of subject matter and an unwillingness to deviate in her technique appear to be what kept Nora in her niche. While completing her master's thesis, Kate Nockels admits that she was searching to support the theory that Nora had been overlooked because she was a woman but she concluded in her view that she was eclipsed because of the subject matter she had chosen:

> I wanted to reinstate this woman who had been overlooked because she was female, because she was the daughter of a famous artist—but I resiled from that ... I found a competent and professional artist but [after] the innovation and excitement in *Corn cobs* ... she retracted like an anemone—she could have gone down this innovative path [of *Corn cobs*] along with Jeffrey Smart and some of her other mates, but she chose not to.[19]

It is Nockels' view that Nora's subject matter positioned her out of sight. This appears to have foundation, but the fact that Nora chose not to explore the innovative excitement of *Corn cobs* raises the question—what did prompt her subject choices? How much had she endured? She never stopped working but she chose to paint for herself. As Barry Pearce puts it: 'For her, painting was about an exploration of the world, not about being famous or being hung in museums'.[20] Lola Wilkins also expands on notions that women's art was often seen as 'feminine, decorative and pretty'. She suggests that Nora choosing flowers as subject matter often resulted in the superior execution of her work being missed:

> Nora probably fell into that chasm that a lot of women artists did. They were all lumped together and weren't given the same amount of focus that the men were given—by the commentators, the critics and the historians. They were treated as second class citizens.

Wilkins observed that Nora's work did not fit this 'feminine' generalisation. Sybil Craig and Nora in particular were given the task of representing the women in the war effort, but according to Wilkins it does not follow that their work is particularly feminine:

> Nora's work shows the dedication of the women ... how women really took what they were doing seriously. In her portrait of the transport driver—it's the strength and the femininity at the same time, that she portrays—the women as serious, that they're strong, that they're focussed on their work—but their femininity is part and parcel of them ... Her work is strong and I don't think you would look at her work and think 'oh yes, this work is done by a woman'. Her own strength comes out in her work along with her determination to show the strength of the women.[21]

Wilkins offers a simple observation in relation to Hans Heysen that possibly penetrated every choice Nora made. He was her main guide and mentor from the start of her career when she was a teenager and his perspective and experience coloured her own:

> I don't think he saw her perspective at all—what it was like as a woman trying to survive in what was still largely a masculine world because he saw the world from his perspective as a man! He never realised what a huge uphill battle it was for her. The entrée for any woman was just not as easy as it was for a man.[22]

The subject choices Nora made, that Nockels refers to, must be embedded in the female experience.

During her visits to The Chalet, Nockels observed how the garden was central to Nora's daily routine and how it provided all the inspiration she required to continue her work. Though this subject matter pleased Nora for over fifty years, there came a point when she fell out of step with the art-buying public and the judges of the competitions she entered. In 1959 Nora commented after her unsuccessful entry in the Melrose Prize, 'I've long since given up hope of winning prizes—my work is far too unexciting and conventional'.[23] Apart from her Pacific Island paintings, Nora chose to remain behind her garden wall, her easel set firmly in the domesticity of flower pieces and still lifes, and in the realm of portraiture.

Hylton suggests that each of Nora's works painted at The Chalet, offers an insight to the structure of her life and state of mind.[24] After dealing with 'all that',[25] as she understatedly describes the reality of marriage, Nora seized for herself what was left in the domestic realm that she could call her own: her garden and her compromised opportunities for painting. Modjeska explores painter Grace Cossington Smith's late works of the interiors of her home, where she lived alone, in a similar vein to Hylton's notion of Nora's still-life paintings as self portraiture. Modjeska describes the detailed interiors and how they can be read:

> Do we see here the representation of spinsterly existence: single beds, neat cupboards, empty hallways? Or the richness of solitude: empty rooms filled with possibilities? Doors opening onto hallways ... allowing us to glimpse their treasures? To my eye these interiors are by way of being self-portraits of a woman who has resolved the tension between her own ability to see and the seeing, or being seen, that is required of her. [26]

Similarly, the interiors that Nora produced of The Chalet show a woman who has navigated the territories of mistress and wife, insisting that the role of artist was still available to her. Schlusser notes that Nora painted continually:

> ... recording the colours, the forms and the effects of time on all living things large and small. But she was living a double life—as artist and wife with a husband who was indifferent to art.

Nora revealed that she was acutely aware of the impact her marriage had on her chosen career. She called it a 'great disruption' saying 'a marriage has got to interfere with a career as long as your partner is not in the same field'.[27] Black's chosen field was supplemented by his passion for ham radio operating, and anecdotal evidence from friends reveals a clutter of equipment that occupied valuable space in The Chalet, just as Smart had observed in the College Street flat. The hobby consumed hours of Black's spare time and it did not include his wife.[28]

When Black had left Nora and Steven was travelling, Steven need not have worried about his friend's compatibility with Nora's preferred way of living, though his consideration was typical. Craig Dubery was sensitive to the artist's needs, to the 'richness of solitude' that she had reaped after Black's final abandoning of her, and that is referenced by Modjeska and echoed by Steven. Dubery became Nora's friend in those years and later her carer following Steven's death. In conversation with me, he reflected on the vicissitudes of the garden and the vagaries of the weather on any given day and how central it was to Nora's routine.[29] He remembered roses, pin cushions, aquilegias, jonquils, purple and white irises, pots of crocus, bluebells and nasturtiums all equally loved, though white irises were especially prized and the Souvenir de la Malmaison rose reigned supreme. The Souvenir often sat in the mixed bunch beside a single-petalled magenta floribunda rose, and one of the finest musk roses, the apricot Buff Beauty: 'It was big, it was like a tree, near the clothes line in the back corner of the garden', says Dubery. He recalled that Nora valued hyacinths because of the scent. People would bring them to her as gifts. He said there were gardenias, hydrangeas 'like women's bathing caps from the 1960s—the white ones', yellow climbing roses, foxgloves and delphiniums that Steven would have carefully shielded from the wind. Nora's rendering of her dahlias has echoes of the garden at The Cedars that Josephine tended so well. Dubery's observation of Nora's relationship with her chosen subject matter supports Jane Hylton's idea of Nora's still lifes as self portraiture:

> One word that describes it perfectly would be 'calming'—her calming environment was still life. With that, is the understanding of life and how it influences different times of the day. It is a portrait of her without her being in it because it is her environment surrounding her which is definitively her. There is a calmness, a quietness, and a love and a beauty of things that surrounded her. You can lose yourself within your own environment. I think that's probably the way the hurt was dissipated from what happened prior ...[30]

Dubery regularly accompanied Nora to exhibitions and recalls the last he took her to just six months before she died was by Australian surrealist James Gleeson at AGNSW, *James Gleeson: drawings for paintings.* Nora had insisted they went before the exhibition finished and Dubery was surprised that she found the work so appealing:

> We went ... and I was just completely overwhelmed by how fantastic it was even though some of the paintings, to my way of thinking, I could not live with. It was so far removed from the style in which Nora worked that I thought what's the attraction for her? It was the early drawing that James had done—when I saw that, I understood.

Her passion for engaging with her artistic world never faltered. A few months before the Gleeson exhibition, Dubery drove Nora to Canberra, into a 'howling wind and driving rain' to view the Bonnard exhibition at the National Gallery that opened in March 2003. Dubery says Nora smoked all the way there, keen with anticipation to see *Pierre Bonnard: observing nature* whom Nora held in the highest regard for his style and interpretation. It was an eventful visit with Nora's enthusiasm at age ninety-one still irrepressible:

> We nearly got thrown out of the National Gallery. She became so animated and so excited. She had recuperated from a fall in her garden and was using a walking stick ... as soon as we got within cooee of the first painting she was lifting her stick up and saying 'look at that light in his work' and pointing things

> out. The [security] guards were circling and they kept seeing this elderly woman's stick aimed at the paintings—not a good idea—and the guards starting coming towards us. I said Nora you had better cool it ... I've never seen anyone that had the injury she had and still be able to move about. She went from one side of the gallery to the other with such excitement. [31]

Dubery said that the security camera footage of Nora's visit to the National Gallery that day would have made excellent viewing.

Nora had taken another drive to Canberra when she had filled a car with smoke, talked art, and observed the countryside as a potential canvas with every changing view. It was July 1994 when the Australian War Memorial sent a Commonwealth car to deliver her to its exhibition *Through women's eyes: Australian women artists and war 1914–1994.* Of the three women official war artists from World War II that included Stella Bowen and Sybil Craig, Nora was the only one living, aged eighty-three. She had long refused to fly and sending a car was the only way the organisers could convince her to travel. As head of Art, Lola Wilkins curated the exhibition and was keen for Nora to attend the opening. She recruited Peter Duff from the War Memorial's office of Ceremonial Protocol and he was despatched to Hunters Hill in the assistant director's car. Peter Duff has fond memories 'of driving the grand lady' who became his friend and whom he came to call 'Dame Nora' after she received her Order of Australia in 1998. Duff had quipped to Nora it should have been the DBE (Dame Commander of the Most Excellent Order of the British Empire) so he promoted her. When he arrived at The Chalet for the first time he said he could see the grandeur of the home but was moved by the decay he observed, respectfully referring to the state of the place as 'genteel poverty':

> It had just decayed ... there was no maintenance ever done on the house, the paintwork was gone, the windows had gone, it was just unbelievable—but I could see the beauty of the house ... she only lived in a couple of rooms. Upstairs had been closed off for years and that was full of possums and rats and at the back there was this lovely old stable block that was half fallen over covered in bougainvillea and a beautiful overgrown garden.

50. In January 2004 Sydney Living Museums (Historic Houses Trust of NSW) photographed The Chalet for the Caroline Simpson Library & Research Collection shortly after Nora died and before the house was auctioned in its original state. Photographs: Brenton McGeachie.

Her paintings were stacked up against the walls—there was a kitchen area out the back where she sat all the time and off that there was a room that she used as a bedroom—there was the verandah where she would sit and paint—there were broken panes of glass and the wind would whistle through ... and then a little morning room. In the kitchen there was a line of red boxes three deep of Johnnie Walker twenty or so, masses of them lined up. That was her thing—a whiskey and a cigarette.

I don't think she could actually see the decaying part of the house, she couldn't see the finer things of the windows and around outside, the house breaking down. She had this world that she was still in ... she was still looking at this lovely garden—although it was overgrown she was still looking at it and she knew she could sit there and paint something.[32]

Eugene Schlusser commented that The Chalet had not been touched for years. He said the kitchen was never updated and that her studio was 'very rudimentary' with an easel, a lot of books, a couple of reproductions and little comfort: 'Her bedroom was also quite decrepit ... It hadn't been painted for years. She didn't want it painted. She liked the peeling paint, the pattern of peeling paint'.[33] Schlusser believes her observations of nature extended to the elements and the passing of time and the effect this had on her surroundings. The patina on a surface that only comes with time held special appeal.

According to Lola Wilkins, the arrival of Nora in Canberra for the exhibition resulted in increased media attention that escalated after the AWM exhibition. This 'national treasure' who had long been out of sight was not overly pleased with the attention:

> She was wonderful at the opening, very gracious, she was beautiful. She had white hair pulled back with this great big velvet bow and she was absolutely stunning ... the press really starting to pick up on her and it got to the stage when she got fed up. There she was in her eighties and every time it was ANZAC Day or what—everybody wanted to talk to her. All the accolades were happening in her eighties and she was like 'I don't need this anymore'.[34]

It was eighteen months later that Mary Eagle had gone to see Nora at the urging of Kate Nockels in 1996. Nockels might initially be viewed as one of the academics referred to by Barry Pearce that saw Nora as 'a hero of sorts ... perfect for a new generation anxious to correct the historical neglect of women'.[35] Nockels herself initially stated she wanted to address the gender bias issue but found other reasons for Nora's years of obscurity. Whatever Nockels' intentions, her persistence in generating renewed interest in Nora from the art institutions of the nation's capital was significant for the most practical of reasons. Some of the more urgent repairs needed at The Chalet were undertaken, Dubery says, with the proceeds from the sale of *London breakfast* to the National Gallery.

Peter Duff's experience of driving 'Dame Nora' and being invited in to her private world—'we became such great mates within a day'—appears to be a shared one with the few fortunate to have spent time with Nora in her final years:

> I gained so much from just that short visit down to Canberra and back to Sydney, just two people sitting in a car. She was a very determined woman. I think she basically loved life, in the sense that she loved the world, she loved nature—because everything was a painting to her, and she just loved the countryside. Most of the trip down was, 'look at that beautiful thing, Peter', 'look at those hills, look at the colour', she loved the countryside.
>
> You either hit it off with her or you didn't. I think she was the type of person who had so much experience with people and the world, that at her age she was nobody's fool. She knew what was important in life and what wasn't.[36]

Peter Duff drove Nora back to Sydney two days after their departure from her home. She had spent the night with Meredith Stokes in Canberra. Duff said that Nora reported on the drive home that the opening had been successful but that she was nonplussed by the attention from the large number of people who wanted to meet her, though she appreciated the recognition given to her work and other women artists by the War Memorial. For Nora it had always been about the work.

In 1999, Nat Williams, as director of exhibitions at the NLA, was introduced to Nora by Lou Klepac at The Chalet. The men were there to propose the 2000 retrospective to Nora and outline their ideas. Williams' experience of meeting Nora echoes that of many who had gone before him. In conversation with me he described the wilderness of the garden, 'overgrown, green and verdant'. He was led around to the back of the house where visitors entered; the front entry hall and rooms were overtaken by paintings and paraphernalia and all Nora's living was done at the rear, in the small kitchen, sitting room and mostly on the verandah. Nat Williams said he had been warned that she was 'pretty reclusive' and initially, sitting at the kitchen table, she was resistant to the idea of an exhibition. Williams reassured her that it need not be an intrusive process and that she could determine her level of involvement:

> We worked on the show ... we roughed out a check list of what we could afford to borrow and we managed to get most of the things on the list. Most people were happy to lend because they liked Nora and respected her and her family. They saw that the moment to acknowledge her had arrived.[37]

In November 2000 Nora returned to Canberra once more by car to the National Library for the opening of her retrospective. Billowing from the library's façade was a gigantic vertical banner announcing the event. It was printed with an image of Nora's *Self portrait* 1932 (AGNSW), her penetrating gaze looked directly out to the tree-lined boulevard leading to the National Gallery a kilometre away, over the heads of the visitors as they walked up the steps of the library forecourt. Williams remembered the satisfaction after working on the project for over a year and seeing it finally hung: 'It's one thing to work on a project for a long time—to see the list, to read the insurance agreements, the correspondence—but when you finally walk in there ... it's quite overpowering'. Nora arrived in the late afternoon to preview her show before the official opening by Sasha Grishin in the evening. Williams described Nora as being 'visually acute ... with all that pedigree of artistic heritage that goes back to the Renaissance, making the link through her father, through the Pissarro connection and Cézanne, then you think—here is this person who is part of a continuum of art practice of the realistic type—like Vermeer'. That 'realistic type' approach that Williams refers to had precluded Nora from so much for so many years. This was a triumphant moment, she was on show in the capital and she walked through the media preview, taking in the sample of her life's work. With her characteristic reserve she told Williams and Klepac that she would not be participating in any way in the public proceedings in the evening but as Williams explains the moment overtook her:

> That was typical [of her] as you would expect, no self-aggrandisement, she just wanted to be there—and then the extraordinary thing happened—I was standing with her by the stage, she had an adoring crowd, people then saw her and thought it was marvellous. And then she got up and spoke. Everyone, especially Lou, just about fell over. She said how

> wonderful it was to be recognised and how much it meant to her ... After drinks and greetings, we had dinner and she expressed, 'No! I didn't speak'—she was convinced; so total was that sense she had of her own personality, but she did—and she did it well.[38]

This retrospective was the culmination of Lou Klepac's continuous support of Nora and her work since first meeting her in 1986 and regenerating interest in her work with his monograph and the curation of the 1989 exhibition in Sydney. Williams said that everyone involved in the 2000 project had benefited from the experience, that she was finally recognised in her eighties and nineties provoked more interest in her work and as a result that continues to build. In 2019 the NGV joint retrospective of Nora's and her father's work stands as a testament to the place they both hold in Australian art.

In *Morning sun* 1965 (Private collection), five languid white cats stretch on a Persian rug, bathing in sunshine that warms them through glazed window panes, a white saucer off to one side is empty as the larger of the cats licks, satiated, at one paw. There is a hint in the scene that no-one else is at home, that this ritual occurs when the house is quiet and the artist can capture the scene without fear of it being disturbed. During their marriage, Black spent months at a time away for research, attending conferences, and delivering papers. These were the times that allowed Nora freedom to paint though she openly missed her husband and wished he would return. She wrote to that effect to her parents in January 1957 when Black was en route to India and would not return until early May:

> ... with Robert leaving ... I spent it [my birthday] ironing and packing ... Robert should have arrived in Kuala Lumpur by now. He has a long strenuous journey ahead ... he hates flying ... so you can imagine he set out with very mixed feelings, and I was equally upset and reluctant to see him go. I must begin to think of the job I've undertaken to do, the painting of Professor Lambie ... As the finished picture is to

> hang in the Great Hall of the University, I'll have to put my best foot forward.[39]

Putting her best foot forward was something Nora knew how to do. Repeatedly, throughout her life, she shrugged off personal setbacks from different quarters, mostly from men who held the balance of power, starting with her art teachers, her army superiors, to the father who wanted his child's portrait altered before he would pay, to art critics, and to the man she had fought so hard to be with and sacrificed so much for.

Nora Heysen was a woman interrupted. She was interrupted by winning the most prestigious art prize in the country and the expectations that were associated with a win of that kind; by her country's declaration of war that redirected her work out of the public eye; by love and the associated heartache of falling for a married man in the 1940s. She submitted to the expectations placed on a woman as a homemaker in the 1950s and was devastated by the abandonment by a husband she had waited ten years to marry, for a younger woman in a workplace romance. The final assault was her grief over the death of her beloved Steven, from an AIDS-related illness.

Craig Dubery shared the intimacy of Nora's days during her final years. He reflects on her life:

> I think she was permanently interrupted and she was loyal to what needed to be done. The loyalties ran far deeper than a lot of generations that have come since would even consider—seeing things through and sticking to the commitment. Nora also remained true to knowing that there would be a time when she would be able to concentrate back onto the things that gave her the most joy. She had enormous patience. When you befriended her, part of the process was her showing you about the act of being patient with things. It is very easy when you are young to be impatient. You just don't know… but to do something well you need to devote time and not be conscious of that time that you are using to make that possible. I think that that is something that anybody that was close to her learnt. She would impart the importance of it, the patience that you did need to do something of real worth.[40]

51. Nora's appreciation of nature and flowers began as a child and framed her lifelong work. Papers of Nora Heysen, National Library of Australia.

Nora's continuum of flower paintings and still lifes describes and maps her adult life. Firstly, Nora as mistress is on full display in her oil painting *The flower ship* 1944, painted in New Guinea just over a year into her relationship with Black. Hylton describes it as a 'luxuriant still life ... a great mass of tropical blooms overflowing out of the container ... two hibiscus flowers sit side by side amid the chaotic abundance'.[41] Nora stood fast against the army movement order until the painting was finished. She would not be moved on.

Postwar, and ensconced at The Chalet as a married woman, her confidently arranged *Spring flowers* 1956 is clearly defined and bold, steady in a strong, white pottery jug—an errant daffodil bloom sits brightly on the purple-blue tablecloth just fallen from the bunch that sits in front of boldly depicted wood-panelled walls of the house that defines her status. Spring bunches make regular appearances over the following years: *Anemones* 1981 (Private collection) appear in the same jug in front of the same panelling, she has progressed in status and is neither mistress nor wife, for over five years unattached, the flowers are freely formed, their stems twisting and curving naturally and splendidly rendered against a lighter-coloured panelling; a brighter, textured cloth suggesting an ikat weave, hinting at the exotic, covers the pedestal table; a notebook sits with loose leaves protruding, an apple lies outside the bowl, the jug itself has the lustre of nacre. *Freesias* 1985 (Private collection), *Spring bunch* 1992 (Private collection) and *Apples on a chair* 1995 (NHFC) are just a few of the oils that reveal Nora in the manner Hylton and Modjeska suggest. These flowers are Nora.

In late May 2003, Nora returned for what she knew would be a final visit to The Cedars. She was surrounded by family including three surviving siblings, Deirdre, Stefan and Michael, as the coffee was poured and the cake served on the scrubbed pine table that had seen so many family meals served from the time of her childhood. She had been reluctant to make the trip but with encouragement from Allan Campbell, she was persuaded. She had also been reluctant to establish the Nora Heysen Foundation, preferring still to defer to her father as the great artist of the family, but on visiting her old studio she was moved and impressed with what had been accomplished. When she returned to Sydney, she prepared a list of artefacts, paintings and furniture to be returned to Hahndorf to recreate the authentic space that had launched her career in 1926. Her palette from Melba has been returned daubed with over seventy years of accumulated oil paint that had been thoughtfully selected and blended and then applied by a serious hand. The Delft vase that features in her flower compositions is carefully positioned and displayed with her brushes, and her equipment box stamped Captain Nora Heysen leans against a wall as if she might just be back for it one day.

EPILOGUE

After a brief illness, Nora died on 30 December 2003. The Chalet was her setting, the home she never wanted to leave. A young family bought her beloved home at auction and have meticulously restored the original structure. There is a half grand piano in the front room where recitals are given. No doubt Mozart is on the program.

WORKS MENTIONED

Note: page numbers in **bold** indicate illustrations.

LIST OF ILLUSTRATIONS

ABBREVIATIONS OF COLLECTIONS AND SOURCES

AGNSW	Art Gallery of New South Wales, Sydney, NSW
AGSA	Art Gallery of South Australia, Adelaide, SA
AWM	Australian War Memorial, Canberra; acquired under the Official War Art Scheme 1945
HHFC	Hans Heysen Foundation Collection, The Cedars, Hahndorf, SA
HHT	Historic Houses Trust of New South Wales
NERAM	New England Regional Art Museum, Armidale, NSW
NGA	Papers of Nora Heysen, National Gallery of Australia, Canberra, ACT
NHFC	Nora Heysen Foundation Collection, The Cedars, Hahndorf, SA
NLA	Papers of Nora Heysen, National Library of Australia, Canberra, ACT
NPG	National Portrait Gallery, Canberra
QAGOMA	Queensland Art Gallery | Gallery of Modern Art, Brisbane, QLD
SLSA	State Library of South Australia, Adelaide, SA
TMAG	Tasmanian Museum and Art Gallery, Hobart, TAS

IMAGES IN ORDER OF APPEARANCE

1 The Heysen family at The Cedars, early 1930s. Papers of Nora Heysen, NLA, image supplied courtesy of Wakefield Press.

2 Heysen family in the lower paddock at The Cedars. MS10041, NLA.

3 Family picnic in 'Heysen Country'. Manuscripts Collection MS10041, NLA.

4 Freya Heysen in the *stoep* at The Cedars, Ambleside. Photo: Harold Cazneaux. PRG 899/2/11, SLSA.

5 Josephine, Freya and Deidre Heysen in the garden at The Cedars, Ambleside. Photo: Harold Cazneaux. PRG 899/2/12, SLSA.

6 *Hahndorf gums* 1930, study in pencil and wash, Private collection.
7 *A portrait study* 1933, oil on canvas, 86.5 × 66.7 cm. Purchased with funds provided by the Art Foundation of Tasmania, 1986. AG5025, TMAG.
8 *Eggs* 1927, oil on canvas, 36.6 × 52.5 cm, gift of Howard Hinton, 1934. The Howard Hinton Collection, NERAM.
9 *Self portrait* 1934, oil on canvas, 43.1 × 36.3 cm, NPG. Purchased 1999.
10 *Ruth* 1933, oil on canvas, 81.5 × 64.2 cm, AGSA. South Australian Government Grant 1934 © AGSA 0.810.
11 *London breakfast* 1935, oil on canvas, 4.07 × 53.5 cm, NGA. Purchased 1996 © Lou Klepac.
12 *Self portrait* 1938, oil on canvas laid on board, 39.5 × 29.5 cm. Acc. 2011.080. Purchased 2011 with funds from Philip Bacon AM through the Queensland Art Gallery Foundation. Collection: QAGOMA © Lou Klepac. Photo: Natasha Harth, QAGOMA.
13 *Corn cobs* 1938, oil on canvas, 40.5 × 51.3 cm, AGNSW. Purchased 1987 © Lou Klepac. Photo: AGNSW 485.1987.
14 *Spring flowers* 1938, oil on canvas on hardboard, 75.5 × 65.2 cm, AGNSW. Purchased 1938 © AGNSW. Photo: AGNSW, Ray Woodbury 6603.
15 *Mme Elink Schuurman* 1938, oil on canvas, Private collection.
16 *Quinces* 1991, pastel, 44.0 × 56.5 cm, Private collection.
17 Photograph of Nora, Hans and Sallie Heysen, 1934, in Wales, NLA.
18 *Portrait of Evie* 1935, conté crayon on ivory wove paper, 34.0 × 26.0 cm, AGNSW. Gift of Meredith Stokes 2008 © Lou Klepac. Photo: AGNSW, Christopher Snee.
19 Busts of Everton Stokes and Nora Heysen. MS10041, Series 3, Box 23, File 12, Papers of Nora Heysen, NLA.
20 *Down and out in London* 1937 (AGSA), MS1004, NLA.
21 Artist Nora Heysen on 21 January 1939 with her winning Archibald Prize entry. MS10041, Papers of Nora Heysen, NLA. © Fairfax Media, FXJ126604. Photo: Tim Clayton.
22 Nora in dress uniform, Melbourne 1944, 062802, AWM.
23 *Study for Bluey* 1944, charcoal, sanguine crayon on paper, 61.5 × 49.0 cm, ART22663, AWM.

43 *Robert H. Black MD* c.1950, oil on canvas laid on composition board, 78.0 cm × 59.0 cm, NPG. Gift of the artist 1999. Donated through the Australian Government's Cultural Gifts Program.

44 Nora and Jeffrey Smart at The Cedars, c.1940s. NHFC.

45 *Verandah and garden at The Chalet at Hunters Hill, New South Wales, c.1968*, © Wes Stacey, <http://nla.gov.au/nla.obj-151856130>, NLA 09/703.

46 Nora and David Heysen prepare to hang the 1963 Millicent exhibition. NHFC.

47 Steven Coorey in San Francisco. Image courtesy of Craig Dubery.

48 Nora Heysen and *A portrait study* 1933, MS10041, NLA.

49 FXT69379. Eighty-year-old Australian artist Nora Heysen is photographed at her home in Hunters Hill, Sydney, 14 August 1991. FXT69380 (Nora smoking), FXT69379 (Nora seated). Photo: Tim Clayton / Fairfax Media.

50 Sydney Living Museums (Historic Houses Trust of NSW). Photos: Brenton McGeachie, Caroline Simpson Library & Research Collection.

51 Nora Heysen. MS10041, NLA.

NOTES

INTRODUCTION: NORA SPEAKS

1. Nora Heysen interviewed by Eugene Schlusser in *Of art and men: Nora Heysen*, dir. Eugene Schlusser, Seven S Productions 2007 (DVD).
2. Jane Hylton, *Nora Heysen: light and life*, Wakefield Press, 2009, p. 34.
3. Catherine Speck (ed.), *Heysen to Heysen: selected letters of Hans Heysen and Nora Heysen*, NLA, 2011, p. 135.
4. ibid.
5. AWM Series Number AWM 315, Item 206/002/01702, Papers relating to artists: VFX94085 Cpt Heysen, Nora, Miss.
6. Nora Heysen interviewed in Schlusser, *Of art and men.*
7. <https://www.awm.gov.au/wartime/58/friends-sisters-and-pioneers>.
8. <http://bwm.org.au/nurses.php>.
9. <https://www.awm.gov.au/wartime/58/friends-sisters-and-pioneers>.
10. L. Stewart, Museum of Australian Democracy, <http://www.womenaustralia.info/leaders/biogs/WLE0338b.htm>.
11. <http://www.diggerhistory.info/pages-conflicts-periods/ww2/pages-2aif-cmf/awas1.htm>.
12. Speck, *Heysen to Heysen*, p. 136, Nora Heysen letter to her parents, 19 January 1944.
13. Catherine Speck, *Painting ghosts: Australian women artists in wartime*, Thames and Hudson, 2004, p. 131.
14. Speck, *Heysen to Heysen*, pp. 137–138, Nora Heysen letter to her parents, November 1943; Nora Heysen letter to her parents, Sunday (?) 1943.
15. Speck, *Painting ghosts*, p. 131.
16. ibid., p. 132.
17. ibid., p. 128.
18. Speck, *Heysen to Heysen*, p. 140, Nora Heysen letter to her parents, Sunday (?) 1944.
19. Speck, *Painting ghosts*, pp. 128–131.
20. ibid., p. 127.
21. Schlusser, *Of art and men.*

ONE: IN THE NAME OF THE FATHER

1. Colin Thiele, *Heysen of Hahndorf*, Hyde Park Press, 2001, p. 302. Hans Heysen letter to his friend Lionel Lindsay, 19 August 1942.
2. Schlusser, *Of art and men.*
3. Sue Heysen, *Heysen: recollections of the Cedars*, North Adelaide, 1991, p. 4.

4 David Meagher, 'Nora Heysen: a cautious gaze', *The Australian Financial Review Magazine*, 10 November 2000, p. 12.

5 ibid.

6 Lou Klepac interviewed by ALW, Roseville, NSW, 26 October 2017.

7 Meagher, 'Nora Heysen', p. 14.

8 Kate Nockels interviewed by ALW, Batemans Bay, NSW, 13 March 2017. Nockels completed a Master of Letters, Fine Art History, with her thesis 'Hidden from view: Nora Heysen twentieth century Australian artist', ANU, 1997.

9 Nora Heysen interviewed in Schlusser, *Of art and m*en.

10 Meagher, 'Nora Heysen', p. 12.

11 Angus Trumble interviewed by ALW, Canberra, by telephone, 21 March 2017.

12 Thiele, *Heysen of Hahndorf*, pp. 3–13.

13 ibid., pp. 3–9.

14 <http://www.germanaustralia.com/e/why-emi.htm>; <http://www.southaustralianhistory.com.au/hahndorf.htm>.

15 <http://www.germanaustralia.com/e/why-emi.htm>.

16 <http://www.southaustralianhistory.com.au/hahndorf.htm>.

17 Thiele, *Heysen of Hahndorf*, pp. 10–15.

18 ibid., pp. 15–19.

19 ibid., pp. 20–22.

20 ibid., p. 93.

21 ibid., pp. 30–39.

22 ibid., p. 84.

23 ibid., p. 170.

TWO: THE CEDARS

1 Thiele, *Heysen of Hahndorf*, p. 129.

2 ibid., p. 178.

3 ibid., p. 138.

4 Allan Campbell, Curator of The Cedars, suggests that the name was changed during the Winnerah family ownership before the turn of the century. Allan Campbell interview by ALW, Adelaide, by telephone, 29 July 2018.

5 <https://www.artsy.net/gene/ruckenfigur-slash-figure-from-the-back/artworks?for_sale=false&include_medium_filter_in_aggregation=true>.

6 Lou Klepac, *Nora Heysen*, The Beagle Press, Sydney, 1989, p. 16.

7 Thiele, *Heysen of Hahndorf*, p. 289.

8 Sue Heysen, *Heysen: recollections of The Cedars,* p. 8.

9 Thiele, *Heysen of Hahndorf*, p. 297.

10 ibid., p. 312.

11 Papers of Allan Campbell, Papers of Nora Heysen, NHFC.

12 ibid., p. 168.

13 ibid.

14 Hylton, *Nora Heysen*, p. 13.
15 Thiele, p. 217.
16 Thiele, *Heysen of Hahndorf*, p. 226.
17 Schlusser, *Of art and men.*
18 Phyllis McKillup, PhD thesis, 'Four contemporary South Australian women artists', Flinders University of South Australia, Women's Studies Department, 2001, p. 48.
19 Schlusser, *Of art and men.*
20 Klepac, *Nora Heysen*, p. 9.
21 NLA MS ACC 11,155, Papers of Josephine Heysen, Josephine Heysen letter to Jacqueline Whyte, March 1936.
22 Thiele, p. 116. See also <http://www.musee-orsay.fr/en/collections/works-in-focus/painting/commentaire_id/flowers-and-fruit-20516.html?cHash=a008e29012>.
23 Thiele, p. 188.
24 Josephine Heysen letter to Jacqueline Whyte, 20 November (1926?).
25 NLA MS ACC 11.155, Papers of Josephine Heysen, Nora Heysen letter to Jacqueline Whyte, 29 January 1930.
26 Meredith Stokes interviewed by ALW, Lara, Victoria, by telephone, 3 November 2017.
27 NLA MS ACC 11.155 Papers of Josephine Heysen, Josephine Heysen letter to Jacqueline Whyte, day/month undated 1928.
28 Tim Heysen interviewed by ALW, Derrymore, Kalangadoo, South Australia, 18 April 2012.
29 Thiele, *Heysen of Hahndorf*, pp. 170–171.
30 ibid., p. 191.
31 ibid.
32 <https://www.historylearningsite.co.uk/a-history-of-medicine/antibiotics/>.
33 Thiele, *Heysen of Hahndorf*, pp. 192–193.
34 NLA MSACC 11.155, Folders 6 and 7, Papers of Josephine Heysen 1927–1938.
35 ibid., Josephine Heysen letter to Jacqueline Whyte, 3 December 1928.
36 ibid., Josephine Heysen letter to Jacqueline Whyte, Tuesday 22, month (?), 1930.
37 Thiele, *Heysen of Hahndorf*, pp. 225–226.
38 NLA MSACC 11.155, Josephine Heysen letter to Jacqueline Whyte, 3 December 192(?).
39 ibid., Josephine Heysen letter to Jacqueline Whyte, 21 January 193(?).
40 Thiele, *Heysen of Hahndorf*, p. 168.
41 NLA MSACC 11.155, Josephine Heysen letter to Jacqueline Whyte, 2 May 1938.
42 ibid., letter, 15 March 1938.
43 Josephine Heysen Wittenburg interviewed by ALW, Maui, Hawaii, 10 September 2015.

44 NLA MSACC 11.155, Josephine Heysen letter to Jacqueline Whyte, (?) June 1938.
45 Josephine Heysen Wittenburg interviewed by ALW.
46 Meredith Stokes interviewed by ALW.
47 Thiele, *Heysen of Hahndorf*, p. 258
48 Josephine Heysen Wittenburg interviewed by ALW.
49 Papers of Josephine Wittenburg, Maui, Hawaii.
50 Josephine Heysen Wittenburg interviewed by ALW.
51 Peter Heysen interviewed by ALW, Glenelg, South Australia, 23 September 2017.
52 ibid.
53 Peter Heysen interviewed by ALW.
54 Josephine Heysen Wittenburg interviewed by ALW.
55 Meredith Stokes interviewed by ALW.
56 Thiele, *Heysen of Hahndorf*, p. 242.
57 Thiele, *Heysen of Hahndorf*, p. 243.
58 Thiele, *Heysen of Hahndorf*, pp. 248–249.
59 Speck, p. 95. Nora Heysen letter to her parents, Monday (October?) 1938.
60 Nora Heysen interviewed by Eugene Schlusser (dir.) *Hans Heysen recollections*, Seven S Productions, 2007.

THREE: ART SCHOOL, TWO DEALS AND PAINTING HERSELF

1 Kate Nockels interviewed by ALW.
2 Meagher, 'Nora Heysen: a cautious gaze', p. 14.
3 Nora interviewed in Schlusser, *Of art and men*.
4 <http://www.portrait.gov.au/people/sydney-ure-smith-1887>.
5 Nora interviewed in Schlusser, *Of art and men*.
6 Nora Heysen interviewed by Hazel de Berg, (place unspecified), 8 November 1965, <https://nla.gov.au/nla.obj-214420381/listen>.
7 ibid.
8 Nora Heysen interviewed by Heather Rusden, Hunters Hill, NSW, 25 August 1994, <http://nla.gov.au/nla.obj-217201668/listen>.
9 Nora Heysen interviewed by Hazel de Berg.
10 Papers of Allan Campbell, notes from conversations with Nora Heysen at The Chalet, Sydney, 2000.
11 Nora Heysen interviewed by Hazel de Berg.
12 Peter Heysen interviewed by ALW.
13 ibid.
14 Nora Heysen interviewed by Hazel de Berg.
15 Nora Heysen interviewed by Michael Cathcart, *'Arts Today'*, ABC Radio National, 12 January 2001. Cassette recording, NHFC.
16 McKillup, PhD thesis, 'Four contemporary South Australian women artists', p. 48.
17 Meredith Stokes interviewed by ALW.
18 Papers of Allan Campbell.

19 Nora Heysen interviewed in Schlusser, *Of art and men.*
20 Nora Heysen interviewed by Heather Rusden.
21 Klepac, *Nora Heysen*, p. 9.
22 Nora Heysen interviewed by Heather Rusden.
23 Hendrik Kolenberg interviewed in Schlusser, *Of art and men.*
24 Schlusser (dir), *Hans Heysen recollections.*
25 Nora Heysen interviewed by Heather Rusden.
26 Thiele, *Heysen of Hahndorf*, p. 221.
27 Hylton, *Nora Heysen*, p. 16.
28 Nora Heysen interviewed by Mary Eagle, papers of Mary Eagle, sent electronically from Mary Eagle to ALW, 10 May 2017.
29 Jane Hylton interviewed by ALW, Hahndorf, 9 March 2016.
30 Nora Heysen interviewed by Heather Rusden.
31 'An artist's wife' (1935, May 23). *The Sydney Morning Herald* (NSW: 1842–1954), p. 11 (Women's Supplement), <http://nla.gov.au/nla.news-article17146663>.
32 Papers of Allan Campbell.
33 Craig Dubery interviewed by ALW, Sydney, 16 March 2016.
34 NLA MS ACC 11, 155 Nora Heysen letter to Jacqueline Whyte, 4 August 1929.
35 Klepac, *Nora Heysen*, p. 9.
36 Nora Heysen interviewed by Heather Rusden.
37 Thiele, *Heysen of Hahndorf*, p. 221.
38 Nora Heysen interviewed by Michael Cathcart.
39 Anne Gray interviewed by ALW, Lawrence Wilson Art Gallery, UWA, Crawley, 14 November 2017.
40 Frances Spalding, *Vanessa Bell: portrait of the Bloomsbury artist*, Tauris Parke, London, 2016, p. 37.
41 Chris Heysen interviewed by ALW, NGV, 18 September 2017.
42 Anne Gray interviewed by ALW.
43 Meagher, 'Nora Heysen: a cautious gaze', p. 14.
44 Nora Heysen interviewed by Heather Rusden.
45 <https://www.artgallery.nsw.gov.au/collection/works/943/>.
46 Hylton, *Nora Heysen*, p. 18.
47 <https://www.theage.com.au/news/entertainment/arts/heysen-out-of-her-fathers-shadow/2009/08/11/1249756303549.html>.
48 Frances Borzello, *Seeing ourselves: women's self-portraits*, Thames and Hudson, 1998. Frances Borzello visited Australia in December 2001 and delivered a keynote paper at the National Portrait Gallery Symposium 'Portrait and Place' in Hobart.
49 <http://www.portrait.gov.au/magazines/2/personal-politics>.
50 Meagher, 'Nora Heysen', p. 14.
51 <http://splash.abc.net.au/home#!/digibook/1778131/look-within-self-portraiture>.
52 Kate Nockels interviewed by ALW.

53 Papers of Mary Eagle.
54 <http://www.portrait.gov.au/content/trumble-tour-part-7>.
55 Drusilla Modjeska, *Stravinsky's lunch*, Pan Macmilllan, 1999, p. 171.
56 Meagher, 'Nora Heysen', p. 12.
57 Research papers of Jane Hylton, NHFC, *Adelaide Advertiser*, 6 November 2000, p. 89.
58 ibid., <www.canberratimes.com.au>.
59 Lou Klepac interviewed by ALW.
60 Drusilla Modjeska, *Stravinsky's lunch*, p. 173.
61 Hylton, *Nora Heysen*, p. 17.
62 Thiele, *Heysen of Hahndorf*, p. 155.
63 Nora Heysen interviewed by Hazel de Berg.
64 Schlusser, *Of art and men*.
65 Papers of Allan Campbell, notes from conversations with Nora Heysen at The Chalet, Sydney, 2000.
66 Kate Nockels, interviewed by ALW, 13 March 2017, Batemans Bay, NSW.
67 <http://www.smh.com.au/entertainment/art-and-design/secret-society-becomes-open-book-for-its-20th-birthday-20110213-1ary1.html>.
68 Margaret Woodward interviewed in Schlusser, *Of art and men*.
69 Papers of Allan Campbell.
70 Hylton, *Nora Heysen*, p. 20.
71 <https://www.theage.com.au/news/entertainment/arts/heysen-out-of-her-fathers-shadow/2009/08/11/1249756303549.html>.
72 Hylton, *Nora Heysen*, p. 20.
73 ibid., p. 15.
74 Schlusser, *Of art and men*.
75 *The Canberra Times*, 12 November 1997, Papers of Nora Heysen, NLA, Canberra, page number not shown.
76 Nora Heysen, travel diary, 20 March 1934, NHFC.
77 ibid., 1 May 1934.
78 ibid., 16 April 1934.
79 ibid., 5 April 1934.
80 ibid., 19 April 1934.
81 ibid., 20 April 1934.
82 ibid., 28 April 1934.
83 ibid., 2 May 1934.
84 ibid., 4 May 1934.
85 ibid., 11 May 1934.
86 ibid.
87 ibid., 4 June 1934.
88 Nora Heysen, travel diary, 6 June 1934.
89 ibid., 30 May 1934.
90 <http://www.tate.org.uk/art/artworks/epstein-epping-forest-t05760>.

FOUR: TRUTH, ART AND HITLER

1 Thiele, *Heysen of Hahndorf*, p. 312.
2 Nora Heysen interviewed in Schlusser, *Of art and men*.
3 <http://www.historic-uk.com/CultureUK/Bright-Young-Things/>.
4 <http://www.iwm.org.uk/history/how-britain-hoped-to-avoid-war-with-germany-in-the-1930s>.
5 <https://www.communist-party.org.uk/history/262-1930-36-daily-worker-and-great-depression.html>; <www.holocaustresearchproject.org/holoprelude/mosley.html>.
6 <https://www.wcml.org.uk/our-collections/protest-politics-and-campaigning-for-change/unemployment/national-unemployed-workers-movement/>.
7 F.M.L Thompson (ed.), *The Cambridge social history of Britain 1750–1950. Volume 1: regions and communities*, Cambridge University Press, 1990, p. 530.
8 Schlusser, *Of art and men*.
9 Thiele, *Heysen of Hahndorf*, p. 297.
10 <http://www.metmuseum.org/toah/hd/bfpn/hd_bfpn.htm>.
11 <https://www.tate.org.uk/art/art-terms/m/modernism>.
12 ibid.
13 Jane Hylton and John Neylon, *Hans Heysen: into the light*, Wakefield Press, 2008, pp. 18–19.
14 Thiele, *Heysen of Hahndorf*, p. 307.
15 Nora Heysen, travel diary, 7 June 1934.
16 <http://www.liverpoolmuseums.org.uk/walker/about/>.
17 Nora Heysen, travel diary, 7 June 1934.
18 Thiele, *Heysen of Hahndorf*, p. 231.
19 Nora Heysen, travel diary, 7 June 1934.
20 Thiele, *Heysen of Hahndorf*, p. 231.
21 Nockels, 'Hidden from view: Nora Heysen twentieth century Australian artist', p. 23.
22 Nora Heysen, travel diary, 22 July 1934.
23 Thiele, *Heysen of Hahndorf*, p. 233.
24 Nora Heysen, travel diary, 24 July 1934.
25 Lou Klepac, *Hans Heysen*, The Beagle Press, 2016, p. 11.
26 Nora Heysen, travel diary, 24 July 1934.
27 ibid., 28 July 1934.
28 <https://www.historylearningsite.co.uk/nazi-germany/the-night-of-the-long-knives>.
29 Thiele, *Heysen of Hahndorf*, p. 231.
30 Nora Heysen, travel diary, 25 July 1934.
31 Nora Heysen, travel diary, 6 July 1934.
32 ibid., 13 July 1934.

33 Josephine Heysen postcard to Max Williams, September 1934, private collection of Josephine Heysen Wittenburg, Hawaii.
34 <https://rarehistoricalphotos.com/nazi-rally-cathedral-light-c-1937/>.
35 Josephine Heysen postcard to Max Williams, September 1934, private collection of Josephine Heysen Wittenburg, Hawaii.
36 Mary Eagle and John Jones, *A story of Australian painting*, Macmillan, 1994, pp. 146–147.
37 <http://www.ngv.vic.gov.au/essay/the-lost-art-of-federation-australias-quest-for-modernism/>.
38 Eagle and Jones, *A story of Australian painting*, p. 146.
39 <http://www.friendsofbanyule.org/about-banyule/the-arts.aspx>.
40 <http://www.ngv.vic.gov.au/essay/the-lost-art-of-federation-australias-quest-for-modernism/>.
41 Thiele, *Heysen of Hahndorf*, p. 96.
42 ibid., p. 302.
43 ibid., p. 310.
44 ibid., p. 96.
45 Thiele, *Heysen of Hahndorf*, p. 307. Hans Heysen letter to Sydney Ure Smith, 20 November 1934.
46 <http://www.ngv.vic.gov.au/essay/the-lost-art-of-federation-australias-quest-for-modernism/>.
47 Thiele, *Heysen of Hahndorf*, pp. 306–307. Letter to Sydney Ure Smith, 30 November 1934.
48 Hans Heysen, 'Some notes on art with special reference to Australian landscape painting in Australia', *Art in Australia,* 15 June 1932, p. 18.
49 Thiele, *Heysen of Hahndorf*, p. 307. Hans Heysen letter to Sydney Ure Smith, 20 November 1934.
50 Eagle and Jones, *A story of Australian painting*, p. 147.
51 <https://www.artgallery.nsw.gov.au/collection/artists/de-maistre-roy/>.
52 David Marr, *Patrick White: a life*, Random House, Sydney, 1991, p. 148.
53 <https://www.artgallery.nsw.gov.au/collection/artists/de-maistre-roy/>.
54 Speck, *Heysen to Heysen*, p. 76. Nora Heysen letter to her parents, 14 April 1937.
55 ibid., p. 145.
56 ibid., p. 149.
57 Ashleigh Wilson, *Brett Whiteley: art, life and the other thing*, The Text Publishing Company, 2016, p. 182, quoting Patrick White letter to Margery Williams, 21 June 1970. In David Marr (ed.), *Patrick White Letter*s ,Vintage, 1996.
58 NLA MS 1004, Series 5, Box 34, Papers of Nora Heysen, NLA, Canberra.
59 Meredith Stokes interviewed by ALW.
60 Ashleigh Wilson, *Brett Whiteley: art, life and the other thing*, pp. 72–73.
61 Marr, *Patrick White*, p. 150.
62 Nora Heysen, travel diary, 2 August 1934.
63 ibid., 4 August 1934.

64 ibid., 21 August 1934.
65 ibid., 30 July 1934.
66 ibid., 6 September 1934.
67 Thiele, *Heysen of Hahndorf*, pp. 235–236.

FIVE: PISSARRO, EVIE AND THOSE OTHER MEN

1 Frances Borzello, *A world of our own: women as artists since the Renaissance*, Watson-Guptill Publications, 2000, p. 174.
2 Speck, *Heysen to Heysen*, p. 74, Nora Heysen in a letter to her parents, 19 February 1937, after having her work dismissed by Sir Charles Holmes, Director of the National Gallery, London.
3 Nora Heysen interviewed by Mary Eagle, October 1996, papers of Mary Eagle.
4 Janine Burke, *Australian women artists 1840–1940*, Greenhouse Publications, 1980, pp. 37–41.
5 <https://www.bl.uk/romantics-and-victorians/articles/daughters-of-decadence-the-new-woman-in-the-victorian-fin-de-siecle>.
6 Hylton, Nora Heysen, p. 97.
7 Speck, *Heysen to Heysen*, p. 62. Hans Heysen letter to Nora Heysen, 19 July 1936.
8 Nora Heysen interviewed by Mary Eagle, October 1996, papers of Mary Eagle.
9 ibid.
10 ibid.
11 <http://www.smh.com.au/articles/2004/01/05/1073267962306.html>.
12 Papers of Allan Campbell.
13 Meagher, 'Nora Heysen: a cautious gaze', p. 12.
14 Meredith Stokes interviewed by ALW.
15 <https://dictionaryofsydney.org/entry/lesbians>.
16 Speck, *Heysen to Heysen*, p. 34, Nora Heysen letter to her parents, 21 March 1935.
17 Hylton, Nora Heysen, p. 22.
18 Speck, *Heysen to Heysen*, p. 31, Hans Heysen letter to Nora Heysen, 18 February 1935.
19 ibid., p. 33, Nora Heysen letter to her parents, 20 March 1935.
20 ibid., p. 34, Nora Heysen letter to her parents, 21 March 1935.
21 Kate Nockels interviewed by ALW.
22 Meredith Stokes interviewed by ALW.
23 MS10041 Series 1.6 Box 13, Folder 84, Papers of Nora Heysen, Everton Stokes to Nora Heysen, 14 October 1934.
24 Meredith Stokes interviewed by ALW.
25 Papers of Mary Eagle.
26 MS10041 Series 1.6 Box 13, Folder 84, Papers of Nora Heysen, Everton Stokes letter to Nora Heysen, 14 October 1934.
27 Klepac, *Nora Heysen*, p. 10.

28 MS10041 Series 1.6 Box 13, Folder 84, Papers of Nora Heysen, Everton Stokes letter to Nora Heysen, 14 October 1934.
29 ibid., Everton Stokes letter to Nora Heysen, 25 March 1934.
30 ibid., 23 April 1934.
31 Nora Heysen, travel diary, 15 May 1934.
32 MS10041 Series 1.6 Box 13, Folder 84, Papers of Nora Heysen, Everton Stokes letter to Nora Heysen, 11 May 1934.
33 Speck, *Heysen to Heysen*, p. 28.
34 ibid., pp. 34–35. Nora Heysen letter to her parents, 28 March 1935.
35 Nora Heysen interviewed by Heather Rusden.
36 Meredith Stokes interviewed by ALW.
37 <http://www.tate.org.uk/art/research-publications/camden-town-group/lucien-pissarro-r1105344>.
38 <https://www.pissarro.art/artistdetails/231909/orovida-camille-pissarro>.
39 Speck, *Heysen to Heysen*, p. 36, Nora Heysen letter to her parents, 5 May 1935.
40 ibid., p. 48, Nora Heysen letter to her parents, 30 October 1935.
41 Hylton, *Nora Heysen*, p. 26; and Speck, *Heysen to Heysen*, p. 51.
42 Schlusser, *Of art and men.*
43 <http://www.camillepissarro.org/camille-pissarro-quotes.jsp>.
44 Speck, *Heysen to Heysen*, p. 48, Nora Heysen letter to her parents, 30 October 1935.
45 ibid., p. 51. Nora Heysen letter to her parents, 10 December 1935.
46 Schlusser, *Of art and men.*
47 ibid.
48 Nora Heysen interviewed by Heather Rusden.
49 See Borzello for a discussion of the barriers women faced, *Seeing ourselves* and *A world of our own*; also Janine Burke, *Australian women artists 1840–1940.*
50 See Hylton, *Nora Heysen,* p. 30 for an example of a student bust of Nora Heysen by Everton Stokes.
51 Meredith Stokes interviewed by ALW.
52 Speck, *Heysen to Heysen*, p. 38. Nora Heysen letter to her parents, 10 June 1935.
53 ibid., p. 56. Nora Heysen letter to her parents, 22 April 1966.
54 ibid., p. 58. Nora Heysen letter to her parents, 3 June 1936.
55 Hylton, Nora Heysen, p. 26.
56 NGA submission for acquisition dated 21 November 1996, papers of Mary Eagle.
57 Nora Heysen interviewed by Mary Eagle, papers of Mary Eagle.
58 Speck, *Heysen to Heysen*, p. 41, Nora Heysen letter to her parents, 10 August 1935.
59 <http://www.dailymail.co.uk/femail/article-3353558/Can-save-beloved-Jaeger-British-brand-struggling-trying-recover.html>.

60 Speck, *Heysen to Heysen*, pp. 41–42, Nora Heysen letter to her parents, 10 August 1935.
61 Hylton, *Nora Heysen,* p. 25.
62 NGA submission for acquisition dated 21 November 1996, papers of Mary Eagle.
63 Mary Eagle, transcription of handwritten notes, papers of Mary Eagle.
64 Speck, *Heysen to Heysen*, p. 45, Nora Heysen letter to her parents, 25 September 1935.
65 NGA submission for acquisition, papers of Mary Eagle.
66 Anne Gray, *Face: Australian portraits 1880–1960*, NGA, Canberra, 2010.
67 <https://artsearch.nga.gov.au/detail.cfm?irn=10533>.
68 Speck, *Heysen to Heysen*, p. 51.
69 McKillup, PhD thesis, p. 53.
70 ibid., p. 43.
71 Hylton, *Nora Heysen,* p. 24.
72 Speck, *Heysen to Heysen,* p. 43, Nora Heysen letter to her parents, 6 September 1935.
73 ibid., p. 51, Nora Heysen letter to her parents, 12 January 1936.
74 ibid., Nora Heysen letter to her parents, 20 January 1936.
75 ibid., p. 53, Nora Heysen letter to her parents, 23 January 1936.
76 ibid., p. 53, Hans Heysen letter to Nora Heysen, 29 January 1936.
77 ibid., p. 35, Nora Heysen letter to her parents, 30 April 1935.
78 ibid., p. 37. Hans Heysen to Nora Heysen, 6 June 1936.
79 Frances Borzello, *A world of our own*, pp. 167–170.
80 ibid., pp. 170–171.
81 ibid., p. 173.
82 Speck, *Heysen to Heysen,* p. 27. Nora Heysen letter to her parents, 21 October 1934.
83 Borzello, *A world of our own*, pp. 174–176.
84 Janine Burke, *Australian women artists 1840–1940*, p. 74.
85 Borzello, *A world of our own* p. 176.
86 ibid. p. 174.
87 Nora Heysen interviewed by Hazel de Berg.
88 Nockels, p. 27.
89 ibid.
90 Spalding, *Vanessa Bell*, p. 36.
91 NLA MS 5073 Box 18 Folder 146 n.d. Papers of Hans Heysen, Nora Heysen letter to her parents, 1934.
92 <http://www.artbiogs.co.uk/2/societies/new-english-art-club>.
93 Schlusser, *Of art and men.*
94 NLA MS No. 5073, series 2, folder 146, Nora Heysen to her parents, 19 May 1935.
95 Hylton, *Nora Heysen*, p. 28.
96 Schlusser, *Of art and men.*
97 Hylton, *Nora Heysen,* p. 28.

98 Schlusser, *Of art and men.*
99 Speck, *Heysen to Heysen*, p. 70, Nora Heysen letter to her parents, 30 November 1936.
100 Spalding, *Vanessa Bell*, p. 36.
101 Schlusser, *Of art and men.*
102 ibid.
103 Rosemary Heysen, MA Art History thesis, *Nora Heysen in the Pacific 1953–1962,* University of Adelaide, July 2006, biography.
104 Thiele, *Heysen of Hahndorf*, p. 68.
105 Speck, *Heysen to Heysen*, p. 81, Hans Heysen letter to Nora Heysen, 25 July 1937.
106 Speck, *Heysen to Heysen*, p. 82, Nora Heysen letter to her parents, 27 July 1937.
107 Nora Heysen interviewed by Heather Rusden.
108 Speck, p. 77, Nora Heysen letter to her parents, 4 May 1937.
109 Speck, *Heysen to Heysen*, p. 80, Nora Heysen letter to her parents, June(?) 1937.
110 Schlusser, *Of art and men.*
111 Hylton, *Nora Heysen*, p. 92.

SIX: NORA TAKES HER LEAVE

1 McKillup, PhD thesis, p. 59.
2 Speck, *Heysen to Heysen*, p. 85, Nora Heysen letter to her parents, 19 August 1937.
3 <http://www.bbc.co.uk/history/british/timeline/worldwars_timeline_noflash.shtml>.
4 Speck, *Heysen to Heysen*, p. 54, Nora Heysen letter to her parents, 30 January 1936.
5 ibid., p.72, Nora Heysen letter to her parents, 4 January 1937.
6 ibid., p. 70, Nora Heysen letter to her parents, 6 December 1936.
7 ibid.
8 <http://culturedarm.com/1937-paris-international-exposition/>.
9 <http://www.arthurchandler.com/paris-1937-exposition/>.
10 ibid.
11 <http://culturedarm.com/1937-paris-international-exposition/>.
12 Speck, p. 76.
13 <http://culturedarm.com/1937-paris-international-exposition/>.
14 <http://www.menziescollection.esrc.unimelb.edu.au/biogs/E000045b.htm>.
15 Speck, *Heysen to Heysen,* p. 58, Nora Heysen letter to her parents, 19 May 1936.
16 ibid., p. 67, Hans Heysen letter to Nora Heysen, 3 November 1936.
17 <http://www.contemporaryartsociety.org.au/home/history>.
18 Nockels, p. 46.
19 <http://www.menziescollection.esrc.unimelb.edu.au/biogs/E000045b.htm>.

20 <http://handle.slv.vic.gov.au/10381/139310>.
21 Nockels, p. 50.
22 Kate Nockels interviewed by ALW.
23 McKillup, PhD thesis, p. 45.
24 ibid., p. 50.
25 Kate Nockels interviewed by ALW.
26 Meredith Stokes interviewed by ALW.
27 McKillup, PhD thesis, p. 84.
28 Klepac, *Nora Heysen*, p. 13.
29 Lou Klepac, *Nora Heysen*, catalogue introduction, NLA, 2000, p. 4.
30 Kate Nockels interviewed by ALW.
31 Schlusser, *Of art and men*.
32 Hylton, *Nora Heysen*, p. 31.
33 Nockels, p. 47.
34 Klepac, *Nora Heysen*, p. 7.
35 ibid., p. 14.
36 Hylton, p. 31.
37 Klepac, *Nora Heysen*, p. 13.
38 Kate Nockels interviewed by ALW.
39 Nora Heysen interviewed by Heather Rusden.
40 <http://adb.anu.edu.au/biography/meldrum-duncan-max-7553>.
41 First published in 1932, *A curate in Bohemia* was Norman Lindsay's first novel, a comedy of manners and sex set in Melbourne cafe society of the 1890s.
42 Nora Heysen interviewed by Hazel de Berg.
43 <http://www.lwgallery.uwa.edu.au/collections/ccwa>.
44 Meredith Stokes interviewed by ALW.
45 Klepac, *Nora Heysen*, p. 18.
46 Angela Goddard interviewed by ALW, Canberra, by telephone, 2 June 2017.
47 <https://artsearch.nga.gov.au/Detail.cfm?IRN=204031>.
48 <https://nga.gov.au/AboutUs/Development/PDF/Masterpieces2011.pdf>.
49 <https://artsearch.nga.gov.au/Detail.cfm?IRN=204031>.
50 ibid., Article 2.
51 <https://www.nla.gov.au/blogs/behind-the-scenes/2017/06/16/a-glimpse-into-the-heysen-archive>.
52 Hylton, *Nora Heysen*, p. 25.
53 <https://www.sothebysaustralia.com.au/list/AU0813B/78>.
54 <https://www.menziesartbrands.com/items/interior-josephine-london>.
55 <http://www.adelaidenow.com.au/news/south-australia/nora-heysen-painting-unearthed-after-50-years-fetches-50500-at-auction-in-adelaide/news-story/fbd2bfbb371092f888acfcfc8b6e5acb>.
56 Thiele, *Heysen of Hahndorf*, p. 221.
57 Nora Heysen interviewed by Heather Rusden.

SEVEN: MAD MAX, MARY AND THE ARCHIBALD

1 <http://www.trove.nla.gov.au/newspaper/article/98237346>.
2 Nora Heysen, interviewed in Schlusser, *Of art and men.*
3 <https://aso.gov.au/titles/home-movies/australias-150th-anniversary/clip2/>.
4 <https://dictionaryofsydney.org/entry/day_of_mourning_1938>.
5 <https://theconversation.com/capturing-the-lived-history-of-the-aborigines-protection-board-while-we-still-can-46259>.
6 <www.naa.gov.au/collection/fact-sheets/fs150.aspx>.
7 <https://www.dailytelegraph.com.au/news/black-sunday-1938-hundreds-washed-out-to-sea-on-bondi-beach-as-freak-waves-kill-five-injure-dozens/news-story/2f584af7365abc298d039d42e5f2ddf1>.
8 <http://athletics.com.au/About-Us/Hall-of-Fame/Decima-Norman>.
9 <http://www.websterworld.com/websterworld/aust/1/1938213.html>.
10 <http://primeministers.naa.gov.au/primeministers/menzies/before-office.aspx>.
11 <https://www.awm.gov.au/articles/encyclopedia/prime_ministers/menzies>.
12 Speck, *Heysen to Heysen,* p. 87.
13 <http://adb.anu.edu.au/biography/boxall-arthur-dauvergne-5317>.
14 Speck, *Heysen to Heysen*, pp. 88–89, Nora Heysen letter to her parents, 15 (June?) 1938.
15 ibid., p. 90, Nora Heysen letter to her parents, 21 June 1938.
16 ibid., p. 91, Nora Heysen letter to her parents, 14 July 1938.
17 ibid., p. 88.
18 ibid., p. 91, Nora Heysen letter to her parents, 5 (August ?) 1938.
19 McKillup, PhD thesis, p. 58.
20 Speck, *Heysen to Heysen*, p. 96, Hans Heysen letter to Nora Heysen, 20 November 1938.
21 ibid., p. 95, Nora Heysen letter to her parents, Tuesday (November?) 1938.
22 ibid., p. 89, Nora Heysen letter to her parents, Wednesday 15 (June?) 1938.
23 ibid., p. 99, Nora Heysen letter to her parents, 7 December 1938.
24 ibid., p. 103, Nora Heysen letter to her parents, 26 February 1939.
25 Scott Bevan, *Bill: the life of William Dobell*, Simon and Schuster, 2014, pp. 84–85.
26 Speck, *Heysen to Heysen*, p. 92, Nora Heysen letter to her parents, 10 August 1938.
27 ibid., p. 106, Nora Heysen letter to her parents, 2 May 1939.
28 ibid., p. 91, Nora Heysen letter to her parents, 14 July 1938.
29 ibid., p. 94, Nora Heysen letter to her parents, 11 September 1938.
30 Meredith Stokes interviewed by ALW.
31 ibid., p. 26.
32 <http://adb.anu.edu.au/biography/longstaff-sir-john-campbell-7230>.
33 <https://www.artgallery.nsw.gov.au/prizes/archibald/history/who-was-jf-archibald/>.
34 <http://adb.anu.edu.au/biography/smith-sydney-george-ure-8485>.

35 Klepac, *Nora Heysen,* p. 14.
36 ibid.
37 Jeffrey Smart, interviewed by ALW, La Posticcia Nuova, Pieve a Presciano, Italy,
17 November 2012.
38 Speck, *Heysen to Heysen*, p. 25.
39 <http://adb.anu.edu.au/biography/smith-sydney-george-ure-8485>.
40 ibid.
41 <http://trove.nla.gov.au/newspaper/article/64308970>.
42 <http://adb.anu.edu.au/biography/smith-sydney-george-ure-8485>.
43 ibid.
44 Speck, *Heysen to Heysen*, p. 91, Nora Heysen letter to her parents, 14 July 1938.
45 ibid., p. 92, Nora Heysen letter to her parents, 10 August 1938.
46 ibid., p. 94, Nora Heysen letter to her parents, 5 September 1938.
47 Hylton, *Nora Heysen*, p. 31.
48 ibid. See also <https://www.smh.com.au/articles/2003/12/30/1072546533012.html>.
49 Hylton, *Nora Heysen*, p. 31.
50 Speck, *Heysen to Heysen*, p. 96, Nora Heysen letter to her parents, (?) (November?) 1938.
51 ibid., p. 101, Nora Heysen letter to her parents, (?) January 1939.
52 ibid.
53 Hylton, *Nora Heysen*, p. 31.
54 Kate Nockels interviewed by ALW, Batemans Bay, NSW, 13 March 2017.
55 Nora Heysen interviewed in Schlusser, *Of art and men.*
56 <http://nla.gov.au/nla.news-article55464841>.
57 Craig Dubery interviewed by ALW, Sydney, September 2012.
58 <http://www.trove.nla.gov.au/newspaper/article/98237346>.
59 Speck, *Heysen to Heysen,* p. 101, Nora Heysen letter to her parents, (?) January 1939.
60 Nora Heysen, interviewed in Schlusser, *Of art and men.*
61 Speck, *Heysen to Heysen,* p. 101, Nora Heysen letter to her parents, (?) January 1939.
62 ibid., p. 108, Nora Heysen letter to her parents, 13 June 1939.
63 Margaret Woodward interviewed in Schlusser, *Of art and men.*
64 Hylton, *Nora Heysen*, p. 33.
65 Nat Williams, interviewed by ALW, 27 March 2015.
66 Speck, *Heysen to Heysen,* p. 102; Nora Heysen letter to her parents, 29 January 1939.
67 Schlusser, *Of art and men.*
68 Speck, *Heysen to Heysen*, p. 110, Nora Heysen letter to her parents, 14 August 1939.
69 ibid., p. 111, Nora Heysen letter to her parents, 25 August 1939.
70 ibid., p. 111, Nora Heysen letter to her parents, 11 September 1939(?).

71 ibid., p. 114, Nora Heysen letter to her parents, 28 October 1939.
72 Speck, *Heysen to Heysen*, p. 115, Nora Heysen letter to her parents, 1939.
73 ibid., p. 115, Nora Heysen letter to her parents, 24 November 1939.
74 ibid., p. 118, Nora Heysen letter to her parents, Tuesday [April?] 1940.
75 ibid., p. 115, Nora Heysen letter to her parents, [November/December?] 1939; p. 118, Nora Heysen letter to her parents, Tuesday [April?] 1940; p. 119, Nora Heysen letter to her parents, Monday [April/May?] 1940.
76 ibid., p. 122, Nora Heysen letter to her parents, [August/September?] 1940.
77 ibid., p. 125, Nora Heysen letter to her parents, [?] Tuesday [October?] 1940.
78 <https://trove.nla.gov.au/newspaper/article/17702286.
79 ibid.
80 Speck, *Heysen to Heysen*, p. 124, Nora Heysen letter to her parents, 5 October 1940.
81 ibid., p. 112, Nora Heysen letter to her parents, 1 October 1939.
82 ibid., p. 120, Nora Heysen letter to her parents, (?) (May?) 1940.
83 ibid., Nora Heysen letter to her parents, (?) 1940.
84 Meredith Stokes interviewed by ALW.
85 Speck, *Heysen to Heysen*, p. 120, Nora Heysen letter to her parents, (?) 1940.
86 ibid., p. 126, Nora Heysen letter to her parents, 18 July 1941.
87 <https://www.theage.com.au/entertainment/art-and-design/heysen-out-of-her-fathers-shadow-20090812-ge81do.html>.
88 Hylton, *Nora Heysen*, p. 33.
89 <http://www.hamiltongallery.org/collection/detail.asp?Artist_LastName=h&Artist_Name=Nora+Heysen&AccNumber=0817>.
90 ibid.
91 Hylton, *Nora Heysen*, p. 34.
92 Speck, *Heysen to Heysen*; p. 131, Nora Heysen letter to her parents, 16 March 1942.
93 Nora Heysen, interviewed in Schlusser, *Of art and men*.

EIGHT: WAR AND LOVE

1 Nora Heysen, interviewed in Schlusser, *Of art and men*.
2 <https://www.warhistoryonline.com/world-war-ii/world-war-twos-long-struggle-new-guinea.html>.
3 <http://ajrp.awm.gov.au/ajrp/remember.nsf/Web-Printer/58EBD6D993E15CE8CA256D05002671FD?OpenDocument>.
4 ibid.; <https://www.awm.gov.au/articles/blog/remembering-war-new-guinea>.
5 ibid.
6 ibid.
7 Thiele, *Heysen of Hahndorf*, p. 164.
8 ibid., p. 154.
9 ibid., p. 162.
10 Klepac, *Hans Heysen*, p. 120.

11 Thiele, *Heysen of Hahndorf*, p. 163.
12 Catherine Speck, 'Nora Heysen: a German-Australian success story', in Monteith, P. (ed), *The German presence in South Australia*, Wakefield Press, 2009.
13 Thiele, *Heysen of Hahndorf*, p. 164.
14 <http://www.abc.net.au/news/2017-03-05/hans-heysen-accused-of-war-time-treachery/8326096>.
15 Trevor Schaefer, 'The Treatment of Germans in Australia, 1914–1924', honours degree thesis, Department of History, University of Adelaide, 1982, p. 28.
16 <http://www.abc.net.au/news/2017-03-05/hans-heysen-accused-of-war-time-treachery/8326096>.
17 Thiele, *Heysen of Hahndorf*, p. 164.
18 ibid., p. 166.
19 ibid., p. 165.
20 ibid., p. 183.
21 Craig Dubery, interviewed by ALW, Sydney, 2012.
22 McKillup, PhD thesis, p. 65.
23 Catherine Speck, *Beyond the battlefield: women artists of the two world wars*, Reaktion Books, 2014, p. 112.
24 Speck, 'Nora Heysen: a German-Australian success story'.
25 Hylton, *Nora Heysen*, p. 34.
26 <http://adb.anu.edu.au/biography/mccubbin-louis-frederick-7329>.
27 McKillup, PhD thesis, p. 59.
28 <http://adb.anu.edu.au/biography/mccubbin-frederick-fred-7328>.
29 <http://adb.anu.edu.au/biography/mccubbin-louis-frederick-7329>.
30 Speck, *Beyond the battlefield*, p. 113.
31 McKillup, PhD thesis, p. 62.
32 ibid., p. 59.
33 ibid., pp. 61–64.
34 Speck, 'Nora Heysen: a German-Australian success story'.
35 Nora Heysen, interviewed in Schlusser, *Of art and men*.
36 Margaret Woodward, interviewed in Schlusser, *Of art and men*.
37 Nora Heysen, interviewed in Schlusser, *Of art and men*.
38 NLA MS 1004, Series 5, Box 34, Papers of Nora Heysen, cutting from *The Australian*, 13 March 1989, p. (?).
39 McKillup, p. 65.
40 Speck, *Heysen to Heysen*, p. 139, Nora Heysen letter to her parents, (?) January 1944.
41 ibid., p. 135, Nora Heysen letter to her parents, 12 October 1943.
42 McKillup, p. 60.
43 ibid.
44 Speck, *Heysen to Heysen*, p. 140. Nora Heysen letter to her parents, Menzies Hotel, Melbourne, Wednesday, 19 January 1944.

45 ibid., p. 138. Nora Heysen letter to her parents, (?) November 1943.
46 ibid., p. 142, Nora Heysen letter to her parents, (?) (March) 1944.
47 Speck, 'Nora Heysen: a German-Australian success story'.
48 Speck, *Painting ghosts*, p. 125.
49 McKillup, p. 66.
50 ibid., p. 142, Nora Heysen letter to her parents, 4 April 1944.
51 ibid., p. 143, Nora Heysen letter to her parents, 8 April 1944.
52 ibid.
53 Speck, 'Nora Heysen: a German-Australian success story'.
54 Nora Heysen, interviewed in Schlusser, *Of art and men.*
55 Speck, *Heysen to Heysen,* p. 145, Nora Heysen letter to her parents, 1 May 1944.
56 Frank Fenner, 'Fairley, Sir Neil Hamilton (1891–1966)', *Australian dictionary of biography*, National Centre for Biography, Australian National University, <http://adb.anu.edu.au/biography/fairley-sir-neil-hamilton-10145> published first in hard copy 1966.
57 Speck, *Heysen to Heysen*, p. 171, Nora Heysen letter to her parents, (?) (November?) 1945.
58 Fenner, 'Fairley, Sir Neil Hamilton (1891–1966)'.
59 Adele Shelton Smith, 'Volunteers help experts to fight dreaded malaria', *The Australian Women's Weekly*, 1 July 1944, p. 12,<https://trove.nla.gov.au/newspaper/article/47218545?browse=ndp%3Abrowse%2Ftitle%2FA%2Ftitle%2F112%2F1944%2F07%2F01%2Fpage%2F4727433%2Farticle%2F47218545>.
60 Yvonne Cossart, 'Black, Robert Hughes (1917–1988)', *Australian dictionary of biography*, National Centre of Biography, ANU, <http://adb.anu.edu.au/biography/black-robert-hughes-12217/text21907> published first in hard copy 2007.
61 NLA MS 10041 Series 1, Subseries 1.2 File 7, Papers of Nora Heysen, letter from QX36074 Captain R.H. Black to Nora Heysen, 3 February 1945 (Cairns?).
62 Speck, *Heysen to Heysen*, p. 170, Nora Heysen letter to her parents (?) (November) 1945.
63 ibid., p. 143, Nora Heysen letter to her parents, 8 April 1944.
64 ibid., p. 144, Nora Heysen letter to her parents, 17 April 1944.
65 ibid., p. 148, Nora Heysen letter to her parents, 8 May 1944.
66 ibid., p. 144, Nora Heysen letter to her parents, 17 April 1944.
67 ibid., p. 147, Nora Heysen letter to her parents, 8 May 1944.
68 ibid., p. 149, Nora Heysen letter to her parents, 30 May 1944.
69 Speck, *Painting ghosts*, p. 134.
70 ibid., p. 135.
71 Speck, *Heysen to Heysen*, p. 152, Nora Heysen letter to her parents, 29 July 1944.
72 McKillup, p. 68.

73 Speck, *Painting ghosts*, pp. 134–135.
74 Speck, *Heysen to Heysen*, p. 152.
75 NLA MS 10041 Series 1, Subseries 1.2 File 7, Papers of Nora Heysen, letter from QX36074 Captain R.H. Black to Nora Heysen, Sydney, 18 August 1944.
76 McKillup, p. 69.
77 AWM PR89/023 Memoir of Flying Sister Beryl Chandler RAAFNS 502237 First Medical Air Evacuation Unit, p. 54, 1977–1978. Collection of the AWM, Canberra.
78 Speck, *Heysen to Heysen*, p. 149, Nora Heysen letter to her parents, 30 May 1944.
79 ibid., p. 150, Nora Heysen letter to her parents, 29 June 1944.
80 Hylton, *Nora Heysen*, p. 38.
81 Nora Heysen interviewed by Michael Cathcart.
82 Schlusser, *Of art and men*.
83 Papers of Nora Heysen, NHFC, letter from Robert Black to Nora Heysen, 13 August 1944.
84 William Dobell was the controversial winner of the 1943 Archibald Prize. The missing portrait referred to by Black is of artist Joshua Smith and was the subject of a court case that argued it was caricature as opposed to portrait. The case was dismissed. *The Sydney Morning Herald* report is on the Allied Works Council exhibition of works by artists representing the war effort at home. <https://trove.nla.gov.au/newspaper/article/17925719>.
85 Papers of Nora Heysen, NHFC, Robert Black letter to Nora Heysen, (?) 1944.
86 ibid.
87 Robert B.T. Black, written responses to ALW via email, 5 November 2018.
88 ibid. Robert Black letter to Nora Heysen, 15 August 1944.
89 Speck, *Heysen to Heysen*, p. 160, Nora Heysen letter to her parents, 7 (December?) 1944.
90 ibid., p. 155.
91 NLA MS 10041 Series 1, Subseries 1.2 File 7, Papers of Nora Heysen, letter from QX36074 Captain R.H. Black to Nora Heysen, 11 July 1944.
92 ibid., 27 August 1945.
93 Speck, *Heysen to Heysen*, p. 155, Nora Heysen letter to her parents, 12 August 1944.
94 ibid., p. 156.
95 McKillup, p. 68.
96 Speck, p. 156, Nora Heysen letter to her parents, 12 August 1944.
97 ibid., p. 154, Nora Heysen letter to her parents, 9 August 1944.
98 ibid., p. 156, Nora Heysen letter to her parents, 12 August 1944.
99 ibid., p. 157, Nora Heysen letter to her parents, 31 August 1944.
100 ibid., p. 156, Nora Heysen letter to her parents, 12 August 1944.
101 ibid., p. 158, Nora Heysen letter to her parents, 18 September 1944.
102 McKillup, p. 70.
103 ibid.

104 ibid.
105 ibid.
106 NLA MS 10041 Series 1, Subseries 1.2 File 7, Papers of Nora Heysen, letter from QX36074 Captain R.H. Black to Nora Heysen, 30 April 1945.
107 Speck, *Painting ghosts*, p. 142.
108 Thiele, *Heysen of Hahndorf*, pp. 257–258.
109 Speck, *Heysen to Heysen*, p. 165. Nora Heysen letter to her parents, 16 March 1945.
110 <https://www.awm.gov.au/collection/P65062>.
111 <https://www.awm.gov.au/collection/P10676776>.
112 <https://www.awm.gov.au/collection/P65062>.
113 McKillup, p. 71.
114 ibid.
115 Speck, *Heysen to Heysen*, p. 163, Nora Heysen letter to her parents, 21 February 1945.
116 Speck, *Painting ghosts*, p. 142.
117 ibid.
118 <https://www.awm.gov.au/sites/default/files/Devotion.pdf>.
119 Speck, p. 142.
120 Speck, *Heysen to Heysen*, p. 168.
121 AWM PR89/023 *Memoir of Flying Sister Beryl Chandler RAAFNS 502237 First Medical Air Evacuation Unit*, p. 142, 1977–1978. Collection of AWM, Canberra.
122 <https://www.awm.gov.au/articles/blog/beryl-maddock-flying-sister>.
123 Nora Heysen interviewed by Michael Cathcart.
124 Speck, *Painting ghosts*, p. 142.
125 <https://www.pacificwrecks.com/aircraft/c-47/A65-54/song-for-sister-sheah.html>.
126 Speck, *Painting ghosts*, p. 144.
127 Yvonne Cossart, 'Black, Robert Hughes (1917–1988)', *Australian dictionary of biography*, National Centre of Biography, Australian National University, <http://adb.anu.edu.au/biography/black-robert-hughes-12217/text21907>, published first in hard copy 2007.
128 David Ferguson, 'Tribute to Emeritus Professor Robert H. Black on his retirement', *The Medical Journal of Australia*, 13 October 1984, p. 487.
129 Speck, *Heysen to Heysen*, p. 170, Nora Heysen letter to her parents, (?) (November) 1945.
130 <http://nga.gov.au/federation/Detail.cfm?WorkID=26277>.
131 NLA MS 10041 Series 1, Subseries 1.2 File 7, Papers of Nora Heysen, letter from QX36074 Captain R.H. Black to Nora Heysen, 19 August 1945.
132 NLA MS 10041 Series 1.2, File 7, Papers of Nora Heysen, letter from QX36074 Captain R.H. Black to Nora Heysen, 19 August 1945.
133 Speck, *Heysen to Heysen,* p. 171. Nora Heysen letter to her parents, 23 January 1946.

134 ibid., p. 172.
135 McKillup, p. 73.
136 Erin Litvik, Assistant Curator, Art Section, AWM, Canberra. 22 October 2018.

NINE: RATIONS AND REVISITATIONS

1 Speck, *Heysen to Heysen*, p. 183, Nora Heysen letter to her parents, 26 August 1948; Nockels, interviewed by ALW.
2 <http://www.atua.org.au/timeline.html>.
3 <https://trove.nla.gov.au/newspaper/article/49361832>.
4 <https://thesocialist.org.au/the-balmain-ironworkers-strike-of-1945/>.
5 <https://quadrant.org.au/magazine/2014/01-02/treachery-unions-second-world-war/>.
6 <http://www.solidarity.net.au/unions/workers-and-the-second-world-war-trotskyism-and-the-1945-balmain-docks-dispute/>.
7 <https://trove.nla.gov.au/newspaper/article/40872588>.
8 <http://www.solidarity.net.au/unions/workers-and-the-second-world-war-trotskyism-and-the-1945-balmain-docks-dispute/>.
9 <http://www.atua.org.au/timeline.html>.
10 <https://trove.nla.gov.au/newspaper/article/82370967>; <https://trove.nla.gov.au/newspaper/article/27000190>.
11 <https://www.marxists.org/subject/stalinism/into-mainstream/ch02.htm>.
12 <https://trove.nla.gov.au/newspaper/article/17969307/997529>.
13 <sa.org.au/interventions/rebelwomen/homefront.htm>.
14 <https://www.solidarity.net.au/unions/workers-and-the-second-world-war-trotskyism-and-the-1945-balmain-docks-dispute/>.
15 <http://www.atua.org.au/timeline.html>.
16 <http://john.curtin.edu.au/legacyex/women.html>.
17 <http://www.naa.gov.au/collection/snapshots/find-of-the-month/2009-march.aspx>.
18 <www.slsa.sa.gov.au/women_and_politics/sa1.htm>.
19 <http://www.naa.gov.au/collection/snapshots/find-of-the-month/2009-march.aspx>.
20 ibid.
21 <http://www.smh.com.au/articles/2004/01/05/1073267962306.html>.
22 <https://www.quora.com/What-were-the-technological-advancements-of-World-War-2>.
23 <https://www.bl.uk/world-war-one/articles/changing-lives-gender-expectations>.
24 Papers of Josephine Heysen, Josephine Heysen letter to Jacqueline Whyte, (192?).
25 Thiele, *Heysen of Hahndorf*, p. 230.
26 ibid., p. 234.

27 <http://www.smh.com.au/articles/2004/01/05/1073267962306.html>.
28 <http://trove.nla.gov.au/newspaper/article/17997986/1001378>.
29 Speck, *Heysen to Heysen*, p. 178, Nora Heysen letter to her parents, 26 October 1946.
30 <http://adb.anu.edu.au/biography/black-robert-hughes-12217>.
31 ibid.
32 Meredith Stokes interviewed by ALW.
33 ibid., p. 178.
34 NLA MS 10041 Subseries 1.2 File 20, Papers of Nora Heysen, letter from Robert Black to Nora Heysen, 5 April 1947.
35 ibid., Letter Robert Black to Nora Heysen, 23 January 1947.
36 ibid., Letter Robert Black to Nora Heysen, 24 January 1947.
37 Speck, *Heysen to Heysen*, p. 179, Nora Heysen letter to her parents, 28 March 1948.
38 <http://econ.economicshelp.org/2010/02/post-war-economic-britain.html>.
39 <http://trove.nla.gov.au/newspaper/article/52610210>.
40 Speck, *Heysen to Heysen*, p. 179, Hans Heysen letter to Nora Heysen, 12 April 1948.
41 Hylton, *Nora Heysen*, p. 38.
42 ibid.
43 Papers of Mary Eagle.
44 Speck, *Heysen to Heysen*, p. 179, Hans Heysen letter to Nora Heysen, 12 April 1948.
45 ibid., p. 181, Hans Heysen to Nora Heysen, 1 June 1948.
46 ibid., p. 180, Nora Heysen to her parents, 9 May 1948.
47 Nora Heysen Foundation Collection, letter from James McGregor to Nora Heysen, 3 May 1948.
48 Speck, *Heysen to Heysen*, p. 181, Hans Heysen letter to Nora Heysen, 1 June 1948.
49 <http://www.neram.com.au/hinton.html>; <http://adb.anu.edu.au/biography/hinton-howard-6681>.
50 Speck, *Heysen to Heysen*, p. 181.
51 ibid., p. 182, Nora Heysen letter to her parents, 26 July 1948.
52 <https://history.state.gov/milestones/1945-1952/berlin-airlift>.
53 Speck, *Heysen to Heysen*, p. 182, Nora Heysen letter to her parents, 26 July 1948.
54 ibid.
55 ibid., p. 181, Hans Heysen letter to Nora Heysen, 1 June 1948.
56 ibid., p. 210, Nora Heysen letter to her parents, 1 September 1952.
57 ibid., p. 182, Nora Heysen letter to her parents, 26 July 1948.
58 Robert B.T. Black, written responses to ALW via email, 5 November 2018.
59 Speck, p. 182, Nora Heysen letter to her parents, 26 July 1948.
60 Speck, *Heysen to Heysen*, p. 183, Nora Heysen letter to her parents, 26 August 1948.

61 Kate Nockels interviewed by ALW, 13 March 2017.

62 <http://www.smh.com.au/comment/obituaries/smart-put-a-new-iconography-in-the-frame-20130621-2oncl.html>.

63 Jeffrey Smart, *Not quite straight: a memoir*, Random House Australia, 2008, p. 197.

64 ibid.

65 Speck, *Heysen to Heysen,* p. 183, Nora Heysen letter to her parents, 17 October 1948.

66 <http://adelaidepedia.com.au/wiki/John_Martin_and_Company>.

67 <http://www.carrickhill.sa.gov.au/the-story/social-history>.

68 <http://www.carrickhill.sa.gov.au/the-story/social-history/the-haywards>.

69 Rose Wilson, 'Hayward, Sir Edward Waterfield (Bill) (1903–1983)', *Australian dictionary of biography*, National Centre of Biography, Australian National University, <http://adb.anu.edu.au/biography/hayward-sir-edward-waterfield-bill-12611/text22717> published first in hard copy 2007.

70 ibid.

71 <http://www.carrickhill.sa.gov.au/house-gardens>.

72 Speck, *Heysen to Heysen,* p. 183, Nora Heysen letter to her parents, 17 October 1948.

73 ibid., p. 185, Nora Heysen letter to her parents, 22 November 1948.

74 ibid.

75 <https://www.nytimes.com/1983/05/22/obituaries/kenneth-clark-is-dead-at-79-wrote-civilisation-tv-series.html>.

76 Speck, *Heysen to Heysen,* p. 185, Nora Heysen letter to her parents, 22 November 1948.

77 <https://www.daao.org.au/bio/paul-haefliger/biography/>.

78 Speck, *Heysen to Heysen,* p. 186, Nora Heysen letter to her parents, 22 November 1948.

79 ibid.

80 ibid., p. 187, Nora Heysen letter to her parents, 12 December 1948.

81 NHFC, Elder Smith & Co letter to Nora Heysen, 1 December 1948.

TEN: LETTERS FROM A FRIEND

1 Papers of Nora Heysen, NHFC, Jeffrey Smart letter to Nora Heysen, 15 March 1949.

2 Speck, *Heysen to Heysen,* p. 188, Nora Heysen letter to her parents, 11 January 1949.

3 ibid., Nora Heysen letter to her parents, 9 February 1949.

4 Speck, *Heysen to Heysen,* p. 189 footnote; Papers of Nora Heysen, NHFC, Jeffrey Smart letter to Nora Heysen, 15 May 1949.

5 Speck, *Heysen to Heysen,* p. 190, Nora Heysen letter to her parents, 10 May 1949.

6 Jeffrey Smart interviewed by ALW, 17 November 2012.

7 Papers of Nora Heysen, NHFC, Jeffrey Smart letter to Nora Heysen, 15 March 1949.

8 Gloria Strzelecki, *Jacqueline Hick: born wise,* Wakefield Press, 2013, p. 123.
9 Speck, *Heysen to Heysen,* p. 190, Nora Heysen letter to her parents, 10 May 1949.
10 ibid., Hans Heysen letter to Nora Heysen, 16 May 1949.
11 ibid., p. 192, Nora Heysen letter to her parents, 17 August 1949.
12 Jeffrey Smart interviewed by ALW, 17 November 2012.
13 Mark Finnane, 'Cilento, Sir Raphael West (Ray) (1893–1985)', *Australian dictionary of biography*, National Centre for Biography, Australian National University, published first in hard copy 2007, <http://adb.anu.edu.au/biography/cilento-sir-raphael-west-ray-12319>.
14 <https://www.daao.org.au/bio/margaret-cilento/biography/>.
15 <http://oxfordindex.oup.com/view/10.1093/oi/authority.20110803100539615>.
16 <http://www.smh.com.au/comment/obituaries/smart-put-a-new-iconography-in-the-frame-20130621-2oncl.html>.
17 For a detailed account including comment by Dobell, released 20 years after his death on his instruction, and comment by Joshua Smith regarding Dobell's statement, see <http://www.smh.com.au/good-weekend/gw-classics/a-portrait-in-pain-20140903-10c76n.html>.
18 Scott Bevan, *Bill: the Life of William Dobell*, p. 185.
19 Ermes De Zan email to ALW, 29 October 2012.
20 Jeffrey Smart interviewed by ALW.
21 ibid.
22 Speck, *Heysen to Heysen*, p. 76, Nora Heysen letter to her parents, 14 April 1937.
23 Jeffrey Smart interviewed by ALW, 19 November 2012.
24 <https://www.pablopicasso.org/night-fishing-at-antibes.jsp>.
25 Smart interviewed by ALW.
26 Speck, p. 186, *Heysen to Heysen*, Hans Heysen letter to Nora Heysen, 1 December 1948.
27 ibid., p. 184, Nora Heysen letter to her parents, 17 October 1948.
28 Smart, *Not quite straight,* p. 200.
29 ibid., p. 272.
30 ibid.
31 ibid., p. 295.
32 ibid., p. 351.

ELEVEN: MARRIAGE, HOME AND ANOTHER WOMAN

1 Speck, *Heysen to Heysen*, p. 236, Nora Heysen letter to her parents, 1 July 1954.
2 Meredith Stokes interviewed by ALW.
3 Speck, *Heysen to Heysen*, p. 192, Nora Heysen letter to her parents, 8 February 1950.
4 ibid.

5 ibid., p. 194, Nora Heysen letter to her parents, 1 May 1950.
6 Jeffrey Smart interviewed by ALW, 18 November 2012.
7 Speck, *Heysen to Heysen*, p. 209, Nora Heysen letter to her parents, 29 May 1952.
8 Schlusser, *Of art and men.*
9 Kate Nockels, interviewed by ALW, 13 March 2017.
10 Speck, *Heysen to Heysen*, p. 213, Nora Heysen letter to her parents, 21 January 1953.
11 Josephine Heysen Wittenburg interviewed by ALW.
12 Catherine Speck interviewed by ALW, Stirling, South Australia, 14 July 2015.
13 Speck, *Heysen to Heysen*, p. 214, Hans Heysen letter to Nora Heysen, 29 January 1953.
14 ibid., p. 215, Nora Heysen letter to her parents, 2 February 1953.
15 ibid., p. 225, Nora Heysen letter to her parents, 25 September 1953.
16 ibid.
17 ibid., p. 229, Nora Heysen letter to her parents, 2 December 1953.
18 ibid., p. 227, Hans Heysen letter to Nora Heysen, 29 October 1953.
19 ibid., p. 228, Nora Heysen letter to her parents, 17 November 1953.
20 ibid., p. 230, Nora Heysen letter to her parents, 24 February 1954.
21 Rosemary Heysen, 'Nora Heysen in the Pacific 1953–1962', Master of Arts in Art History, Faculty of Humanities and Social Science, University of Adelaide, July 2006, p. 1.
22 Speck, *Heysen to Heysen*, p. 231, Nora Heysen letter to her parents, 13 March 1954.
23 Rosemary Heysen, 'Nora Heysen in the Pacific 1953–1962', p. 2.
24 Hendrik Kolenberg interviewed by ALW.
25 Speck, *Heysen to Heysen*, pp. 220–221, Nora Heysen letter to her parents, 23 March 1953.
26 ibid., p. 247, Nora Heysen letter to her parents, 22 May 1956.
27 Speck, *Heysen to Heysen*, pp. 220–221, Nora Heysen letter to her parents, 23 March 1953.
28 <https://sydneylivingmuseums.com.au/documenting-nsw-homes/chalet>.
29 Speck, *Heysen to Heysen*, p. 228, Nora Heysen letter to her parents, 17 November 1953.
30 ibid., p. 236, Nora Heysen letter to her parents, 1 July 1954.
31 ibid., p. 240, Nora Heysen letter to her parents, 26 October 1954.
32 ibid., p. 239, Nora Heysen letter to her parents, (?) (August) 1954.
33 ibid., p. 245, Nora Heysen letter to her parents, (?) (March) 1955.
34 ibid.
35 ibid., p. 238, Nora Heysen letter to her parents, 8 July 1954.
36 ibid.
37 ibid., p. 239, Nora Heysen letter to her parents, (?) (August) 1954.
38 Linda Emery, *Pictorial history Hunters Hill*, Kingsclear Books, 2011, p. 126.
39 ibid., p. 241, Nora Heysen letter to her parents, 26 October 1954.
40 Meredith Stokes interviewed by ALW.

41 ibid., *Heysen to Heysen*, p. 246, Nora Heysen letter to her parents, 12 July 1955.
42 ibid., p. 247, Nora Heysen letter to her parents, 12 January 1956.
43 ibid., p. 249, Nora Heysen letter to her parents, (?) (December?) 1956.
44 ibid., p. 252, Nora Heysen letter to her parents, 17 March 1957.
45 ibid., p. 256, Nora Heysen letter to her parents, 2 August 1957.
46 ibid., p. 265, Nora Heysen letter to her parents, 2 July 1959.
47 ibid., p. 264, Nora Heysen letter to her parents, 2 July 1959.
48 ibid., p. 265, Nora Heysen letter to her parents, 21 July 1959.
49 Catherine Speck interviewed by ALW.
50 Speck, *Heysen to Heysen*, p. 270, Nora Heysen letter to her parents, 18 February 1960.
51 <adelaidefestival.ruciak.net/archive/1960%20Booking%20Guide.pdf>.
52 ibid., p. 273, Nora Heysen letter to her parents, 27 August 1960.
53 Meredith Stokes interviewed by ALW.
54 ibid.
55 Hendrik Kolenberg interviewed by ALW.
56 Meredith Stokes interviewed by ALW.
57 NLA Oral history interview with Hazel de Berg, tape 138, 8 November 1965.
58 Thiele, *Heysen of Hahndorf*, p. 276.
59 ibid., p. 277.
60 ibid.
61 ibid., p. 278.
62 ibid., p. 279.
63 ibid.
64 ibid.
65 ibid., p. 278.
66 <http://www.hansheysen.com.au/rembrandtia_5.pdf>.
67 ibid.
68 Thiele, *Heysen of Hahndorf*, p. 210.
69 ibid., p. 208.
70 Tim Heysen interviewed by ALW.
71 Speck, *Heysen to Heysen*, p. 323, Nora Heysen letter to her father, 19 June 1968.
72 ibid., p. 326.
73 ibid.
74 Allan Campbell, interviewed by ALW, Hahndorf, April 2012.
75 Craig Dubery interviewed by ALW, 2016.]
76 <http://adb.anu.edu.au/biography/black-robert-hughes-12217>.
77 Catherine Speck interviewed by ALW.
78 Hendrik Kolenberg interviewed by ALW.
79 Meredith Stokes interviewed by ALW.
80 Schlusser, *Of art and men*.
81 Catherine Speck interviewed by ALW.
82 Drusilla Modjeska, *The orchard*, Macmillan, 1994, p. 54.

83 Catherine Speck interviewed by ALW.
84 Stella Bowen, *Drawn from life*, first published Collins 1941. Picador edition 1999, p. 92.
85 Speck, *Heysen to Heysen*, p. 232, Nora Heysen letter to her parents, Easter Sunday 1954.
86 Craig Dubery interviewed by ALW, 2012.
87 ibid.
88 Meredith Stokes interviewed by ALW.
89 NLA MS 10041, Series1, Subseries 1.4, Folder 64, Papers of Nora Heysen 1913–2003, Steven Coorey postcard to Nora Heysen, 13 March 1980.
90 Chris Heysen interviewed by ALW.
91 NLA MS 10041, Series 1, Subseries 1.4, Box 9, Folder 57, Papers of Nora Heysen, Steven Coorey letter to Nora Heysen, 2 May 1988.
92 ibid.
93 NLA MS 10041, Series 1, Subseries 1.4, Box 9, Folder 57, Papers of Nora Heysen, Steven Coorey letters to Nora Heysen.
94 ibid., Steven Coorey letter to Nora Heysen, 1 September 1986.
95 ibid.
96 NLA MS 10041, Series 1, Subseries 1.4, Box 9, Folder 57, Papers of Nora Heysen, Steven Coorey letter to Nora Heysen, July 15 1986.
97 ibid., Steven Coorey letter to Nora Heysen, 6 April 1985.
98 ibid., Steven Coorey letter to Nora Heysen, 3 June 1988.
99 ibid., Steven Coorey letter to Nora Heysen, 9 March 1985.
100 ibid., Steven Coorey letter to Nora Heysen, 23 September 1987.
101 Craig Dubery interviewed by ALW, 2016.
102 ibid.
103 Meredith Stokes interviewed by ALW.
104 Hendrik Kolenberg interviewed by ALW.
105 ibid.
106 ibid.
107 Klepac, *Nora Heysen*, catalogue introduction, p. 6.
108 Craig Dubery, interviewed by ALW, Sydney, March 2016.
109 Tim Heysen, interviewed by ALW.
110 Allan Campbell, interviewed by ALW, Hahndorf, April 2012.
111 Craig Dubery, interviewed by ALW 2012.

TWELVE: SACRED GROUND

1 Nat Williams interviewed by ALW, 27 March 2015.
2 <https://www.smh.com.au/articles/2003/12/30/1072546533012.html>.
3 Nora Heysen, interviewed by Michael Cathcart.
4 Chris Heysen, interviewed by ALW.
5 Speck, *Heysen to Heysen*, p. 266, Nora Heysen letter to her parents, 30 December 1959.
6 Nora Heysen interviewed by Heather Rusden.
7 Allan Campbell journal, The Cedars, Hahndorf.

8 Craig Dubery, interviewed by ALW.
9 Chris Heysen interviewed by ALW.
10 Craig Dubery, interviewed by ALW.
11 Nora Heysen interviewed by Eugene Schlusser.
12 Angus Trumble interviewed by ALW.
13 Yvonne Cossart, 'Black, Robert Hughes (1917–1988)', *Australian dictionary of biography*, National Centre of Biography, Australian National University, <http://adb.anu.edu.au/biography/black-robert-hughes-12217/text21907>, published first in hard copy 2007.
14 Klepac, *Nora Heysen*, p. 18.
15 Nora Heysen interviewed by Michael Cathcart.
16 Lola Wilkins interviewed by ALW, Canberra, December 2017.
17 Speck, *Heysen to Heysen*, p. 288, Nora Heysen letter to her parents, 30 December 1959.
18 Lola Wilkins, interviewed by ALW.
19 Kate Nockels, interviewed by ALW.
20 <https://www.smh.com.au/articles/2003/12/30/1072546533012.html>
21 Lola Wilkins interviewed by ALW.
22 ibid.
23 Speck, *Heysen to Heysen*, p. 217.
24 Jane Hylton interviewed by ALW.
25 Nora Heysen interviewed by Michael Cathcart.
26 Modjeska, *The orchard*, p. 136.
27 Schlusser, *Of art and men.*
28 Allan Campbell interviewed by ALW, Hahndorf, September 2013.
29 Craig Dubery interviewed by ALW, 2016.
30 Craig Dubery interviewed by ALW, 2012.
31 Craig Dubery interviewed by ALW, 2016.
32 Peter Duff interviewed by ALW, Canberra, 7 May 2018.
33 Eugene Schlusser interviewed by ALW, Carlton, 18 March 2016.
34 Lola Wilkins interviewed by ALW.
35 <http://www.smh.com.au/articles/2004/01/05/1073267962306.html>.
36 Peter Duff interviewed by ALW.
37 Nat Williams interviewed by ALW.
38 ibid.
39 Speck, *Heysen to Heysen*, p. 250, Nora Heysen letter to her parents, 15 January 1957.
40 Craig Dubery interviewed by ALW, 2016.
41 Hylton and Neylon, *Hans Heysen*, p. 38.

INDEX

Notes: Page references in **bold** refer to illustrations.
Titles starting with The or A are filed by the next word (e.g. *A world of our own* files under W).
Works by Nora Heysen are not listed in this index. Please refer to **Works Mentioned** (p. 340).

ACKNOWLEDGEMENTS

I would like to thank members of the Heysen family and Nora Heysen Foundation Trustees who authorised this work, in particular Peter Heysen who shared his memories and on reading this work gave his reassuring seal of approval. My thanks to Tim Heysen who paved the way for this biography, and Robin Heysen McLaughlin and Chris Heysen, who all shared memories of their aunt. Josephine Heysen Wittenburg's contribution to this book is poignant and I thank her for her heartfelt reminiscences. Nick Heysen provided his father Stefan's written recollections of his sister, and it was a special day when I met Nora's late brother Michael, then ninety, full of warmth and vigour as he remembered his sister.

I am grateful for the enduring support of Allan Campbell in his capacity as Chairman of the Nora Heysen Foundation, and as Nora's friend. Thank you to Jill Swann, art historian and archivist at The Cedars in Hahndorf, for her meticulous records, and for her shared forensic knowledge of my subject. My conversation with Lou Klepac was a highlight in getting to know Nora and I thank him for that, along with his generosity in allowing the reproduction of images where he holds copyright. Craig Dubery offered a view of Nora's life that few were privileged to witness and my work is the richer for his most personal of views. To Robert B.T. Black, my sincere thanks for his willingness to share his memories of his father Robert, and of Nora. Meredith Stokes' candid contribution reveals the essence of a life well lived, it is this intimacy that a biographer values so highly. Peter Duff's memories of driving Nora and of their friendship also enhanced this story. To the current owners of The Chalet, thank you for allowing me to visit Nora's home and 'seeing' her there. It was my privilege to interview the late Jeffrey Smart and my heartfelt thanks for his gracious assistance lie with Ermes De Zan.

I owe a debt of gratitude to the researchers who have gone before me, informing my work on many levels. Catherine Speck's publications provide the foundation for my research and her invaluable resource includes her leviathan work as editor of the hundreds of letters between Nora and her father that anchors the chronology. Jane Hylton's published works on Nora and Hans Heysen also belong in this category of indispensable sources. I thank both women for their generosity in face-to-face interviews, a space where nuanced meaning can be garnered and highlights exposed. The sensitive Heysen documentaries of Eugene Schlusser allowed me to see and hear Nora in conversation, an invaluable resource, and I appreciate the interview time he gave me. Scholars' manuscripts I have accessed include those of Kate Nockels (with thanks for her personal insights in our interview), Rosemary Heysen, Trevor Schaefer, and the late Phyllis McKillup, and I thank them for their rigour.

Support for this work has been generously given by Australian curators and art historians Mary Eagle, Anne Gray, Christopher Menz, Angus Trumble, Barry Pearce, Hendrik Kolenberg, Nat Williams, Lola Wilkins, Angela Goddard, Ted Snell and Alex Torrens.

I acknowledge the librarians and staff of the National Library of Australia and the Australian War Memorial who manage these extraordinary archives and where my repeated requests for assistance were met with equanimity. My thanks also to the galleries who assisted with this work in supplying information and also permissions to reproduce art works: National Gallery of Australia, National Portrait Gallery, Art Gallery of New South Wales, National Gallery of Victoria, Art Gallery of South Australia, New England Regional Art Museum, Tasmanian Museum and Art Gallery, Queensland Art Gallery | Gallery of Modern Art.

I am indebted to Brenda Walker for her encouragement throughout this work from its inception. The value of her guidance is immeasurable.

Working with Fremantle Press has been a seamless and rewarding experience and I thank the team for their professional execution at all levels of production. In particular, I would like to thank Fremantle Press publisher Georgia Richter for her exceptional work as editor and for her commitment to this project.

My family and friends supported this work and my depth of gratitude cannot be measured. These relationships are the framework that holds this writer together. To you all and to TJW, thank you for the faith.

First published 2019 by
FREMANTLE PRESS

Fremantle Press Inc. trading as Fremantle Press
25 Quarry Street, Fremantle WA 6160
(PO Box 158, North Fremantle WA 6159)
www.fremantlepress.com.au

Cover design: Carolyn Brown, www.tendeersigh.com.au
Cover images: FRONT: *A portrait study* 1933, oil on canvas, 86.5 × 66.7 cm. Purchased with funds provided by the Art Foundation of Tasmania, 1986, AG5025, TMAG.
BACK: *Transport driver (Aircraftwoman Florence Miles)* 1945, oil on canvas, 66.6 × 81.8 cm, AWM.

Printed by Everbest Printing Investment Limited, China

A catalogue record for this book is available from the National Library of Australia

Nora Heysen: a portrait
ISBN 9781925815207

Fremantle Press is supported by the State Government through the Department of Local Government, Sport and Cultural Industries.

Australia Council for the Arts

Publication of this title was assisted by the Commonwealth Government through the Australia Council, its arts funding and advisory body.